Cloud-Native Application Design

Cloud-Native Application Design

Mohammad Ashique Azad

ARCLER PRESS

www.arclerpress.com

Cloud-Native Application Design

Mohammad Ashique Azad

Arcler Press
4164 Lakeshore Road
Burlington, ON L7L 1A4
Canada
www.arclerpress.com
Email: orders@arclereducation.com

ISBN: 978-1-77956-963-9 (Hardcover)

ABOUT THE AUTHOR

Mr. Mohammad Ashique Azad serves as Assistant Professor in the Department of Computer Science and Engineering at K.L. University, Vijayawada, Andhra Pradesh, India, where he combines academic excellence with cutting-edge research in quantum technologies. He is currently pursuing his doctoral research (PhD) in Quantum Computing from the National Institute of Technology (NIT), Jamshedpur, positioning himself at the forefront of this transformative field. His research expertise encompasses Quantum Computing with specialized focus on Quantum Machine Learning (QML), Quantum Cryptography, Quantum Sensing, and Quantum Convolutional Neural Networks (QCNN). With over five years of distinguished teaching experience across premier engineering institutions and universities in India, Mr. Azad has cultivated a reputation for academic rigor and innovative pedagogy. His unique multidisciplinary foundation spanning B.Sc (Zoology), B.Tech and M.Tech in Computer Science and Engineering, MBA (Human Resource Management), PGDEMA, and Diploma in Quantum Computing enables him to approach complex research challenges with diverse perspectives. He has established an impressive scholarly portfolio with numerous publications in prestigious national and international journals and conferences, complemented by multiple patents, books and book chapters that underscore his ability to translate theoretical insights into practical innovations, making significant contributions to the advancement of quantum technologies and computational science.

TABLE OF CONTENTS

LIST OF FIGURES

PREFACE

The software development landscape has also undergone its own foundational transformation in the past few years as organizations move towards architectures and methods prioritizing scalability, resiliency, and flexibility. Traditional monolithic systems, while sufficient for much of business need in the past, struggle to keep up with the velocity of digital transformation, shifting user expectations, and growing data-driven complexity. To meet these demands, developers and architects are embracing design patterns that leverage distributed computing, modular design, automation, and cloud platforms as first-class citizens in the application development lifecycle. This has transformed not only the way applications are developed but also deployed, secured, and run in different ecosystems.

At the center of this revolution is a realization that software cannot be written anymore as static or independent. Applications must be designed to adapt, adapting traffic flows, responding to failures, and scaling seamlessly when opportunities arise. This calls for a strategy where modular services, automated pipelines, and robust data management come together under practices that are always cloud-savvy. These practices have enabled companies across various industries to shrink release cycles, increase reliability, and rapidly test new features. So, the new paradigm offers discipline and flexibility—discipline in adherence to principles that result in sustainability and performance in distributed systems and flexibility in how systems are allowed to change.

Cloud-Native Application Design aims to provide a structured yet practical exploration of these ideas, combining the foundational knowledge with applied methods for building contemporary software systems. The book discusses significant architectural patterns, technology, and best practices that characterise the cloud-native era while preparing readers with the conceptual clarity they need to put them into practice. Each chapter builds on the previous, progressively taking readers from introductory ideas to advanced techniques in orchestration, security, monitoring, and scalability. The intention is to strike a balance between theoretical models and pragmatic design choices so that the material is both intellectually challenging and industry-relevant.

Chapter 1 is an introduction to cloud-native thinking and the beginning of understanding what makes applications cloud-native and why the approach is different from its traditional equivalents. It looks at the most important distinguishing characteristics of cloud-native design, which are modularity, elasticity, and automation, but places them within the general trend toward distributed systems.

Chapter 2 is focused on microservices architecture, the basis of most cloud-native applications. The subject highlights advantages of dividing systems into extremely small, independent services and touches on design patterns, service communication, and problems such as data consistency and service discovery. Students learn why microservices became the most favorite method of achieving agility and scalability.

Chapter 3 describes containerization and orchestration, the two pillars of cloud-native deployment. Containers provide a standard package unit for deploying and running applications, and orchestration environments such as Kubernetes coordinate deployment, scaling, and high availability. The chapter covers the transition from virtual machines to containers, best practices in container design, and the fundamental role of orchestration in the management of distributed, complex workloads.

Chapter 4 is about API design and management. Since APIs are the cloud-native system's glue, the chapter is devoted to strategies for designing good, secure, and versioned APIs. It also mentions API gateways, management platforms, and maintaining the communication uniform across heterogeneous microservices.

Chapter 5 addresses cloud-native data management, which is an area where the traditional approaches fall short in distributed systems. It addresses database selection, partitioning strategies, consistency models, and data synchronization between services. It addresses how to balance scalability against reliability in managing large, distributed data sets.

Chapter 6 discusses DevOps and CI/CD pipelines, highlighting the significance of continuous delivery and integration in modern software development. The chapter quotes the symbiosis between technical automation and cultural practices and how the team can build pipelines that reduce human intervention, accelerate releases, and offer quality assurance through automated deployment and testing.

Chapter 7 brings in observability and monitoring as fundamental aspects of cloud-native applications. It emphasizes metrics, logging, and tracing as the three tenets of observability and offers advice to embrace monitoring systems that provide actionable insights. The discourse illustrates how observability identifies problems beforehand, makes the system reliable, and improves user experience.

Chapter 8 examines security in cloud-native systems, including topics such as distributed attack surfaces, trustworthy communication between services, and compliance requirements. The chapter provides principles of zero trust, runtime security, and container vulnerability management so that readers are aware of how to architect systems that are data-protecting and trust-enabling.

Chapter 9 covers scalability, resilience, and performance. It introduces approaches to architecting systems in a way that they can adapt dynamically to shifts in load, recover from failure gracefully, and remain responsive when stressed. The chapter identifies design practices like autoscaling, redundancy, load balancing, and resilience testing as critical components in keeping high-performance applications in check.

Chapter 10 introduces serverless computing and examines its role in the future of cloud-native architecture. Serverless models, by further abstracting infrastructure management, enable developers to concentrate on business logic and let scaling and provisioning fall to the platform. This chapter examines the benefits, downsides, and trends surrounding serverless and where it will be going to shape application development in the coming years.

Target audience for the book are software developers, system administrators, architects, and technology leaders who want to learn more about application design in today's world. It is also sufficient for computer science, information system, and engineering students and researchers seeking to acquire expertise in cloud-age technologies. Combining conceptual depth with practical application, the book equips its audience with insight and a sense of confidence to develop, design, and deploy applications that thrive in fast-evolving, distributed, and highly scalable settings.

CHAPTER 1

INTRODUCTION TO CLOUD-NATIVE CONCEPTS

Contents

INTRODUCTION

Cloud-native is a software development approach that fully leverages cloud computing to enable organizations to create, deploy, and run applications in a highly efficient and scalable manner. Cloud-native applications are different from the majority of traditional software development practices based on monolithic architecture since they are designed with microservices, containers, and dynamic orchestration. This principle of design not only enhances flexibility and agility in responding to different market demands but also facilitates seamless integration and delivery of software, which is essential in the fast-paced digital age. Moreover, cloud-native is also favorable for resiliency and scalability, allowing applications to adapt with ease to fluctuating workloads and resource needs, which is essential for business continuity and performance enhancement. When defining cloud-native applications, there is a need to highlight their innate traits, including scalability, resilience, and flexibility. The applications are meant to fully leverage the distributed resources of clouds, avoiding downtime and maximizing performance through automatic scaling and self-healing processes. But this move toward a cloud-native architecture comes with its challenges. Restrictions imposed by vendors can lead to vendor lock-in, which is a risk to organizations that are reliant on specific cloud service providers. It is crucial, numerous studies illustrate, including one that addresses enterprise architecture, for organizations to understand such probable pitfalls and avoid them successfully in order to leverage the disruptive potential of cloud-native applications without sacrificing future flexibility and responsiveness (Kratzke et al., 2017). The embrace of cloud-native strategies has profound implications, spreading beyond the technical aspect to organizational culture and operational approaches. Cloud-native technologies necessitate that organizations transform their culture toward more collaborative and agile practices, silo-busting, and evangelizing the DevOps culture. This transformation can be particularly relevant in cases requiring innovative solutions to complex social problems, such as delineated in the research of the SELFSERV platform, which merges old practices with new models of operation (Bensbaa et al., 2016). By its interconnectedness of old methodologies with modern models of operation, a cloud-native strategy can provide wiser organizational models for greater responsiveness and effectiveness in reacting to market needs as well as citizen demands.

Explanation of Cloud-Native Architecture

Cloud-native design emerged in the last few years as a groundbreaking method of software development and deployment. Essentially, it leverages the native characteristics of cloud computing to enable developers to create elastic, scalable, and resilient applications. Perhaps the most interesting aspect of cloud-native architecture is its emphasis on microservices, wherein applications are broken down into smaller, independently deployable services that can work together in harmony. This module-based architecture allows organizations to improve their responsiveness to user demands and evolving market trends. Also, cloud-native architecture allows for the use of containers that encapsulate microservices in such a way that they can run uniformly on different environments. By adopting such strategies, businesses are in a position to acquire a better working model with the ability for rapid innovation but without losing stability and security in the course of digital transformation processes, as further outlined by Yanamadala (2025). Another vital component of cloud-native architecture is its alignment with modern DevOps disciplines aimed at integrating development and operations to promote cooperation and effectiveness. In this paradigm, automation is the foundation, streamlining activities such as deployment, monitoring, and scaling. CI/CD pipelines facilitate regular updates and enhancements to applications so they remain responsive to users' demands. The architecture also employs service meshes to manage communication between microservices so that they can offer observability, security, and traffic management without overly complicating the services. Through such practices, organizations can develop a culture of ongoing improvement, removing the bottlenecks that typically plague traditional development approaches. As companies adopt cloud-native philosophies, they are in a better position to leverage opportunities in the market more effectively, as noted in Oyeniran et al. (2024).

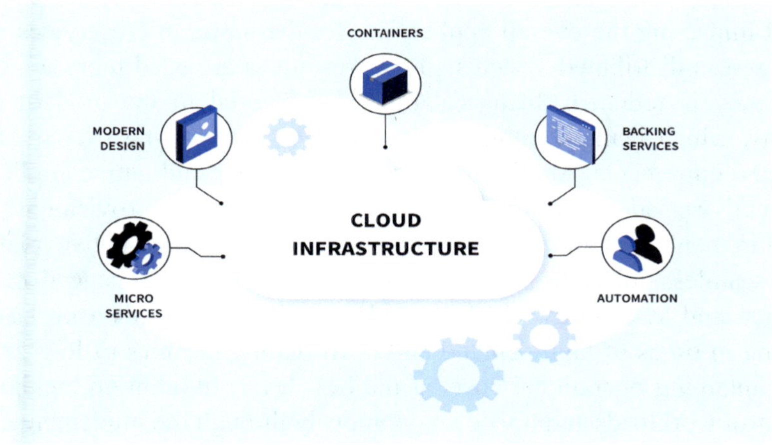

Figure 1.1. *Explanation of cloud-native architecture.*

Source: https://nix-united.com/wp-content/uploads/2022/05/1920_1280_1.jpg.

Finally, cloud-native architecture is an end-to-end solution for companies seeking to manage the complexities of modern software development. By embracing the paradigms of flexibility, scalability, and resilience, organizations can move away from monolithic structures to more agile architectures. This movement not only optimizes operational efficiency but also fosters a culture of innovation, where development teams can test and iterate quickly. Moreover, as businesses expand, the cloud-native approach allows them to make use of elastic computing resources in a dynamic fashion, balancing costs and performance. Basically, cloud-native architecture is a building block for companies seeking to thrive in a more digital era, as well as encouraging strategic rethinking around how technology can aid business objectives. This capability for transformation identifies the necessity of adapting cloud-native methods to sustainable development within the digital era, most famously explained within the frameworks set out in Yanamadala, (2025) and Oyeniran et al. (2024) (Figure 1.1).

Key Characteristics of Cloud-Native Applications

Cloud-native apps are defined by their ability to utilize cloud environments to their fullest potential, changing the paradigm of software development and deployment fundamentally. Microservices architecture is one of the predominant features, where applications are broken down into discrete, independent services that can be developed, tested, and deployed independently. Modularity allows greater agility, with teams able to push updates and innovate more quickly without impacting the overall application. Furthermore, microservices can be spread across distributed systems so that resources are used more effectively and latency is reduced. Such scalability is essential in the modern digital economy, which demands immediate responses to changing user needs and business requirements. Another intrinsic property of cloud-native applications is their native elasticity, which is a feature enabling dynamic provisioning based on requirements. As the 4CaaSt project highlights, cloud-native platforms ensure seamless lifecycle management for services with enhanced resource utilization and availability (Andrikopoulos et al., 2012). This aspect enables upscaling in times of high demand and downscaling in times of low demand, thus maintaining operational costs at the best level. In addition, applications can control workloads and traffic autonomously through the implementation of cloud-native services. Such responsiveness not only improves user experience but also assists in ensuring system stability, as programs can adapt to changing situations in a quick and efficient manner. Security issues are part of cloud-native application design as such systems introduce novel threats. The application of GPUs, while helping in performance improvement, also brought security concerns as it is a possible attack point by malware concealed within the high-performance computing hardware (Abhinaya et al., 2018). This being the case, cloud-native applications necessitate robust security mechanisms that consider the distinct architecture and model of functioning for the cloud environment. The implementation of broad security strategies such as services isolation and constant monitoring for vulnerabilities is imperative. Mitigating such security concerns not only protects the integrity of the application but also establishes user trust, thus making the cloud-native solutions more reliable and dynamic overall.

Importance of Cloud-Native in Modern Software Development

In the present era of rapid technological advancement, the importance of cloud-native approaches in modern software development cannot be emphasized more. Cloud-native development provides the framework that allows organizations to build scalable applications that can adapt freely to evolving requirements. This shift allows developers to take advantage of microservices architecture that breaks down programs into smaller sized, more manageable pieces. All of these microservices are independently deployable, developable, and scalable, resulting in increased agility and efficiency. As companies need to attain faster release cycles with predictability, adopting cloud-native principles has become essential in meeting these demands. Cloud-native development also enables better team collaboration, significantly cutting down on the friction that results from traditional software development patterns. With containerization and orchestration tools such as Docker and Kubernetes, developers can create standardized environments for all deployment phases.

The consistency ensures applications become predictable in their behavior regardless of where they are deployed, either in production or test environments. Teams thus direct their resources towards coding new features rather than debugging environment problems. Thus, cloud-native culture not only makes the workflow easier but also enhances operational support as well as developing an innovation culture. Additionally, the evolving scene of data management and computing requires efficient management of the quantity and complexity of data generated these days. Organizations are increasingly being confronted with the need to possess excellent data tools and libraries in order to handle massive datasets efficiently.

Cloud-native architecture is particularly beneficial in this context since it facilitates easy integration with various data services like graph databases that are capable of supporting strong querying capabilities required to comprehend complex relationships within data (Dries et al., 2017). Supported by the necessity for computational capability that has been driven in domains such as high energy physics, where computational requirements for data processing are enormous, cloud-native strategies play a central role in establishing agile infrastructure to address these evolving requirements (Asai et al., 2015). Cloud-native development thus plays a critical role in modern software frameworks, which goes much beyond specific applications and shapes the future of how business operates with technology in the era of data excess (Figure 1.2).

Figure 1.2. *Advantages-of-cloud-application-development.*

Source: https://media.excellentwebworld.com/wp-content/uploads/2025 /01/3006 312 6/Advantages-of-Cloud-Application-Development.webp.

1.1. HISTORICAL CONTEXT

The historical context of cloud-native concepts brings into focus the evolution of paradigms in computing and their radical impacts on software deployment and software development. The concept emerged from increasing requests for scalable and flexible services amidst escalating digital needs felt towards the later part of the 20th century. Early cloud structures began emerging as the internet matured, creating space for shifting from on-prem infrastructures to distributed systems. This change brought about a turning point as the explosive expansion of data and devices demanded an evolvable solution beyond what static architectures could provide. Because of that, understanding this context is significant in comprehending the cloud-native model, which focuses on rapid iterations and microservices, enabling organizations to respond in real-time to emerging user and market demands. The emergence of cloud-native technology is also characterized by the landmark advancements in virtualization and containerization technologies, which have made it possible for the platform to construct failure-tolerant applications. Virtualization initially emerged with mainframe computing during the 1960s, making it possible for multiple operating systems to run on a single piece of hardware. This paved the way for more advanced cloud infrastructure. The entry of container technology like Docker in the early 2010s accelerated the momentum towards the cloud-native space through enabling lightweight, portable, and reproducible runtime environments across a range of computing infrastructures. These allude to a technological maturity and reflect the increasing capability to process and manage large sets of data, which is indispensable in current digitized business environments. Secondly, the context of cloud-native concepts reveals significant trends that have shaped current business models, particularly in the context of circular economy principles. Contemporary models emphasize sustainability and resource conservation and point to how technology can be leveraged to create value without depleting resources. The concept manifests itself in the creation of business models that not only aim for profitability but also ecological impacts and social obligations. This technological alignment with sustainability principles is a manifestation of a broader societal trend toward responsible consumption and production. As detailed in more recent works, synthesizing these viewpoints generates an integrated understanding of contemporary business practice and contributes to the creation of circular adaptive models as a countermeasure to environmental pressures on a global scale (Aguayo-González et al., 2020). Therefore, understanding this historical development is crucial in order to successfully navigate the nuances of cloud-native ideas.

1.1.1. Evolution of Software Development Practices

The evolution of software development practices has been significantly influenced by technological and methodological innovations that facilitate quicker and better production cycles. Previously, it was dominated by monolithic architecture but later developed to encompass microservices architecture, which allows for greater modularity and scalability. Such a change aligns with the principles of agile development, wherein iterative processes and continuous feedback are paramount. The use of DevOps practices also enhances collaboration between development and operations teams, creating a culture of shared responsibility. It is observed, through case studies, that the transition of current systems into microservices architecture demands thorough planning and execution to minimize disruption and achieve maximum improvement in performance. The use of DevOps not only streamlines processes but also allows teams to deploy at high velocity, thus guaranteeing responsiveness and innovation within software environments (Balalaie et al., 2016). Apart from structural changes, the constant migration to cloud-native technologies is a key move towards the future of software development. Cloud-native practices emphasize the importance of leveraging the cloud infrastructure to create applications that are deployable, scalable, and resilient. With growing organizations adopting cloud solutions, they are forced to shift their development strategy in a bid to harness the real potential of cloud capabilities. Among them is the implementation of containerization and orchestration tools that ease resources management and deployment. Beyond their technical impact, such technologies encourage a culture shift from a traditional working environment to one that is collaborative and agile. Evidence shows that such migrations also entail overcoming challenges such as system integration and cloud resource management effectively (Johnson et al., 2009). Ultimately, the trajectory of software development practices reflects a broader trend towards greater agility, collaboration, and innovation. Challenges with migrating legacy systems to modern architectures can be overwhelming, leading organizations to reevaluate their plans for operations. As can be observed, the cloud-native development iterative process facilitates continuous adjustment and improvement, making deployments and updates easier for teams. By embracing technological advancements along with cultural changes, organizations position themselves to respond to evolving market requirements and user demands. It is clear that with the continued unfolding of cloud-native concepts, they will increasingly shape the future of software development and herald not only a shift in practice but also in the fundamental philosophies that inform development processes (Balalaie et al., 2016) (Figure 1.3).

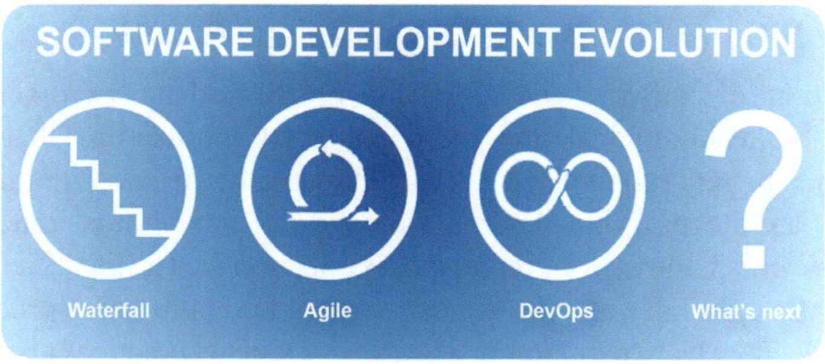

Figure 1.3. *The evolution of software development practices.*

Source: https://media.licdn.com/dms/image/v2/C4D12AQFgwkkq-GYKhw/article-cover_image-shrink_600_2000/article-cover_image-shrink_600_2000/0/1535125603262?e=2147483647&v=beta&t=qMVidK9UpfTaJd2d1bu_Z8HpIDrL-eemu2H2gKMP6leA.

1.1.2. Transition from Traditional to Cloud-Native Approaches

The transition from legacy to cloud-native approaches is a significant organizational IT infrastructure and application management change.

Legacy applications are often rooted in monolithic, tightly coupled, and rigid architectures that are resistant to responsiveness to changing business requirements. Cloud-native architectures leverage microservices architecture and allow for applications to be broken down into smaller, standalone services that can be developed, deployed, and scaled individually. This decomposition not only ensures greater flexibility but also makes it possible for faster iteration in sync with market changes. Applying cloud-native methods, organizations can leverage complete scalability and flexibility of cloud infrastructures, resulting in more creative solutions in synchronization with evolving customer demands and industry expectations.

The evolution to cloud-native solutions allows organizations to adopt modern data management practices that facilitate greater operational efficiency and enhanced analytical power. For instance, the majority of industries, like insurance, are leaving behind their old systems for cloud-native data models that support real-time processing of information and adaptive analytics. The platforms utilize containerization and serverless architecture to construct event-based data pipelines that optimize the use of resources and minimize operational costs. The transformation is not merely technological but also calls for organizations to experience cultural change, altering the way groups collaborate and resolve issues.

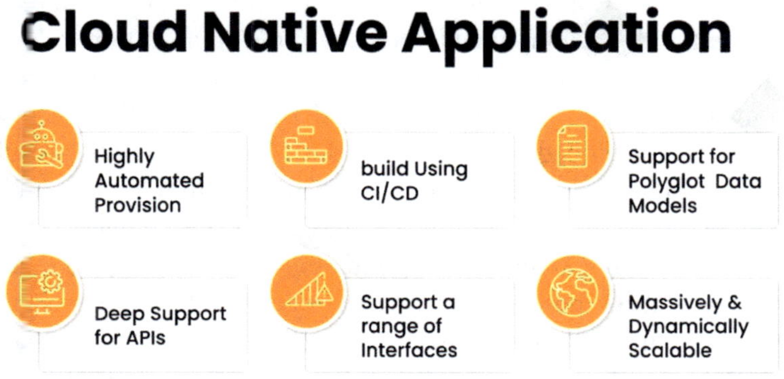

Figure 1.4. *Transition from traditional to cloud-native approaches.*

Source: https://www.moontechnolabs.com/blog/wp-content/uploads/2023/11/Cloud-Native-Applications.webp.

As businesses embrace cloud-native products, they gain deep insights into consumer behavior and trends within the market, guiding more efficient decision-making that powers competitive advantage in rapidly changing landscapes

(Malipeddi, 2025). Besides, security is of topmost priority while migrating to cloud-native architectures, necessitating new frameworks for maintaining data integrity and compliance. Traditional perimeter-based security approaches lack in dynamic cloud environments, necessitating the implementation of identity-based security controls such as Zero Trust Architecture (ZTA). ZTA emphasizes continuous verification and adaptive authentication, allowing organizations to secure their cloud-native applications while maintaining user privacy. This shift highlights a growing realization that security must be built into the design and implementation of applications. Emerging technologies such as blockchain for identity and decentralized models for security are at the forefront in providing robust defense against modern-day cyber attacks. As businesses navigate this multiverse of complexity, the movement toward cloud-native offers not merely engineering complexities, but also key opportunities for enhanced security posture and resilience (Ganapathi, 2025) (Figure 1.4).

1.1.3. Impact of Virtualization on Cloud-Native Concepts

The impact of virtualization on cloud-native concepts is profound, spanning from the management of infrastructure right up to the deployment of applications. Virtualization provides an underlying abstraction layer that allows for numerous virtual machines to be hosted on a single physical server. Not only does this save hardware costs, it also facilitates the scalability of applications that are typical of cloud-native deployments. As the world's organizations adopt cloud-native paradigms, they depend more on microservices architecture that thrives on the convenience and adaptability offered by virtualization. Applications can therefore be developed, rolled out, and scaled individually, resulting in faster time-to-market and better resistance to faults. With these game-changing capabilities, however, comes complexity, including the demand for efficient orchestration tools that can interoperate and assist in managing the relationship between virtualized components and microservices faultlessly. Hence, realizing the principle of virtualization is key to unlocking the full potential of cloud-native principles. Additionally, the relationship between virtualization and cloud-native principles is more than technical infrastructure. Virtualization enables an ecosystem that is simply designed for continuous integration and continuous deployment (CI/CD), thus enabling organizations to embrace rapid iteration cycles and regular application updates. Such a transformation is imperative in a cloud-native environment, where the ability to respond quickly to customer feedback and market trends can be an organization's defining competitive edge. Virtualized infrastructures isolate application dependencies and configurations from each other, permitting seamless shift between development, testing, and production processes. Such deployment pipeline control encourages a culture of innovation, since developers are able to prototype new features and functions within isolated environments that do not disrupt current services. But as these advancements are implemented in organizations, they must deal with monitoring and security issues so that the advantages of virtualization do not generate new risks. In addition to operational efficiency, virtualization is also an accelerator for enabling collaborative workflows between remote teams. Utilizing cloud-native and virtualized infrastructures, companies can enable developers and stakeholders to share common environments, enabling synergy and effectiveness. This capability to co-ordinate in real-time aligns with the tenets of DevOps, which emphasizes breaking silos between development and operations teams. However, as the line separating virtual and physical environments gets weak, organizations are confronted with problems associated with data governance and compliance. Applications of virtualization technologies can inadvertently render regulatory compliance more difficult, especially in industries having stringent data privacy mandates. Organizations, thus, need to give the highest priority to governance policies so that the fast pace of innovation that accompanies cloud-native concepts does not overshadow fundamental ethical and legal responsibilities, resulting in a balanced strategy toward modernization and compliance.

1.2. CORE PRINCIPLES OF CLOUD-NATIVE DEVELOPMENT

The fundamental principles of cloud-native application development effectively redirect application development and deployment in pivotal ways, with a concentration on agility, scalability, and resilience. It promotes development of applications that are tailored to operate in cloud infrastructure, rather than porting existing applications onto the cloud. Utilizing microservices architecture, cloud-native applications enable developers to create independent, interdependent service components that are able to be developed and updated independently. This modularity also fosters innovation since it is easier for small teams to experiment on specific services without disrupting the entire app. Also, cloud-native development takes advantage of containerization such that applications can reap faster environments from development through production, ultimately leading to smoother deployment processes and improved resource optimization since applications can dynamically be allocated based on demand. Monitoring and observability then become keystones in ensuring cloud-native apps keep running. With the advanced logging, metrics, and tracing, engineers can gain insight into application performance and user experience, allowing them to perform proactive maintenance and optimization. Continuous integration and continuous deployment (CI/CD) is also crucial since it offers a culture that enables rapid testing and deployment of code changes. Rapid feedback loop is significant so that developers can observe how applications are performing and how to improve them with time. Therefore, those teams implementing these practices are not only able to respond rapidly to customer feedback but also proactively work on resolving potential issues beforehand, greatly improving overall application stability. Adopting these tenets helps organizations become more attuned to the needs of the market, thus creating a culture of constant improvement and innovation. Finally, a much higher focus on security throughout development is the top priority in cloud-native strategies. Security by design philosophy embeds security into every step of application development, right from the very first design to deployment and even after deployment. Coupled with the complexity of cloud systems and greater cybersecurity threats, the inclusion of automated security scans within CI/CD pipelines ensures that vulnerabilities are detected and remediated earlier in the development lifecycle. This forward-thinking attitude is particularly relevant to the question of the ethical concerns of cloud technologies, whereby organizations must deal with the implications of data protection and privacy issues. In the absence of an effective security mechanism, the advantages of scalability and agility can be overridden by the risk of data breaches and compliance breaches, it is critical that cloud-native developers prioritize security first while adopting these revolutionary development paradigms (Figure 1.5).

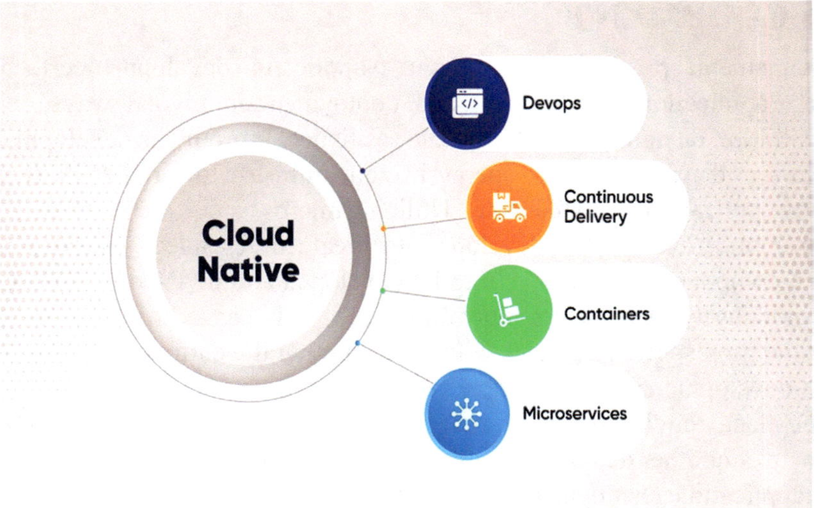

Figure 1.5. *The core principles of cloud-native.*

Source: https://www.netsolutions.com/wp-content/uploads/2025/04/key-pillars-of-cloud-native-development.webp.

1.2.1. Microservices Architecture

One of the cloud-native concepts, microservices architecture is a new way of application designing and deployment. Microservices architecture breaks monolithic apps into loosely coupled small services interacting with one another through properly documented APIs. Microservices are independently deployable, allowing development teams to be responsive with iteration and innovation. This responsiveness addresses the fast-changing demands of modern applications, particularly in FinTech industries, where being responsive is crucial. As industries go more towards digitization, microservices companies have a successful ability to make their maintainability and scalability easier to handle. This type of architectural pattern not only contributes to better performance but also addresses characteristics such as security and compliance, which are the utmost in financial services, and therefore are compatible to be implemented into a cloud-native approach (Molleti, 2025). The strengths of microservices extend beyond flexibility alone; they also provide greater fault isolation and resilience. By distributing functionalities over multiple services, the failure of a microservice does not bring down the entire application. This is particularly beneficial in critical environments, such as healthcare or finance services, where availability is critical and system crashes result in significant loss. Further, newer orchestration tools like Kubernetes enable efficient microservice management, deployment, scaling, and operations in containerized environments through automation. This capacity to choreograph enhances resource utilization and operating efficiency further, further supporting business objectives. Microservices architecture and cloud-native tool complementarity provide an environment where businesses are able to respond quickly to market development and customer requirements, a strategic advantage in today's competitive world (Sana, 2025).

Deploying microservices architecture, however, is not without difficulties. Organizations need to contend with issues such as coordination of services, data management, and ensuring consistent performance for distributed services. For instance, while microservices allow scalability, they can also complicate data consistency and integrity, requiring advanced ways to manage transactional behavior between services. In addressing these challenges, innovations such as adaptive transaction isolation algorithms are emerging that dynamically adjust isolation levels based on workload and data criticality. By implementing such advanced methodologies, businesses are able to unlock the full potential of microservices without losing any form of efficiency or consistency. With businesses encountering such complexities, it is evident that careful planning and thoughtful execution of microservices must be implemented in order to achieve the full benefits of cloud-native concepts within a dynamic technological landscape (Molleti, 2025; Sana, 2025) (Figure 1.6).

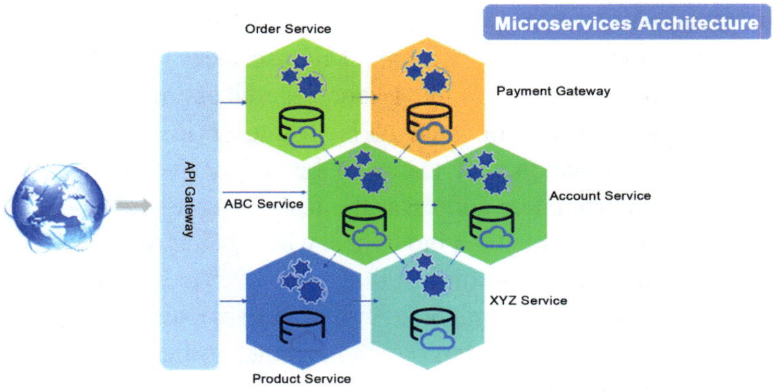

Figure 1.6. *Microservices architecture.*

Source: https://www.c-metric.com/wp-content/uploads/2020/10/Microservices-1.png.

1.2.2. Containerization and Orchestration

Containerization is a primary technology in the cloud-native world, through which applications are deployed into independent environments known as containers. This minimal virtualization technique enables developers to package applications alongside their dependencies so that applications run in a consistent and reproducible environment on any platform. Among all the various containerization technologies, Docker stands unique due to having low overhead and flexibility that facilitates rapid deployment and scaling of applications. Its ease of integration with orchestration tools keeps Docker at the forefront of this field, providing optimized application performance, particularly in complex structures where services interact with one another. It is significant to get the nuances of the containerization tools because they play a great role in the efficiency of the development pipelines and in the operational stability of the cloud, hence representing the requirement of well-informed decisions in choosing technology for application deployment into heterogeneous environments (Beltre et al., 2019). Orchestration is a component of the management of containerized applications, particularly within complex, distributed environments. This facilitates the automated scaling, management, and deployment of containerized applications, thereby enabling organizations to efficiently manage resources as well as ensure application resilience. Kubernetes is the most widely used orchestration platform and supports a wide feature set that can manage millions of containers, ensuring that they function in harmony with one another. With load balancing, self-healing, and service discovery features, Kubernetes enhances the operational effectiveness of organizations with the capability to deploy rapidly but out of reach of failed deployment risks. Literature on deployment strategies shows that effective orchestration exerts a significant impact on containerization by making complex workflows manageable and promoting the adoption of DevOps culture that can further facilitate the alignment of development and operations (Alavilo et al., 2025). Besides, containerization and orchestration technologies converge to offer new deployment models that augment the general cloud-native architecture. Deployment can be automated through CI/CD pipelines that deploy and test containerized applications automatically, thereby lowering the frequency of releases and enhancing the quality assurance. Tekton is an example of such a tool that integrates into this space and offers continuous integration and delivery through extensible and flexible application-specific pipelines. A case study in real life shows that such container-based approaches not only reduce the deployment times but also set up a uniform development environment regardless of the environment. Such alignment of orchestration and containerization is the disruptive potential of cloud-native technologies as the foundation for scalable, efficient, and fault-tolerant applications in the new technological landscape, further accentuating the necessity of extensive knowledge and use of the technology (Alavilo et al., 2025) (Figure 1.7).

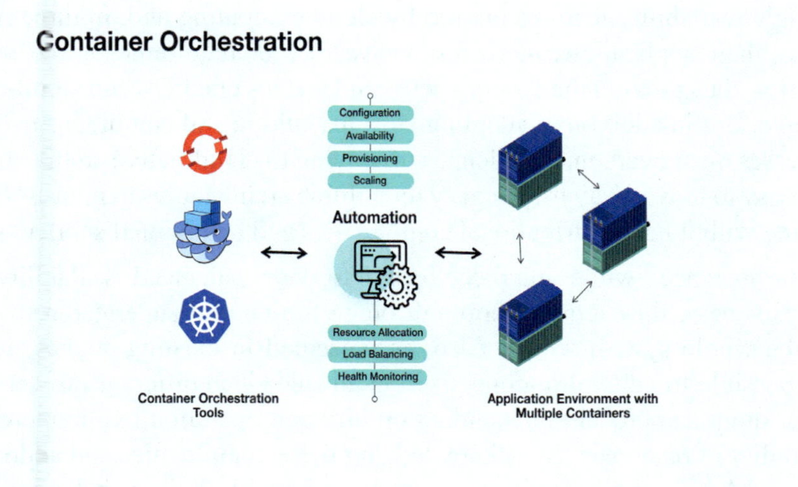

Figure 1.7. *The container-orchestration.*

Source: https://www.simform.com/wp-content/uploads/2022/05/automation-with-container-orchestration.png.

1.2.3. DevOps Practices and Continuous Delivery

DevOps practice has revolutionized software development by bringing operations and development teams together. This practice emphasizes ongoing communication, enabling quick reaction to market and customer feedbacks, thereby enhancing product quality. The core principles of DevOps like automation, continuous integration, and continuous delivery enable the organizations to streamline their processes and save significant time-to-market. Through integration of these practices, teams can enjoy more cyclical development, with code edits tested and released rapidly without compromise on reliability or performance. Not only does this integration trigger a culture of shared responsibility but it also boosts overall productivity levels, showing the main advantages of DevOps compliance in cloud-native apps. Continuous delivery (CD) is an essential part of the DevOps model that keeps accelerating software releases so that code is always deployable. CD practices involve deploying straight into production environments, which minimizes human error and intervention.

This automation supports quick iterations and feedback loops, which result in higher-quality software and a more responsive development process. In this, cloud-native designs, such as microservices, significantly enhance the scope for continuous delivery by the possibility of deploying each piece separately. When businesses shift towards such designs, they can better leverage the scalability and high availability features offered by cloud computing and, in turn, end up making their applications more responsive to user requirements and market scenarios, thus proving the synergy between DevOps practices and cloud-native concepts. But in addition to adopting DevOps culture and continuous delivery, businesses must overcome challenges of moving to cloud-native architecture. It is not easy to move away from legacy monolithic architectures to microservices, bringing with it new distributional complexities and operational subtleties.

For instance, while microservices introduce enhanced scalability and responsiveness, they require thorough orchestration and supervision to make sure the whole system works. Also, as presented in existing studies, it may be impossible to adhere to a one-size-fits-all rule since different projects may call for unique approaches depending on different operation requirements and availability of resources. By acknowledging these complexities and addressing them in advance, organizations can make informed choices that align their DevOps initiatives with their overall migration plans and facilitate a smoother move to cloud-native thinking while delivering long-term benefits (Balalaie et al., 2016; Evans et al., 2015) (Figure 1.8).

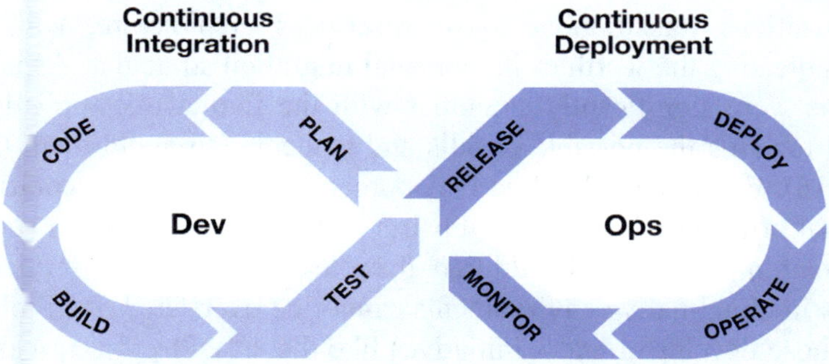

Figure 1.8. *DevOps practices and continuous deliver.*

Source: https://www.simform.com/wp-content/uploads/2022/01/cicd-in-devops.png.

1.3. BENEFITS OF CLOUD-NATIVE APPROACHES

The cloud-native strategies have revolutionized application development, deployment, and management into a far better way of working with numerous benefits that enhance efficiency in operations. Microservices is the core of the strategies, which breaks down applications into fewer independent deployable services. Not only does it simplify continuous integration and deployment, but it also allows development teams to scale up different components of an application independently, hence enhancing the utilization of resources. Besides, cloud-native designs improve resilience and agility, enabling organizations to respond rapidly to market shifts and technological advancements. Through such methodologies, businesses have the capacity to leverage the intrinsic cloud resource elasticity to result in a significant decrease in overhead expenses on traditional infrastructure. Thus, adoption of cloud-native practices has the capability to invigorate organizational capabilities, with increased innovation and competitiveness in the rapidly evolving digital business environment. Moreover, cloud-native solutions also encourage DevOps practices that complement one another by streamlining IT operations with software development. This integrated collaboration encourages cooperation, whereby teams can make quick iterations and implement changes with greater ease. With a DevOps culture, organizations can cushion risk while rolling out incremental updates, hence minimizing the probability of catastrophic disruptions in deployment. The strength of such integration is highlighted by the experience of organizations transitioning to microservices architecture, with lessons learned indicating the worth of incremental migration strategies. As noted, the migrations were significantly smoother with the framework applied since it indicated towards the possible pitfalls and strategies to avoid them (Balalaie et al., 2016). Embracing cloud-native approaches thus not only contributes to operational efficiency but also establishes a strong foundation for innovation and constant improvement. In addition, the role of Platform as a Service (PaaS) platforms in cloud-native environments cannot be overstated. PaaS platforms, such as those developed under initiatives like the 4CaaSt project, make cloud services and applications easier to market, deploy, and manage.

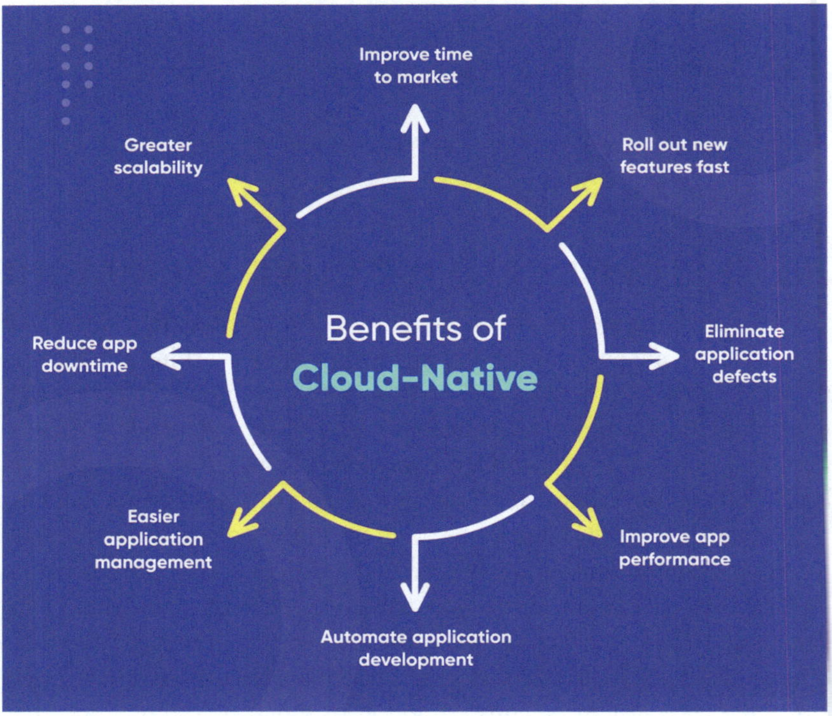

Figure 1.9. *The benefits-of-cloud-native-development.*

Source: https://www.netsolutions.com/wp-content/uploads/2025/04/benefits-of-cloud-native-development.webp.

This structure allows for flexibility as companies can deploy resources dynamically according to demand fluctuations. With an assortment of pre-composed cloud-native services integrated into an end-to-end lifecycle management system, companies can focus on developing their applications without being encumbered by the challenges associated with underlying infrastructures (Andrikopoulos et al., 2012). By leveraging these advanced PaaS capabilities, companies can accelerate their development cycles, deploy superior applications with improved efficiency, and ultimately enhance their responsiveness to their customers. By these multi-aspect benefits, cloud-native approaches support robust and adaptive business processes in today's cloud-driven era (Figure 1.9).

1.3.1. Scalability and Flexibility

Among cloud-native concepts, scalability and flexibility emerge as underlying characteristics that exert significant influences on system design and deployment patterns. Scalability refers to the capacity of a system to handle an increase in the volume of work or its capacity to handle greater levels of demand without compromising performance. In cloud environments, where the applications must dynamically redistribute their resources to accommodate fluctuating user traffic, this characteristic assumes particular importance. With organizations making the move to cloud-native infrastructures, the need for high-capacity scalability solutions has grown, enabling companies to extend or reduce their technology infrastructure to meet operations requirements, thereby maximizing cost and efficiency. Scalability is supplemented by flexibility, which allows the system to respond to developments in the marketplace and changing technology. Cloud-native platforms typically utilize microservices architecture, which disaggregates applications into smaller, independently deployable services. This approach not only facilitates agility in deployment and development but also allows organizations to modify or scale specific elements without it having a cascading effect on the overall system. 4CaaSt exemplifies this idea by its focus on flexible deployment and management of cloud offerings, creating possibilities for a more flexible IT environment. By promoting environments that make it easy to reallocate resources and modify services independently, companies can easily adapt to the needs of users and trends in the market. Scalability and flexibility synergistically contribute to the business environment for cloud-native applications. As seen in the incremental migration and architecture reworking of a business mobile backend into a microservices architecture, the integration of DevOps practices raises this to enable smoother transitions and rollouts. Under such a system, organizations are positioned to harness both flexibility and scalability, leading to more innovative and more resilient SaaS solutions. The ability to scale rapidly without relinquishing on a malleable architecture puts businesses in a better position in a strongly competitive digital landscape such that they remain proactive, as well as reactive, in service delivery and technology adoption (Andrikopoulos et al., 2012; Balalaie et al., 2016) (Figure 1.10).

Figure 1.10. *Cloud-flexibility-and-scalability.*

Source: https://www.xovient.com/blog/wp-content/uploads/2024/02/Cloud-Flexibility-and-Scalability.png.

1.3.2. Improved Resource Utilization

The concept of increased usage of resources forms the basis of cloud-native architecture, which deals with efficiency and flexibility of app deployment. Conventional architectures instead lead to resource underutilization or even bottlenecks but cloud-native implementations leverage sophisticated technologies such as containers and microservices to optimize resources dynamically. With the decoupling of apps into separately deployable smaller pieces, cloud-native environments can actually allocate resources according to real-time demands. This means high savings on unused capacity and overall operating costs. For instance, a service-based approach allows applications to scale automatically, responding quickly to fluctuations in user demand. As such, organizations achieve improved performance simultaneously with the use of only needed resources, thus fulfilling the potential of cloud-native computing in efficiently optimizing resource utilization. Also, resource management in cloud-native ecosystems depends on advanced scaling techniques. With traditional vertical scaling methods, over-provisioning and decreased efficiency can occur, particularly in variable usage scenarios. Here, the implementation of proactive scaling tools becomes very crucial. The adoption of machine learning algorithms introduces a complex way of predicting resource demands and allowing organizations to scale resources up or down precisely. As explained in Balázs et al. (2025), employing machine learning-capable solutions for microservice scaling has the potential to significantly enhance resource utilization without compromising on Service Level Agreements (SLAs). Not only does this cutting-edge strategy enhance performance but also wards off the risks from unexpected spikes in user traffic, ensuring responsiveness and availability in real-world scenarios that are crucial to maintaining competitive advantage in the fast-digitizing marketplace. Apart from scaling, integration of intelligent frameworks for provisioning resources is central to the enhancement of efficiency of utilization. Application of artificial intelligence-based solutions can potentially automate resource orchestration and thus the conversion of resource management to a more efficient, automated process from its traditional labor-intensive, human-error nature. Services such as Smart Fabric Provisioning, as highlighted in Nandi (2025), capitalize on the application of AI to model dynamic infrastructures that are able to develop as circumstances evolve. This technology not only reduces human error but also increases the effectiveness with which resources are provisioned, leading to faster deployment cycles. With automatic testing and configuration of network fabrics, organizations derive better resource utilization without the clunky physical reconfigurations traditionally required. These efforts then emphasize the pivotal role of greater resource utilization within cloud-native environments, leading to a better aggregate operational efficiency and responsiveness (Figure 1.11).

Figure 1.11. *The concept of improved resource utilization.*

Source: https://i0.wp.com/kantata.marketing/wp-content/uploads/2022/11/white-aper-30-60-90-1.jpg?fit=2560%2C1152&ssl=1.

1.3.3. Enhanced Collaboration and Faster Time-to-Market

In the context of cloud-native ideas, increased collaboration greatly drives organizations toward faster time-to-market. Through the use of cloud technologies, teams are able to collaborate more effectively across different geographic locations, sharing resources and information easily. This collaborative setup allows an ecosystem in which different people from different backgrounds and expertise meet to address complicated issues in an efficient manner.

Cloud-native architectures are enabled by tools and platforms that support real-time communication, and immediate feedback enables rapid iteration on projects. Just as in sectors like banking and information technology, the synergic productivity created through such combinations can result in enhanced workflow efficiencies and innovation. Therefore, businesses can bring products and features to market faster than ever, effectively reducing the amount of time it takes to respond to changing market requirements, thereby enhancing their competitive edge and providing optimal customer satisfaction. Faster time-to-market is more about efficiency than speed; it has a very close relationship with processes and methodologies adopted by companies. Cloud-native concepts, such as microservices and continuous integration/continuous deployment (CI/CD), provide development teams with the ability to design and deploy software in an efficient manner.

The systemic concept allows for smaller and more manageable code changes that are deployable and testable within a quicker environment. Organizations minimize latency associated with typically lengthy development lifecycles by embracing such paradigms. Furthermore, the knowledge acquired through rapid deployment provides for iterative refinement through user feedback in real time, enhancing product relevance and quality. As such, the fusion of cloud-native technologies with agile approaches leads to innovative solutions that address the needs of the market with increased speed. Aside from this, cloud-native principles enable greater organizational-level resilience and scalability. In the event of a shift in market conditions, firms are required to react with swift turnaround in order to remain relevant. New collaboration technologies enable groups to reroute attention and resources in real-time, making innovation ongoing even as priorities change. The capability of cloud-native infrastructure to offer more flexibility enables organizations to scale operations rapidly in response to increasing demand or pivot strategically without a protracted interval of operational dislocation. To this extent, safe data storage and protection, as also demonstrated with blockchain technologies, provide additional impetus to the cooperative effort of securing competitive edge in the fast-changing digital world. As organizations increasingly benefit from the strength of cloud-native concepts, their ability to work in concert and provide faster time-to-market becomes the prime focus for future growth and prosperity in their respective business markets.

1.4. CHALLENGES IN ADOPTING CLOUD-NATIVE TECHNOLOGIES

Cloud-natives' migration is beset with great obstacles that organizations must navigate through to experience the promised scalability and resilience. Foremost among these obstacles is the complexity of adopting new architectural designs such as microservices and containerization. These platforms necessitate a wholesale revolution of the traditional application design, which requires great expertise and understanding of cloud ecosystems. Later, most organizations are forced to deal with steep learning curves that can hinder timely implementation. Additionally, team realignment in the new structures can lead to communication and cooperation disruptions from role and responsibility changes. Such is the multi-faceted intricacy that not only hinders deployment but also threatens integration errors as teams adapt to new workflows and tools, thereby defeating hoped-for gains in efficiency in operations (Oyeniran et al., 2024). Another hurdle is the presence of legacy systems already deployed, typically existing in parallel with newer cloud-native applications. Organizations must decide how to migrate such legacy systems as easily as possible, or how to ensure their continued compatibility with new technologies. The hybrid setup can complicate deployment pipelines and introduce additional latency into processes. Besides, legacy systems may not be architecturally built to hold the rapid iteration cycles cloud-native technologies thrive on, thereby constraining their scalability. The uncertainty in integrating these incommensurable systems may lead to increased costs and operational risks, which discourage companies from embracing a complete cloud-native shift. Mitigation of such challenges requires proper planning and time and funds investment in order to achieve an integrated infrastructure (Jordanov et al., 2023). Compliance and safety are also paramount in the adoption of cloud-native technologies. The distributed and dynamic nature of the cloud environment poses limitations in using classical security models, whereby it is hard to monitor and protect applications against various types of threats. Organizations must weigh compliance with regulations against the requirement that their cloud-native applications are well secured against exploits. Moreover, as applications become increasingly microservices-based, attack surfaces increase, and there is a greater need for sophisticated security measures. All of this becomes even more challenging when organizations exist across multiple cloud vendors or hybrid environments, where differences in security controls introduce gaps that can be targeted by attackers. Therefore, developing an effective security plan that addresses both technical and compliance requirements of cloud-native deployments remains one of the primary difficulties for organizations that undertake this exercise (Oyeniran et al., 2024) (Figure 1.12).

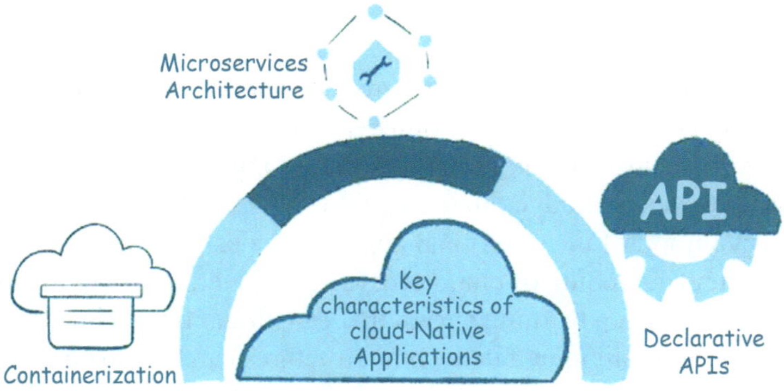

Figure 1.12. *The transition to cloud-native technologies presents significant challenge.*

Source: https://cdn.prod.website-files.com/64f059c734c83a7232cacfab/66a0e442 29ec5570365ebdc0_key-char.webp.

1.4.1. Complexity of Microservices Management

Microservice management introduces a layered sophistication that manifests in the world very differently than with monolithic designs. A microservices solution typically involves dividing applications into smaller, loosely connected services that are independently deployable and scalable. This architecture adds flexibility but is more difficult to manage the services as an ensemble. For instance, microservices require sophisticated orchestration to deal with interactions and interdependencies so that a failure in one service does not cascade and take down the entire system. Further, ensuring consistency among multiple microservices is a significant challenge since data must be handled in a distributed manner, i.e., gobs of communication protocols and state management methods are required. Addressing these complexities not only entails system design with great resilience but also organizational culture transformation to greater collaboration and lean thinking in an effort to best utilize the benefits of microservices management. Additionally, the process of migrating legacy applications to microservices architectures—typically called microservitization—also delineates the technical challenges of this migration. Legacy applications might not have been designed for stand-alone service operation, and therefore they will need deep analysis of service granularity and interfaces. As suggested, the emergence of microservices is intended to improve technical design consistency with business value, but discrepancies in the alignment may introduce significant implementation challenges. Organizations tend to find it difficult to correlate functionality with appropriate service boundaries, which can influence not only performance but also the deployment cycle. Understanding the principles and workings of microservitization is crucial to counteract such complexities because proper granularity is required to avoid over-communication between services, which could negate the very benefits of a microservices structure, like scalability and resilience (Andrawos et al., 2019). Last but not least, the workings of microservices can trigger unexpected operational complexities that, if not properly controlled, could undermine the touted benefit of cloud-native environments. For instance, microservices inherently support scalability and high availability, but these are lost in the challenges of distributed system monitoring, logging, and debugging. Traditional IT operations need to adapt to a world where services write their operations on their own, making it time-consuming to monitor issues across service boundaries. Apart from this, the inclusion of CI/CD pipelines becomes both required and complicated because each service may have unique configurations and testing frameworks. Without giving any special consideration to these operational intricacies, organizations risk being unable to take full advantage of the benefits that cloud-native architectures bring and thus underscore the importance of a strategic approach in adopting microservices management (Evans et al., 2015).

1.4.2. Security Concerns in Cloud Environments

With organizations increasingly migrating into cloud environments, assured safeguarding of sensitive information remains at the fore. Outsourcing data storage and processing to third-party cloud service providers is essentially relinquishing control of an organization's infrastructure. Trust becomes a matter of key concern, where clients must trust that CSPs possess the capability to safeguard data from potential internal and external threats. Nowadays, such confidence is rooted primarily on the CSPs recommended security controls, which cannot be verified by customers directly. The idea of enabling customers to validate the integrity of virtual machine (VM) instances and their corresponding environments emerged as a key step toward building reliable security infrastructures within public clouds. These measures not only guarantee client confidence but also help in adequately controlling risks in the event of data tampering or breaches (Paladi et al., 2012). The multi-tenant nature of cloud infrastructure further adds complexity to cloud security and tends to expose more. In typical cloud computing, multiple different customers will be sharing the same physical resources and thus require robust security measures able to offer separation and data integrity of data belonging to each user. Current cloud infrastructures are primarily built on the Infrastructure as a Service (IaaS) model of deployment, where the users receive virtualized resources on demand. However, such a model becomes problematic when attempting to pursue secure data traversals between multiple cloud domains or when attempting to implement dynamic service topologies between several providers. Lacking any standard framework, the provision of secure communications and resource bookings between disparate cloud environments can become cumbersome and subject to security attacks. Inter-cloud security then must be considered to allow effortless, secure communications across platforms (Dimitrakos et al., 2012). To enhance security in cloud settings, existing innovations focus on incorporating trusted computing initiatives and advanced virtualization platforms. Leveraging a trusted launch protocol that enables verification of VM integrity at launch time significantly enhances the security posture of cloud services. This protocol, according to the Trusted Platform Module (TPM) usage principle, offers a root of trust, allowing users to ascertain that their VM images are not tampered with and authentic. These developments are addressing immediate security demands by providing organizations with a significant mechanism to ensure they are secure in a cloud-based model of operations. As the cloud computing industry matures, there is a need for both clients and CSPs to place utmost importance on establishing good security practices so that scalability and usability of cloud computing are not compromised at the expense of security and integrity of data (Paladi et al., 2012).

1.4.3. Skills Gap and Training Requirements

The rapid rate of growth in cloud-native technology has created an increasing demand for skilled IT professionals who are capable of designing, deploying, and managing complex cloud infrastructures. But it has also demonstrated enormous skill gaps in available talent. All these institutions do not synchronize their curriculum with industry needs, and this results in their graduates being technically capable but lacking the practical capabilities to thrive in a cloud environment. As highlighted earlier, employers' expectations vs. graduates capabilities is a critical issue that requires immediate intervention. Plugging this skills gap requires collaboration between industry and academia to continuously update the curriculum of education in a way that equips students to meet the challenges that accompany the rapidly changing digital economy (Zatonskiy et al., 2025). Besides, targeted training programs play a significant role in addressing the skills gap in cloud-native ideas. Organizations should invest in comprehensive professional development programs that emphasize experiential learning of cloud platforms and tools. A good strategy is to offer workshops, certification programs, and mentorship schemes under the guidance of experienced professionals of the industry. One instance is that of pushing novel systems, such as DRACSC, into the limelight, and hence the focus on practical training alternatives that not only include theory but also practical examples. Such training will be instrumental in enhancing problem-solving and analytical skills, resulting in an effective workforce that can handle the complexities associated with cloud infrastructure management (Reina et al., 2024). Hand-on training is a must for organizations to equip their workforce with the skills necessary to thrive in a competitive environment. Incorporation of data-driven analysis in program design is instrumental in further mitigation of the skills gap.

Research indicates that systematic methods of IT specialist training management can lead to improved alignment between learning outcomes and the needs of industry (Zatonskiy et al., 2025). Employing methods such as machine learning and big data analysis, schools can maintain updated curricula according to evolving employer needs. This planning provides a mechanism for developing training programs that are both effective and meaningful. Moreover, the inclusion of stakeholder feedback in the use of education programs ensures that students have the necessary competence to perform well in the workplace, curving the skills gap, as well as enhancing the quality of the education system. Prioritization of agility and responsiveness in education programs will ultimately lead to a more competent, efficient workforce, well-positioned to succeed in the ever-evolving landscape of cloud-native technologies (Figure 1.13).

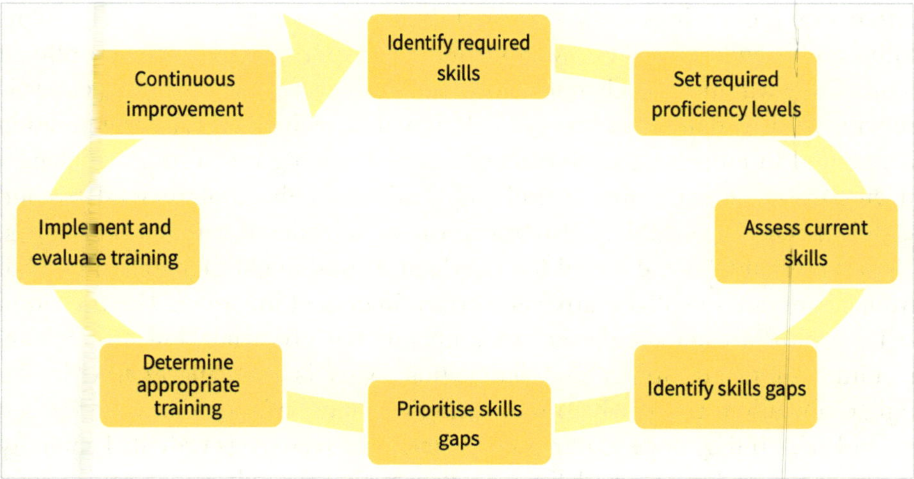

Figure 1.13. *The rapid evolution of cloud-native technologies has created an increasing demand for skilled IT professionals capable of designing.*

Source: https://www.vettimes.co.uk/app/uploads/2024/02/245_fig1.png.

1.5. TOOLS AND TECHNOLOGIES

In cloud-native concepts, the technologies and tools required for effective deployment and monitoring of applications are key. Cloud-native application development is inherently associated with microservices architecture, which emphasizes the development of applications as a collection of loosely integrated services. This is made possible by providing greater scalability and fault tolerance since the architects have the option to scale or make changes in individual pieces without affecting the entire system. Technologies such as Kubernetes and Docker have become fairly common in orchestrating and managing these microservices. Kubernetes, with its robust orchestration capabilities, provides deployment, scaling, and management of the containers, while Docker facilitates simple creation and sharing of application containers to provide uniform environments between production and development. These solutions combined are the very embodiment of cloud-native design through their propagation of agility, flexibility, and resource utilization optimization. Besides, the creation of cloud-native technology has been fueled by the pervasiveness of automation and DevOps adoption. Automation tools such as Jenkins and GitLab CI/CD are at the core of the CI/CD pipeline, hence fueling the speed and quality of software delivery. Menial tasks' automation enables development teams to focus more on innovation and code quality, reducing the risk of human error. Furthermore, the integration of cloud services and such automation tools brings forth a cyclical development cycle that heavily aligns with current agile practices. With businesses requiring themselves to remain competitive within a fast-changing technology landscape, adopting such tools is imperative. This dynamic synergy of cloud-native technologies and automation is essential in unlocking fresh efficiencies and driving transformative change in enterprises. Finally, the overall implications of the tools extend beyond technical benefits since they also transform organizational cultures and shapes. Cloud-native methods demand the overhaul of traditional IT paradigms, with groups being more collaborative and cross-functional in nature. The transition to DevOps does not merely enhance operational efficiency but also fosters a culture of responsibility and innovation. This is particularly true in the higher education arena, where the institutions must adapt to new trends and technologies if they hope to remain relevant. A keen analysis provided annually by the Horizon Report shed light on this evolving landscape, demystifying upcoming technologies that will shape higher education over the course of the next several years. The report emphasizes acquiring knowledge and integrating these tools to handle the complexity of today's educational demands (Johnson et al., 2009). Therefore, it is essential to comprehend the application of cloud-native tools for organizations to thrive in the digital age (Figure 1.14).

Figure 1.14. *The tools and technologies required for effective deployment and management of applications are pivotal.*

Source: https://www.ryadel.com/wp-content/uploads/2020/10/cloud-computing-tech-firm-laptop-notebook.jpg.

1.5.1. Overview of Popular Cloud-Native Platforms

The arrival of cloud-native platforms is a milestone in information technology history, offering organizations the scalability and agility to handle a changing market. At the forefront of these platforms are Docker and Kubernetes, which offer container orchestration and application deployment to numerous environments. Kubernetes is an open-source platform that automates application deployment, scaling, and management within containers and offers a robust platform for developers seeking to streamline operations. Docker completes this toolset by offering a means to build and deploy slim, portable containers that package up applications and their dependencies. These tools in combination form the foundation of cloud-native strategy, allowing businesses to become more productive while creating a culture of continuous integration and delivery. The more these platforms are used by businesses, the more they not only achieve technological advantages but also creative ways of deploying services. In addition to Docker and Kubernetes, OpenShift and Cloud Foundry also play critical roles in the cloud-native ecosystem. OpenShift is an application platform built on top of containers and a base of Kubernetes, with the aim of providing developers a simple workflow and advanced enterprise features. It supports continuous integration, delivery, and application lifecycle management tools that allow organizations to rapidly deploy applications without compromising on security. Cloud Foundry, on the other hand, emphasizes rapid application development and deployment via abstraction of infrastructure complexity. It supports multiple programming languages and frameworks and is therefore a development team favorite with heterogeneous languages and frameworks. Both offerings emphasize developer experience as well as operational effectiveness to serve the growing demand for scalable, agile solutions in the evolving digital landscape today. In addition, projects like 4CaaSt also postulate further innovations in cloud-native platforms via lifecycle management and promoting cloud services. Through the creation of an environment that enables cloud applications to be defined, deployed, and managed with versatility, 4CaaSt aims to enhance the service delivery with value-added aspects for developers as well as end-users. With an offering of a portfolio of cloud-native services ready to use, developers are provided with tools that support quick deployment and innovation. When these platforms are embraced by organizations, they not only receive the technological benefits but also strategic benefits in terms of agility and responsiveness to the market. By integrating diverse tools and frameworks within the cloud-native ecosystem, companies are well-positioned to overcome the complexities of modern application development with greater efficiency and competitiveness (Andrikopoulos et al., 2012; Dries et al., 2017).

1.5.2. Role of Kubernetes in Orchestration

Kubernetes has emerged as the core orchestrator for cloud-native applications where Kubernetes is making deployments and application management much more different for developers. Effectively, Kubernetes enables developers to automate application management, deployment, as well as scaling so that development teams can focus more on development and less on infrastructure complexity of operations. By abstracting the underlying infrastructure and promoting a microservices architecture, Kubernetes facilitates elastic and transient workloads in addition to optimized resource utilization. The strong capabilities of the platforms—with the self-healing characteristics and autoremediations—ensure that applications remain resilient and available even when there is failure. Therefore, Kubernetes not only streamlines DevOps processes but also enhances the general performance of applications, which is crucial in the digital economy of today, thereby solidifying its position as the de facto orchestration platform for businesses transitioning to cloud-native operations. The scalability and flexibility of Kubernetes are also enhanced by its orchestration capabilities, particularly through use of Pods and Deployments. Pods group together similar containers for efficient communication while Deployments manage the life cycle of these Pods, configuring them correctly and scaling them according to existing demand. Such a framework supports organizations to implement advanced deployment strategies like rolling updates and canary releases, thereby minimizing risks in altering the application. Autoscaling feature in Kubernetes further enhances performance by adjusting resources automatically according to changes in traffic patterns. These features are crucial to ensuring reliability of service in heavy loads and cost management by ensuring resources are used only where needed. With companies increasingly moving towards microservices architecture, Kubernetes is a critical component, streamlining the process of handling complex application environments with its orchestrative feature.

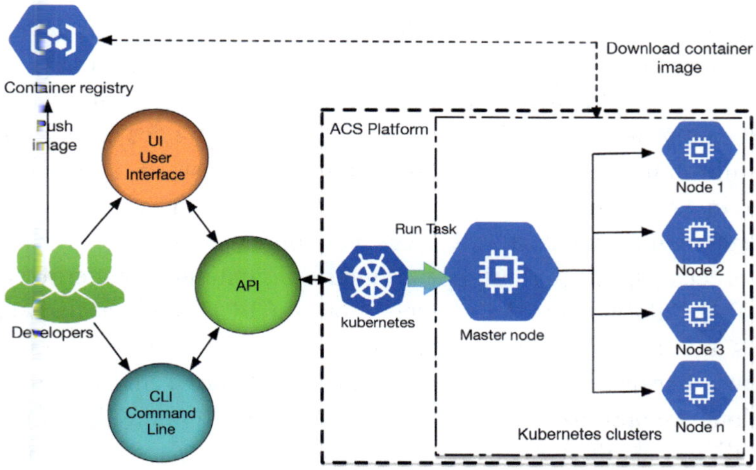

Figure 1.15. *Role of Kubernetes in orchestration.*

Source: https://www.researchgate.net/profile/Uchechukwu-Awada/publication/325737011/figure/fig1/AS:637005562142722@1528885369411/Kubernetes-orchestration-overview.png.

As Kubernetes gains pace, applying artificial intelligence and machine learning to orchestration is becoming more and more of a top priority for maximizing operational efficiency. Traditional methods of monitoring are found to be lacking in the distributed and dynamic cloud-native application environments, and as such, efficient uptake of fresh innovations with the help of AI technologies has become necessary. With the addition of predictive analytics and AI-driven log analytics, organizations are able to transition from reactive to proactive operations, significantly increasing the mean time to resolution for incidents. This shift not only improves system uptime but also allows teams to more effectively watch application health and performance. Its ongoing development in observability practices within Kubernetes environments reflects the platforms flexibility and ability to adapt to incorporate new methodologies, solidifying its position as a dominant force in orchestrating cloud-native technologies (Mohammed, 2025; Lakka, 2025) (Figure 1.15).

1.5.3. Importance of CI/CD Tools in Cloud-Native Workflows

In today's cloud-native software development environment, Continuous Integration and Continuous Deployment (CI/CD) tools are a fundamental component in optimizing workflow performance. The tools enable developers to automate code change integration throughout the entire software development process. Through establishing a productive process of code merge, testing, and application deployment, CI/CD practices avoid integration issues as well as significantly minimize release cycles. This strategy goes well with cloud-native philosophies because they lay so much emphasis on agility and quick iteration in software deployment. With CI/CD pipelines, as organizations embrace them, they will be able to focus more on innovation and less on tedious manual processes, thereby building a culture of continuous betterment (Liang et al., 2024). Additionally, the incorporation of CI/CD in cloud-native models promotes more collaboration between development and operations teams, leading to better-quality software releases. In cloud-native environments, where applications are optimized to maximally use cloud computing benefits, CI/CD tools facilitate seamless deployment of microservices as well as containerized applications. Among the most significant advantages of implementing CI/CD is that it makes it easy to handle complicated dependencies, enabling developers to be able to collaborate with multiple related services without wasting too much time. This orchestration is crucial in microservices architectures, where individual scaling and deployment of services rely on coherent integration patterns. Additionally, CI/CD tools provide developers with the capability to execute automated tests at every stage in the pipeline, providing rapid feedback and ensuring vulnerabilities are identified and corrected early in the development cycle (Azariah et al., 2024). Thus, the organizations can minimize the risks of software releases and provide a promise that performance, security, and compliance are not sacrificed. Furthermore, the role of CI/CD tools in cloud-native development pipelines is also in their role of developing an elastic and high-performing software delivery pipeline. With the automation of the deployment process, CI/CD minimizes the chances of human error, which is the cause of issues in legacy deployment practices. This reliability is of utmost importance for businesses that employ cloud services for customer-facing applications and services. Secondly, CI/CD enables infrastructure as code

(IaC), where teams provision and manage environments programmatically. Not only does this enhance consistency and traceability but also supports rapid scaling and compliance with changing demands (Liang et al., 2024). In general, strategic application of CI/CD tools is at the center of cloud-native concepts, reinforcing overall agility and productivity in modern software development processes.

1.6. CASE STUDIES OF CLOUD-NATIVE IMPLEMENTATIONS

The research into cloud-native technologies has yielded numerous case studies that show the power of change that this model can exert on various domains. One such example is the OpenDreamKit project, which is centered on the development of a solid open-source math software ecosystem. Through facilitating the development of Virtual Research Environments, the project seeks to customize environments for solving different research needs ranging from pure mathematics to applied fields. At its center is system interoperability, allowing researchers to utilize a shared vocabulary and functionality in a variety of mathematical tools. It illustrates how cloud-native methods can facilitate collaboration and imagination, ultimately contributing to productivity and efficiency in mathematics research and related fields (Dehaye et al., 2016). An additional indicative case study is found in the field of high energy physics (HEP), where the HEP Forum for Computational Excellence (HEP-FCE) outlines strategic objectives for raising computational competence. In HEP, as volume and complexity of data grow, the community feels the urgent need for greater software and infrastructure. The HEP-FCE roadmap finds synergy in the interplay between software efficiency and infrastructure advances in cloud-native platforms. Through the development of specialized working groups focused on applications, libraries, and systems, the HEP community is establishing a cloud-native future. This response illustrates how scalability and coordination generate robust computational tools that are particularly tailored for science excellence, illustrating the significance of cloud-native deployments to address global challenges (Asai et al., 2015). Aside from this, combined, these case studies reinforce a critical conclusion: cloud-native architectures can significantly enhance the scalability, reliability, and efficiency of any application. Using microservices, containerization, and orchestration, organizations can manage variable workloads and accelerate development cycles. A case in point is the use of several mathematical systems in the OpenDreamKit project which exemplifies the user-friendly flow of functionality and data, symbolizing the flexibility needed in modern research environments. In contrast, HEP-FCEs projects illustrate how the improvement of infrastructural and software foundations can transform high energy physics environments. Finally, these implementations prove to be representations of the pillars and benefits embodied by cloud-native principles, thus confirming their relevance in a number of scientific and technological sectors (Dehaye et al., 2016; Asai et al., 2015) (Figure 1.16).

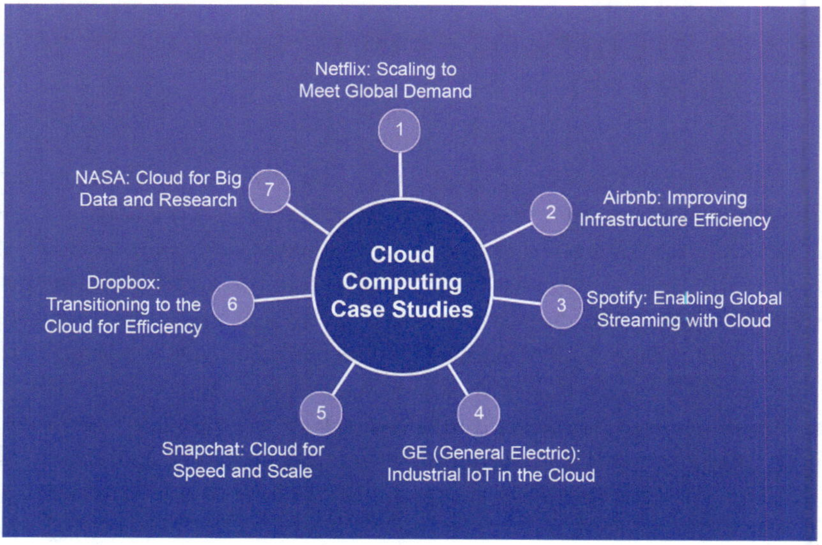

Figure 1.16. *Success stories from leading tech companies.*

Source: https://cdn.prod.website-files.com/670cbf146221ee06c3cdd761/6762803c6e7bb09774490904_676280227b6b0ca3fc3ac8ac_Cloud%2520Computing%2520Case%2520Studies.webp.

1.6.1. Success Stories from Leading Tech Companies

The cloud-native adoption journey sheds light on the phenomenal success stories of leading tech players, which reflect on how they use cloud technologies to innovate. Netflix and Airbnb are the best examples of the benefits of cloud-native architectures, which provide them with scalability and flexibility. Netflix moved to a microservices architecture, which allowed it to roll out updates quickly and efficiently and deal with varying viewer needs without going down. This shift not just enhanced user experience but also established Netflix as a streaming giant. This kind of successful implementation emphasizes the potency of cloud-native principles in revolutionizing business functions and facilitating easy expansion in the cutthroat tech landscape. Similar success can be seen in the example of Dropbox, which initially employed traditional data storage methodologies. The company shifted to a cloud-native model, leveraging its own infrastructure as well as that of public clouds. This transition allowed Dropbox to simplify its file-sharing capabilities and enhance synchronization of users across devices. Besides this, by adopting microservices as well as containerization, the company was able to adopt the practice of continuous delivery, leading to overall operational efficiency. This shift illustrates the capability of cloud-native approaches to bring dramatic performance, resource consumption, and user experience enhancements to technology companies. The impacts of cloud-native technologies are experienced even beyond typical software solutions, as noticed in current attempts to address key global challenges. Technology companies operating in the Arctic region impacted by climate change and energy shortage have started utilizing cloud-native solutions to develop sustainable energy infrastructure in isolated villages. Cloud capabilities enabling innovation surrounding renewable energy projects are also enabling capabilities in data analysis and monitoring of live energy use. By taking example from the case studies in regions like Canada and Alaska, there is evident evidence that efficient deployment of cloud-native concepts has the potential to initiate community resilience and sustainability programs in challenging environments, showcasing the broader adoption of these technologies towards addressing real-world issues (Johnson et al., 2009; Strand et al., 2018).

1.6.2. Lessons Learned from Cloud-Native Migrations

The shift to cloud-native architectures also has a tendency to reveal important learnings that significantly help the operational effectiveness and responsiveness of an organization. One of the most important lessons derived from such shifts is the need to adopt a culture of DevOps to remove the chasm between development and operations groups. Organizations that adopt DevOps practices find that they facilitate seamless shifts by removing collaboration roadblocks and removing the silos that have a tendency to decelerate. As demonstrated by Balalaie et al. (2016), the use of DevOps to refactor the architecture of a mobile backend service enabled a seamless migration to a microservices topology. Such a collaborative process not only accelerates deployment cycles but also enables improved responsiveness to changing business needs, eventually leading to enhanced customer satisfaction and retention. Another important takeaway concerns service dependency awareness in cloud-native environments. Most organizations are challenged by the intricate web of dependencies that accompany microservices architecture. It is critical that teams conduct a comprehensive analysis of these dependencies before making attempts at migration. Lack of adequate identification and analysis of these relationships may lead to unnecessary downtime or degradation in performance upon migration. As shown in various case studies, including those described in Allan et al. (2018), organizations that successfully handle service dependencies are more aware of system architecture, and scaling and resource utilization become more efficient. By prioritizing such knowledge, companies can develop robust mechanisms to deal with future performance bottlenecks. Finally, security must be the top priority when moving to cloud-native infrastructures. Once organizations shift their operations onto cloud platforms, they are likely to face more stringent security requirements and regulatory compliance concerns, particularly when handling confidential data. Lessons learned from a few migrations highlight the importance of adopting end-to-end security measures right from the design phase. For example, the development of the Stratus cloud environment highlighted the importance of implementing tiered security protocols and two-factor authentication to comply with controlled-access data policies, as mentioned in Allan et al. (2018). Through embedding security into the cloud-native migration DNA, not only are sensitive data safeguarded, but trust and confidence are also built between users and stakeholders.

1.6.3. Industry-Specific Applications of Cloud-Native Concepts

The adoption of cloud-native principles has several implications on various industries, particularly in facilitating innovation across industries such as construction and engineering. In these industries, cloud-native applications can facilitate better collaboration and interoperability through the integration of web technologies with Building Information Modeling (BIM). Emerging technologies such as Linked Data and Semantic Web technologies have been outstanding due to their capability to generate interlinked data environments. These technologies enable stakeholders to manage complex projects by using cloud-based software that streamlines communication and access to data. Through the creation of mutually acceptable mechanisms for automated retrieval and communication, such as GraphQL-based solutions, industries can overcome historical interoperability barriers and achieve improved project outcomes. This shift towards cloud-based, collaborative models is vital to driving practices and improving efficiencies in the construction sector, thereby revolutionizing the way industry stakeholders interact with data and technology (Beetz et al., 2019). In healthcare, cloud-native thinking is revolutionizing data management, patient treatment, and business procedures. The sector increasingly utilizes microservices architecture to design scalable and fault-tolerant applications that can support growing demands of modern healthcare systems. By migrating to this architecture, healthcare workers are able to respond at pace to patient demand or to regulatory updates and accelerate the delivery of services. The benefits of having DevOps processes during the migration are of utmost importance; organizations are able to automate development activities, enhance the quality of software, and decrease disruption to active operations. By adopting cloud-native concepts, health organizations simplify combining various services, including electronic health records, telemedicine platforms, and patient engagement platforms, towards the final goals of improved patient outcomes and business agility. The game-changer impact of cloud-native concepts in health accentuates the ability of these technologies to address the specific challenges of the industry (Balalaie et al., 2016). The banking industry is also the sector-specific applications of cloud-native concepts. Since financial institutions are subject to increasingly stringent regulatory requirements as well as demands for responsive responses to market conditions, the deployment of cloud-native architectures is a must. These structures enable organizations to deploy and offer services faster, cheaper, and securely simply by having fine-grained control over microservices. Also, the use of cloud-native approaches can lead to improved customer experience through facilitating financial institutions to deploy features in sync with evolving consumer demands in a timely manner. Data-driven intelligence can inform decision-making effortlessly when applications scale well and interact with advanced analytics tools. While the financial services landscape keeps transforming and shaping, the industry's embrace of cloud-native thinking not only makes it more competitive but also allows it to move towards more innovative and robust service offerings, to the benefit of both institutions and their customers.

SUMMARY

It is apparent that these technologies are not merely a trend but a fundamental shift that's reshaping the future of software development and deployment. With an emphasis on scalability, flexibility, and resilience, cloud-native architecture enables the seamless integration of services and applications, enabling organizations to respond quickly according to the changing requirements of the market. The foundation principles of microservices, containers, and orchestration platforms are the key drivers of such transformation, enabling resources to be managed and run more effectively. With such architectures, businesses have not just the ability to become more agile but also create the platforms for game-changers that leverage data and technology in unprecedented ways, illustrating the pervasive impact of cloud-native concepts on modern businesses. Deeper examination highlights the socioeconomic impact of adopting cloud-native technologies, uniquely as an enabler for environmental sustainability and democratized access to technological resources. As organizations shift toward cloud-native infrastructure, they experience a reduction in resource consumption and carbon footprint, with a huge contribution to sustainability goals. This reshapes not only business practice but also societal norms on large scale toward responsible consumption and environmental care. Furthermore, cloud-native platforms provide emerging companies and emerging economies an opportunity to engage in innovations that, before, were hindered by expensive capital and infrastructure costs. Overcoming such barriers, cloud-native technologies allow a broader set of voices to join the technological universe, generating an environment of collaboration and innovation that drives industries ahead. Lastly, it is critical to deal with the ethics and governance problems presented by the shift toward cloud-native applications. As with any revolutionary technology, data sovereignty, privacy, and compliance become more complex since companies are operating in multi-tenant systems. All of these problems require a proactive way of treating governance and ethics policies that respect user privacy but make data accessible. As evident from recent overviews, overcoming these difficulties in an effective manner has the potential to enhance the integrity and trustworthiness of cloud-native applications. Policymakers and leaders in technology must join hands to design strategies that do not merely provide maximum gains of cloud-native technologies but also work towards minimizing associated risks, ultimately contributing to a more equitable and secure digital future (Mohammed, 2025; Munteanu, 2024).

In considering cloud-native concepts, there are a few important considerations that elucidate the revolution of cloud computing. Firstly, the inherent nature of cloud-native architecture is that it is built with dynamic scalability and resiliency in mind. Unlike more conventional infrastructures that are static and prone to bottlenecks, cloud-native systems use microservices and containerization to create modularized applications. Through modularity, applications can be deployed and developed at high speed, which allows for faster innovation and responsiveness to changing market conditions. Moreover, these architectures allow for CI/CD, which enables smooth updates and improvements without grueling system downtime. These are the essentials of businesses that need assistance to remain competitive in the world of rapid-fire digital change. The importance of security in cloud-native systems is another essential aspect. While the cloud infrastructure inherently offers flexibility and efficiency, it also presents particular vulnerabilities, particularly through aspects like graphics processing units (GPUs). As has been emphasized by research, GPUs can be a starting point of malicious actions and become a weakest link for an organization's security posture. They must be patched with full awareness of the potential threats and with proper security controls tailored specifically for cloud-native applications. Hence, organizations must place highest importance on the security of their cloud systems through constant assessment and adoption of best practices for securing clouds, ultimately establishing trust in their web-based operations (Abhinaya et al., 2018). Further, projects such as the 4CaaSt project reflect the evolution of platform as a service (PaaS) platform to enhance cloud-native deployments. This project gives emphasis to elasticity and lifecycle management, which are critical to guaranteeing performance and flexibility in a PaaS system. Through such innovations as the blueprint generation and management of resources, 4CaaSt provides the marketing and deployment of cloud services and applications, thus rendering users capable of utilizing cloud-native technology efficiently. These models provide plug-and-play functionality that is essential to organizations looking to transition into cloud-native models without invoking massive overhead or complexity (Andrikopoulos et al., 2012). Collectively, these components encapsulate the essence of cloud-native concepts: cultivating operational effectiveness with adopting modernization as well as weathering future security challenges.

REFERENCES

1. Abhinaya, S. B., Ali, I., Mittal, S., Reddy, A., et al. (2018). A survey of techniques for improving security of GPUs. http://arxiv.org/abs/1804.00114 (accessed on 11th September 2025).
2. Aguayo-González, F., Lama-Ruiz, J. R., Martín-Gómez, A. M., Ávila-Gutiérrez, M., et al. (2020). Eco-holonic 4.0 circular business model to conceptualize sustainable value chain towards digital transition. https://core.ac.uk/download/299807283.pdf (accessed on 11th September 2025).
3. Alavilo, A., & Puutonen, E. (2025). Containerization and Deployment of a Web Platform: via Red Hat OpenShift. https://core.ac.uk/download/657107253.pdf (accessed on 11th September 2025).
4. Allan, G. T., Benson, R. M., Bollig, E. F., Huerta, E., et al. (2018). Leveraging OpenStack and Ceph for a controlled-access data cloud. http://arxiv.org/abs/1807.08657 (accessed on 11th September 2025).
5. Andrawos, M., Aßmann, U., Bass, L., Behara, D. G. K., Betts, T., Bianco, P., Bryant, D., et al. (2019). Microservice transition and its granularity problem: A systematic mapping study. https://core.ac.uk/download/426749569.pdf (accessed on 11th September 2025).
6. Andrikopoulos, V., Biro, J., García-Gómez, S., Jiménez Gañán, A., et al. (2012). Challenges for the comprehensive management of cloud services in a PaaS framework. http://oa.upm.es/15893/ (accessed on 11th September 2025).
7. Asai, M., Bauerdick, L., Borgland, A., Calafiura, A., et al. (2015). High Energy Physics Forum for Computational Excellence: Working group reports (I. Applications software II. Software libraries and tools III. Systems). http://arxiv.org/abs/1510.08545 (accessed on 11th September 2025).
8. Azariah, W., Bimo, F. A., Lin, C. W., Cheng, R. G., Nikaein, N., & Jana, R. (2024). A survey on open radio access networks: Challenges, research directions, and open-source approaches. Sensors, 24, 1038–1038. https://doi.org/10.3390/s24031038 (accessed on 11th September 2025).
9. Balalaie, A., Heydarnoori, A., & Jamshidi Dermani, P. (2016). Microservices architecture enables DevOps: An experience report on migration to a cloud-native architecture. https://core.ac.uk/download/77019042.pdf (accessed on 11th September 2025).
10. Beetz, J., Bourreau, P., Senthilvel, M., Van Berlo, L., et al. (2019). Semantic query languages for knowledge-based web services in a construction context. https://core.ac.uk/download/225020751.pdf (accessed on 11th September 2025).

11. Beltre, A., Govindaraju, M., Saha, P., Uminski, M., et al. (2019). Evaluation of Docker containers for scientific workloads in the cloud. http://arxiv.org/abs/1905.08415 (accessed on 11th September 2025).
12. Bensbaa, S., De Florio, V., Le-Phuoc, D., Rakay, R., & Yalgashev, O. (2016). Towards a smarter organization for a self-servicing society. http://arxiv.org/abs/1701.04616 (accessed on 11th September 2025).
13. Dehaye, P. O., Kohlhase, M., Konovalov, A., Lelièvre, S., et al. (2016). Interoperability in the OpenDreamKit Project: The Math-in-the-Middle approach. http://arxiv.org/abs/1603.06424 (accessed on 11th September 2025).
14. Dimitrakos, T., Nair, S. K., Rajarajan, M., Sajjad, A., et al. (2012). Secure communication using dynamic VPN provisioning in an Inter-Cloud environment. https://core.ac.uk/download/9559393.pdf (accessed on 11th September 2025).
15. Dries, A., Gutiérrez, A., Iosup, A., Morari, A., Poulovassilis, A., Zhu, A. D., Mendelzon, A. O., et al. (2017). An introduction to graph data management. http://arxiv.org/abs/1801.00036 (accessed on 11th September 2025).
16. Dwivedi, Y. K., Hughes, L., Baabdullah, A. M., Ribeiro-Navarrete, S., Giannakis, M., Al-Debei, M. M., Dennehy, D., et al. (2022). Metaverse beyond the hype: Multidisciplinary perspectives on emerging challenges, opportunities, and agenda for research, practice and policy. International Journal of Information Management, 66, 102542–102542. https://doi.org/10.1016/j.ijinfomgt.2022.102542 (accessed on 11th September 2025).
17. Dwivedi, Y. K., Kshetri, N., Hughes, L., Slade, E., Jeyaraj, A., Kar, A. K., Baabdullah, A. M., et al. (2023). Opinion paper: "So what if ChatGPT wrote it?" Multidisciplinary perspectives on opportunities, challenges and implications of generative conversational AI for research, practice and policy. International Journal of Information Management, 71, 102642–102642. https://doi.org/10.1016/j.ijinfomgt.2023.102642 (accessed on 11th September 2025).
18. Evans, E., Hohpe, G., Humble, J., Nygard, M., Stine, M., Mendonca, N., Jamshidi, P., et al. (2015). Migrating to cloud-native architectures using microservices: An experience report. http://arxiv.org/abs/1507.08217 (accessed on 11th September 2025).
19. Evans, E., Hohpe, G., Humble, J., Nygard, M., Stine, M., Mendonca, N., Jamshidi, P., et al. (2015). Migrating to cloud-native architectures using microservices: An experience report. http://arxiv.org/abs/1507.08217 (accessed on 11th September 2025).

20. Fodor, B., & Sonkoly, B. (2025). Improved performance control of cloud-native microservices in the edge with proactive autoscaling. NOMS 2025–2025 IEEE Network Operations and Management Symposium. https://www.semanticscholar.org/paper/388367b6a00f5fb6e4559f2c52a8b3e1c3a25f77 (accessed on 11th September 2025).
21. Ganapathi, A. (2025). Zero trust evolution: Advanced architectures for resilient cloud-native IAM systems. International Journal of Scientific Research in Computer Science, Engineering and Information Technology. https://www.semanticscholar.org/paper/6d8b10cad316539ae029cd07cdd0aa9b4e37366f (accessed on 11th September 2025).
22. Huynh-The, T., Gadekallu, T. R., Wang, W., Yenduri, G., Ranaweera, P., Pham, Q.-V., da Costa, D. B., et al. (2023). Blockchain for the metaverse: A review. Future Generation Computer Systems, 143, 401–419. https://doi.org/10.1016/j.future.2023.02.008 (accessed on 11th September 2025).
23. Johnson, L., Levine, A., & Smith, R. (2009). Horizon Report 2009. https://core.ac.uk/download/13285380.pdf (accessed on 11th September 2025).
24. Jordanov, J., & Petrov, P. (2023). Domain driven design approaches in cloud native service architecture. TEM Journal. https://www.semanticscholar.org/paper/9f7f4a0e93215281e236eaa579c04098057e9126 (accessed on 11th September 2025).
25. Kratzke, N., & Peinl, R. (2017). ClouNS–A cloud-native application reference model for enterprise architects. http://arxiv.org/abs/1709.04883 (accessed on 11th September 2025).
26. Lakka, M. (2025). Kubernetes for enterprise: Mastering cloud-native container orchestration at scale. European Modern Studies Journal. https://www.semanticscholar.org/paper/74a3ca9455cc80bf046672aebb75d949412773b9 (accessed on 11th September 2025).
27. Liang, P., Wu, Y., Xu, Z., Xiao, S., & Yuan, J. (2024). Enhancing security in DevOps by integrating artificial intelligence and machine learning. Journal of Theory and Practice of Engineering Science, 4, 31–37. https://doi.org/10.53469/jtpes.2024.04(02).05 (accessed on 11th September 2025).
28. Malipeddi, A. R. (2025). The shift to cloud-native data architectures in the insurance industry: A technical review. World Journal of Advanced Research and Reviews. https://www.semanticscholar.org/paper/36c6eb54c5decd71cbd9d547e7d67902f2a43789 (accessed on 11th September 2025).
29. Mohammed, N. A. (2025). Cloud-native technologies AI-enhanced observability: Machine learning pipeline for Kubernetes

log analytics in EKS environments. World Journal of Advanced Research and Reviews. https://www.semanticscholar.org/paper/acdfd38a959bfbb622928849f4160ca04fd5201a (accessed on 11th September 2025).

30. Mohammed, N. A. (2025). The convergence horizon: Cloud-native technologies reshaping society and infrastructure. World Journal of Advanced Engineering Technology and Sciences. https://www.semanticscholar.org/paper/36c2cd1366e5f5de58322c15347c7fafbbe18543 (accessed on 11th September 2025).
31. Molleti, R. (2025). Comparing serverless and microservices architecture patterns in fintech space. International Journal of Scientific Research in Engineering and Management. https://www.semanticscholar.org/paper/e501bc346b73632783b704c9ce173e9409cb825e (accessed on 11th September 2025).
32. Morillo Reina, J. D., & Mateo Sanguino, T. J. M. (2024). Cloud-based automatic configuration and disaster recovery of communication systems applied in engineering training. Electronics. https://www.semanticscholar.org/paper/8ca576eb90c9b6fb049a4b4753684f29521d80b6 (accessed on 11th September 2025).
33. Munteanu, A. (2024). Data cubes and cloud-native environments for Earth observation: An overview. Scalable Computing: Practice and Experience, 25. https://www.semanticscholar.org/paper/dcbc300fae7c3c37612a492fa1dd40a8ca2c89df (accessed on 11th September 2025).
34. N/A. (2017). SciTech News, 71(1). https://core.ac.uk/download/83049835.pdf (accessed on 11th September 2025).
35. Nandi, S. P. (2025). Serverless databases: Architectural evolution, implementation strategies, and future directions in cloud-native data management. World Journal of Advanced Research and Reviews. https://www.semanticscholar.org/paper/e6098fa25fd5cc8e68bbd44c1018c6dd0ed18fa5 (accessed on 11th September 2025).
36 Oyeniran, O. C., Adewusi, A. O., Adeleke, A. G., Akwawa, L. A., & Azubuko, C. F. (2024). Microservices architecture in cloud-native applications: Design patterns and scalability. Computer Science & IT Research Journal. https://www.semanticscholar.org/paper/62cf8cdf0051c8d4e68e1cf8cac402fc5626e723 (accessed on 11th September 2025).
37. Oyeniran, O. C., Modupe, O. T., Otitoola, A. A., Abiona, O. O., Adewusi, A. O., & Oladapo, O. J. (2024). A comprehensive review of leveraging

cloud-native technologies for scalability and resilience in software development. International Journal of Science and Research Archive. https://www.semanticscholar.org/paper/45d7d25f6184feaedb5347bd150650621dcdff76 (accessed on 11th September 2025).

38. Paladi, N. (2012). Trusted computing and secure virtualization in cloud computing. https://core.ac.uk/download/11435290.pdf (accessed on 11th September 2025).

39. Sana, S. K. (2025). Pioneering adaptive transaction isolation in cloud-native microservices: A dynamic algorithm achieving optimal consistency-performance balance. World Journal of Advanced Engineering Technology and Sciences. https://www.semanticscholar.org/paper/774c59c5e0a6532ce757bb9bdcb267e6efe8f243 (accessed on 11th September 2025).

40. Strand, H. (2018). Breaking Barriers to Renewable Energy Production in the North American Arctic. https://core.ac.uk/download/213020138.pdf (accessed on 11th September 2025).

41. Wang, C. X., You, X., Gao, X., Zhu, X., Li, Z., Zhang, C., Wang, H., et al. (2023). On the road to 6G: Visions, requirements, key technologies, and testbeds. IEEE Communications Surveys & Tutorials, 25, 905–974. https://doi.org/10.1109/comst.2023.3249835 (accessed on 11th September 2025).

42. Yanamadala, P. (2025). Demystifying cloud-native enterprise architecture: A framework for digital transformation in complex organizations. World Journal of Advanced Research and Reviews. https://www.semanticscholar.org/paper/36aaa423ac52699d5d03295128cdf8b10565d23a (accessed on 11th September 2025).

43. Zatonskiy, P. A., Shakleina, R. V., & Krasovskiy, R. V. (2025). Modern methods of collecting and analyzing employers' requirements for training IT workers. Bulletin of the South Ural State University. Ser. Computer Technologies, Automatic Control & Radioelectronics. https://www.semanticscholar.org/paper/092a8aecbd6eeb43eaede0101b3f010dbbeada55 (accessed on 11th September 2025).

CHAPTER 2

MICROSERVICES ARCHITECTURE

Contents

INTRODUCTION

Microservices architecture is a cutting-edge software design and development paradigm optimally suited to the demands of modern applications. Traditional monolithic architectures put all functions into a single, tightly coupled unit that constrains agility and scalability. Microservices, however, are advocates of a distributed pattern in which applications are made up of small, independent services that are built, deployed, and scaled separately. This degree of detail allows teams to work on different pieces simultaneously, thereby accelerating collaboration and minimizing release cycles. Additionally, microservices facilitate better fault isolation; if a single service fails, it does not necessarily impact the entire app. By embracing a microservices architecture, companies are in a better place to respond to evolving market demands as well as maximize their operational effectiveness. Furthermore, adopting microservices entails changing the development style towards application architecture and administration. This pattern of architecture is compatible with cloud-native technologies that focus on dynamic sharing of resources, continuous integration, and continuous delivery. Such technologies make it possible for companies to utilize microservices effectively as part of a cloud environment, streamlining operations and ensuring that resources are utilized to their fullest. Modular design of microservices makes it possible to employ several programming languages and frameworks, giving developers the freedom to choose the best tools for each service. Orchestration and control of microservices play a vital role in maintaining smooth interactions and are made possible through sophisticated tools and platforms for their deployment and scalability. With organizations now venturing into cloud-native technology, the integration of microservices becomes part and parcel in unleashing the actual value of their applications (Zheng et al., 2024). Despite the huge benefits, the transition to a microservices architecture has its drawbacks. Firms must overcome service orchestration, data management, and communication between services complexities as well as maintaining security and compliance. The distributed nature of microservices can make it difficult to have uniform governance and management, which adds complexity to regulatory compliance. Further, as more services are proliferated, network traffic and service dependencies increase, potentially leading to performance bottlenecks. Organizations therefore must invest in good monitoring and logging infrastructures to manage the complexities effectively. By addressing these challenges head-on, companies are then able to realize the full potential of microservices architecture, positioning themselves for future innovation and operational excellence in an increasingly digitized future (Randhi, 2025).

Definition of Microservices

Microservices architecture is a paradigm shift for software development, independent deployable services that communicate through well-defined APIs. This is in contrast to traditional monolithic methods, where a single unit manages everything about an application. By breaking up the capabilities into smaller bits that are manageable, developers can use agile methodologies for continuous deployment and integration with ease. Each microservice performs a particular functionality, allowing teams to work separately on various parts of the application, thereby boosting productivity and speeding up delivery cycles. This modularity not only makes room for innovation via speedy experimentation but also enhances system resilience by isolating risks of failure when services collapse, thus guaranteeing the overall application stability.

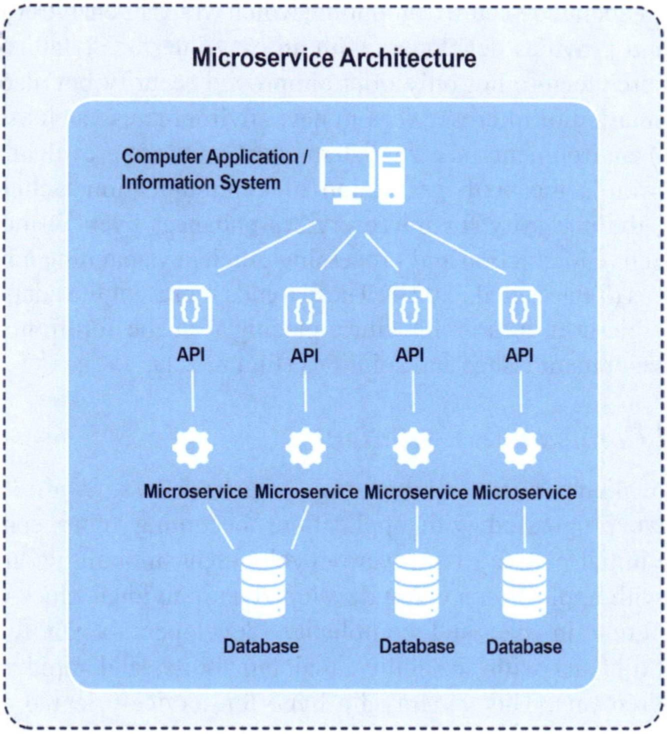

Figure 2.1. *Microservices architecture represents a paradigm shift in software dev.*

Source: https://bi-insider.com/wp-content/uploads/2021/09/Microservice-Architecture.png.

The sense of definition is also increased by the fact that microservices have the ability to enhance scalability and flexibility in complex systems. Rather than requiring the rewriting of the application during scaling, organizations have the ability to enhance individual microservices. The ease with which this can be done without interrupting the whole system makes it simple to maintain and change. Also, microservices' pluralistic characteristic enables them to be coded using different programming languages such that the most effective tools and frameworks can be employed that suit each services requirements. For instance, certain services require optimization in performance, whereas others require better security implementations, which makes for a more secure overall application framework that can keep up with changing technological environments and needs of the users. Bridging sophisticated technologies, microservices tend to employ middleware solutions that manage intensive interactions among services to provide security and efficient resource management. An example of this is the utilization of Federated Secure Computing, which wraps intensive cryptographic operations and provides developers with an easy interface (Ballhausen et al., 2023). This architecture not only offers improved security but also facilitates the implementation of microservices in new environments, such as Internet of Things (IoT) environments, where system constraints are prevalent. Moreover, as efforts towards the sixth generation of communication technologies are progressing, the necessity for microservices enhances even further, with the need for effective interaction and processing efficiency spanning a broad range of applications (Tataria et al., 2021). These trends represent the adaptability and potential of microservices architecture, placing it at the forefront of modern software development issues and solutions (Figure 2.1).

Historical Context and Evolution

The history of microservices architecture goes back to how software development methods have progressed with applications becoming more complex with time. In the initial phases of software development, monolithic architectures were used, with applications being developed as individual blocks. However, as systems grew in size and complexity, developers began to encounter significant problems with scalability, maintainability, and rapid response to market requirements. This generated a hype for service-oriented architecture (SOA) during the early 2000s that made possible the design of loosely coupled services. The fundamental building blocks of SOA established a platform for microservices based on modularization and interoperability among different software components. The transition from SOA to microservices architecture has been a huge step forward in software engineering practice. While SOA promoted service consumption, microservices also recommended that services be expressed as small, standalone units of work, which may be independently deployed and scaled. This architecture caters to the shifting technological landscape and the needs of companies to adapt rapidly to new business situations. Cloud computing and containerization were among the facilitators of microservices because they provided simple deployment and management of different applications. Furthermore, the advancements reflected advancements in mobile communication, where advancement to 5G further supported calls for systems that ought to be capable of adapting to high-data-rate exchanges and low-latency requirements, leading to amplified use of microservices in existing software solutions (Tataria et al., 2021). Future technologies also underscore the future of microservices, where they join forces with edge computing and advanced networking in a bid to deliver solutions for existing application issues. In the case of the Internet of Everything (IoE), microservices architecture is increasingly crucial for managing huge data transmissions and interconnected devices. The limitations of conventional systems led to the need for innovative approaches in terms of agility, redundancy, and security. With microservices being compatible with technologies such as artificial intelligence and blockchain, organisations can leverage cross-disciplinary approaches to discover better software ecosystems. This kind of evolution is a call to address the demand for systems that can handle complexity introduced by next-generation networks and applications, with microservices being one methodology to simplify application design and delivery in today's digital age (Kong et al., 2022).

Importance in Modern Software Development

The software development methodologies have changed with time, which has driven the growing importance of microservices architecture for contemporary applications that are required to be highly scalable and versatile. Monolithic structures fail to keep up with evolving needs, making it hard for organizations to scale applications. Microservices, however, decompose applications into smaller, isolated deployments, which enables teams to create various services concurrently. This modular design not only enhances agility but also allows for easy updating and deployment of each component separately without affecting the overall system. As more and more organizations respond to market forces, the ability to iterate and deploy faster with microservices is a competitive advantage that supports further innovation and responsiveness in a high-speed environment (Gite, 2025). In addition to supporting agility, microservices architecture significantly enhances reliability and fault tolerance of computer systems. Since every microservice executes independently, the failure in one service does not necessarily endanger the entire application. This separation-of-concern minimizes the possibility of system failures and allows selective responses to issues in real time. Pattern design also calls for the implementation of service orchestration and API management, which can further serve to enhance the process of streamlining interaction between services. Microservices also facilitate better resource allocation, enabling dynamic optimization of performance by implementing some of the services on suitable infrastructures that meet their requirements. The cloud-native application has further added to these benefits, whereby organizations can leverage superior technologies such as container orchestration and serverless computing to increase their microservices deployments (Singhal, 2024). Microservices architecture has also changed the way collaboration occurs between operations and development teams, a practice commonly referred to as DevOps. This paradigm change leads to a shared responsibility culture and effective communication, which is necessary for high-quality software management in dynamic environments. Microservices enable continuous integration and continuous deployment (CI/CD) pipelines, with more frequent updates and short delivery cycles. This constant collaboration speeds up innovation while keeping issue resolution and new feature delivery time low. Furthermore, tuning microservices to specific business needs enhances efficiency because businesses can tailor solutions to address unique demands and industry requirements. As microservices architecture gains popularity in modern software development, its importance lies in its capacity to drive efficiency, collaboration, and rapid growth (Gite, 2025) (Figure 2.2).

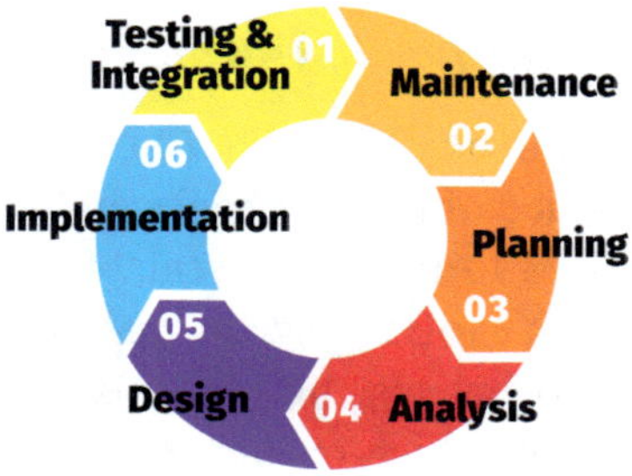

Figure 2.2. *The evolution of software development practices.*

Source: https://fortyseven47.com/storage/2021/04/fs-1.svg.

2.1. KEY CHARACTERISTICS OF MICROSERVICES

One of the most fundamental characteristics of microservices is modularity, allowing for the division of large-scale applications into smaller, independent units. Each microservice would usually be tied to a specific business function, and teams can therefore develop, deploy, and scale services in isolation. Separation enhances development team agility, as changes or patches are able to be made without disrupting the overall application. Microservices modularity adheres to the Rational Unified Process (R.U.P) fundamentals, which emphasize a systematic, iterative approach to building software and is central to keeping everyone who gets involved in the manufacturing process aligned. Through this method, microservices architecture can maintain a clear focus on user requirements as well as facilitate a very flexible development environment that can be mapped to evolving business needs (Dimitrios et al., 2022). Yet another basic characteristic of microservices is that they can be decentralized data management. Instead of the centralized database system, each microservice can handle its database, which not only enhances data ownership but also reduces the risks of bottlenecks associated with shared database systems. This decentralization allows every service to choose its database technology autonomously based on its specific needs, practicing polyglot persistence—a method in which different data storage technologies sit together in harmony. This autonomy brings improved performance, as services can store and retrieve data in the optimal manner for their processes. Moreover, decentralized data management favors the objective of fast deployment as developers can modify individual services without interfering with the overall system (Tataria et al., 2021). Lastly, resiliency is a marker of microservices architecture, and it is characterized by its ability to endure function in the event of failure. Since the services are split during design for an application, the architecture itself acts as a counter for the possibility of a system failure due to a point of failure. In microservices, if a service is down, other services can still be run in order to maintain system continuity. This is usually boosted with additional mechanisms such as circuit breakers and service discovery protocols, all of which work towards high availability and load balancing. As more companies adopt cloud-native technologies, the importance of microservices resilience is greater than ever before, prompting innovation in monitoring and recovery strategies to enable companies to foresee and prepare for unforeseen interruptions and build a robust application ecosystem that supports user requirements (Tataria et al., 2021).

2.1.1. Decentralization and Autonomy

Autonomy and decentralization are critical concepts to enhance the performance of microservices architecture so that systems are able to operate efficiently and autonomously. Microservices decentralization allows for various elements to operate autonomously, with reduced reliance on the central server. Microservices architecture is incredibly beneficial for businesses that want to scale applications. Through decentralization of tasks into several services, issues such as performance bottlenecks and single points of failure are significantly minimized. Secondly, with the increasing demand for rapid scalability, decentralized systems offer the elastic flexibility to adapt to changes in requirements without needing full overhauls. This level of autonomy enables development teams to deploy services in isolation, which nurtures a culture of innovation and rapid iteration crucial in today's fast-paced technology environment. Autonomy in microservices does not only increase efficiency in operations but also increases system resilience. Services in microservices architecture can handle their own states and recover from failures on their own without complete coordination. For instance, in a decentralized system, when a service encounters some issue, it can fail gracefully but allow other services to execute, thereby maintaining global system integrity. This autonomy is amenable to continuous integration and deployment approaches, where the parts can be modified or replaced individually. Incorporation of autonomous processes ensures services are able to change freely without compromising the overall architecture, thus making the system more flexible. As argued in disputes regarding the Cyber Physical Supply Chain Planning System (CPS2), application of autonomous microservices can potentially ensure maximum resource usage and optimize process effectiveness (Demartini et al., 2021). In addition, decentralization combined with autonomy facilitates novel mechanisms for addressing complicated issues, such as in Space Traffic Management (STM). Within such a context, decentralized microservices architecture constructed on open Application Programming Interfaces (APIs) facilitates simple interactions between varied stakeholders, promoting cooperation while maintaining autonomous individuality. The integration of automated systems in decision-making and data exchange enhances the ability to take proactive control of future space collisions, illustrating how flexible architectures can be constructed to optimize outcome in various areas. By utilizing modern development practices, as demonstrated in the STM prototype, organizations can harness the power of microservices to adapt to rapidly evolving challenges, contributing to safer and more efficient operations in ever-increasing spacecraft populations (Kopardekar et al., 2025).

2.1.2. Scalability and Flexibility

Scalability and flexibility become essential traits in microservices architecture, enhancing an organization's ability to respond and stay alive in an increasingly dynamic technological world. Microservices make it possible to decompose monolithic applications into small, independent services, which can be developed, deployed, and scaled independently. This type of architecture enables teams to address explicit business needs without the need for systemic redesign. Where workloads are changing, dynamic resource allocation can be applied, keeping the performance level stable under alternate requirements. This type of flexibility becomes enormously useful in areas like medicine, where there are chances for sudden spikes in usage of applications to impact operational effectiveness and outcome of patient care. Emphasizing such characteristics, studies emphasize the intrinsic strengths of microservices, specifically their ability to provide responsive and adaptive solutions to complex systems in a dynamic environment, thus enhancing overall resilience (Akerele et al.,

2024). Moreover, inherent flexibility in microservices architecture allows firms to innovate at a rapid pace by introducing new features or services without disrupting ongoing operations. Microservices enable teams to employ diverse programming languages, databases, and frameworks aligned with service requirements, promoting technological flexibility culture. This diversity enhances the potential for the use of the most appropriate tool for every task and hence optimum performance and utilization of resources. As more organizations abandon monolithic Digital Experience Platforms (DXPs) for microservices-based systems, they are presented with various challenges to plan to implement successfully. By focusing on business capabilities and decomposing service components in a step-by-step manner, organizations can mitigate transformation risk and enjoy the benefits of scalability and flexibility inherent in microservices (Sethi et al., 2024). In addition, strategic adoption of microservices not only addresses immediate performance and scalability challenges but also lays the groundwork for future innovation. When companies undergo digital transformation, the demand for rapid response to market swings builds up, and thus organizations need to embrace the flexibility of microservices architecture. Due to continuous integration and deployment, microservices facilitate organizations to accelerate the development cycle easily, allowing them to prototype their products at never-before-seen speeds. Such operational efficiencies not only contribute to increased customer satisfaction but also lead to competitiveness in their respective markets. With microservices revolutionizing organizational software development, emphasis on scalability and adaptability becomes even more crucial in order to ensure that companies remain sustainable and responsive amid constant technological evolution (Akerele et al., 2024; Sethi et al., 2024).

2.1.3. Technology Diversity

Diversity in technology within microservices architecture plays a pivotal role in enhancing the resiliency and scalability of a system. With a polyglot strategy, organizations are able to operate with multiple programming languages, frameworks, and tools that best fit certain service requirements. This provides flexibility in selecting the best technology stack for a specific microservice, making it perform best and optimize the use of resources. Consequently, overall reliability of distributed systems improves because the effects of potential failures can be neutralized by heterogeneous technologies. Technology diversity adoption further enables teams to cooperate more effectively and innovate because diverse skills and perspectives enable continuous improvement culture. Ultimately, the practice results in a stronger architectural foundation that can handle evolving market demands and technological advancements. Deployment of microservices architecture is directly linked with the adoption of multiplicity of technology in order to address unique problems that accompany distributed systems. Automated testing practices, for instance, become crucial in ensuring the verification of the functionality and performance of microservices developed with diverse languages and frameworks. As noted in the definition of testing practices, tiered testing methods like unit, integration, contract, and end-to-end testing methods are crucial to verification of guaranteeing completeness. Various tools and technologies—such as API test framework and observability tools—must be merged into a common testing strategy to effectively cater to heterogeneity microservice ecosystems.

Figure 2.3. *Technology diversity.*

Source: https://media.istockphoto.com/id/1209869264/photo/click-here-and-it-should-direct-you-further.jpg?s=612x612&w=0&k=20&c=Ro4bJAAyRslFJSEvHLST6joJS2Ho2ThQg9GNTGzSQhE=

The intricate relationship between technology heterogeneity and test methodologies indicates the imperative of adopting a holistic and adaptable approach to quality assurance in microservices architecture, ultimately culminating in system reliability and user satisfaction (Dhandapani, 2025). Additionally, technology heterogeneity in microservices architecture is best exhibited with the rise of machine learning technologies. Incorporating machine learning algorithms, such as K-Nearest Neighbors and Bayesian Personalized Ranking, into container scheduling algorithms yields optimal resource usage and effectiveness, especially in edge computing. This heterogeneity allows organizations to take advantage of advances in machine learning to enable improved decision-making and optimization strategies. The comparative analysis of container scheduling methods reveals dramatic improvements in scheduling time and accuracy using machine learning techniques. This reflects the transformative power of technology diversity in enabling microservices to automatically adjust to real-time data and user demand, resulting in a more agile and responsive system that can counter the complexity of modern computing environments (Baker et al., 2025) (Figure 2.3).

2.2. BENEFITS OF MICROSERVICES ARCHITECTURE

Embracing microservices architecture benefits organizations with more scalability, a critical factor in the ever-changing market today. Microservices facilitate independent scaling of separate components based on demand, as opposed to monolithic systems, which require extensive rework to grow. With such adaptability, businesses can more effectively allocate resources in response to desired infrastructure support for high-demand services without overwhelming less-trafficked functions. Because each service operates in its own environment, the ability to scale computer resources becomes not only easier but also more cost-effective. By providing tailored scalability, microservices allow companies to respond rapidly to increases in user traffic, thus enhancing general application performance and user experience. Apart from that, this architectural style also aligns with current trends towards cloud solutions wherein microservices' modularity and thinness lean towards convenience in deployment and scaling approaches as supported by the findings of Busi (2025) findings. The second benefit of microservices architecture lies in its enhanced resilience of software programs. With monolithic applications, a failure in one component has the potential to take the whole application down, meaning downtime and user inconvenience. Microservices are designed to be independent in a way that if one service fails, others will still be able to function normally, thereby reducing the potential for failure of the whole system. This isolation permits the application of updates and patches to single services without having to bring down the entire application, thus enabling more predictable stability and uptime. In addition, this type of resilience is also vital for companies operating in those industries where service continuity is paramount, such as finance and healthcare. With added fault tolerance and simplified recovery mechanisms, microservices form an integral component of a robust application infrastructure, as evident in the best practices discussed in Njina et al. (2025). Microservices architecture also promotes technological diversity and team autonomy, allowing firms to leverage the best tools and frameworks for specific functions. Microservices architecture gives the development teams the liberty of choosing the best technology suited for their services without being restrained by a single tech stack. It not only drives innovation but also facilitates incorporating new and future technologies and programming languages into existing systems. Moreover, the independence of the services encourages cross-functional teams to be self-sufficient, increasing the development cycles and resulting in productivity. Since groups are less reliant and more accountable for their work, they can better collaborate and drive collective energy. The culmination of all of these advances ultimately yields a more responsive company that can rapidly adapt to market demand and technological shifts, further validating the arguments in favor of adopting a microservices architecture as detailed at greater length in Busi (2025) (Figure 2.4).

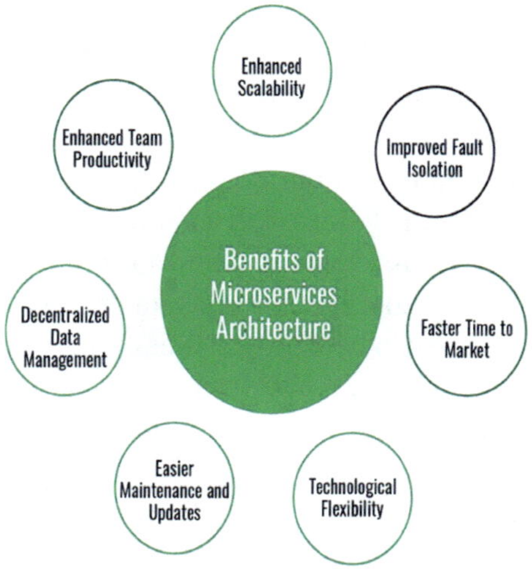

Figure 2.4. *Benefits of microservices architecture.*

Source: https://www.mega.com/sites/tera/files/inline-images/benefits-of-microservices-architecture.webp.

2.2.1. Improved Development Speed

Increased velocity of development is most notable in microservices architecture, a radical departure from the monolithic software systems of yesteryears. Microservices enable teams to develop different components of an application simultaneously without interfering in the development of the other. This parallel development not only accelerates the rate of innovation but also facilitates rapid iteration based on feedback, hence quicker deployment. Therefore, organizations can respond faster to the needs of the market, innovate due to regulatory adjustments, or add new features that make their products relevant and competitive. Decoupling of services enables efficiency as it enables teams to focus on their area of expertise and have repositories and deployment pipelines instantiable as independent units, thus reducing lead time across the entire development lifecycle. Apart from that, microservices allow one to integrate new development methodologies such as DevOps and continuous integration/ continuous deployment (CI/CD). This integration offers a platform where code changes are capable of being tested and deployed with minimal resistance, hence enhancing collaboration between developers, testers, and operations personnel. Consequently, the risk of deployment failure decreases since small, manageable updates replace large, complex releases. Also, native scalability in microservices gives teams the power to allocate resources dynamically and optimize operations as required.

Figure 2.5 *Improved development speed.*

Source: https://media.licdn.com/dms/image/v2/D4E12AQFkY-rMCx6b6A/article-cover_image-shrink_720_1280/article-cover_image-shrink_720_1280/0/1682410092491?e=2147483647&v=beta&t=GZAZVAVHtZNgFLOS8wLwgsfGhTsMFScoPXonXN-X5CY.

The teamwork culture supported by CI/CD pipelines easily integrates with microservice deployments in a manner that incremental enhancement can easily be made. This is most evident in sectors like healthcare, where the effective integration of technologies equates to improved outcomes, such as when chatbot technologies are utilized to improve interactions and workflow design that are central to delivering quality care (Xu et al., 2021). Further, microservices architecture helps facilitate increased scalability for development processes, which translates beautifully into reduced delivery cycles. With decomposition of applications into smaller, individually deployable services, organizations can scale development resources according to particular workloads and requirements. This offers flexibility to development teams to concentrate on those key services that require immediate attention while spreading resources evenly across various areas of an application, which is most required during usage periods when there is peak demand. This type of system is also pertinent in the environments where rapid technological advancement is needed, as highlighted in the case of smart cities based on the Internet of Things (IoT) for efficiency and sustainability (Bellini et al., 2022). These development advancements support the manner in which microservices lead to large gains in development speed, bearing testament to the architecture acting as a catalyst to innovation and operational efficiency in most industries (Figure 2.5).

2.2.2. Enhanced Fault Isolation

In the case of microservices architecture, heightened fault isolation is one of the primary mechanisms for enhancing system resilience and guaranteeing operational continuity. Unlike monolithic systems, where an individual point of failure will lead to complete system down-time, microservices facilitate function encapsulation within independent services. This decoupling enables more detailed fault management wherein faults in one service do not propagate to others, hence lower systemic risks. By efficiently isolating faults, organizations can maintain high levels of availability and performance, which is especially vital in conditions demanding quick response to evolving conditions. As stressed, fault isolation's ability to enhance supports a robust software development cycle that further reinforces the overall reliability of distributed systems (Gundala, 2025). Improved fault isolation is also another main advantage supported by its continuous deployment and integration strategy. With microservices architecture, each service may be scaled or upgraded without undermining the stability of the entire application. This agility is a selling point for modern development teams since new features can be added, and bugs resolved with minimal inconvenience to end-users. Real-time monitoring of these services enables developers to discover, diagnose, and resolve issues in real time, enhancing user experience and satisfaction. Reusable services do necessitate, however, the execution of sophisticated monitoring tools and processes that deliver insight into service health and performance. For instance, the utilization of sophisticated observability frameworks facilitates detection of bottlenecks as well as optimization of resource allocation, ultimately for the aim of continuous service provision (Kumar, 2025). Secondly, the application of enhanced fault isolation serves a greater purpose than solely the immediate advantage of increased performance; it also facilitates playing a critical function in furthering innovations for companies. By creating a risk-tolerant culture where teams can experiment with new ideas without risking the entire system, companies can best take advantage of technological advancements. The innovation is particularly significant in e-commerce and digital services industries where flexible and responsive solutions are required to respond to customer demands. With use cases such as cloud-based ordering processing systems, the benefits of microservices architecture in supporting fault isolation are demonstrated, with notable operational efficiencies compared to legacy systems. Thus, as firms weather the storms of digital transformation, the strategic implementation of enhanced fault isolation remains key to sustaining competitive advantage in an increasingly complex landscape (Kumar, 2025) (Figure 2.6).

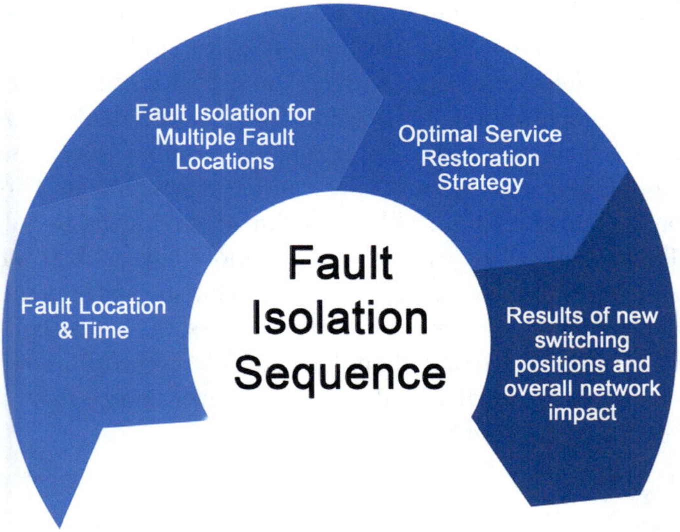

Figure 2.6. The *fault-isolation-sequence.*

Source: https://etap.com/images/default-source/product/fault-isolation-service-restoration/fault-isolation-sequence.jpg?sfvrsn=41efb97f_14.

2.2.3. Better Resource Utilization

Microservices architecture provides a key transition towards improved utilization of resources in software development by encouraging distributed and loosely integrated systems. It enables organizations to deploy their applications as separate services so that they can be managed and allocated more efficiently. Individual microservices can be scaled as needed, which is especially useful in cloud environments where resources can be provisioned and de-provisioned on the fly. The intrinsic malleability of microservices supports dynamic scaling that handles different loads efficiently, hence avoiding wastage of resources and minimizing overall operational expenditure, which is a key factor emphasized in recent research (Blinowski et al., 2022). Strategic allocation of microservices also improves the use of idle computing resources. Since microservices enable different parts of an application to execute independently, companies are able to manage workloads more effectively across available hardware. Since microservices can be independently developed, updated, and deployed, this architectural benefit enables developers to maximize the performance of individual services, thus resulting in more efficient CPU and memory utilization. This is an optimized resource usage that can result in tremendous cost reduction and enhanced application reliability, with resources being used per real-time requirement instead of static provisioning methods commonly applied in monolithic structures (Tataria et al., 2021). In addition, microservices architecture also maximizes the use of resources by the use of automation and orchestration tools which simplify the deployment process. Such tools as Kubernetes not only automate resource allocation but also allow for monitoring, scaling, and microservice management. Through such orchestration, organizations are able to optimize workloads distribution and automatically adjust to changes in demand without any manual intervention, greatly improving on responsiveness and agility. This smooth interaction among services fosters a more efficient usage of resources, such that computational resources are not overloaded or underutilized, which is critical for organizations seeking to attain operational excellence in the ever-competitive digital age (Blinowski et al., 2022) (Figure 2.7).

Figure 2.7. *The resource-utilization-mistakes-graph-scaled.*

Source: https://www.ganttic.com/wp-content/uploads/2018/10/resource-utilization-mistakes-graph-scaled-1.jpg.

2.3. CHALLENGES OF IMPLEMENTING MICROSERVICES

Introduction of microservices architecture brings along a list of serious issues to be resolved by organizations if they want to realize its anticipated benefits. One of the significant issues of concern is the inherent complexity pertaining to handling a distributed system. When compared to traditional monolithic architecture, microservices require a broad perspective on service orchestration, inter-service communication, and data management. As services are loosely connected, organizations often lack the ability to keep different components consistent and reliable. This complexity can exacerbate issues such as latency and failover response time, which makes operational efficiency increasingly harder to attain. Hence, careful planning and robust architecture design are extremely important to prevent the traps associated with this complex environment.

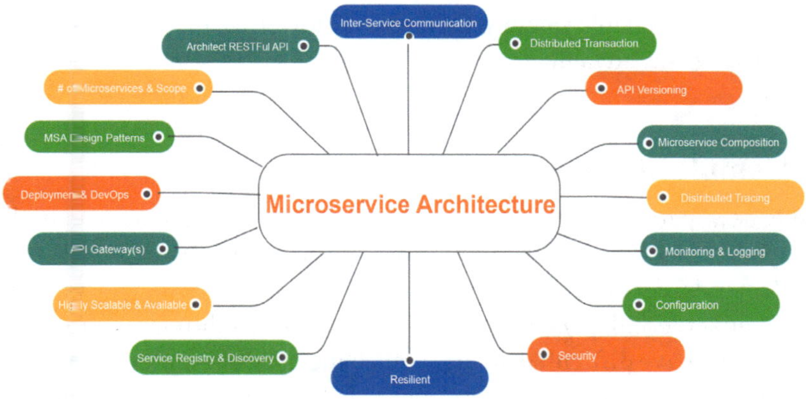

Figure 2.8. *The implementation of microservices architecture.*

Source: https://media.licdn.com/dms/image/v2/D5612AQGqJTfTvKzcWg/article-cover_image-shrink_600_2000/article-cover_image-shrink_600_2000/0/1702242470323?e=2147483647&v=beta&t=o3SC8YmmexgasBt3lj-Woh8Wv6Ev5gPX-P9iChffWFCc.

Additionally, the transition to microservices architecture is a profound change in cultural and procedural practices in organizations. Enactment of this architecture could be accompanied by the adoption of DevOps practices, which promotes collaboration between development and operations. This type of cultural change can be resisted as well, as the former ways and duties might get blurred. Organizations might find it difficult to adapt existing workflows and procedures to enable continuous integration and deployment practices necessary for microservices. Delay in transition and even project failure may result from resistance if proper management is not exercised. Creating a culture of innovation and agility is key to successfully implementing microservices and realizing their full potential. Companies must also deal with skills and tooling to execute microservices. The architectural transition requires knowledge about cloud computing, containerization, and orchestration technology such as Kubernetes and Docker. Finding skilled personnel with expertise in these areas can be quite challenging, particularly in industries where technical personnel are needed in large numbers. Also, existing personnel might need to be completely retrained, an exercise that takes resources and time away from other essential operations. This is reinforced in the implementation of microservices with a telco's experience, where a market-leading company faced setbacks due to inadequate preparation and skills gaps, and this resulted in a three-month project delay (Amri et al., 2024). It is, therefore, crucial to address the skills gaps in developing deployment effectiveness, lowering transition complexity, and actualizing the advantages vowed by microservices architecture (Figure 2.8).

2.3.1. Complexity in Management

With the new paradigm of software development, management complexity is hugely driven by adoption of microservices architecture. The pattern of design demands departure from monolithic applications to loosely coupled services that serve independent functionalities. Although making a transition, companies also have difficult management challenges, particularly coordination and communication among microservices. Decentralized control can lead to inconsistencies and mismatch in organizational behavior, for which managers will have to use sophisticated strategies to bring harmony among teams. In addition, hierarchical management models could be less effective, which would require reconsideration of leadership functions and relationships in an attempt to develop a harmonious setting where microservices can thrive (Andrawos et al., 2019). Besides, with the adoption of microservices, companies must deal with the subtleties involved in the management of technological innovation and operational effectiveness. Each microservice is a stand-alone entity, but at the same time it has its dependency on interactions with other services to offer end-to-end functionalities. Interdependence creates vulnerabilities since changes in one service can inadvertently affect others' functionality. To counter these risks, effective management involves a sharp awareness of service granularity and its influence on system performance as a whole. Managers are responsible for deploying an elastic strategy, adapting their strategies to keep pace with the constantly shifting nature of microservices while making sure teams are always locked in with higher organizational goals (Hoque et al., 2018). This calls for adopting practices that ensure constant integration and deployment, developing a resiliency against the perpetually changing alterations. Further, the complexity of managing microservices is compounded by the need for robust analytical frameworks for enabling data-driven business decision-making. As businesses leverage microservices in processing and analyzing huge amounts of data, management must develop mechanisms for harnessed high scalability and maintainability of such architectures. The emergence of a multi-layered microservices design, as established in present studies, accentuates the degree of high cohesion and low coupling as being integral to effectively managing data flows. These types of architectures not only enhance scalability but facilitate better monitoring and managing of microservices. By incorporating precisely defined analytics into their operational models, organizations can overcome the challenges of microservices management while encouraging innovation and efficacy in their processes (Hoque et al., 2018).

2.3.2. Data Consistency Issues

In microservices architecture, data consistency becomes one of the most critical issues for developers and architects. Decentralization of microservices gives flexibility and scalability but makes it much harder to manage data. It is extremely hard when services are autonomous to keep all instances of data in sync. Traditional database management policies operated in monolithic setups tend to fail in the distributed environment. Application developers then resort to using eventual consistency models, which prioritize system availability and partition tolerance at the expense of real-time data correctness. This paradigm calls for a shift in the manner in which applications handle state management and transactions and sensitivity to the trade-offs needed to guarantee data consistency between services (Narv et al., 2025). To reconcile data consistency between microservices, several patterns and practices have been proposed. The Saga pattern is one approach, whereby transactions are broken down into a series of individual, distributed operations that can be managed independently. Though this pattern creates a vehicle to maintain consistency in the face of distributed microservices, it introduces complexity in the guise of error management and compensating transactions. In addition, use of techniques such as event sourcing and CQRS (Command Query Responsibility Segregation) can enhance data correctness with flexible writes and reads support. However, their enforcement requires thoughtful consideration of the underlying architecture because the overhead incurred comes at a cost to overall system performance. Accordingly, even though such solutions attempt to solve data consistency issues, they also compel developers to trade off between the competing needs for performance, reliability, and consistency (Iovescu et al., 2024). Further, the application of artificial intelligence (AI) in microservices development has begun to introduce new solutions to data consistency problems. Machine learning is one type of AI technology that can predict potential data synchronizing discrepancies and suggest proactive measures for avoiding inconsistency before they result in a noticeable effect in the user interface. However, one must be well familiar with both the architecture of microservices and data operations performed within them to implement AI successfully. In addition, the need for robust security mechanisms in AI implementations cannot be overstated, especially since data integrity violations could have devastating effects. While AI is a promising field to enhance data consistency in microservices, it needs ongoing research to address integration issues and ensure that solutions work effectively as well as remain secure (Narv et al., 2025) (Figure 2.9).

Figure 2.9. *The data consistency issues.*

Source: https://moldstud.com/_next/image?url=https%3A%2F%2Fmoldstud.com%2Fuploads%2Fimages%2Funderstanding-dynamodb-data-consistency-common-issues-explained-for-be.webp%3Fw%3D1216%26h%3D912&w=3840&q=75.

2.3.3. Network Latency and Performance

Network latency is crucial in determining system performance and the user experience in microservices architecture. Microservices communicate through the network, so the time it takes for packets of data to travel from one service to another highly impacts efficiency. High latency can lead to bottlenecks, resulting in delayed response times that annoy users and undermine system reliability. This becomes particularly vital in applications involving real-time interactions, where the latency of a few milliseconds can prove to be catastrophic. Following the emergence of serverless functions that draw upon stateless architecture as a service deployment paradigm, certain complexities regarding latency have come into the mix. Although serverless platforms appear to be a suitable substitute, their runtime latencies pose challenges in achieving low latency needed for interactive microservices, supporting the need for optimized architectural choices in latency-sensitive environments (Jia et al., 2021). Advances in mobile communication technology also contribute to characterizing network latency and performance in microservices.

The transition from fourth-generation (4G) to fifth-generation (5G) systems, and the emerging interest in sixth-generation (6G) systems, is sure to raise throughput and reduce latency significantly, thus addressing crucial performance parameters of microservices. With 5G systems now being commercially deployed, such technology holds out the promise of ultra-reliable low-latency communications (URLLC), which are necessary for applications with timed constraints. The integration of such next-gen networks under microservices architecture would likely minimize communication latency among distributed services, ultimately paving the way for smoother interactions and improved user experiences. However, the envisioned variability in network conditions requires a profound sense of the underlying infrastructure and its impact on service latency, highlighting the need for adaptive design principles in microservices frameworks (Tataria et al., 2021). With microservices architecture increasingly being used in organizations, addressing network latency and performance is necessary for ensuring good system performance. Some mechanisms can be used to neutralize latency, such as utilizing caching mechanisms and optimizing data formats to reduce the payload size while transmission is in progress. In addition, content delivery networks (CDNs) may help enhance performance by caching services opportunistically in close proximity to users, thus lowering latency that comes with geographical distances. Furthermore, the utilization of asynchronous communication patterns, such as messaging queues, allows for decoupling of service interactions and therefore minimizes wait times during processing. Through design and infrastructure considerations focused on network efficiency, organizations are able to achieve agile responsiveness and performance characteristic of contemporary microservices applications to make them realize their potential to fully meet user expectations in today's competitive digital economy (Jia et al., 2021) (Figure 2.10).

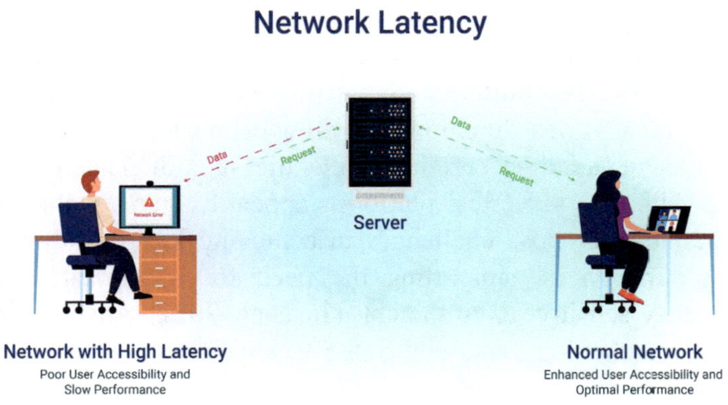

Figure 2.10. The *network latency plays a pivotal role in determining overall system performance and user experience.*

Source: https://io.hfcl.com/blog/wp-content/uploads/2023/07/1-01-scaled.jpg.

2.4. MICROSERVICES VS. MONOLITHIC ARCHITECTURE

With the investigation into the design patterns of monolithic architecture and microservices, it is crucial to mention the inherent disparities that establish their respective implementation and functional traits. Monolithic architecture structures applications as a complete, indivisible entity, with everything tightly coupled with each other. This can be very problematic, particularly as the application scales up. Larger systems become cumbersome, rendering updates an ordeal and causing increased downtime. Conversely, microservices architecture gives a more modular structure, breaking applications into individual services that are independent. This modularity not only facilitates updating without interfering with the entire system but allows services to be deployed at various levels of complexity and scale, leading to overall system performance and adaptability improvement, as put forth in Barua et al. (2024). The transition from monolithic to microservices architecture is not without its challenges but is also full of opportunities. Breaking down a monolithic application into microservices enhances agility and programmer productivity significantly in high-scale organizations. Microservices possess the intrinsic scalability that allows organizations to react quickly to fluctuating demands of their users without leading to system decline. It is not a simple change; extensive planning and an in-depth understanding of domain-driven development concepts are needed. The complexities present may result in tremendous pressure on existing resources and require new skill sets within development teams. From research evidence, while microservices may ease operational efficiency, organizational readiness to make such a transition must be strategically evaluated, especially where legacy systems are involved, as noted in Seedat et al. (2023). Moreover, microservices deployment makes system resiliency and fault tolerance much higher. By decoupling the services, they are independent, and failures won't cascade to take down the application. Segregation enables more immediate error recovery mechanism, which enables quick detection and repair of faults. Microservices also leverage technologies such as containerization and orchestration, which are built upon further efficiency in deployment and improved utilization of resources. Microservices flexibility drives businesses to cutting-edge software development methodologies to accelerate continuous delivery and integration. However, as seen in both (Barua et al., 2024; Seedat et al., 2023), migration to frameworks involves new challenges in terms of service management and operational consistency, requiring good planning and strategic vision to get maximum utilization advantages of microservices architecture (Figure 2.11).

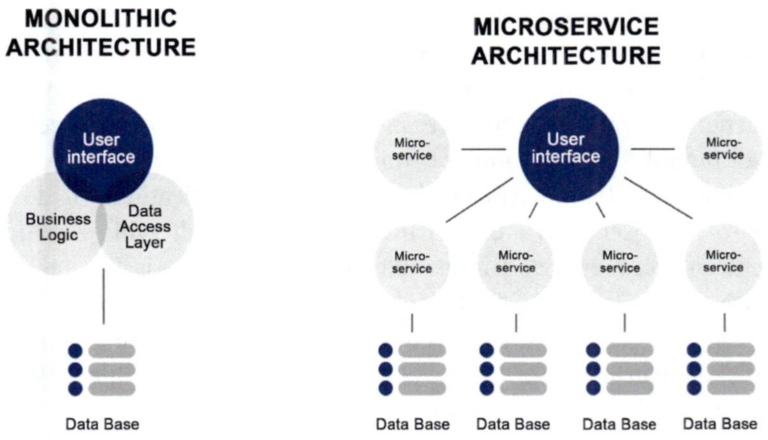

Figure 2.11. *The architectural paradigms of microservices and monolithic architecture.*

Source: https://www.cloudflight.io/app/uploads/2024/10/frame-1-4.png.

2.4.1. Comparison of Structure and Design

In software architecture, the paradox between monolithic and microservices approaches provides a fascinating dichotomy of form and design. Monolithic architectures generally come in one piece, where all elements are interdependent on one another, such that they are simpler in deployment and maintenance. Microservices architecture, on the other hand, breaks down applications into smaller, standalone services communicating through APIs. This level of granularity offers greater scalability and fault tolerance but introduces complexity in the inter-service communication and service orchestration. Migration from a monolithic architecture to microservices is not only a technological change but also a philosophical one, as organizations attempt to increase responsiveness and agility to evolving market demands. Yet, for smaller groups, the perceived advantages are overstated, particularly when they are not industry leaders' scale (Blinowski et al., 2022). The architectural implications of microservices versus a monolithic approach go deep. A monolithic approach can enjoy rapid development cycles in the early stages due to its single design, whereby teams can easily deploy and implement patches. On the other hand, microservices have independent updates, which prefer flexibility among technology stack choices for an individual service. However, the load for maintenance increases, particularly regarding service dependencies and life cycles of individual services. It is vital to realize these structural differences since they influence decision-making in application design intended to scale and fulfill performance demands in the future. In addition, while microservices architecture entails gigantic benefits regarding resilience and flexibility, the performance metrics might favor monolithic styles under certain circumstances with low concurrent usage environments (Blinowski et al., 2022). The implications of design in migrating to microservices are also made more difficult with variations in deployment environments and implementation technologies. The technology stack, whether it be Java or C#.NET, plays a pivotal role in how performance and scalability outcomes are achieved. For instance, monolithic applications can be quicker than microservices when running on one machine since they have less overhead in communicating between services. Moreover, as noted with cloud implementations, vertical scaling proves more efficient than attempting horizontal scaling on systems like Azure, adding yet another wrinkle of sophistication to architectural decisions. This crossover between structural design options and performance characteristics requires advanced understanding of both microservices and monolithic approaches, eventually bringing organizations to their optimal architecture based on their specific use cases and operational requirements.

2.4.2. Advantages and Disadvantages of Each

Microservices architecture possesses several well-known advantages that contribute to its growing popularity among organizations moving away from the monolithic system. The major advantage is its enhanced modularity, by which application developers can build, test, and deploy individual elements independently. The modular structure also facilitates continuous integration and delivery, which leads to accelerated release cycles as well as increased flexibility regarding adapting to evolving market demands. Furthermore, microservices architectures enable teams to utilize diverse technology stacks optimized for the needs of specific services, which promotes optimization and innovation. However, this decentralization introduces complexity in service management, necessitating good orchestration tools to make clear, consistent communication among services possible, as evidenced by a study done by μBench which illustrates how architectural choices affect performance in microservices (Detti et al., 2023). Thus, while the advantages of microservices are attractive, organizations must weigh these against the cost of operation and potential problems with distributed elements. Monolithic designs, however, have certain inherent sole advantages which might be better suited for smaller organizations or systems with lower levels of scalability needed. A single codebase enables streamlined development and testing process since everything runs under a single framework. This interconnectedness usually translates into improved performance on individual machines, as seen in performance comparisons which indicate monolithic applications may be more efficient than their microservices counterparts, particularly when isolated to a single computing environment (Blinowski et al., 2022). Additionally, the initial deployment of monolithic applications can be accomplished with less resources and less sophisticated orchestration tools, hence reducing build and deployment complexity. But as organizations expand and require more flexibility, monolithic systems become cumbersome, wherein enormous refactoring projects are required to change towards microservices, which may or may not necessarily produce the desired outcome. Whether microservices or remaining with a monolithic architecture is selected depends on a meticulous review of both designs' pitfalls. For microservices, increased operational complexity will strain existing infrastructure and demand high expenditure on monitoring, logging, and configuration management to maintain performance levels. This can lead to communication problems between services, particularly when not properly controlled through correct service meshes or API gateways. Conversely, while monoliths are easy to build and deploy, as system demands change over time, they can hinder user requirement responsiveness and agility, leading to bottlenecks in software development. Thus, organizations intending to adopt microservices must research their specific use cases and future growth habits with utmost care. This decision is significant in that the transition from monolithic architecture to microservices entails both strategic risk and logistical complexity that would weigh extremely heavily on operational efficiency and innovation capacity in the long term.

2.4.3. Use Cases for Each Architecture

Microservices architecture is particularly useful in situations where there are requirements for scalability at high speed and reliability. For instance, online shops prefer using this pattern to cope with changing traffic from the users during peak holiday seasons such as Black Friday or Cyber Monday. Multisided sections of the store such as product catalogs, shopping baskets, and payments can be developed, deployed, and scaled individually. This allows developers to optimize individual services without affecting the overall system, thereby enhancing overall efficiency and performance. Microservices further enable organizations to implement continuous integration and continuous deployment (CI/CD) practices, which result in faster release cycles. Consistent with latest studies, utilization of microservices in these areas slashes average deployment time considerably, thereby allowing access to new features and improvements in user experience at a faster rate (Singh et al., 2023). On the other hand, monolithic traditional architectures may be more suitable for less complicated applications or systems with well-determined functionalities that do not require frequent updates. For example, a simple content management system would not be enhanced by the sophistication of microservices. In such scenarios, the simplicity of development and testing offered by a single codebase may prove more beneficial than the modularity of scalability offered by microservices. Nevertheless, with increasing applications, scalability becomes increasingly difficult to achieve. The threat of monolithic applications, including extended deployment time and potential downtime during maintenance, urges organizations to explore the transition to microservices. A well-designed process will lead the migration process without compromising existing functionalities. Multiple case studies reveal that companies handle the transformation effectively by employing incremental deconstruction techniques and leveraging tools like API gateways in order to interface with legacy systems (Murilo et al., 2022). Also, microservices deployment is accompanied by specific security concerns organizations must address. Every microservice constitutes an independent unit of deployment, thereby escalating the attack surface and necessitating individual security configurations for each entity. Since these services communicate, an unauthorized access to one microservice would compromise the entire system. For this reason, it is essential that developers include stringent authentication and authorization practices for all services. These processes such as OAuth 2.0 and JWT have been effective methods to enhance security without detracting from responsiveness and agility that defines microservices architecture. Existing literature suggests the necessity for a secure security framework to manage the trust relationships as well as inter-service communication, hence bolstering the integrity of microservices-based systems against impending threats (Murilo et al., 2022).

2.5. TOOLS AND TECHNOLOGIES FOR MICROSERVICES

The move toward microservices architecture has called for a resilient ecosystem of tools and technologies intended to make development, deployment, and management more streamlined. Of these, containerization has proven to be a key technology. Docker and Kubernetes are some of the tools that enable the creation, deployment, and orchestration of microservices and provide developers with the ability to bundle applications and their dependencies into a light and portable package. Such packaging not only ensures consistency across multiple environments but also enhances scalability by making services easily replicated and scaled whenever required. With the increased adoption of microservices, integration of continuous integration and continuous deployment (CI/CD) tools also accelerates the development cycle further, so updates are being delivered efficiently and seamlessly without compromising system performance and stability. Besides containerization, API management software is a vital component of microservices as well. They serve as the communication framework, enabling different microservices to talk to each other securely and reliably. API gateways and service meshes are technologies that simplify service-to-service communication management by providing capabilities such as traffic management, security policy, and monitoring. For instance, Istio and Envoy include observability functionality that allows developers to trace requests through several microservices, simplifying debugging and performance optimization. This effective API management is most essential in situations involving numerous interdependent services, where watching out and safeguarding communications might otherwise be cumbersome. With such tools continuing to evolve, they come a long way in building fault-tolerant and efficient microservices architectures. Also, microservices deployment has been enhanced by leaps and bounds with the advent of serverless computing platforms. AWS Lambda, Azure Functions, and Google Cloud Functions are some of the services that allow developers to focus on code without needing to provision server infrastructure. This abstraction eliminates the overhead of provisioning, scaling, and managing servers, thereby enhancing the responsiveness and agility of development teams. In addition, serverless architectures go well with the concept of microservices because they assist in developing small, stateless, and event-driven pieces that can scale independently. As the industry keeps exploring the crossing points between serverless computing and microservices, possibilities for developing unique service architecture extend far, contributing further impetus towards more scalable and efficient application deployments within a dynamic technology landscape (Figure 2.12).

Figure 2.12. *The shift toward microservices architecture.*

Source: https://hcltech.imgix.net/sites/default/files/rich-snippet/facebook/2024-11/devops-tools-and-technologies-1200x630.jpg?auto=compress&fit=crop&ixlib=php-3.3.1.

2.5.1. Containerization (e.g., Docker)

Containerization has changed the deployment and management of applications in a microservices ecosystem, providing a robust model for modular development. Through encapsulation of functionalities into standalone containers, developers can ensure that each microservice operates independently, regardless of the underlying infrastructure. This independence provides for consistency across environments, reducing the differences in development and production environments. Besides, the light nature of containers enables greater scalability because they may rapidly be spun up or down based on resources. Therefore, organizations enjoy greater efficiency and flexibility in their deployments and have the ability to react faster to changing demands. The nature of containerization itself encourages microservices' principles with its emphasis on loose coupling and autonomy, which leads to continuous integration and delivery practices that improve software quality as well as deployment velocity. In big data application scenarios, the need for containerization becomes critical even more. Utilization of platforms like Docker in these cases can maximally benefit resource utilization as well as application performance. The need for effective load balancing is critical since increased workloads in data can devastate typical server architecture. As indicated in the literature, the integration of Docker Swarm and microservice architecture presents a novel scheduling mechanism to handle the workload associated with big data applications.

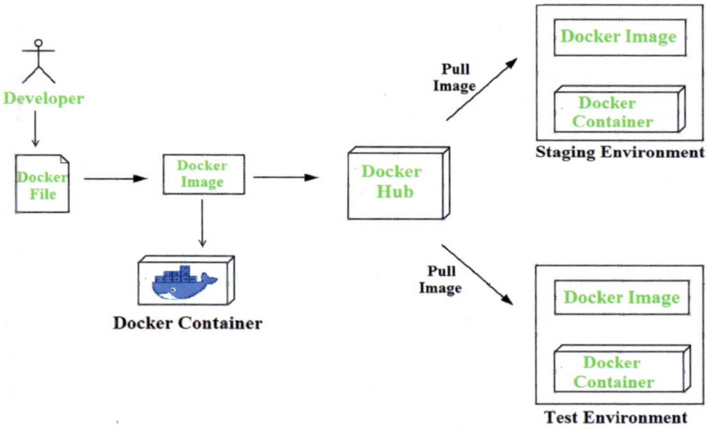

Figure 2.13. *Containerization has reshaped the deployment and management of applications in a microservices architecture.*

Source: https://media.geeksforgeeks.org/wp-content/uploads/20190915151739/docker_flowchart-1024x640.png.

This ensures services are maximally available and responsive under changing workloads, since Docker Swarm efficiently manages container instances based on real-time demand. Therefore, managing heavy data applications in container environments leads to optimized operational costs and improved service delivery, thereby demonstrating the scalability and elasticity of microservices in managing large amounts of data (Singh et al., 2023). Further, using containerization in the Industrial Internet of Things (IIoT) context demonstrates the flexibility of this technology across various industries. The union of containerization and edge computing is the greatest proof of microservices architecture's innovative nature since the applications can be seamlessly shifted from centralized cloud infrastructures to localized edge devices. The transition not only enhances response times by lessening latency but also offers improved resource optimization, particularly in scenarios where real-time data processing is a crucial imperative. The use of Docker together with orchestration platforms such as Kubernetes further accelerates the deployment process, enabling applications to take advantage of edge functionality hassle-free. By enabling the deployment of applications in the edge, containerization allows businesses to take full advantage of the potential of IIoT, and it is thus a vital element in the transformation of smart industries (Muthanna et al., 2022) (Figure 2.13).

2.5.2. Orchestration Tools (E.g., Kubernetes)

The microservices architecture has given rise to the necessity to create and adapt orchestration tools, and here, Kubernetes is one of the leading solutions in this regard. Kubernetes is an open-source system designed in particular to manage applications based on containers to deploy, scale, and manage them over host clusters. Through the utilization of Kubernetes, businesses can enable a higher degree of automation and resource management that is essential to the seamless operation of microservices. The capacity for scaling service discovery, load balancing, and automated rollouts and rollbacks makes Kubernetes an indispensable utility for developers who want to guarantee system reliability and operational efficiency. Secondly, the use of Kubernetes mitigates some complexities of microservices such that teams can focus on programming without considering infrastructure, a feature that is particularly convenient in high-speed development environments (Aybuyev et al., 2025). Other than Kubernetes, the orchestration environment is complemented by many other tools with the aim of enhancing container orchestration capabilities. Such tools are more likely to support continuous integration and continuous deployment (CI/CD) pipelines, which are required to maintain agile and quick-response development pipelines. Integrating CI/CD practices into container orchestration makes testing, integration, and deployment of microservices easier, such that with each new release, production is updated smoothly. Such integration results in a more reliable software delivery process, such that teams can iterate and innovate rapidly without impacting system stability. The orchestration solutions not only provide automated scaling and self-healing capabilities but also provide assurance to developers to deploy microservices as orchestration tools will handle failures and deliver consistent performance (Fehlis et al., 2025). Further, the incorporation of orchestration tools like Kubernetes provides improved monitoring and profiling of microservices, one of the most important considerations for ensuring functioning digital systems. These tools are shipped with native monitoring features that allow businesses to track application health, performance, and resource utilization in real-time.

Based on observability metrics, teams can identify probable bottlenecks and areas for optimization, leading to better application performance. Orchestration tool integration also allows for a microservices architecture that is horizontally and vertically scalable, and offers businesses the feature of scaling resources as per demand. This adaptability is especially important in the modern digital age, when users' traffic can fluctuate wildly. As companies advance their digital transformations, the role of orchestration tools cannot be overemphasized, since they provide the framework necessary to manage more complex microservices environments effectively (Aybuyev et al., 2025) (Figure 2.14).

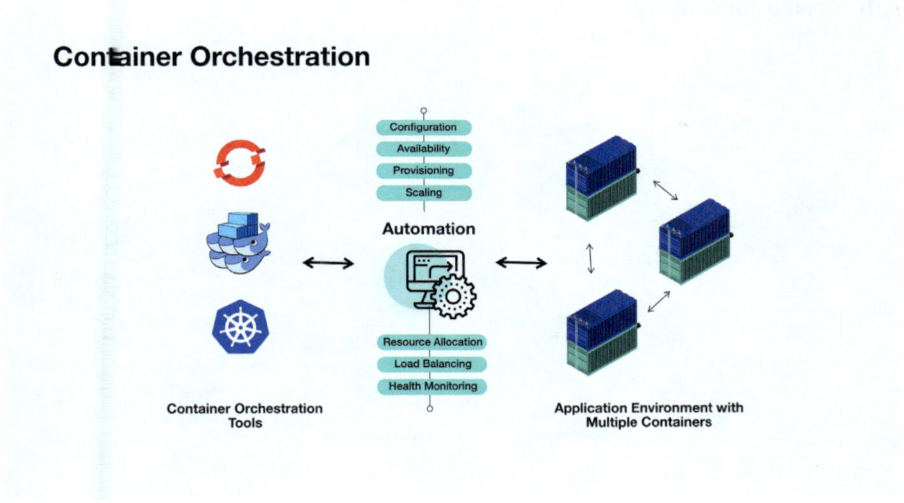

Figure 2.14. *The container-orchestration.*

Source: https://www.simform.com/wp-content/uploads/2022/05/automation-with-container-orchestration.png.

2.5.3. API Management Solutions

In microservices architecture, API management tools play a critical role in facilitating communication between the various services comprising an application. The dynamic and distributed nature of microservices in an application can generate numerous APIs, which have to be well managed to ensure smooth operation. API management tools provide a framework for securing, monitoring, and analyzing these APIs and hence enhance reliability as well as performance. These solutions enable streamlining the process of deployment so that it becomes easy for development teams to manage changes and updates as the application scales up. Therefore, organizations embracing microservices architecture need to ensure that API management solutions are a high priority so that their systems continue to be efficient and scalable as demand increases. API management solutions also become crucial for security fortification in microservices architectures. Security issues are caused by the decentralized nature of microservices, as several services talk to each other using multiple protocols. With the usage of API management tools, organizations can apply security functions like authentication, authorization, and encryption to their APIs as a systematic approach. Such solutions provide centralized management over API access so that administrators can apply security policies to all services uniformly.

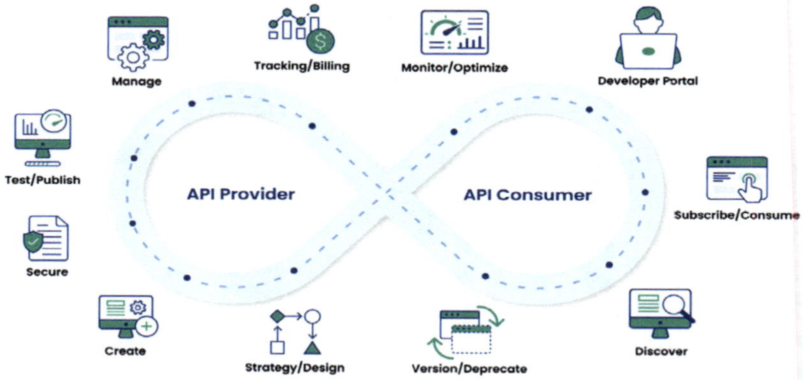

Figure 2.15. *API management solutions.*

Source: https://www.snaplogic.com/wp-content/uploads/2019/02/What-is-API-Management.png.

With growing emphasis on data privacy and security, especially in the case of developing technologies such as 6G, robust API management platforms can limit vulnerabilities from inappropriate access and data leaks, thereby encouraging greater trust from users and stakeholders (Porambage et al., 2021). In addition to performance and security, API management platforms also enable enhanced analytics and insights for microservices architecture. With these solutions, businesses can gather huge volumes of data on API usage patterns, response time, and error rates. This type of analytics is crucial for identifying bottlenecks and optimization opportunities within the architecture. Additionally, this data can be utilized for long-term development and strategic planning, enabling businesses to improve their services to be more tailored towards meeting the needs of users. As increasing numbers of industries welcome digital twins and other pioneering tech models (Minerva et al., 2020) to their operations, the role of API management solutions becomes more crucial in maintaining agility and responsiveness required in today's speedy digital age. Effective API management, aside from enhancing the operations' efficiency, also facilitates innovation life cycles, which allow organizations to respond quickly to the expectations of the market (Figure 2.15).

2.6. BEST PRACTICES FOR DEVELOPING MICROSERVICES

Microservices architecture design needs a disciplined approach to ensure scalability and resiliency in intricate systems. Perhaps the most important best practice is adopting decoupling principles that allow separate services to be self-sufficient. Autonomy assists in faster deployment as well as greater fault tolerance since one microservice failure won't crash the overall system. Use of APIs as the communication mechanism between services is essential to maintaining such autonomy, so modular development and adding new functionalities become easier. Furthermore, use of containerization tools like Docker facilitates consistent environments for development as well as production, which makes deployment an easier task. These strategies not only enhance performance but also enable the flexibility to adapt to changing user requirements and emerging technological advancements, solidifying microservices as a mainstay in modern software development (Aybuyev et al., 2025). Ensuring rigorous monitoring and observability practices is another core component of microservices construction. Given the decentralized nature of microservices, there is a need to utilize end-to-end logging and monitoring features that provide visibility into system performance. Profiling and load testing automation tools are essential to detect bottlenecks within the architecture, thereby facilitating timely optimizations. Through ongoing observation of data movement and service interaction, developers can determine the points of optimization and ensure smooth functioning across varying loads. Blending metrics and logs into central platforms offers real-time visibility that allows teams to respond before problems may arise. This focus on observability not only enhances the maintenance of system health but also supports a culture of continuous evolution in the development lifecycle (Cherukuri, 2024). Lastly, security must be considered from the beginning of the microservices development lifecycle. Since services run independently and may frequently communicate across networks, points of potential weakness can exist at multiple points across the system. A security-first approach includes taking practices like service-to-service authentication, encryption of data in transmission, and periodic security audits. Having strict access controls in place and using conceptually well-founded communication protocols can also counter risks that come with interservice interactions. Besides, making sure that each microservice is implemented with the minimum privilege rules can limit exposure to vulnerabilities. This enables organizations to design secure microservices that not only meet the functional specifications but also safeguard against the ever-rising cyber threats (Aybuyev et al., 2025).

2.6.1. Designing for Failure

In microservices architecture, the "design for failure" ideology is most critical in developing systems that are fault-tolerant. This ideology also recognizes that failures are not random events but are part of what distributed systems are made of. Preparing beforehand against potential points of failure and having mechanisms to deal with them allows organizations to develop more resilient applications. Utilization of redundancy, circuit breakers, and graceful degradation provides sustained service in spite of the failure of specific services. This strategy shifts the design emphasis from merely preventing failure to actually dealing with their impact and, as a result, minimizing their effect on end-users and overall service quality. Therefore, microservices resilience not only strengthens the operational reliability but also reinforces trust between the users and the service provider and provides a more reliable experience in case of unexpected failures. Making use of observability and monitoring is more important when designing for failure in microservices. A strong observability plan allows developers and operators to detect issues before they emerge as significant outages, hence allowing timely interventions. The complexity of the distributed system demands robust monitoring systems that gather information on various services and components. Instrumenting microservices with tools that provide visibility into levels of performance and user activity enables teams to diagnose more effectively their capacity to recover quickly from failure. This is in line with the standards described in recent works whereby the witnesses of distributed edge infrastructures applied containerization and microservices to guarantee continuity in operations (Usman et al., 2022). Such foresight not only minimizes the risk of service interruption but also minimizes the troubleshooting process, resulting in more sustainable microservices architecture. Lastly, embracing a culture of failure among development teams is essential to improve microservices architecture. By developing a culture whereby team members see failure as learning, organizations will be facilitated to catalyze innovation and responsiveness. Teams capable of experimentation and quick iteration are better placed to find flaws in their systems and optimize processes from experiential realities. Such cultural reform goes hand in hand with best practices in Configuration Management (CM) that promote flexibility and collaboration

(Farayola et al., 2023). As businesses cope with evolving technological landscapes, those who possess the culture of learning from failure continually will definitely enjoy a competitive edge. Hence, designing for failure is not merely about technical implementations but permeates organizational culture, ultimately resulting in resilient and innovative microservices architecture that can adapt to future challenges.

2.6.2. Continuous Integration and Deployment

Integration of CI/CD practices into a microservices architecture completely alters the software development lifecycle. CI/CD is centered around automating the steps involved in software delivery to make rapid application development, testing, and deployment possible. In microservices, this works extremely well with the architectural principle of supporting independent, small-sized services. With CI/CD pipelines, organizations can have each microservice continuously updated, thoroughly tested, and reliably deployed, thus enhancing overall productivity and quality. The automation process facilitates it to be simpler to carry out the integration of new features as well as bug fixes rapidly, with less downtime and faster value delivery to the end-users, vital in today's fast technological era (Daki, 2024). The challenges of microservices management have a tendency to make the CI/CD pipelines more complex since individual services may have special requirements and dependencies. Thus, constructing an efficient CI/CD pipeline is necessary to guarantee the efficacy and effectiveness of software development. This requirement can be met by implementing total strategies encompassing all stages ranging from version control to automated testing and deployment. With effective integration of the right tools and compliance with the best practices, teams can automate deployments to a variety of environments, thereby always ensuring compliance as well as operational standards. As firms further innovate using the microservices model, building culture centered on well-defined CI/CD processes remains fundamental to successful software delivery as well as operational excellence (Nandigam, 2024). Aside from minimizing deployment pipelines, the use of CI/CD also fosters cultural change across organizations. This paradigm is characterized by increased synergy between development, operations, and security teams, encapsulated in the philosophies of DevOps and DevSecOps. Through the inclusion of security practices within all phases of the deployment process, teams are able to preclude threats while ensuring maximum overall deployment performance. This synergetic environment promotes innovation and encourages teams to be adaptive to market demands and customer needs. Besides, organizations that manage to effect such cultural transformations tend to experience spectacular improvements in the pace and quality of software releases. By investing in CI/CD platforms, organizations position themselves to thrive in a competitive market defined by accelerating technological transformation, further solidifying the strategic importance of continuous integration and delivery in a microservices architecture (Nandigam, 2024) (Figure 2.16).

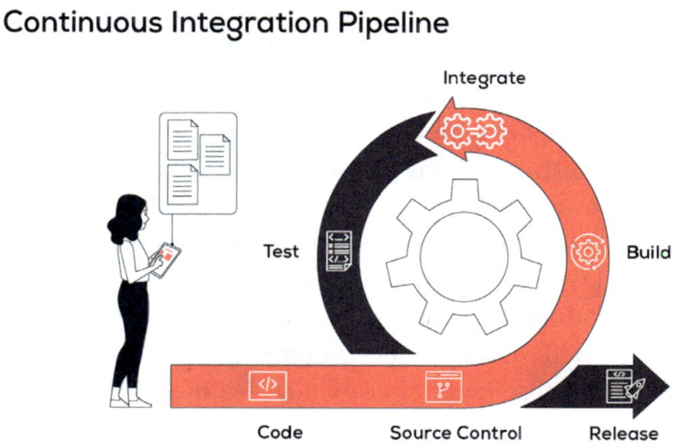

Figure 2.16. *Continuous integration and deployment.*

Source: https://www.inspirisys.com/uploads/blog_image/Continuous-Integration-Pipeline.png.

2.6.3. Monitoring and Logging Strategies

In the context of microservices architecture, good logging and monitoring practices are key to providing system stability and performance. Because microservices are distributed in nature, traditional monitoring practices are generally not sufficient in handling complexity caused by independent functioning of individual services. A good strategy would involve live monitoring tools that provide insights into health and performance of various microservices. This approach ensures that performance bottlenecks or outliers can be identified and resolved in time, thereby minimizing downtime and enhancing the user experience. With a mix of proactive alerting and monitoring of performance metrics, organizations can create an open observation environment that encourages agility and responsiveness across the microservices landscape. Logging is an essential complement to monitoring strategies under microservices architecture to enable end-to-end view of operational events. A good logging system saves valuable data from all microservices, which can be analyzed in real-time as well as after the fact. The log information is invaluable for debugging and trouble-shooting because it provides a time-correlated perspective on the sequence of events that result in service crashes. Effective logging also must prioritize the collection of structured information that lends itself to simple querying and analysis. Such disciplined approach enhances cooperative collaboration among development and operations teams since it allows them to trace down faults effectively and measure the impact of change across service boundaries, thus offering a more efficient development cycle. Moreover, the use of cutting-edge logging techniques can significantly enhance predictive ability in microservices systems. Using log data from the past, machine learning algorithms can be applied to identify patterns and predict future service behavior or future failure. For instance, learning that is derived by using logging data can be utilized to drive adaptive resource allocation policies and tune system configurations for handling varying workloads. In these cases, concepts outlined in Soosaar et al. (2025) highlight that AI-based predictive maintenance and diagnostics require structured data in order to be enabled. As companies continue to build their microservices architecture, using good monitoring and logging practices is no longer merely a technical need but a building block of ensuring operational excellence and allowing innovation in the software development process, as contended in Gundala (2025).

SUMMARY

The microservices architecture discovery reveals its revolutionary potential across all business lines, particularly digital technologies. Microservices enable applications to be better developed, deployed, and scaled, and from this, they provide a solid base upon which systems can be built to be highly resilient. Not only does the architecture support continuous delivery and integration but also fault tolerance and security through independent, manageable services. Adoption of microservices, particularly in performance-intensive spaces, demands proper understanding of interservice communication and containerization technologies, such as Docker and Kubernetes. Literature emphasizes that companies embracing digital transformation need to consider these styles of architecture as a prime element in achieving scalability and efficiency in operations (Aybuyev et al., 2025). For specific industries, such as banking, the role of microservices architecture becomes even more prominent. As financial institutions come under greater pressure to innovate and build better customer experiences, microservices' modular architecture facilitates the rapid deployment of new features and services. In addition to this approach supporting organizations' ability to react to certain operation-specific issues, it finds its place among the overall goals of responsiveness and agility that today's competitive business environment demands. Real-world observations validate the fact that banks like JPMorgan Chase and HSBC have successfully employed microservices to enhance the performance of their applications and elevate customer satisfaction levels (Kulkarni, 2025). Thus, embracing microservices can be labeled as a strategic benefit in reshaping the digital financial services universe. Microservices architecture, in general, is at the center of modern application building, providing a strategic pattern that promotes innovation and responsiveness. The ability of architecture to split functionalities into individualized services allows organizations to respond rapidly to changing market demands and the dangers of monolithic systems. As empirical studies and real-world experience have uncovered, microservices transformation is not a hype but a reorganization that can introduce sweeping operational efficiencies. Therefore, organizations interested in remaining competitive in their line of business must prioritize the implementation of microservices architecture in order to take advantage of scalability, resilience, and improved user experiences in the digital transformation process.

In microservices architecture, the greatest problem is request processing latency, particularly for cloud systems. Latency can easily be affected by the speed of communication among services as well as the absence of efficient computation resource handling. For instance, research indicates an improved particle swarm optimization (PSO) algorithm supplemented by an enhanced Round Robin (RR) algorithm as effective solutions to the problems. By the deployment of these steps, network traffic, latency, and resource consumption have been observed to be better. The testing uncovered considerable declines by up to 35% of network traffic and over 80% latency decreases in fixed environments, showcasing the way scheduling optimization can enhance microservices systems' performance and fault tolerance by a significant margin to an advantage ultimately for developers and system architects seeking to optimize performance within cloud infrastructure (Iurchenko, 2025). The other key aspect of microservices architecture is the need for end-to-end observability systems. As these structures scale and get bigger, they become critical in terms of monitoring performance and reliability. The value of good observability practices becomes apparent, as distributed systems tend to provide multiple paths to failure and paths to bottlenecks. Recent studies talk about some frameworks that are designed to address these challenges and mention logs, traces, and metrics as primary sources of data for good monitoring. Notably, thematic taxonomy groups observability approaches, examining how they work together in different deployment environments and architectural patterns. Such a comparison draws out the pros and cons of solutions currently in hand to make a soundly educated judgment on how observability may be enhanced in microservices architecture deployed within cloud, edge, and fog environments

(Faseeha et al., 2025). Finally, the utilization of both performance optimization methods and observability tools is imperative in realizing the full potential of microservices architecture. As much as techniques such as PSO and RR algorithms optimize the handling of requests and the use of resources, they are supplemented by sound observability practices. Such two-sided approach not only mitigates the very nature of distributed systems but also fosters an environment where there is constant improvement and innovation. While businesses increasingly move towards cloud-native platforms, guide of action to adopt observability can assist system architects as well as DevOps teams. Solving performance and monitoring problems comprehensively, one can maximize the reliability and effectiveness of microservices systems within a technologically sophisticated environment, paving the way for potential innovation in the field (Iurchenko, 2025; Faseeha et al., 2025).

REFERENCES

1. Abdul-Khalid, A. M., & Aybuyev, A. Z. D. (2025). Developing scalable microservices on Go: Architecture, performance, and best practices. Ekonomika I Upravlenie: Problemy, Resheniya. https://www.semanticscholar.org/paper/5fc420c96b699d50626ae7a9b7aae332af4ce8a2 (accessed on 11th September 2025).
2. Akerele, J. I., Uzoka, A. C., Ojukwu, P. U., & Olamijuwon, O. J. (2024). Improving healthcare application scalability through microservices architecture in the cloud. International Journal of Scientific Research Updates, 8, 100–109. https://doi.org/10.53430/ijsru.2024.8.2.0064 (accessed on 11th September 2025).
3. Amri, M. G., Raharjo, T., Fitriani, A. N., & Hutasuhut, N. R. P. (2024). Critical success factors of microservices architecture implementation in the information system project. International Journal of Advanced Computer Science and Applications. https://www.semanticscholar.org/paper/1dc13a69f2865e48bde34996545634b2ace5aaae (accessed on 11th September 2025).
4. Andrawos, M., Aßmann, U., Bass, L., Behara, D. G. K., Betts, T., Bianco, P., Bryant, D., et al. (2019). Microservice transition and its granularity problem: A systematic mapping study. https://core.ac.uk/download/426749569.pdf (accessed on 11th September 2025).
5. Baker, O., Li, W., Ma, H., Subaramaniam, K., Lopez, D., & Palaniappan, S. (2025). Machine learning-driven container scheduling for edge-empowered microservices. 2025 IEEE International Conference on Robotics and Technologies for Industrial Automation (ROBOTHIA). https://www.semanticscholar.org/paper/643213fb0e063c86e56e9855c68898d62a502a2d (accessed on 11th September 2025).
6. Ballhausen, H., & Hinske, L. C. (2023). Federated secure computing. Informatics, 10, 83–83. https://doi.org/10.3390/informatics10040083 (accessed on 11th September 2025).
7. Barua, B., & Kaiser, M. S. (2024). *A Methodological Framework of Containerized Microservices Orchestration and Provisioning in The Cloud: A Case Study of Online Travel Platforms*. CRC Press eBooks. https://doi.org/10.1201/9781003606260-33 (accessed on 11th September 2025).
8. Bellini, P., Nesi, P., & Pantaleo, G. (2022). IoT-enabled smart cities: A review of concepts, frameworks and key technologies. Applied Sciences, 12, 1607–1607. https://doi.org/10.3390/app12031607 (accessed on 11th September 2025).

9. Blinowski, G., Ojdowska, A., & Przybyłek, A. (2022). Monolithic vs. microservice architecture: A performance and scalability evaluation. IEEE Access, 10, 20357–20374. https://doi.org/10.1109/access.2022.3152803 (accessed on 11th September 2025).

10. Busi, S. P. (2025). Understanding microservices architecture: A comprehensive guide. International Journal of Scientific Research in Computer Science, Engineering and Information Technology. https://www.semanticscholar.org/paper/eb267e129a4ebd8a5ac9614bc91d0bcadd6a70a0 (accessed on 11th September 2025).

11. Cherukuri, B. R. (2024). Building scalable web applications: Best practices for backend architecture. International Journal of Science and Research (IJSR). https://www.semanticscholar.org/paper/9cc3af006aba6a48eb1d2d05beeb81a57d4bde6b (accessed on 11th September 2025).

12. Dakić, P. (2024). Software compliance in various industries using CI/CD, dynamic microservices, and containers. Open Computer Science, 14. https://www.semanticscholar.org/paper/db6a876e19764593bf2388935443d2603e86864e (accessed on 11th September 2025).

13. Demartini, M., Lala, R., Pacella, M., & Tonelli, F. (2021). Cyber-physical systems (CPS) in supply chain management: From foundations to practical implementation. https://core.ac.uk/download/521186798.pdf (accessed on 11th September 2025).

14. Detti, A., Funari, L., & Petrucci, L. (2023). µBench: An open-source factory of benchmark microservice applications. IEEE Transactions on Parallel and Distributed Systems, 34, 968–980. https://doi.org/10.1109/tpds.2023.3236447 (accessed on 11th September 2025).

15. Dhandapani, A. (2025). Automated testing in microservices environments: A comprehensive approach. Global Journal of Engineering and Technology Advances. https://www.semanticscholar.org/paper/3097c23e49f77cf725be242215fd2ca255bc0bac (accessed on 11th September 2025).

16. Farayola, O. A., Hassan, A. O., Adaramodu, O. R., Fakeyede, O. G., & Oladeinde, M. (2023). Configuration management in the modern era: best practices, innovations, and challenges. Computer Science & IT Research Journal, 4, 140–157. https://doi.org/10.51594/csitrj.v4i2.613 (accessed on 11th September 2025).

17. Faseeha, U., Syed, H. J., Samad, F., Zehra, S., & Ahmed, H. (2025). Observability in microservices: An in-depth exploration of frameworks, challenges, and deployment paradigms. IEEE Access, 13, 72011–72039. https://www.semanticscholar.org/paper/

fb7a25a8206be0e67729e1c2c22ae2e0ab99f464 (accessed on 11th September 2025).

18. Fehlis, Y., Crain, C., Jensen, A., Watson, M., Juhasz, J., Mandel, P., Liu, B., et al. (2025). Technical implementation of Tippy: Multi-agent architecture and system design for drug discovery laboratory automation. arXiv (abs/2507.17852). https://www.semanticscholar.org/paper/94f62979ef01002239716239882e7c11041b4ec5 (accessed on 11th September 2025).

19. Gite, K. (2025). Monolithic vs. microservices architecture: A comparative study of software development paradigms. International Scientific Journal of Engineering and Management. https://www.semanticscholar.org/paper/cd3d9827a93a71b8f2cc16ca9f9ae71f905595fc (accessed on 11th September 2025).

20. Góes de Almeida, M., & Canedo, E. D. (2022). Authentication and authorization in microservices architecture: A systematic literature review. Applied Sciences, 12, 3023–3023. https://doi.org/10.3390/app12063023 (accessed on 11th September 2025).

21. Gundala, S. K. (2025). Microservices architecture: A comprehensive guide to modern distributed systems. International Journal of Scientific Research in Computer Science, Engineering and Information Technology. https://www.semanticscholar.org/paper/d1e1aae6275f2cd9210c87b153e6c0aa1821c94f (accessed on 11th September 2025).

22. Hoque, S., & Miranskyy, A. (2018). Architecture for analysis of streaming data. http://arxiv.org/abs/1805.01025 (accessed on 11th September 2025).

23. Iovescu, D., & Tudose, C. (2024). Real-time document collaboration—System architecture and design. Applied Sciences, 14, 8356–8356. https://doi.org/10.3390/app14188356 (accessed on 11th September 2025).

24. Iurchenko, A. (2025). Methods for minimizing request processing latency in microservices architecture. Universal Library of Innovative Research and Studies. https://www.semanticscholar.org/paper/ed3e17bda47356b0f0be1ed9ef6d0f6e389d1985 (accessed on 11th September 2025).

25. Jia, Z., & Witchel, E. (2021). Night core: Efficient and scalable serverless computing for latency-sensitive, interactive microservices. https://doi.org/10.1145/3445814.3446701 (accessed on 11th September 2025).

26. Kong, X., Wu, Y., Wang, H., & Xia, F. (2022). Edge computing for Internet of Everything: A survey. IEEE Internet of Things Journal, 9, 23472–23485. https://doi.org/10.1109/jiot.2022.3200431 (accessed on 11th September 2025).

27. Kopardekar, P. H., Lifson, M. T., Marker, N. A., Murakami, L., et al. (2025). Prototyping operational autonomy for space traffic management. https://core.ac.uk/download/pdf/286393023.pdf (accessed on 11th September 2025)

28. Kulkarni, V. (2025). Microservices in banking: Challenges and best practices in scaling core applications. International Journal of Scientific Research in Engineering and Management. https://www.semanticscholar.org/paper/bc7ac99db57ea4aa8bc91c65a0b5bcf5596f1eeb (accessed on 11th September 2025).

29. Kumar, F. P. (2025). Scalable microservices architecture for high-volume order processing in cloud environments. International Journal of Innovative Science and Research Technology. https://www.semanticscholar.org/paper/72e83aa1f034c90ece2eeb87b6f53de31fdb11e1 (accessed on 11th September 2025).

30. Minerva, R., Lee, G. M., & Crespi, N. (2020). Digital twin in the IoT context: A survey on technical features, scenarios, and architectural models. Proceedings of the IEEE, 108, 1785–1824. https://doi.org/10.1109/jproc.2020.2998530 (accessed on 11th September 2025).

31. Muthanna, M. S. A., & Tselykh, A. (2022). Development of Docker and Kubernetes orchestration platforms for industrial internet of things service migration. IEEE, 11, 1–6. https://doi.org/10.1109/monetec55448.2022.9960769 (accessed on 11th September 2025).

32. Nandigam, V. D. G. (2024). DevOps and DevSecOps practices in microservices deployment. International Journal for Multidisciplinary Research. https://www.semanticscholar.org/paper/87c4444041b715b43845c9f6b49b581c5fc3cd1c (accessed on 11th September 2025).

33. Narváez, D. D., Battaglia, N., Fernández, A., & Rossi, G. (2025). Designing microservices using AI: A systematic literature review. Software, 4, 6–6. https://doi.org/10.3390/software4010006 (accessed on 11th September 2025).

34. Njira, A., & Munialo, S. (2025). Modernizing legacy enterprise resource planning systems using the microservices architecture: A review. Journal of Innovation, Technology and Sustainability. https://www.semanticscholar.org/paper/ff418b7f3a8c6e681fa9a8f43e5183d713816737 (accessed on 11th September 2025).

35. Panagoulias, D. P., Virvou, M., & Tsihrintzis, G. A. (2022). nuhealthsoft: A nutritional and health data processing software tool from a patient's perspective. https://doi.org/10.1109/sitis57111.2022.00065 (accessed on 11th September 2025).

36. Porambage, P., Gür, G., Moya Osorio, D. P., Liyanage, M., Gurtov, A., & Ylianttila, M. (2021). The roadmap to 6G security and privacy. IEEE Open Journal of the Communications Society, 2, 1094–1122. https://doi.org/10.1109/ojcoms.2021.3078081 (accessed on 11th September 2025).
37. Randhi, K. (2025). Empowering scalable AI and generative innovation with data mesh architecture. The Edge Review. https://www.semanticscholar.org/paper/ae233b87a26357a8df4a8c4bb1fffc8c41dddcd9 (accessed on 11th September 2025).
38. Seedat, M., Abbas, Q., & Ahmad, N. (2023). Systematic mapping of monolithic applications to microservices architecture. arXiv (Cornell University). https://doi.org/10.48550/arxiv.2309.03796 (accessed on 11th September 2025).
39. Sethi, S., & Panda, S. (2024). Transforming digital experiences: The evolution of digital experience platforms (DXPs) from monoliths to microservices: A practical guide. Journal of Computer and Communications, 12, 142–155. https://doi.org/10.4236/jcc.2024.122009 (accessed on 11th September 2025).
40. Singh, N., Hamid, Y., Juneja, S., Srivastava, G., Dhiman, G., Gadekallu, T. R., & Shah, M. A. (2023). Load balancing and service discovery using Docker Swarm for microservice-based big data applications. Journal of Cloud Computing: Advances, Systems and Applications, 12. https://doi.org/10.1186/s13677-022-00358-7 (accessed on 11th September 2025).
41. Singhal, P. (2024). Mastering microservices architecture and cloud computing: In-depth strategies for domain-specific optimization. International Journal of Scientific Research in Computer Science, Engineering and Information Technology. https://www.semanticscholar.org/paper/91ae21e6928a761402d6600a19e3f3daadf84e34 (accessed on 11th September 2025).
42. Soosaar, G., & Lillerand, T. (2025). An energy-efficient battery monitoring and logging system for agricultural robotics with CAN Bus integration. Environmental and Climate Technologies, 29, 156–170. https://www.semanticscholar.org/paper/e1554cec1d8db07679f5f884c93079f7733968cc (accessed on 11th September 2025).
43. Tataria, H., Shafi, M., Molisch, A. F., Döhler, M., Sjöland, H., & Tufvesson, F. (2021). 6G wireless systems: Vision, requirements, challenges, insights, and opportunities. Proceedings of the IEEE, 109, 1166–1199. https://doi.org/10.1109/jproc.2021.3061701 (accessed on 11th September 2025).

44. Usman, M., Ferlin, S., Brunström, A., & Taheri, J. (2022). A survey on observability of distributed edge & container-based microservices. IEEE Access, 10, 86904–86919. https://doi.org/10.1109/access.2022.3193102 (accessed on 11th September 2025).

45. Xu, L., Sanders, L., Li, K., & Chow, J. C. L. (2021). Chatbot for health care and oncology applications using artificial intelligence and machine learning: Systematic review. JMIR Cancer, 7, e27850–e27850. https://doi.org/10.2196/27850 (accessed on 11th September 2025).

46. Zheng, J., Qu, J., Cai, Z., Xue, Y., & Li, X. (2024). Modelling and simulation of cloud-native-based edge computing terminals for power distribution. IET Generation, Transmission & Distribution. https://www.semanticscholar.org/paper/1ebc5c458d8969ed0b3dd86eaf43c21502c553c9 (accessed on 11th September 2025).

CHAPTER 3

CONTAINERIZATION AND ORCHESTRATION

Contents

INTRODUCTION

The advent of containerization and orchestration has changed the face of software deployment and development. The development of the ability to bundle up programs and their dependencies within light containers enabled developers to provide consistency in computing environments. The technology replaces much of the limitation of conventional virtualization solutions, such as wastage of resources and delays in deployment time. The significance of such developments is greatest in e-commerce and cloud-computing dependent businesses, where reliability and uptime are paramount. Consequently, organizations requiring competitive advantages need to invest in these technologies to gain improved performance and efficiency in application processes. In this essay, we examine the extensive implications of containerization and orchestration, particularly in enhancing system reliability and minimizing operational downtime, thus paving the way for more robust and dynamic service provisioning. One of the central problems for businesses today, particularly online stores, is downtime vulnerability, which may lead to huge financial loss as well as a decline in customer satisfaction. Containerization is the key to mitigating these risks via a standardized environment that enhances application deployment. Isolation and scalability are supported by this technology, allowing businesses to grow resources based on traffic requirements without impacting performance. Moreover, orchestration tools such as Docker Swarm and Kubernetes automate the life cycle of these containers so that app updates and scaling operations are smooth. Through a discussion of the interaction between containerization and orchestration, this paper highlights their core role in facilitating operational resilience, hence addressing the urgent need for continuous service availability in the competitive market (Akerele et al., 2024). Further, with an increasing number of organizations embracing multi-cloud environments, the relevance of containerization increases even more. It not only enhances workload portability but also optimizes utilization of resources across various cloud environments. This paper will describe the issues and benefits of implementing container orchestration across multi-cloud setups. This will include case studies and best practices that create the effectiveness of such technologies in enhancing operational performance and consistency. With the help of the functionalities of orchestration tools, businesses are able to enhance their ability to deploy, manage, and scale applications with ease, hence benefiting from a more efficient infrastructure. The subsequent parts of the paper will offer actionable recommendations and insights to organizations that wish to apply containerization and orchestration to be able to improve innovation and further improve service delivery, paving the way for future innovations in the fast-growing field (S. M. S et al., 2024).

Definition of Containerization

Containerization is now revolutionary software development and deployment technology because it allows packaging of applications and their dependencies together in a single package, a portable software piece known as a container. The revolutionary approach allows developers to package software within a normal context that is independent of the host environment, hence escaping software compatibility and deployment issues in diverse environments. Consequently, applications run perfectly on a variety of systems, either in on-premises servers or cloud setups, for a more responsive and agile software development life cycle. Standardizing deployment by containerization removes much of the friction typically experienced in production, thereby enhancing overall efficiency and reliability of software delivery. In essence, containerization is the inherent aspect of modern DevOps operations, focusing on cooperation and automation within software development. Through the provision of support for multiple containers to run in parallel on a single machine, organizations can optimize resource utilization, leading to cost-effective operations. The technology is also compatible with the concept of microservices architecture, enabling the development of small modules deployable and manageable in isolation. This modularity enables continuous integration and continuous deployment (CI/CD), which are critical to guaranteeing the perpetual velocity of software innovation. Containers enable faster release cycles, which, subsequently, enable an organization to respond to market requirements and technological advancements better. Furthermore, container orchestration is critical in managing complex containerized environments. Orchestrators such as Kubernetes or Docker Swarm automate the deployment, scaling, and management of containerized applications, hence avoiding the complexity of running multiple containers. This orchestration is especially relevant in cloud computing, where scalable and efficient resource usage is of paramount importance. It is noted that cloud computing has revolutionized the IT sector, yet it has problems with energy consumption and environmental pollution (Katal et al., 2022). By therefore combining containerization with orchestration, not only is performance optimized but also sustainable, resulting in more efficient and environmentally friendly data center operation, thereby addressing pertinent challenges in the emerging world of IT and software development.

Importance of Orchestration

Orchestration has emerged as a critical component in the age of containerization, significant in automating the deployment, management, and scaling of apps in containers. With the shift towards microservices architecture, orchestration is required more than ever. Without orchestration, it becomes challenging to deal with several containers across different environments within a limited time frame, and it turns into a mess with issues such as configuration drift, inconsistent deployments, and resource wastage. Through orchestration tools, such as Kubernetes or Docker Swarm, organizations can maintain one cohesive operational model that not only simplifies deployment but also enhances the utilization of resources and system dependability. Therefore, orchestration is not luxury; it is required to keep things in check, efficient, and dependable in complex, ever-evolving application environments (Rajakakuar et al., 2025). Besides improving the efficiency of operations, orchestration is also essential in offering fault tolerance for containerized systems. With applications growing and being developed into complexity, there are greater probabilities for individual component failure. With orchestration, one has automatic recovery methods, such as self-healing mechanisms where the failed containers are retried or replaced automatically without the intervention of human beings. This makes one independent of downtime and provides greater availability for services in general. Besides, orchestration allows for workloads to be evenly distributed across a cluster to address issues of skewed resource deployment. With the presence of intelligent orchestration protocols, organizations not only enhance resilience to failure in their systems but also advance their strategic objective of high availability and performance under constantly changing operating environments. These are the kinds of attributes that are vital in today's competitive business environment where customer satisfaction is a factor of reliability (Gite, 2025). Beyond administrative efficiency and fault tolerance, the applicability of orchestration to containerization also enables easy scaling of applications to meet changing demands. With changing usage traffic, orchestration systems have the ability to easily adjust the number of running containers as needed, with performance being kept at an optimal level without any human effort. This scalability is particularly beneficial for businesses that have variable loads, as it supports immediate allocation of resources in real time based on actual demand. Besides, the orchestration of containerized applications allows for a more structured approach to managing configuration and state, therefore standardizing deployment on various different environments. This degree of control and optimization encourages the broader goals of operational agility and innovation, which allow companies to respond effectively to market changes and technological innovation. Generally, orchestration is crucial in developing an adaptive and resilient model in the area of containerization (Rajakumar et al., 2025).

3.1. HISTORICAL CONTEXT OF CONTAINERIZATION

The history of containerization dates as far back as the 1950s, an era characterized by the high growth of shipping applications that aimed at eliminating inefficiencies in handling cargo. Before containerization, shipping was done through breakbulk, whereby the handling of individual cargo items entailed loading and unloading it manually. This time-consuming exercise not only increased the risk of damage and theft but also took the better part of the time. The invention of standard containers revolutionized this approach, making products packaged with ease for shipment. This technology not only reduced loading time but also reduced costs, contributing to enabling globalization in business. Containerization began gaining ground in use by the 1960s, then came the development of sophisticated shipping methods, paving the way for future logistic innovations later in the century. As the global economy expanded, the 1980s and 1990s were the coming-of-age years for containerization as a part of international business. Container ships emerged, with which thousands of containers could be transported per vessel, making sea freight more efficient and lower in cost. This transformation created a sea change in logistics and supply chain management by making it quicker to deliver and enabling the use of just-in-time manufacturing methods. Also, the use of containerization in port activities opened up room for special terminals, which were equipped with cranes and automated systems, to help quicken cargo handling processes. Through this innovation, containerization established a solid foundation that integrated harmoniously with emerging technologies, opening doors to the orchestration techniques that would dominate the logistics sector in the years that followed. The second half of the 20th century and early 21st century saw containerization cross into its technological actualization as technology began to redefine the handling and utilization of the containers. Emergence of digital technologies, such as the Internet and database networks, enabled the deployment of advanced tracking mechanisms that increased visibility and efficiency across the supply chain. This digital transformation occurred alongside the Configuration Management (CM) principles, where fundamental models and innovation like DevOps began to intersect with logistics practice. Innovations are consistently transforming traditional CM practices to provide solutions for scalability, automation, and flexibility (Farayola et al., 2023). These innovations have challenges, particularly when it comes to cybersecurity in cloud-native environments that are constructed on such orchestration of containerized applications (Θεόδωρος et al., 2023). Knowing this background history is key to knowing the present status of containerization and where it is going in international trade and technology.

3.1.1. Evolution of Software Deployment

Software deployment has also undergone dramatic transformation with the advancement, largely driven by technology innovation and changing organizational needs. Software deployment in the past was practically solely dependent on traditional installation, which entailed time-consuming processes of individual system configuration. Not only was it time-consuming, but also prone to error, leading to inconsistency in software performance and customer satisfaction. As applications grew more complex and large in nature, there was a clear call for deployment strategies to become more effective. This call gave rise to virtual environments, where the developers were able to test complete systems within a simulated environment, thereby reducing compatibility and simplifying deployment across multiple platforms. The strategy still had its limitations with regards to efficiency and scalability of resources and, as such, spawned containerization as an even better solution. Containerization revolutionized software deployment by packaging applications and their dependencies in lightweight, portable containers. This facilitated increased levels of consistency in heterogeneous environments, in effect curing the it works on my machine syndrome that had been a source of anguish to developers for years. Containers run on a shared operating system, radically reducing overhead in terms of system resources over virtual machines.

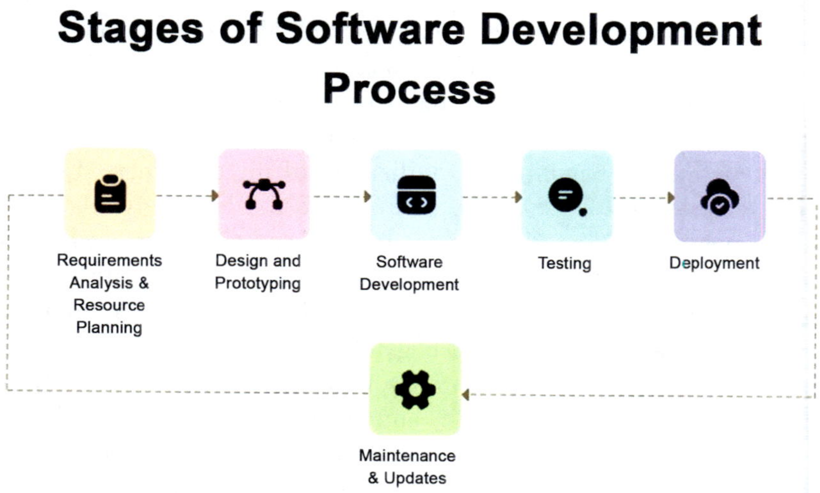

Figure 3.1. *Evolution of software deployment.*

Source: https://media.licdn.com/dms/image/v2/D5612AQHNHGvfMMVCeQ/article-cover_image-shrink_600_2000/article-cover_image-shrink_600_2000/0/1714239044129?e=2147483647&v=beta&t=N95Bhh2vxlu6kym7q1VTB53mJko7OCR7T6w1Qg1JDTA.

This, thus, enables rapid scaling and deployment consistent with the current demand for rapid development methodology. Container orchestration tools such as Kubernetes also enable automated management of containerized applications, which simplifies dynamic resizing of resources to changing workload. This orchestration capability is key for companies that seek to improve their deployment habits while ensuring high availability and reliability of the services in cloud systems, a critical necessity for companies dealing with data-intensive domains. With emerging software deployment, there has continued to be increasing care for energy efficiency and sustainability amidst cloud computing architecture proliferation. The increase in data centers driven by cloud technology has boosted energy usage, and the projections indicate a steep rise in power demands by 2030 (Katal et al., 2022). This has thus necessitated innovation in power management at the software level. Energy consumption optimization in containerized environments is being pursued using different methods, showing promise towards minimizing the environmental impact of software deployment. Besides, with increasing growth in Internet of Things (IoT), security concerns with an enormous number of connected devices also highlight the importance of robust deployment mechanisms for ensuring secure and efficient operation (Schiller et al., 2022). These emerging challenges underscore the imperative necessity of software deployment tactics to enhance not only to meet technical requirements but also to meet broader societal imperatives in terms of security and sustainability (Figure 3.1).

3.1.2. Introduction of Containers in Computing

The arrival of containers in the world of computing is a landmark change in software deployment and management procedures. Containers package programs and their dependencies into one package that promises consistency in different environments, from development to production. This packaging minimizes the complexity in deploying applications and enables the developer to work without worrying about variations in different systems. Because they can run on any environment that supports the container runtime, containers promote scalability and portability. With businesses now embracing agile methodologies and DevOps, containers are now essential in streamlining workflows and reducing deployment time, thereby improving software development and operations effectiveness. Containerization has taken a massive hit in traditional application deployment strategies in contemporary computing. By allowing applications to run inside isolated environments, containers eliminate much of the contention surrounding shared libraries and dependencies in legacy operating systems. In addition to ensuring that applications execute in a safe environment, this isolation enables organizations to achieve horizontal scaling because they can spin up numerous instances of an application with minimal effort. The utilization of container orchestration platforms elevates this capability to another level in that it offers dynamic scaling and management of containerized applications. This containerization is of supreme significance in guaranteeing system stability and optimal resource exploitation, and ultimately assisting organizations to respond to evolving needs with greater agility. The relevance of containerization is also highlighted by its integration with emerging practices such as Machine Learning Operations (MLOps), as it addresses quite a few strategic issues. Machine learning model deployment would usually require tremendous computational resources and integration of heterogeneous systems, which complicates the operational environment. Containerization simplifies the deployment of the models by packaging them with their dependencies and thus reducing failures during changes in the production environment. Moreover, with companies striving to be energy efficient in their data centers, the advantages brought about by containers find their place in overall sustainability goals. Research has indicated that using container-based infrastructure can cut down on energy usage problems, particularly with power demands in data centers consistently increasing, with projections predicting a dramatic spike by 2030 (Katal et al., 2022).

3.1.3. Key Milestones in Container Technology

The past of container technology is marked by some major milestones that have significantly impacted its evolution and adoption in the digital infrastructure world. Container technology was originally popularized by technologies such as chroot in Unix-based systems, which provided a basic environment isolation technique. The dynamics were completely turned around by the arrival of Docker, though, in 2013. Docker brought containerization to everyone's door, where developers could easily develop, deploy, and execute applications in standardized units. Docker technology did not just enhance the pace of development, but it also enhanced the deployment scenario across various computing environments in a more standardized way, thereby paving the way for large-scale adoption in enterprise as well as open-source environments. With development trends evolving, so did the accompanying frameworks, giving rise to converged solutions that balance orchestration, scale, and efficiency, proving container technology's revolutionary potential for propelling software development and operational efficiency. Following Docker, the second important milestone in container technology was with the development of orchestration frameworks, the master key to managing advanced containerized applications. Kubernetes, introduced by Google in 2014, was a leading open-source orchestration platform to address the challenge of deploying, scaling, and running containerized applications on clusters of hosts. The power of Kubernetes lies in its ability to automate application container deployment, scaling, and operations, providing developers with the right tools to manage multi-container applications effortlessly. Its robust architecture supports a wide range of workloads, allows for effective resource utilization, and has robust configuration management features. Additionally, Kubernetes has also provided a vibrant ecosystem of add-on tools and services, propelling the rapid pace of microservices patterns and Continuous Integration/Continuous Deployment (CI/CD) methods. The integration of containerization and orchestration technologies has continued to evolve, shaping modern software development paradigms. Also, with advancing maturity of container technology, compliance and security have become a region of high concern. With widespread use of containerization in production environments, platform and container vulnerabilities have become regions of top interest. Good Configuration Management (CM) practices have never been more imperative, as businesses desire ensuring the integrity and security of applications that are running inside containers. Technologies such as security scanning automation, runtime defense, and compliance auditing software have been adopted in order to address these challenges effectively. Also, industry standards and frameworks are being developed to ensure that container environments are not just optimized but also secure and regulatory compliant. By incorporating these security controls into the life cycle of the container, organizations become more stable and resilient, and that is essential in today's complex and dynamic technology landscape (Farayola et al., 2023). Overall, these high milestones emphasize the revolutionary nature of container technology, its ability to empower sophisticated application building and operational approaches (Figure 3.2).

Figure 3.2. *Containers-technology-speed-up-application-delivery.*

Source: https://www.veritis.com/wp-content/uploads/2019/07/containers-technology-speed-up-application-delivery.jpg.

3.2. CORE CONCEPTS OF CONTAINERIZATION

One of the fundamental principles of containerization is bundling an application and its dependencies together in a single light-weight package called a container. This bundling delivers consistency across different environments from development to production and hence high compatibility reductions, which otherwise normally happen in traditional application deployment. Containers, unlike virtual machines consuming a complete guest operating system, share the kernel of the host OS and are thus very lightweight in terms of resource consumption. Such a structure not only enhances application boot time but also facilitates high-density server deployment, which is essential for modern cloud infrastructures. The coupling of containerization and agile development methodologies further enhances the software development life cycle, allowing teams to release updates and features faster and with greater regularity. As more and more organizations adopt microservices architecture, the need for efficient and repeatable deployment becomes paramount, thus positioning containerization as a core technology in DevOps practice. Container orchestration is another critical concept required to deal with complex applications made up of many containers. Container orchestration tools, such as Kubernetes, automate application container deployment, scaling, and execution. The tools allow for several functions, including load balancing, service discovery, and health monitoring, to ensure applications operate smoothly and effectively in the production environment. Orchestration also provides automatic scaling, enabling organizations to dynamically respond to demand changes. By streamlining the orchestration process, companies can enhance business efficiency, reduce human mistakes, and enhance system robustness. This is more critical as organizations implement Machine Learning Operations (MLOps), where plugging machine learning models into production environments needs to be supported by a robust orchestration platform that can also efficiently manage the lifecycle of such models (Kreuzberger et al., 2023). Generally, container orchestration not only simplifies application management but also serves to further the overall goals of improved operational efficiency and reliability. Further, the green aspect of containerization cannot be overlooked, particularly in today's data centers where energy efficiency is increasingly becoming more desirable. Adoption of container technology has been associated with lower energy consumption compared to traditional virtual machines due to the ability of containers to support higher density and improved resource utilization. By making effective hardware use and allowing improved scalability, organizations are able to reduce their carbon footprint and overall costs tremendously. From research, it has been proven that as data centers become more modern, the implementation of green strategies such as containerization can be a critical factor in enhancing energy efficiency. This aligns with the current push to reduce the environmental footprint of data centers, which are poised for a huge increase in power consumption over the next few years (Katal et al., 2022). The core concepts of containerization, then, are not merely facilitating operational optimization but also making computing more sustainable as the world becomes more aware of its own resource use.

3.2.1. Container vs. Virtual Machine

The decision between virtualization and containerization is based on understanding their native architectures and efficiency of operation. Virtual machines (VMs) deploy a hypervisor to emulate complete hardware environments in order for multiple operating systems to exist simultaneously on a single physical server. Abstraction offers good flexibility and isolated environments but at the cost of higher resource usage and longer boot-up. In contrast, containers borrow the host operating system kernel, enabling them to share system resources but isolate applications in light, isolated environments. This contrasts not merely to enable faster startup and less overhead but also enhance portability and scalability of applications, important factors in modern microservices architecture. Containers' capacity for efficient use of energy and resources is a major contributing factor in their increasing popularity over VMs. Since the host operating system is shared by containers, multiple containers are able to operate on a single server without incurring the cost of resources used in virtualizing entire operating systems using VMs. This leads to reduced power consumption, thus leading to more eco-friendly data center operations. Katal et al. (2022) describes the role of the data center in energy usage, revealing how efficient power management at the software level, particularly with containers, results in lower operational expenses as well as carbon footprint. With increasing focus on sustainability within organizations, containerization is an effective approach in minimizing environmental impacts without compromising on application performance requirements. Furthermore, container orchestration makes them more efficient and operational. Systems like Kubernetes manage the deployment of containers, scaling, and network policies making easy automated process that delivers very high application reliability and performance. Orchestration systems enable software developers to write and not worry about infrastructure management, thus reducing the development cycle very drastically. As demonstrated by recent studies, container orchestration also facilitates the deployment of applications across heterogeneous environments very conveniently with minimal friction and maximum consistency. I. Such frameworks not just enhance operational responsiveness but also strengthen the case for containerization as opposed to legacy VMs, particularly in contexts where there's a need for high degrees of automation and quick iteration of applications. By optimizing both performance and environmental sustainability, containerization continues to redefine the future of contemporary software deployment and orchestration (Figure 3.3).

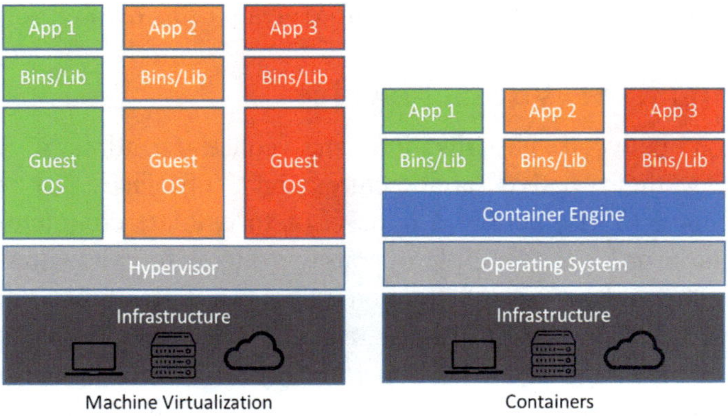

Figure 3.3. *Container vs. virtual machine.*

Source: https://www.netapp.com/media/Screen-Shot-2018-03-20-at-9.24.09-AM_tcm19-56643.png.

3.2.2. Benefits of Using Containers

The use of containers in software development has transformed application deployment through the creation of a consistent and insulated runtime environment. Isolation ensures that applications can be executed on multiple systems with less discrepancy arising from differences in underlying infrastructure. Developers therefore have improved efficiency due to their ability to trust an integrated environment that facilitates testing and deployment. Moreover, container portability supports seamless migration of applications from on-premises data centers to the cloud. This aspect is in line with current workflows, particularly with the fact that organizations are increasingly investing in hybrid cloud strategies whose requirement is agile integration and deployment from different platforms, hence leading to overall operational effectiveness. Besides improving portability and consistency, containers further significantly optimize resources utilization and operational costs in data centers. Traditional VMs are resource-intensive for both the operating system and the hypervisor layer, while containers share the same kernel and thus lack the overhead of VMs. This equates to cost savings in infrastructure along with reduced energy consumption because containers require less space on a server compared to their VM counterpart. Emphasis on energy efficiency in IT operations is especially relevant because the rising energy demands of data centers are among the factors behind increasing CO2 emissions. Its use thus is not only cost-effective but also environmentally friendly in considerations, with strong appeal to implement it in environmentally sustainable cloud computing applications (Katal et al., 2022). Furthermore, the container orchestration optimizes scalability and management, making it possible for organizations to control microservices architecture complexity effectively. Container orchestration tools such as Kubernetes automate deployment, scaling, and the management of applications that run in containers, thereby assisting businesses to accommodate rapid responses to unforeseen workloads. Such responsiveness is crucial in today's fast-moving digital economy where demands fluctuate and technological transformation is extremely rapid. In addition, integration of security controls into orchestration processes is more important, most notably in the Internet of Things (IoT) that carries significant security risks (Schiller et al., 2022). While it streamlines application deployment and scalability, containerization not only boosts productivity but also strengthens the security stance of organizations as a whole, a key component of modern software development and deployment strategies (Figure 3.4).

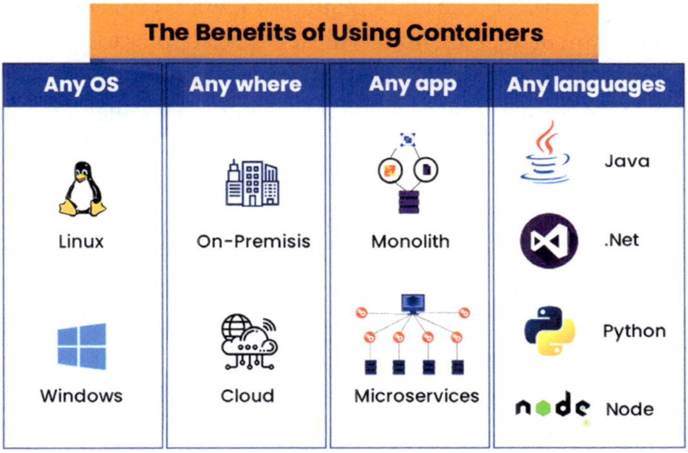

Figure 3.4. *Benefits-of-containers.*

Source. https://www.veritis.com/wp-content/uploads/2021/01/benefits-of-containers.jpg

3.2.3. Popular Container Technologies

Container technologies were soon fundamental building blocks in modern software building, deeply influencing application development, deployment, and running. Container technologies are leading the way, with one of the most powerful being Docker, a product that allows developers to bundle an application along with its dependencies into containers. Doing so creates a culture of consistency across various stages of development, cutting back on compatibility and configuration-related issues. Dockers simplicity and effectiveness have earned it widespread popularity, as it allows teams to develop applications faster and releases innovation at a faster pace. Furthermore, its light footprint ensures resources are utilized optimally, which is crucial for businesses looking to create operational efficiency in a world that is becoming increasingly competitive. As more businesses adopt microservices architectures, orchestration tools have become a prime priority. Kubernetes, the leading orchestration platform, is at the heart of automating scaling, deployment, and management of containerized applications. With Kubernetes, developers can make it easier to manage their microservices with auto-enabled services such as service discovery, load balancing, and rollouts and rollbacks. Kubernetes further provides dynamic scaling, scaling resources based on the needs of an application, thereby optimizing response to fluctuating workloads. This orchestration capability is essential to businesses seeking to enhance their agility and efficiency (Gite, 2025). The combination of Kubernetes and Docker creates a resilient environment that facilitates faster development cycles and fosters continuous integration and deployment (CI/CD) culture. Along with Docker and Kubernetes, there are other container technologies that gain popularity. OpenShift, a Kubernetes-based platform, provides additional capabilities like enhanced security and collaboration tools for developers. Similarly, container runtimes such as containerd and CRI-O focus on resource usage and performance within Kubernetes environments. Each of these technologies brings something unique to the container environment, enabling companies to tailor their DevOps approach in a suitable way. Additionally, through the incorporation of artificial intelligence and machine learning, containerization is evolving with predictive scaling and proactive resource provisioning that are guided by the high demands of new applications. Over time, container technologies will improve to develop more effective processes that will allow organizations to rapidly respond to market fluctuations and enhance their service levels (Gite, 2025).

3.3. INTRODUCTION TO ORCHESTRATION

Containerized app orchestration is a landmark shift in software system deployment and management. While companies increasingly are depending on microservices architecture, the need for sound orchestration grows infinitely greater. Orchestration offers automation through deploying, scaling, and executing application containers to ensure proper resources are allocated in a seamless way based on fluctuating workloads. This automation reduces human errors and optimizes operation, giving developers time to focus on innovating without having to worry about infrastructures. Such frameworks optimize operations in addition to promoting resilience in applications because orchestration solutions can automate recovery processes whenever failures are identified. This groundbreaking shift in the management of apps emphasizes the pivotal significance that orchestration plays in the current DevOps practices, pushing businesses towards more agile and dynamic workloads within a cloud-centric environment.

Figure 3.5. *Datacenter-network-soc-monitoring.*

Source: https://www.e-spincorp.com/wp-content/uploads/2021/06/datacenter-network-soc-monitoring.jpeg.

The core of the new orchestration efforts lies in the practice of Machine Learning Operations (MLOps), which adds to traditional practices by introducing machine learning models into software pipelines. MLOps offers a structured process for deploying and running machine learning models with data science and operations alignment. The principles of MLOps can also enhance orchestration further by providing clarity in defining roles, processes, and workflows that are necessary for operational success. This process addresses some of the main issues concerning deploying machine learning products like the complexities involved in model maintenance and workflow automation. With MLOps principles applied in orchestration platforms, organizations are able to enhance their reactivity to the needs of the market and achieve faster time-to-market, hence sustaining their competitive advantage in the rapidly evolving technology landscape (Kreuzberger et al., 2023). The sustainability aspect of orchestration is also gaining prominence with heightened environmental concern due to technology. Growing energy consumption by data centers, which are expected to grow exponentially in the next couple of years, requires new mechanisms for improving energy efficiency (Katal et al., 2022). Orchestration technology has the potential to be at the forefront of achieving this by optimizing the utilization of resources and minimizing unnecessary applications of compute power in containerized environments. Techniques such as dynamic scaling of containers based on real-time demand will reduce the use of energy significantly without impinging on performance. This is consistent with broader societal goals of reducing carbon footprints and fighting climate change. Thus, through integration of sustainability techniques within orchestration plans, organizations can achieve operational excellence alongside contributing to the propagation of a more sustainable model of computing, further adding to the role of orchestration in the worldwide discussion about sustainable technology practices (Figure 3.5).

3.3.1. Definition of Orchestration in IT

IT orchestration definition also encompasses the coordination and management of dependent tasks across various computing environments. Primarily, it is dynamic application and service deployment, management, and scaling in various architectures, especially in container environments. It utilizes orchestration tools to automate the process of deployment, which otherwise involves a lot of manual work. Apart from making it more efficient, automation also ensures the same configuration and deployment in multiple environments. In contrast to simple container management, orchestration is a more conceptual upper layer that comprises such aspects as resource provisioning, service discovery, and the desired application state. The evolution from manual to sophisticated automated orchestration reflects the enhanced complexity of IT environments today, where organizations can respond rapidly to changing requirements and improve operational stability. Besides, orchestration is key in the Machine Learning Operations (MLOps) practice. By integrating orchestration with containerization, organizations can effectively automate deploying machine learning models. MLOps concentrates on the necessity to automate machine learning product life cycle, such as testing, validation, and deployment phases. The orchestration of the processes is necessary as it addresses collective headaches, such as the need for rapid updates and scaling to meet varying workloads. More specifically, orchestration provides a platform where software engineers and data scientists can collaborate more effectively, enabling machine learning systems to be properly deployed and kept operationally in check. With the rise of MLOps, the interdependence of machine learning and orchestration assumes even greater importance, underscoring the urgency of automation in the IT landscape of today (Kreuzberger et al., 2023). Lastly, the IT applicability of orchestration is not confined to direct application management reach. It also assumes significance while contributing to the ongoing debate regarding data center energy efficiency, particularly in the case of cloud computing. By utilizing orchestration to control their infrastructure, organizations are able to monitor resource usage and maximize energy consumption. With estimates indicating a significant increase in the energy consumption of data centers, it is these challenges that have become increasingly vital to address for environmentally friendly IT practices. By utilizing the power management capabilities of orchestration software tools, IT staff can implement power management at various levels of software, addressing efficiency as well as environmental concerns. This general approach not only aligns with future green computing standards but also emphasizes the imperative nature of how orchestration will play a role in the larger picture of the reduction of the carbon footprint across the IT sector (Katal et al., 2022) (Figure 3.6).

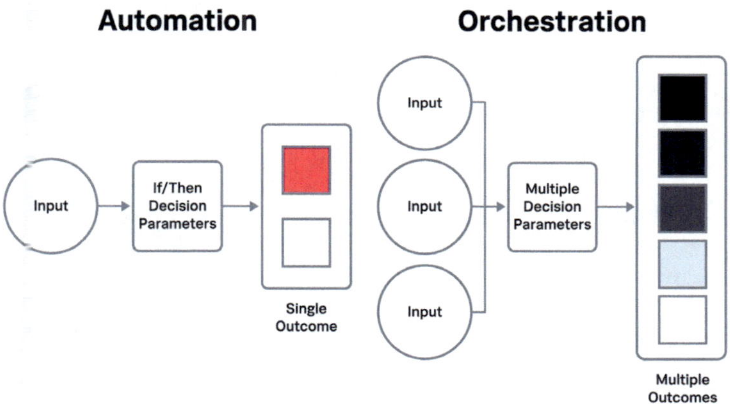

Figure 3.6. *The orchestration/automation-vs-orchestration.*

Source: https://www.splunk.com/content/dam/splunk2/images/data-insider/it-orchestration/automation-vs-orchestration.jpg.

3.3.2. Role of Orchestration in Container Management

Anchor of modern software deployment practices, container orchestration plays a central role in driving the governance and automation of deploying, scaling, and running applications within containers. Through management of the lifecycle of the containers, orchestration software such as Kubernetes enables organizations to optimize both efficiency and reliability. The software enables dynamic scalability, whereby applications automatically scale up or down to fluctuating loads without sacrificing optimal performance. Further, orchestration introduces uniformity to deployment processes, reducing the degree of inconsistency between development, testing, and production environments. Uniformity plays an important role in preventing human error and enhancing overall performance effectiveness, especially in a sophisticated microservices architecture in which numerous containers can work together effectively. Orchestration, in the management of containers, is not a technical enhancement but a strategic necessity at high-level IT infrastructure.

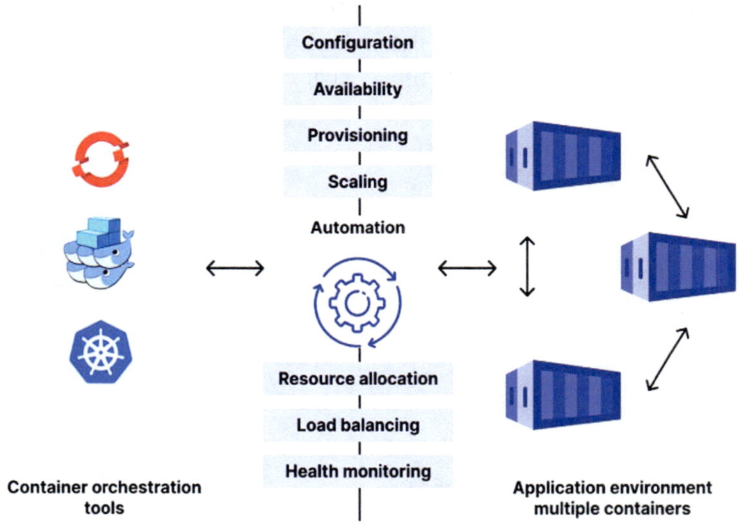

Figure 3.7. *Role of orchestration in container management.*

Source: https://cdn.prod.website-files.com/5ff66329429d880392f6cba2/63bee7de323e0503981d88f9_What%20Is%20Container%20Orchestration.jpg.

The application of automated testing in these orchestration frameworks has been a game-changer, providing enhanced reliability for CI/CD pipelines. A case in point is the role of automated testing in research, which assesses its role in container orchestration efficacy, particularly with the help of frameworks like Kubernetes. These frameworks allow for sophisticated deployment tactics, such as rolling updates and canary releases, which are crucial in risk abatement with regard to potential code malfunction with regards to production changes. This automated testing during integration ensures that deployments are examined step by step, thus promotes a culture of quality assurance in DevOps practices

(Nimdia, 2025). The technicality of manipulating orchestration also appears in the guise of the need for proper specifications, particularly in Kubernetes. Declarative manifest files usage in container deployment orchestration can turn into a challenge for teams without extensive DevOps experience. However, new technologies such as Large Language Models (LLMs) provide the opportunity to make this easier. Automation of generating such manifest files, LLMs eliminate the complexity of the orchestration process, and deployment pipelines become available and more straightforward. Research has indicated that various approaches, including prompt engineering, can optimize the performance of the models to develop correct Kubernetes configurations with minimal human input. Not only does this innovation boost working procedures, but it also unveils promising practices for auto-deployments, representing a significant advancement in container management practices (Kratzke et al., 2024) (Figure 3.7).

3.3.3. Key Features of Orchestration Tools

In containerization, orchestration tools are the source of managing and automating the deployment, scaling, and management of application containers across clusters. One of the most important features of orchestration tools is to offer service discovery and load balancing so that applications with containers can find and communicate with each other efficiently. By directing traffic automatically to various container instances based on prevailing loads, such tools enhance application reliability and performance. Moreover, orchestration platforms such as Kubernetes make it easier to manage the life cycle of containers, which allows developers to focus on application deployment and development rather than infrastructure complexity. This automation not only makes the delivery faster but also reduces the human factor of error, which is important in maintaining stable operation environments necessary for software applications nowadays. Another essential point about orchestration tools is that they support high scaling capacity. When applications experience spikes in demand, the orchestration platforms will scale the number of containers running automatically to adjust. This elastic resource ability is important in optimizing the use of resources and reducing costs. As the demand increases, the orchestration tool will be able to deploy additional containers to take up the load, whereas during off-peak hours it will scale up to conserve resources. With dynamic scaling like this, organizations are able to ensure better service availability and assure levels of performance without unnecessarily burdening costs. Additionally, this characteristic goes hand in hand with sustainable principles, where businesses can manage their use of energy effectively, as detailed in Katal et al. (2022), which discusses approaches to reduce power usage in data centers. Security is paramount in container orchestration, with growing concern about the complexity of cyber-attacks given the Internet of Things (IoT) environment. The ability of orchestration tools to impose security controls—role-based access control, vulnerability scanning, and secure networking—is what keeps applications and their data secure from attempted breaches. Through the provision of a secure operational environment, orchestration tools neutralize risks that interconnectivity presents in environments with IoT devices, as defined in Schiller et al. (2022). This focus on security not only ensures sensitive data is protected but also encourages user trust and regulatory adherence. Therefore, orchestration tools play a crucial role in enabling secure application deployment across cloud-native environments while dealing with the sophisticated challenges presented by emerging technologies (Figure 3.8).

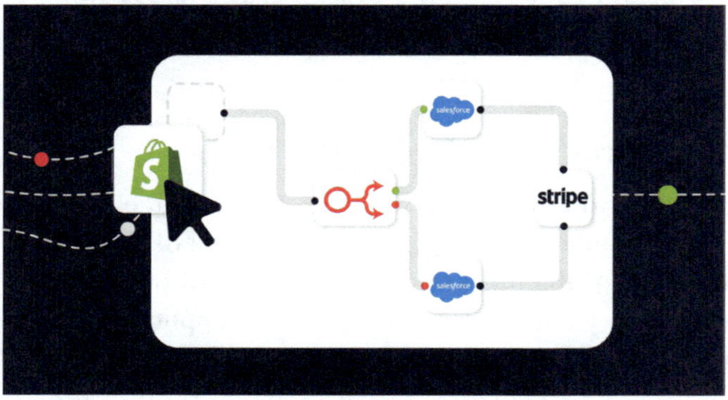

Figure 3.8. *Data-orchestration-tools.*

Source: https://cyclr.com/wp-content/uploads/2022/08/Data-Orchestration-Tools.png.

3.4. POPULAR ORCHESTRATION TOOLS

In the containerization space, orchestration tools play the key role of addressing application deployment, scaling, and networking in complex environments. Kubernetes is arguably the most popular orchestration tool and is currently the industry standard. Kubernetes facilitates automated delivery of containerized applications, with service discovery, load balancing, and rollouts and rollbacks being automatically handled. Through virtualization of the underlying infrastructure, it allows developers to focus on application development rather than server management. Moreover, its extensible nature supports integration with various cloud service providers, hence addressing the heterogeneity of enterprise needs. The rise in popularity of Kubernetes demonstrates the importance of orchestration tools in streamlining contemporary applications to be more efficient and responsive, particularly as businesses increasingly turn towards continuous integration and delivery pipelines. Another leading orchestration tool is Docker Swarm, which is a native Docker tool but offers special features in orchestration by making cluster management more efficient.

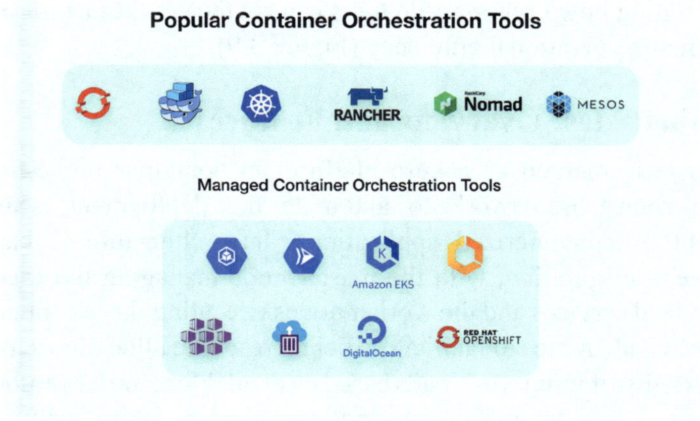

Figure 3.9. *The container-orchestration-tools.*

Source: https://www.simform.com/wp-content/uploads/2022/05/container-orchestration-tools.png.

Compared to Kubernetes, which is hard to set up, Docker Swarm offers a smooth user experience by using the Docker CLI. It is an excellent option for smaller teams or organizations who appreciate ease and swift deployment. With integrated load balancing, service discovery, and scaling support, Docker Swarm is simple to use for developers to manage containerized applications. It lacks the rich feature set of Kubernetes but can decimate operation overhead to get teams to market more quickly. When choosing orchestration tools, Docker Swarms straightforward approach can be particularly beneficial to those new to containerization or that require less functionality. In addition to Kubernetes and Docker Swarm, OpenShift is another robust orchestration tool that merges Kubernetes with an excellent developer experience. OpenShift was developed by Red Hat and provides developers with more functionality, including a CI/CD system integrated right in, security features for containers, and application monitoring software. This unified platform not only simplifies deployment but also facilitates collaboration among development, operations, and security groups. One of the positives of OpenShift is the emphasis it places on the development of a secure and manageable environment for enterprise applications, catering to the needs of organizations that require robust compliance and security solutioning. OpenShift usage is a direction of development towards cloud-native applications, with microservices architecture used to the benefit of organizations to provide them with options for deployment, scaling, and management (Katal et al., 2022; Kuranage et al., 2022). As the organizations are realizing the complexities of software development in the present, OpenShift is a case illustrating how orchestration tools can set the conditions for innovation while enhancing operational efficiency (Figure 3.9).

3.4.1. Kubernetes: Overview and Features

Kubernetes has emerged as a core platform in container orchestration that provides a robust framework to automate the deployment, scaling, and management of containerized applications. Its architecture is based on a master-slave configuration, with the master node managing the orchestration of containerized services and the worker nodes executing these containers. This design allows Kubernetes to facilitate efficient resource allocation across multi-node clusters, distributing workloads based on available resources automatically. Scalability characteristics of Kubernetes allow organizations to easily adjust their applications as a reaction to dynamic demands, an essential aspect in modern cloud computing environments. As cloud services expand, businesses are relying increasingly on Kubernetes because of its potential to automate processes and enhance data center performance optimization, placing it in an invaluable spot for businesses in search of optimal delivery of their services (Senjab et al., 2023). Perhaps the most important feature of Kubernetes is its sophisticated scheduling algorithm, which manages deployment and execution of containers within a cluster. This algorithm examines various metrics and constraints to determine optimal placement such that resources are utilized effectively and loads are distributed evenly. Kubernetes supports various scheduling strategies, such as generic scheduling and multi-objective optimization-based scheduling, that can be formulated to cater to various operational requirements. This is particularly helpful in sophisticated environments where various applications have varying requirements and priorities. By enabling good resource management and allocation, Kubernetes enhances operational efficiency; organizations are hence able to respond faster towards business needs and provide better service quality, hence improving their market competitiveness (Senjab et al., 2023). Kubernetes further transcends orchestration to encourage integration within broader technology frameworks, particularly in the case of Machine Learning Operations (MLOps). As demand grew to deploy machine learning models into production, Kubernetes offers essential functionality that greatly simplifies the lifecycle management of the models. The containerization feature of Kubernetes allows reproducible environments for deployment, removing the issues typically encountered in operationalizing machine learning offerings. Automating the model training, testing, and deployment workloads becomes much simpler with Kubernetes, propelling businesses towards achieving and maintaining better MLOps practices. Such a merger also speaks for the ubiquity and usability of Kubernetess in advancing organizational strategies for harnessing advanced technologies in the framework of containerization and orchestration, thereby promoting business organizations to innovate with greater agility and effectiveness (Figure 3.10).

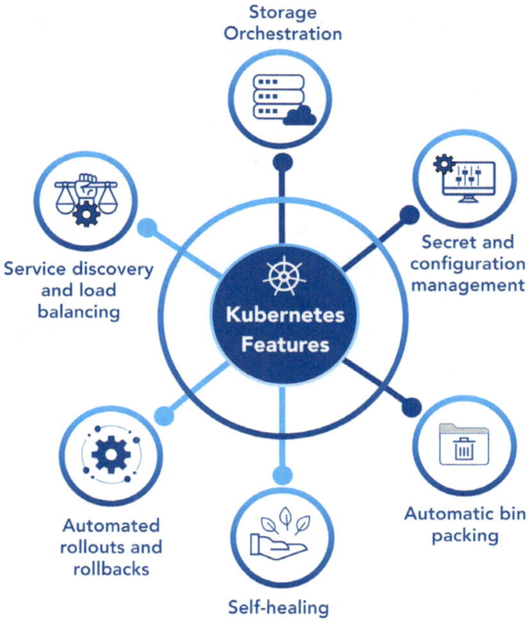

Figure 3.10. *Kubernetes has emerged as a pivotal platform in the realm of container orchestration.*

Source: https://www.opsramp.com/wp-content/uploads/2022/07/Kubernetes-Features-1024x797.png.

3.4.2. Docker Swarm: Use Cases and Benefits

In the rapidly evolving era of today's software development, Docker Swarm comes along as a determinant orchestration solution that facilitates seamless containerized application management. Its architecture facilitates applications' scalability because it allows users easily to deploy, run, and scale containers on numerous hosts. Microservices architecture comes in as one of the prime applications of Docker Swarm, where applications are broken down into smaller, independent deployable services. This module-based approach not only enhances the development cycle with simultaneous work on different services by groups of developers, but also augments application scalability and resilience because each service can be scaled independently according to demand without hampering the system as a whole. With the utilization of Docker Swarms capabilities, organizations gain effective usage of resources, thereby supporting a better more agile and responsive environment for development. The operation efficiency of Docker Swarm is also supplemented by its inherent capabilities of high availability and load balancing. In a scenario where application traffic fluctuates, Docker Swarm logically spread workloads across available containers, thereby streamlining performance and enhancing user experience. Such capability is particularly valuable to businesses with fluctuating workloads, such as e-commerce platforms managing spikes in traffic during holiday shopping promotions. Secondly, Swarms constant container health monitoring allows for automated restarts of condemned services, implying negligible downtime and hence business continuity. With organizations increasingly focusing on operational availability, the uptime reliability that Docker Swarm offers is a differentiator that can increase market competitive advantage.

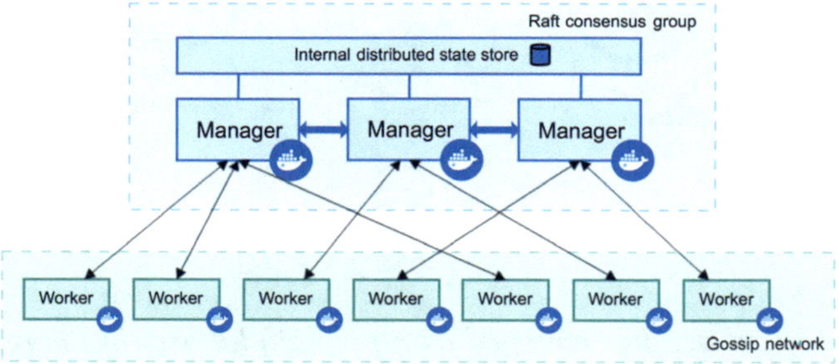

Figure 3.11. *Docker swarm: Use cases and benefits.*

Source: https://cdn.prod.website-files.com/681e366f54a6e3ce87159ca4/687d7a4dc74d8c88972d57f7_image2-52-1170x549.png.

The other essential aspect of Docker Swarm is its role in facilitating cooperative development through the use of the technology of containerization. Through the provision of a consistent environment, Docker Swarm facilitates easier collaboration among operations teams and developers, thereby reducing friction that normally arises between software development and IT operations—a concept known as DevOps. The use of containerization together minimizes inconsistency caused by differences in environments because images built can be directly exported to production without conflicts of compatibility. This effective process is required by organizations which aim to promote productivity and reduce time-to-market for their applications. As the industry shifts towards green cloud innovations, such as those discussed within the energy efficiency model of (Katal et al., 2022), Docker Swarms resource-conscious utilization is appropriate for sustainability objectives, reaffirming the necessity of container orchestration in contemporary software development (Figure 3.11).

3.4.3. Apache Mesos: Architecture and Applications

Apache Mesos architecture forms a robust foundation for modern-day container orchestration, particularly in cloud hosting that is highly demanding in terms of efficiency and scalability. Basically, Mesos is centered around a two-level scheduling architecture dynamically allocating resources to a broad spectrum of workloads. Microservices using organizations are greatly reliant on this functionality, as it supports the dynamic allocation of CPU, memory, and storage resources to numerous containers. The autonomy of resource management over task scheduling not only improves the operations efficiency but also enables hassle-free integration with other frameworks and tools, and therefore becomes the ideal choice for organizations who are working towards maximizing their containerized applications. In addition, the capability of Mesos to manage resources across clusters gives it an edge in handling mixed workloads, which makes it attractive for modern applications that need efficient resource management mechanisms in next-generation distributed systems. Under containerization, Apache Mesos facilitates the management of containerized applications through using its resource management capabilities to ensure containers are well-scheduled and executed. With the increasing adoption of microservices architecture, effective container scheduling paradigms have become increasingly sought after. Mesos avoids this drawback by offering scope for heuristic and meta-heuristic scheduling approaches, which realize better resource utilization by optimizing their allocation based on present demand and availability. This is particularly significant in situations where containers exhibit dataflow interactions and competition for resources. By employing advanced strategies that forecast performance targets, Mesos improves containerized microservices management and is therefore part of the cloud infrastructure ecosystem. Notably, one needs to study container scheduling in this regard so that it enables effective use of resources without causing latency issues between related services, as outlined by modern research regarding container scheduling problems (Prajapati et al., 2024). Furthermore, Mesos plays a vital role in improving the accessibility of machine learning frameworks to containerized applications. As work continues towards improving the discipline of machine learning, there is definitely an imperative for systems to orchestrate the end-to-end development process — from model creation to production deployment. The integration of Apache Mesos with such systems supports transparent access to distributed resources, facilitating the management of big computational tasks which are ubiquitous in machine learning workflows. The architecture supports a serverless model, permitting data scientists and machine learning practitioners to publish and share models easily while still being able to provide strong orchestration. With a DevOps strategy, organizations are able to enhance collaboration and efficiency in the deployment of machine learning models into production, according to contemporary trends in cloud computing towards scalability and resource utilization (Álvaro et al., 2020). The benefits of Apache Mesos thus make it an essential orchestration element within containerized settings, enhancing operational efficiency and the deployment of complex machine learning solutions (Figure 3.12).

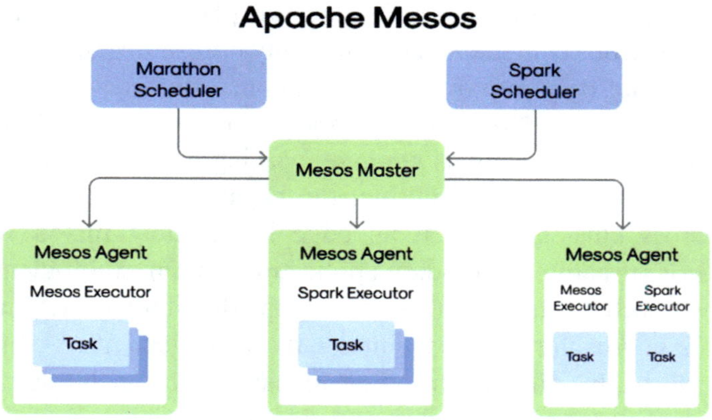

Figure 3.12. *The architecture of Apache Mesos serves as a robust foundation for modern container orchestration.*

Source: https://cdn.prod.website-files.com/5ff66329429d880392f6cba2/661575d0e902e166f1d66ac8_516-min.jpg.

3.5. CHALLENGES IN CONTAINERIZATION AND ORCHESTRATION

The rapid adoption of containerization has transformed software development and deployment trends, but it also has a list of challenges that companies have to confront. One of the bigger challenges is the increased complexity delivered by orchestration technology such as Kubernetes, which, while so potent, demand a steep learning curve for proper implementation and maintenance. When organizations are transitioning to microservices architecture, the more number of containers exacerbates the issues with handling inter-service communications, scalability, and resilience. Further, ensuring that containers are well-configured involves meticulous attention to security parameters, which can easily get compromised in agile environments. Without good comprehension and planning, organizations risk adverse outcomes, including downtime or threats that disrupt service delivery and undermine data integrity in the online space. In addition, the implementation of continuous integration and continuous deployment (CI/CD) patterns complicates the management of containerization and orchestration. Such teams wishing to achieve fast, iterative updates must grapple with the complexity of testing, integration, and deployment automation. This configuration demands structured workflows that can manage repeated changes without compromising on dependability of resulting software releases.

Challenges related to dependency management are not infrequent, nor are test failures due to stale or heavy resource-consuming images. If the dynamics of CI/CD pipelines aren't taken into account by organizations, they will have bottlenecks that will hinder development flow and reduce the speed at which new features get incorporated. Thus, a compromise must be made between stability and speed in terms of tapping the complete potential of containerized applications and orchestration systems (Ali et al., 2024). Finally, security remains a topmost issue in orchestration and containerization due to the fact that traditional practices might prove insufficient in overcoming the singular vulnerabilities brought about by these technologies. Shift-left security practices echo the significance of implementing security controls throughout the development process, particularly in containerized environments where image vulnerabilities and misconfigurations might expose severe exposure risks.

Mandating automated vulnerability scans within CI/CD pipelines is necessary to identify weaknesses at an early stage, but it typically proves challenging for organizations in terms of the complexities in enforcement and remediation. It involves designing policies that would align security standards and operational practices, with the requirements for incessant cross-departmental coordination. As the threat landscape evolves, spending on advanced security solutions for containerized apps can work wonders to enhance resilience but needs dedication and visionary leadership thinking to ensure proactive and reactive robust defenses remain intact (Bhardwaj et al., 2024).

3.5.1. Security Concerns

The expanding adoption of containerization in modern deployment patterns creates severe security risks that need to be addressed head-on by organizations. Certain of the fundamental issues stem from the very vulnerabilities which are posed by container architecture, such as misconfigurations, insecure images, and weak access control. As containers hold applications and their dependents, any defect in the packaging can leave the entire system open to attack. The runtime environment is specifically exposed to attack, as a compromised container could provide unauthorized access to sensitive data or other containers on the same host. To mitigate these threats, there is a need to ensure that strict security practices are taken at every stage in the lifecycle of a container, so that all the images are scanned for vulnerabilities and the configurations are security best-practice compliant, thus securing deployment environments and sensitive organizational data from potential breaches (Mori et al., 2025). Additionally, the orchestration layer in the form of technologies like Kubernetes also has its own security issues.

Though these tools enable scalable and efficient management of containers, they also extend the attack surface unless properly secured. Malicious orchestration can be employed to induce system-wide failures, leading to severe downtime and data loss. This poses security concerns regarding role-based access control and network segmentation in the orchestration system, which, unless properly configured, can potentially allow attackers to abuse privileges and move laterally across containers. Security controls such as allocation controls for resources, automated security scanning, and practices of vulnerability management must be pillars of any orchestration deployment. Through the securing of the orchestration platform, organizations are able to have a symbiotic balance between the containerization agile benefit and security precautions needed to protect key infrastructure (Murali et al., 2025). Finally, organizations must realize that container security is both a technical and a cultural challenge requiring end-to-end training and awareness from development and operations teams.

As the speed of Docker and DevOps style of work grows, the need is to instill a culture of security among teams so that every member is aware of the effect their activity has on the overall security posture. Rolling out ongoing education programs in container security, orchestrator vulnerabilities, and best practices can empower teams to identify and eliminate potential flaws before they can be exploited. Having security safeguards integrated into CI/CD pipelines automates the processes and facilitates rapid deployment without impacting security. By making security a collaborative endeavor across workflows and teams, companies can best position themselves against evolving threats and maintain the integrity of their containerized applications in a world where everything is in a constant state of change (Mori et al., 2025) (Figure 3.13).

Figure 3.13. *The increasing adoption of containerization within modern deployment practices raises significant security.*

Source: https://ophtek.com/wp-content/uploads/2018/02/Top-5-Unnoticed-Network-Security-Risks-to-Your-Business.jpg.

3.5.2. Complexity of Management

The nature of running in the environment of containerization and orchestration is primarily caused by integrating varied technologies and practices that are needed to operate effectively in cloud-native applications. Containerization simplifies deploying applications in isolated environments, making resources used efficiently and eliminating infrastructure discrepancies. However, with increased utilization of container-based solutions by organizations, they are confronted with immense resource management and scaling challenges. The complexity that accrues from balancing these technology developments with business objectives requires management to tread a tight rope of interaction between operational security, user requirements, and service availability. Added to this is the requirement for mature orchestration tools that ensure effective monitoring and management of containerized applications across diverse deployment environments (Nascimento et al., 2024). Adaptive measures must hence be taken by effective leadership in order to mitigate risks as they pursue efficiency and scalability. Furthermore, as organizations transition to cloud-native architecture, end-to-end management frameworks are a vital necessity. Effective management is through understanding that deploying the application containerized is not enough. Instead, organizations must adopt a holistic approach embracing continuous delivery and integration, and also monitoring the running of microservices in orchestrated environments. In this regard is the importance of Machine Learning Operations (MLOps), which provides essential best practices, guidelines, and development culture for successfully operationalizing machine learning products. While businesses are exposed to the natural dynamics in running such systems, they also need to examine existing frameworks to determine if they can accommodate these new ways (Kreuzberger et al., 2023). The management's role changes into that of a facilitator to enable teams to leverage tools and collaborations that promote integration of workflow. Lastly, the effectiveness of the management in containerization and orchestration is contingent upon how it handles the dynamic issues of changing techno-environments. This requires a good understanding of the technical as well as managerial aspects of container-based apps, with the operational challenges such as manual scaling and potential single points of failure in mind. The transition to cloud-native architectures requires organizations not only investing in established orchestration platforms like Kubernetes but also creating organizational culture encouraging ongoing learning and resilience. By accepting such intricacies, management is able to enhance innovation while ensuring operational resilience and security. A well-structured approach in between strategic direction and technical knowledge will enable organizations to thrive in the competitive landscape created through containerization and orchestration (Nascimento et al., 2024).

3.5.3. Resource Allocation Issues

The efficient use of resources is a challenge to organizations utilizing containerization and orchestration technologies. In environments where it is simple to deploy and scale containers, the management of computation and memory resources becomes critical. Resource allocation issues arise with mismatches between available resources and those required by the applications during high loads or unusual patterns of demand. Effective orchestration tools must thus strike this balance of ensuring that applications perform optimally without incurring additional cost or compromising on performance. Customers are also often confronted with the issue of over-provisioning and under-provisioning; the former is wasteful while the latter results in application failures and leaves customers with second-rate experiences. Therefore, building intelligent automation policies that are able to provision resources dynamically according to real-time demands is vital in modern container orchestration setups (Shah et al., 2024). The role of resource scheduling in orchestration engines cannot be ignored, especially as applications increasingly execute in cloud-native setups. The engines must schedule resources to containers with optimality to attain high system utilization and yet guarantee system performance. For instance, a well-designed orchestration platform should leverage algorithms that consider both the resource requirements of containers and the current availability within the cluster. Challenges arise from resource contention, where multiple containers compete for limited resources, potentially leading to bottlenecks. Additionally, some orchestration solutions may struggle with scaling decisions, particularly when workloads fluctuate unpredictably. Integration support for various scheduling policies can mitigate these issues, increasing efficiency and supporting application resiliency.

Figure 3.14. *The efficient allocation of resources is a critical challenge facing organizations utilizing containerization and orchestration technologies.*

Source: https://cdn.prod.website-files.com/5d9ffc249511353e75384 0c9/676305a01fb88fb03fe20cfd_66defe8e746d6cfe29cac118_AD_4nXcRryZc4s9a5VNbMM89r8D0_qmO2vrwxUCbb2F3p2XWZh9xJV0bYux-5tOu-qQEKDHSy9PCuOd5P3pCLWsd5BfvdodsA_hGmtVpwA9o_UR-0SmGbfl_TEEmz1NYeNg7aqyPpWIQED_f0XUvRw_1tdf57rlpR.png.

In the end, a robust resource allocation strategy fosters a condition that is extremely responsive and capable of adapting to both typical operational demands and unforeseen surges in activity (Dave et al., 2024). Also, the complexities involved in microservices architecture further complicate resource allocation issues, particularly when employing container orchestration. In a microservices setup, each piece of software runs autonomously, perhaps requiring diverse resources based on workload patterns. That diversity complicates the resource allocation strategies because different microservices may have varying performance and scalability demands. With orchestration solutions managing hundreds of containers, having each service receive suitable resources involves complicated calculations and real-time allocations. Monitoring and analytics tools need to be integrated to enable data that informs quality resource allocation. With the combination of real-time measurements and advanced machine learning models, organizations can predict resource demands more accurately, hence optimizing the overall system performance. With increasing businesses shifting toward microservices architecture through containerization, addressing such issues of resource utilization becomes essential to achieve operational efficiency and reliability (Shah et al., 2024) (Figure 3.14).

3.6. FUTURE TRENDS IN CONTAINERIZATION AND ORCHESTRATION

With organizations gravitating increasingly towards multi-cloud setups, containerization and orchestration are going to be at the forefront of this development. Multi-cloud infrastructure allows one to leverage various service providers to achieve optimized performance, reduced costs, and redundancy. The transition to multi-cloud strategies is brought about by the need for workload portability in order for businesses to deploy their apps across various infrastructures with ease. Containers are a light-weight virtualization option making this flexibility achievable by packaging up applications with their dependencies. Thus, orchestration tools such as Kubernetes are necessary, as they ease deployment, scaling, and management of containerized applications. This indicates that as firms desire greater operational efficiency and reduced risks of vendor lock-in, there will always be a need for next-generation container orchestration solutions, firmly positioning them at the center of IT strategy transformation in firms (Kumar, 2025). Future orchestrations trends are also shaping the future of containerization, particularly with regard to financial management and compliance frameworks. Organizations must function in a tougher ecosystem where regulatory requirements are high, and budget constraints are universal. With the evolving container orchestration technologies, technologies are becoming more capable of integrating capabilities for cost management, resource optimization, and compliance tracking. For instance, next-generation financial management software can provide insight into resource consumption and optimize costs, aligning technology spending with business objectives. Also, compliance frameworks are being modernized to recognize the unique attributes of containerized environments, thereby facilitating easier compliance with regulatory standards. This union of financial management and compliance management is one manifestation of the intricacy of orchestration, which enables organizations to remain nimble but accountable and responsive (Soleymanzadeh et al., 2025). Another critical trend is the growing focus on energy efficiency and sustainability in containerization processes. While environmental concerns are escalating with climate change, organizations are rising to the challenge of the green profile of their operations. Container-based applications can ensure energy efficiency through optimized utilization of resources through orchestration tools. With dynamic resource utilization optimization, businesses can reduce energy consumption and carbon footprints. In addition, serverless architectures and edge computing are enhancing the chances for energy-saving habits. As businesses embrace these environmentally friendly practices with containerization, they are not just getting greener but also better placed to comply with future carbon emission standards. Lastly, the merging of sustainability and technology between containerization and orchestration will be a defining feature of industry trends as stakeholder expectations continue to evolve (Kumar, 2025).

3.6.1. Advancements in Container Security

As containerization technologies improve, the need for stronger security measures also grows, this time for their respective architectures. Of the most significant developments in this area is further evolution of security tooling that are designed specifically for environments like Kubernetes that remain at the core of cloud-native application orchestration. Recent developments in Kubernetes, including the release of Kubernetes 1.29 and the Kubernetes Gateway API, are major stepping stones toward closing base security vulnerabilities. Beyond streamlining access control, these advancements also improve network traffic management, leading to an overall tighter security position. Moreover, analysis of critical components such as worker and master nodes demonstrates how their designs themselves facilitate scalability while simultaneously supporting serious security loopholes, which then call for continuous improvements in protection methods in such systems (Aksholak et al., 2025). Alongside developments in orchestration platforms are also arising trends in the application of behavioral detection approaches in container security. Early methods, such as Decision Trees and Hidden Markov Models, laid the foundations for more sophisticated ones by highlighting the necessity of behavior-based malware detection. The older methods are still used as a reference point because they shifted the focus from static and signature-based detection to a more fitting direction with the adaptive nature of containerized environments. Modern entries, particularly those centered around eBPF-based monitoring and sophisticated machine learning algorithms, have built upon these foundational concepts. Through the support of orchestrated metadata and cross-container correlation, modern security solutions are better positioned to detect lateral movement within container environments, hence improving the security environment against sophisticated threats (Kamaluddin, 2021). The path to comprehensive container security is lined with emergent tools and methods that attempt to neutralize specific vulnerabilities incorporated into containerized environments. The comparative study of key security tools like Kube-bench and Kube-hunter, consequently, emphasizes how much depends on solutions that, aside from being effective, are also able to adapt to the ever-evolving nature of container orchestration. While there are several tools with significant security features, there is still a gap in their ability to provide end-to-end automated, integrated answers to the intricacies of cloud infrastructure. Thus, subsequent research must emphasize integrating adaptive AI-driven security solutions that can actively identify and thwart risks, thereby creating safety nets for Kubernetes clusters and other similar orchestration environments (Aksholak et al., 2025; Kamaluddin, 2021).

3.6.2. Integration with Cloud Services

Containerization with cloud services has emerged as a major strategy for organizations that want to enhance their application deployment and management operations. With the aid of cloud computings flexibility and scalability, firms are able to bypass the limitations of traditional monolithic systems. Containerization allows apps to be broken down into microservices, which run separately in their individual environments. Such modularity is particularly beneficial for cloud applications where high scalability is essential. Microservices architecture-designed systems are able to distribute resources in the most efficient way possible, with the performance remaining at its best even when the system is fully utilized. As identified in recent research, adopting containerized microservices not only increases the performance of the overall system but also enhances fault tolerance, making cloud services a more reliable choice for current applications (Barua et al., 2024). Furthermore, orchestration of such containerized microservices plays a critical role in optimizing their operation in cloud environments. Applications like Kubernetes provide seamless management of container lifecycles, enabling applications to scale automatically according to real-time demand. The feature is especially critical in verticals such as online travel services where massive bursts of user requests overwhelm traditional infrastructures. By coupling container orchestration with cloud capabilities, businesses are able to build flexible systems that dynamically adjust to changing workloads. The orchestration platforms not only distribute resources but also merge seamlessly with other cloud-native services, such as databases and analytics, to further enhance operational efficiency and resilience (Nascimento et al., 2024). The ability to manage these interdependencies in a manner that is efficient reduces some of the complexities associated with cloud deployment, allowing for a more symbiotic cloud-native environment. Furthermore, although containerization simplifies the deployment of applications, managing it in conjunction with cloud services requires understanding of some of the challenges and limitations.

Although cloud-native architectures allow for greater scalability and fault tolerance, organizations must also contend with potential challenges like resource management and security loopholes. Container-based applications do pose some problems, particularly in the absence of monitoring and orchestration tools that can properly keep performance and security under check. Cloud-native platforms necessitate a deep understanding of these forces and an expenditure on the proper tools and learning. Solutions like Kubernetes address not only the scalability and availability needs but also cover the security position of applications migrating to cloud infrastructures, ultimately allowing organizations to reap full benefits of containerization in correlation with sophisticated cloud services (Nascimento et al., 2024) (Figure 3.15).

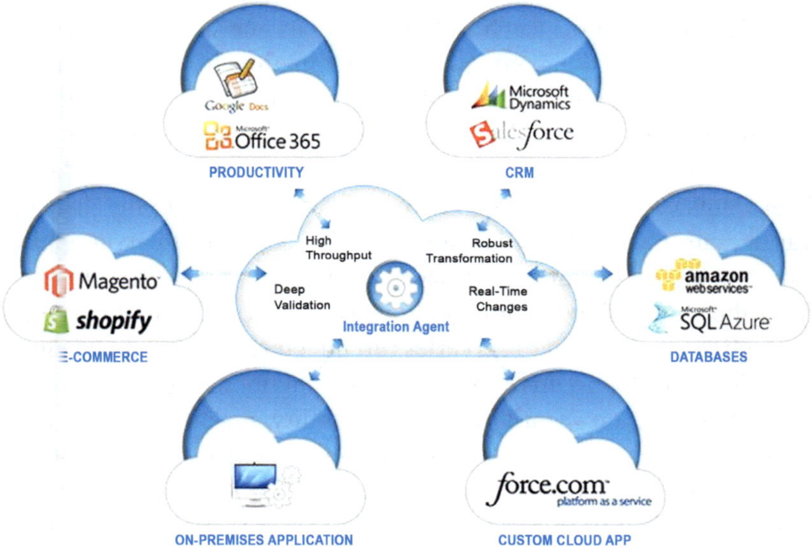

Figure 3.15. *Integration with cloud services.*

Source: https://i.pinimg.com/736x/6f/c9/7a/6fc97aed40d859fa594338d012c07cc4.jpg.

3.6.3. The Rise of Serverless Architectures

The emergence of serverless architecture is a significant leap in the field of cloud computing that has basically transformed the process of deploying and running applications, with developers focusing solely on writing code without having to deal with server management issues compared to traditional architectures where teams often have to provision and manage servers individually. This paradigm shifts the burden of managing infrastructure off customers onto cloud providers, enabling automatic scaling and pay-as-you-go pricing. Serverless architecture is increasing due to advancements in containerization and orchestration technologies, which enable simple deployment and scaling of microservices and functions. With companies increasingly seeking agility and efficiency in software development, serverless architectures become increasingly prevalent in bringing a new flexibility that can immediately adapt to changing market demands. The synergy of serverless architectures and cloud-native technologies lies at the heart of scaling scalability and sustainability in app development. By leveraging automatically scaling services according to user load, developers can avoid a significant amount of resource management and provisioning time. Cloud-native architectures, such as microservices and container orchestration, contribute to this operational efficiency by automating the deployment pipeline. With architectures that are dynamically scalable in response to shifting traffic patterns, high availability and performance can be maintained at lower costs. In addition, serverless transformation encourages a culture of experimentation in which teams can iterate and deploy features quickly. Not only does this fuel innovation, but it also allows developers to develop fault-tolerant applications that are capable of meeting user needs in a more competitive marketplace, verifying the value of such cutting-edge technologies (Oyeniran et al., 2024). To best realize the potential of serverless architecture, organizations must adopt best practices in cloud-native app development focusing on efficiency and reliability. Focusing on security and dependability, developers are encouraged to use mechanisms such as automated testing and continuous integration that collectively create robust systems that can survive failure. Service mesh integration is critical in this case, facilitating secure communication between services while offering observability capabilities to track application health. As noted in resilient architecture discussions, putting these elements together results in developing smart applications that are capable of independently adjusting to changing user demands and environmental factors (Velasco et al., 2021). Lastly, serverless architectures represent an extension of the overall movement towards containerization and orchestration and set the stage for a new application development model with an emphasis on agility, elasticity, and redundancy.

SUMMARY

The discovery of containerization and orchestration highlights their pivotal positions in modern software development and deployment practices. As businesses increasingly demand agility and efficiency, containerization offers an agile way of dealing with application environments by encapsulating software and its dependencies. With the use of light-weight containers, developers are able to deliver consistency across environments, lower compatibility issues, and accelerate deployment cycles. This is particularly important in the fast-paced digital world of today, where sensitivity to changes in the market is imperative to maintaining digital competitiveness. The combination of containerization with robust orchestration solutions further enhances these advantages, allowing automated governance and seamless scalability of application workloads. Furthermore, the integration of advanced automation frameworks into container orchestration is groundbreaking for enterprise operations. Being able to have an end-to-end automation strategy reduces operating expenses while preventing human configuration risks. As demonstrated, technologies such as NVMe-FC display extreme performance boosts in storage management, essentially transforming how organizations architect their data structure. Having orchestration tools, and more so Kubernetes, cannot be overstressed regarding automating said process. They enable organizations to maximize utilization of resources and minimize downtime, thus promoting operational efficiency and resilience in the increasingly complex IT landscape (Suseendran, 2025). Containerization and orchestration's future is ultimately going to be further revolutionized by adopting artificial intelligence and machine learning technologies. It will result in predictive functionality, which can facilitate proactive handling of container environments and offer improved user experience in general. As in this research shown, the integration of automated testing into CI/CD pipelines significantly enhances efficiency and dependability and thus reduces new release deployment risks (Nimdia, 2025). The future course of container orchestration is clear; as companies strive to be more efficient and agile, the integration of advanced technological solutions will continue to propel stronger and faster infrastructures.

The concept of containerization has transformed the deployment of applications by facilitating greater portability and resource utilization. Containerization diverges from traditional virtualization techniques, as it allows applications to run within separate containers that share the kernel of the host operating systems, which leaves them with smaller overhead and faster boot times. This aspect is particularly advantageous to organizations desiring to simplify their DevOps practices. By keeping application lifecycle simple, from coding through deployment and its following scale, containerization allows companies to remain agile regardless of the evolving market needs. In addition, the intrinsic security features of containers provide an excellent plus point because they isolate applications from each other, thereby decreasing the likelihood of vulnerabilities. The systematic deployment of containerized applications closely follows modern cloud computing models, which respond to the urgent need for cost-effective and scalable infrastructure in data centers, as emphasized in recent studies (Senjab et al., 2023). Kubernetes, being one of the top orchestration platforms for containers, is at the center of automating deployment, scaling, and management operations. Its advanced scheduling mechanism provides optimal resource utilization across a node cluster, thereby maximizing data center operation efficiency. Kubernetes' capability to dynamically manage containers enables organizations to react quickly to fluctuating workloads and changing resource needs. Also, the orchestration aspect of Kubernetes allows for the use of multiple scheduling algorithms, which are categorized as generic scheduling, multi-objective optimization-based scheduling, AI-schedule-oriented scheduling, and autoscaling-enabled scheduling (Senjab et al., 2023). Through the implementation of these algorithms, organizations can tune their usage of resources so that applications are not only deployed efficiently but also handled appropriately throughout the whole operational phase. This orchestration capability contributes to the performance and resiliency of cloud solutions overall. With data center power consumption likely to grow significantly, the push towards green methodologies has grown significantly important in the areas of containerization and orchestration. Businesses are becoming more environmentally conscious regarding their IT infrastructure, particularly the CO2 footprint from energy-intensive data center operations. Initiatives aimed at improving energy efficiency are crucial because they contribute to solving environmental problems in addition to presenting cost benefits for organizations. Containerization achieves this by optimizing the utilization of resources and allowing the development of green data centers that prioritize energy management at the software level. Through the use of solutions across every level—virtualization, operating systems, and applications—firms can minimize their environmental impact while continuing to gain efficiencies from containerized architectures. This trend highlights the dual imperative of technological progress and environmental stewardship in enhancing a balanced approach toward future cloud computing practice.

REFERENCES

1. Abdul Raheem, A. K., Osilaja, A. M., Kolawole, I., & Essien, V. E. (2024). Exploring continuous integration and deployment strategies for streamlined DevOps processes in software engineering practices. World Journal of Advanced Research and Reviews, 24, 2813–2830. https://doi.org/10.30574/wjarr.2024.24.3.3988 (accessed on 11th September 2025).
2. Akerele, J. I., Uzoka, A., Ojukwu, P. U., & Olamijuwon, O. J. (2024). Minimizing downtime in e-commerce platforms through containerization and orchestration. International Journal of Multidisciplinary Research Updates. https://www.semanticscholar.org/paper/df3653870a72d40949cca8316c541e6d58bf7124 (accessed on 11th September 2025).
3. Aksholak, G., Bedelbayev, A., & Magazov, R. (2025). Securing Kubernetes: An in-depth analysis of vulnerabilities, tools, and future directions. Physico-Mathematical Series. https://www.semanticscholar.org/paper/4163064f1565c39e56e0f6b38a3d2548fd9a601f (accessed on 11th September 2025).
4. Barua, B., & Kaiser, M. S. (2024). A methodological framework of containerized microservices orchestration and provisioning in the cloud: A case study of online travel platforms. CRC Press eBooks. https://doi.org/10.1201/9781003606260-33 (accessed on 11th September 2025).
5. Bhardwaj, A. K., Dutta, P. K., & Chintale, P. (2024). Securing container images through automated vulnerability detection in shift-left CI/CD pipelines. Deleted Journal, 2024, 162–170. https://doi.org/10.58496/bjn/2024/016 (accessed on 11th September 2025).
6. Dave, S. A., Nadukuru, S., Singiri, S., Goel, O., Tharan, O., & Jain, A. (2024). Scalable microservices for cloud based distributed systems. Deleted Journal, 12, 776–809. https://doi.org/10.36676/dira.v12.i3.132 (accessed on 11th September 2025).
7. Farayola, O. A., Hassan, A. O., Adaramodu, O. R., Fakeyede, O. G., & Oladeinde, M. (2023). Configuration management in the modern era: Best practices, innovations, and challenges. Computer Science & IT Research Journal, 4, 140–157. https://doi.org/10.51594/csitrj.v4i2.613 (accessed on 11th September 2025).
8. Gite, K. (2025). Monolithic vs. microservices architecture: A comparative study of software development paradigms. International Scientific Journal of Engineering and Management. https://www.semanticscholar.org/paper/cd3d9827a93a71b8f2cc16ca9f9ae71f905595fc (accessed on 11th September 2025).

9. Kamaluddin, K. (2021). Fine-grained behavioral analysis for malware detection in containerized environments. American Journal of Computing and Engineering. https://www.semanticscholar.org/paper/802edab5c9fcd475e15c51c4d1e43347c80c5ee1 (accessed on 11th September 2025).
10. Katal, A., Dahiya, S., & Choudhury, T. (2022). Energy efficiency in cloud computing data centers: A survey on software technologies. Cluster Computing, 26, 1845–1875. https://doi.org/10.1007/s10586-022-03713-0 (accessed on 11th September 2025).
11. Kratzke, N., & Drews, A. (2024). Don't train, just prompt: Towards a prompt engineering approach for a more generative container orchestration management. https://www.semanticscholar.org/paper/ee5fb6dce6f665ec0a76ef6711ec7687241472c4 (accessed on 11th September 2025).
12. Kreuzberger, D., Kühl, N., & Hirschl, S. (2023). Machine learning operations (MLOps): Overview, definition, and architecture. IEEE Access, 11, 31866–31879. https://doi.org/10.1109/access.2023.3262138 (accessed on 11th September 2025).
13. Kumar, S. (2025). The rise of multi-cloud architecture: A technical deep dive. International Journal of Scientific Research in Computer Science, Engineering and Information Technology. https://www.semanticscholar.org/paper/d109bf4dd5d97b125c205c269ef4a8c28f0805cd (accessed on 11th September 2025).
14. López García, Á., Marco, J., Antonacci, M., zu Castell, W., David, M., Hardt, M., Lloret Iglesias, L., et al. (2020). A cloud-based framework for machine learning workloads and applications. IEEE Access, 8, 18681–18692. https://doi.org/10.1109/access.2020.2964386 (accessed on 11th September 2025).
15. Morić, Z., Redžepagić, J., Bencarić, I., & Dakić, V. (2025). The role of container security in application development. Edelweiss Applied Science and Technology. https://www.semanticscholar.org/paper/5a89f72c4fdfeb8ea4943d939eaed192ed0fd94d (accessed on 11th September 2025).
16. Murali, N., & Koneru, K. (2025). Containerization best practices–Using Docker and Kubernetes for enterprise applications. Journal of Information Systems Engineering and Management. https://www.semanticscholar.org/paper/72dcf2051a416667e596a02d97a9d25fe147ce45 (accessed on 11th September 2025).
17. Nascimento, B. R., Santos, R., Henriques, J., Bernardo, M. V., & Caldeira, F. (2024). Availability, scalability, and security in the migration from container-based to cloud-native applications. Computers, 13, 192–192.

https://doi.org/10.3390/computers13080192 (accessed on 11th September 2025).

18. Nimdia, A. (2025). Effectiveness of automated testing in container orchestration. The American Journal of Engineering and Technology. https://www.semanticscholar.org/paper/62efbacc003eb44784399a62408cdf2c962162a2 (accessed on 11th September 2025).
19. Oyeniran, O. C., Modupe, O. T., Otitoola, A. A., Abiona, O. O., Adewusi, A. O., & Oladapo, O. J. (2024). A comprehensive review of leveraging cloud-native technologies for scalability and resilience in software development. International Journal of Science and Research Archive, 11, 330–337. https://doi.org/10.30574/ijsra.2024.11.2.0432 (accessed on 11th September 2025).
20. Pati, S., Baid, U., Edwards, B., Sheller, M., Wang, S. H., Reina, G. A., Foley, P., et al. (2022). Federated learning enables big data for rare cancer boundary detection. Nature Communications, 13. https://doi.org/10.1038/s41467-022-33407-5 (accessed on 11th September 2025).
21. Perera Jayasuriya Kuranage, M., Nuaymi, L., Bouabdallah, A., Ferrandiz, T., & Bertin, P. (2022). Deep learning-based resource forecasting for 5G core network scaling in Kubernetes environment. https://doi.org/10.1109/netsoft54395.2022.9844056 (accessed on 11th September 2025).
22. Prajapati, A., & Patel, M. (2024). Container scheduling: A taxonomy, open issues and future directions for scheduling of containerized microservices. https://doi.org/10.2139/ssrn.4699558 (accessed on 11th September 2025).
23. Rajakumar, J., Thason, M., & Kumar, L. (2025). Containerization in modern software architectures: Optimizing scalability, portability, and resource efficiency. International Journal for Research Publication and Seminar. https://www.semanticscholar.org/paper/c0e0b32b5eb89cae506cebfaf8f3587162fb7894 (accessed on 11th September 2025).
24. Saravanan, M. S., & Karumudi, M. (2024). Efficient workload portability and optimized resource utilization using containerization in a multi-cloud environment. 2024 5th International Conference on Data Intelligence and Cognitive Informatics (ICDICI). https://www.semanticscholar.org/paper/19da0ccdbd838111638d9396d485e6abfa3c32f2 (accessed on 11th September 2025).
25. Schiller, E., Aidoo, A., Fuhrer, J., Stahl, J., Ziörjen, M., & Stiller, B. (2022). Landscape of IoT security. Computer Science Review, 44, 100467–100467. https://doi.org/10.1016/j.cosrev.2022.100467 (accessed on 11th September 2025).

26. Senjab, K., Abbas, S., Ahmed, N., & Khan, A. U. R. (2023). A survey of Kubernetes scheduling algorithms. Journal of Cloud Computing: Advances, Systems and Applications, 12. https://doi.org/10.1186/s13677-023-00471-1 (accessed on 11th September 2025).

27. Shah, S., & Jain, U. (2024). Comparison of container orchestration engines. Integrated Journal for Research in Arts and Humanities, 4, 306–322. https://doi.org/10.55544/ijrah.4.6.24 (accessed on 11th September 2025).

28. Soleymanzadeh, O., & Hajipour, B. (2025). A bibliometric analysis of resource orchestration research: Current status, emerging trends and future research agenda. Management Research Review. https://www.semanticscholar.org/paper/043cf7107b2074efcd9ffbd0c8e36245a54bf337 (accessed on 11th September 2025).

29. Suseendran, S. (2025). Automation and orchestration in NVMe over Fibre Channel environments: A comprehensive analysis. World Journal of Advanced Engineering Technology and Sciences. https://www.semanticscholar.org/paper/aa30a83f1228b1e1e5c11fa9c51693997da02834 (accessed on 11th September 2025).

30. Trucillo, P. (2024). Biomaterials for drug delivery and human applications. Materials, 17, 456. https://doi.org/10.3390/ma17020456 (accessed on 11th September 2025).

31. Velasco, L., Signorelli, M., González de Dios, Ó., Papagianni, C., Bifulco, R., Vegas Olmos, J. J., Pryor, S., et al. (2021). End-to-end intent-based networking. IEEE Communications Magazine, 59, 106–112. https://doi.org/10.1109/mcom.101.2100141 (accessed on 11th September 2025).

32. Warnat-Herresthal, S., Schultze, H., Shastry, K. L., Manamohan, S., Mukherjee, S., Garg, V., Sarveswara, R., et al. (2021). Swarm learning for decentralized and confidential clinical machine learning. Nature, 594, 265–270. https://doi.org/10.1038/s41586-021-03583-3 (accessed on 11th September 2025).

CHAPTER 4

API DESIGN AND MANAGEMENT

Contents

INTRODUCTION

The technology environment is constantly evolving, particularly with the Application Programming Interfaces (APIs). API design and management are now key building blocks of modern software development, making integration simple across different platforms and programs. In a bid to enhance interoperability and performance, understanding principles that steer good API design has become increasingly vital. APIs are the bridges that connect various pieces of software in a way that enables them to communicate with one another and share information. In addition to enhancing user experiences, APIs create streams of innovation in sectors. For example, such groundbreaking artificially intelligent gadgets such as ChatGPT show how APIs may create complicated connections, thereby enhancing productivity in the financial and marketing sectors, while concurrently creating ethical concerns that require careful observation (Yogesh et al., 2023). Even though well-designed APIs have apparent advantages, their governance presents a real challenge to organizations. Successful API management involves managing the complete life cycle of an API from its very inception to the final stage of deprecation. This is done through a strategic plan that incorporates versioning, scalability, security, and monitoring to ensure maximum performance and usability. APIs present specific concerns regarding data security and privacy because they frequently handle sensitive information across various applications. Companies must solve these problems while at the same time ensuring that they are adaptable enough to maintain pace with ongoing advancements in technologies as well as user needs. Moreover, as advancements in technologies like robotics also show, most significantly through tools like ROS 2, there are fundamental architectural shifts required in order to bring APIs to fruition (Macenski et al., 2022). This ongoing evolution calls for ongoing learning and adjustment in a bid to harness the full potential of API technologies. Enforcing good API design and management principles will, ultimately, support technological advancement and innovation across various industries in the long run. Aligning technical specifications with business objectives is fundamental in establishing significant relationships among systems. With the increasing reliance on APIs to enhance efficiency and user experience, there is a need for well-defined best practices. Organizations must leverage experience gained from past frameworks as well as iterative testing to make their API strategy better and better with each iteration. With growing demand for robust APIs and the increasing development of technology, stakeholders will be crucial to consider long-term implications of API integration in order to encourage ethical conduct and responsibility. As a whole, these are factors that will underline the key significance of API design and management in shaping the digital technologies future.

Definition of APIs

In the software and technology space, Application Programming Interfaces (APIs) are fundamental tools for enabling interaction between systems and components. An API can be defined as a set of protocols and rules that allow software to communicate with another piece of software, allowing sharing of information and functionality. This definition points to the importance of APIs in their role to increase interoperability among various technologies, and thereby overall software efficacy. They can be used as web services, libraries, or frameworks, each with its own distinctiveness for different programming needs. The advent of APIs has transformed the world of software, as they enable developers to add existing capability without reinventing the wheel, encouraging a culture of coordination and innovation in API Design and Management. Beyond the purposes of interaction, APIs are wrappers for best practices and standards that help developers build solid applications. One needs to understand the intricacies of API design so that not only are the interfaces working, but they are also user-friendly and efficient. Good APIs permit ease of use, with well-documented APIs, versioning, and clean endpoints. This makes a developer's ability to connect several systems smoothly increase. Even more important, as the API economy grows, so does the significance of the metrics for measuring API quality. From latency to error capture, metrics are vital measures of performance that assist developers in continuously refining API strategies (Eder et al., 2025). The dynamicity of APIs also has emergent challenges that require critical analysis and innovative solutions. The need for automation in deriving APIs from customer requirements is a significant step towards simplifying API management. This can be observed through efforts towards automating the process of translating ambiguous customer requests to precise API specifications, ultimately smoothing out processes and enhancing user satisfaction. Such innovation with API technology, including the utilization of models such as Seq2Seq, demonstrates the ongoing effort to better the API design process. By giving precedence to achieving high precision in deriving APIs from natural language, the potential for transforming customer order processing emerges as a key focal point of research, emphasizing the necessity for sound API Management practices to be adopted in modern software development (Omata et al., 2022).

Importance of API Design

API design is at the heart of the integration and functionality of modern software systems, serving as the basis for passing data and functionality between heterogeneous systems. A good API allows developers to talk to various software elements seamlessly, facilitating seamless data exchange and access to functionality. The interoperability is essential, especially in diversified environments comprising diverse technologies and platforms. Through the application of clean and uniform design practices, APIs minimize complexity, therefore improving developer productivity and reducing errors. Furthermore, proper documentation of APIs is instrumental in helping developers get access to the tools that they require in order to effectively utilize an API, facilitating broader adoption as well as simpler collaboration between applications. With continuous development in digital ecosystems, the emphasis on API design is increasingly critical to determining overall success and adaptability of software solutions in a competitive scenario. Good API design also contributes significantly to the scalability and robustness of software systems. With growing uses, a well-designed API will be able to manage larger traffic and volumes of data without loss of performance or dependability. Applying architectural patterns such as microservices can make programs more modular, allowing teams to develop and deploy the pieces independently. Decoupled architecture favors continuous integration and deployment approaches, further facilitating resilience.

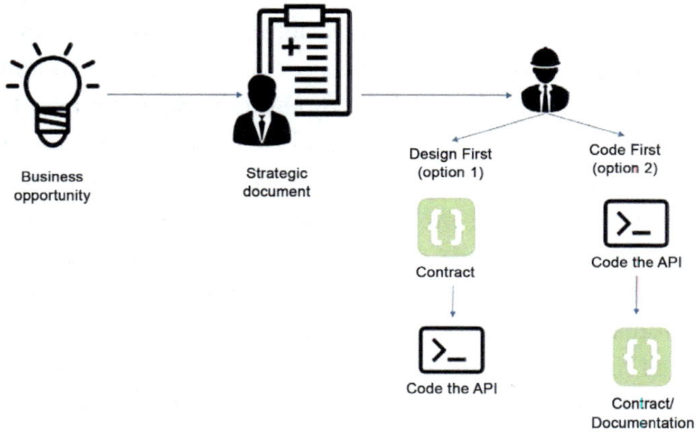

Figure 4.1. *Importance of API design.*

Source: https://blog.axway.com/wp-content/uploads/2019/09/API-Design-importance-photo-3.png.

However, it is important to consider API versioning and backward compatibility effects to facilitate easy transition as updates are applied. Failure to consider these aspects may introduce interruption and fragmentation within the experience of the users. Thus, thoughtful API design not only affects short-term functionality but also gives the foundation for long-term operational viability, so systems can evolve as user demands and technology keep evolving. In addition, API design helps in influencing the user experience, being a bridge between backend functionality and frontend interactions. A thoughtfully designed API can facilitate users to have a natural interface by providing them with the needed data in a reasonable and accessible manner. This alignment enhances user experience since the developers have the ability to create aligned experiences with user expectations without being forced to deal with complex backend processes. In banking services, for example, aggregation platforms rely on stable API interactions to display homogeneous services that make user transactions and interactions easier (Eziamaka et al., 2024). Similarly, the oil and gas sector is more and more using APIs to combine various operating aspects, as seen in significant breakthroughs in Tertiary Reservoir management (Badi et al. 2025). Consequently, effective API design not only meets technical objectives but also strategic business objectives, ensuring user satisfaction and operational efficiency across several industries (Figure 4.1).

Overview of API Management

Within the ever-changing landscape of digital services, API management has become a crucial element for organizations to unlock their infrastructure of technology. It is a comprehensive collection of practices that govern the development, deployment, consumption, and maintenance of Application Programming Interfaces (APIs). It not only helps to integrate independent software systems but also enables organizations to increase their operational efficiency refine user experience, and drive innovation. By having a robust API management in place, businesses can better monitor API performance, implement security protocols, and regulate user access, thereby ensuring their digital services are always up and running as well as resistant to fluctuating market requirements. Underlying effective API management is compliance with the principles of findability, accessibility, interoperability, and reusability (FAIR), which can significantly enhance the utility of APIs in a research environment. As businesses strive to maintain data sharing compliances and standards, APIs must be built with these principles in consideration to foster seamless data exchange and integration between platforms. For example, having approaches that allow for proper data definition and domain-based ontologies can minimize data silos and stimulate more harmonized data management approaches. By placing highest priority on FAIR alignment as argued by Koers et al. (2020), organizations not only increase API efficiency but also become an integral and cooperative part of the digital landscape. Apart from this, the role of API management exceeds the technical installation, as it requires strategic insight and sensitivities towards market realities. Effective API management includes constant monitoring and analytics to determine performance metrics and engagement levels. As identified in Yogesh et al. (2020), these results can be used in making decisions so that organizations can make proactive steps towards problems such as negative electronic word-of-mouth or suboptimal user experiences. With the help of potent analytics and feedback loops, companies can optimize API products so they better fit consumer demands, thereby boosting brand loyalty and competitive advantage. As a result, a healthy API management strategy is the cornerstone of businesses that desire success in a rapidly changing digital landscape.

4.1. PRINCIPLES OF API DESIGN

Solid API design is based on a few governing principles that encourage usability as well as functionality. A solid API needs to be centered around simplicity so that developers can accomplish their work with minimal friction. This encompasses the employment of good naming conventions, documentation, and uniform error handling. Simplicity not only decreases learning time for new consumers but also facilitates maintainability because complexity tends to play a role in increased difficulty in changes and updates. Furthermore, good API design fosters predictability, wherein the behavior of the API adheres to established patterns and nomenclature. This predictability builds trust among developers, as they can rely on an API to function as documented. By maintaining a user-centric focus, API designers can create interfaces that align closely with developer expectations, thereby reducing the potential for errors and enhancing overall satisfaction. Security is also a key principle that applies to API design, particularly because APIs are typically points of entry into sensitive data and functions. Having good authentication and authorization measures in place is crucial to limiting out-of-control access and ensuring data integrity. OAuth 2.0 for delegated access and encryption mechanisms bolster an APIs defense position against potential threats. Moreover, rate limiting may prevent abuse by restricting the number of requests to the API over an interval of time. This defensive design not only guards the API but also promotes reasonable usage among the consumers. A good API never compromises user privacy to any extent; rather, it includes privacy-safeguarding mechanisms to win the trust of users and enable functionality. As APIs continue to grow in complexity and prevalence of use, fundamental security principles must remain paramount in design. Lastly, good API design encourages flexibility and scalability to adapt based on shifting technological and user needs. APIs must be designed with a modular architecture to allow for incremental adjustments without affecting existing functionality. This may be particularly well-suited for cloud-native applications, where loosely connected microservices can modify separately. As pinpointed in recent research, for instance, designs based on domain-driven design principles, proper service boundaries yield business capabilities mapping very naturally with technical implementations. Furthermore, event-driven architecture integration allows for real-time responsiveness so that APIs can more effectively support high-load scenarios and dynamic user interaction. Lastly, an elasticity-friendly, forward-looking API design not only limits potential downtime and performance degradation but also allows developers to keep innovating continuously, and the overall user experience is enhanced in a world with connectivity (Tholoniat et al., 2025; Pillutla, 2025) (Figure 4.2).

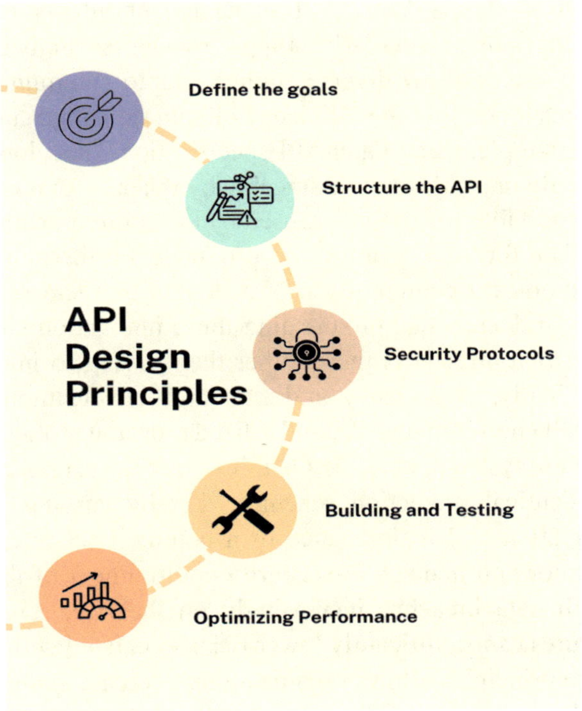

Figure 4.2. *Principles of API design.*

Source: https://favtutor.com/articles/wp-content/uploads/2024/05/image1-11.png.

4.1.1. Consistency and Standards

In API Design and Management, consistency and standards principle is the cornerstone upon which successful communication between systems and users takes place. Consistent APIs allow developers to learn through familiarity in progressing from endpoint to endpoint and function to function, thereby making cognitive loads lighter while integrating or consuming multiple services. Where APIs adhere to standard practices, be it through RESTful conventions, naming conventions, or data formats such as JSON, they thereby promote greater usability and interoperability. Not only does this create a better developer experience but also the maintainability of the API in the future by being able to make adjustments and updates with ease without taking away from usability. Hence, companies concentrating on consistency and adhering to established standards can help facilitate a robust ecosystem allowing cooperation and efficient development processes in diverse groups. Moreover, application of well-established standards in API management allows inter-operability between diverse systems, particularly as apps grow increasingly interdependent. Standardized interfaces allow diverse applications to communicate with each other at once, thus increasing the efficiency of data exchange and collaborative processes. For example, using OpenAPI specifications, developers can design APIs that are easily readable and consumable by other consumers and systems. This minimizes possible frustrations caused by miscommunications and speeds up time-to-market for new features or products. Furthermore, consistency across APIs promotes a community of developers that can rely on common understanding and documentation, creating more innovation since developers can build upon what already is there rather than having to invent everything from scratch. Finally, consistency and standards enable more security and compliance in API environments. A standardized procedure to security measures and authentication systems, such as OAuth or JWT, ensures any interaction occurs under identical protection schemes, thereby curbing vulnerabilities. Through the creation and maintenance of a common scheme, organizations are able to monitor and manage the security environment of their APIs more effectively. With data breaches increasingly on the rise, standardization of security procedures can significantly lower risks associated with API exposure. Practice of these principles allows organizations to create applications that are scalable as well as secure, so APIs not only play the role of function but also serve the greater purpose of safeguarding sensitive information during transit. This judicious thinking on consistency and standardization ultimately becomes the base for long-lasting API ecosystems that are capable of transformation based on transforming technological requirements.

4.1.2. Usability and Developer Experience

The usability-developer interface is the essential part of great API design and management. A good API is not only coded to serve functional demands but should further undergo extreme trials to ensure that developers have no difficulty engaging with it. In this case, usability means the simplicity of learning about the API, simplicity, and how well the developers are able to implement it into projects. Breadth usability testing is likely to reveal valuable insight into the true challenges facing developers in day-to-day use, allowing for iterative improvement to maximize overall satisfaction. Usability-driven development fosters a culture in which organizations facilitate developer-led prioritization, minimizing complexity and improving workflows, which will organically increase the likelihood of successful API integration and implementation. Usability focus suggests an across-the-board transition to a user-led design mindset that ultimately leads to enhanced software development results.

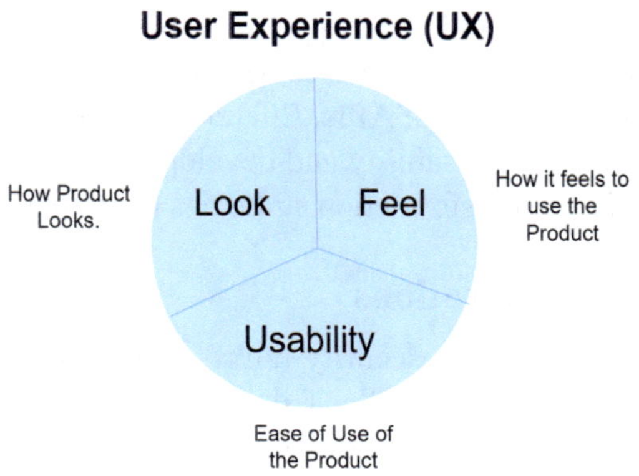

Figure 4.3. *The interplay between usability and developer experience.*

Source: https://public-images.interaction-design.org/literature/articles/materials/6E2NcywDsHnY7Dtr5upZsMCABeXjXHVSm5S96iPs.png.

Developer experience (DX) is directly connected to usability and can significantly determine the success of APIs within organizations. Enabling developers by means of a user-centric API will increase their productivity, thereby generating lower time-to-market for applications and services. Facilitating a good DX is not just about the external design and capabilities of the API but also the documentation, support systems, and community engagement that envelops it. Furthermore, research indicates that APIs created with formal governing mechanisms, such as API Improvement Proposals (AIPs), are much more usable, as surveyed consumers of APIs indicate a strong preference for such formal approaches. Higher alignment with best practices in API development is an indication of a commitment to making developers' experiences more efficient, aligning organizational goals with the fast-paced demands of the digital era (Ahmad et al., 2024). Lastly, it is worth prioritizing developer experience to create and acquire the best developer brains. The growing significance of developer experience and usability further suggests that good API management practice matters. Organizations now demand platforms that facilitate not just the technical use of APIs but also the experiences between the API itself and the developers. As highlighted in a comparative review of tools such as Microsoft's Azure API Management and Google's Apigee, security functionalities, integration possibilities, and performance requirements directly influence the way developers engage with APIs. As the tools evolve further, prioritizing the developer experience from the point of sign-up to usage becomes essential (Addagalla, 2025). Getting the optimum balance between good governance and developer independence is essential here, as businesses that equip developers with user-friendly tools are most likely to see a considerable increase in the use of APIs. Effective API management, therefore, must put maximum focus on usability and developer experience to unleash the entire potential of digital transformation strategies (Figure 4.3).

4.1.3. Security Considerations

In API design and governance, security ranks as the number one priority in safeguarding sensitive data as well as delivering stable functionality. The potential attack from insufficient security mechanisms can easily wear down not only the API but also the faith of its stakeholders and consumers. Organizations therefore must give high importance to an aggressive security-first approach to the entire lifecycle of the API, beginning with threat modeling and secure coding. By detection of potential vulnerabilities from the beginning, developers can embrace appropriate measures, such as rate limiting and data validation, to manage risks in a proper manner. It is a precautionary principle that plays a central role in maintaining good API integrity because it forms the foundation upon which the remaining APIs implementation and monitoring are done, and this should include continuous security scans for compatibility with emerging threats and vulnerabilities. A key feature of securing APIs is the authentication and authorization process that provides access to only trusted users for sensitive resources. The application of common industry protocols such as OAuth 2.0 and OpenID Connect allows developers to create secure access controls, hence minimizing the risk of unauthorized entry. Multi-factor authentication can also be employed to enhance security by requiring users to authenticate using multiple methods before being granted access. The effectiveness of these steps depends on their seamless integration in the broader API framework so that security shouldn't come at the cost of user experience. Moreover, with more and more organizations embracing microservices and serverless architectures, security practices need to be conformist and align with these trends to address the particular problems that these present, like processing service-to-service authentication and having consistent policies between distributed systems.

Apart from this, businesses must monitor evolving regulations and compliance procedures regarding data protection and privacy. As APIs typically deal with sensitive user information, compliance with standards such as GDPR and HIPAA avoids legal consequences and maintains user trust. Regular audits of API security practices can determine loopholes in compliance and enhance areas accordingly. By incorporating solid logging and monitoring in position, companies can create a more comprehensive knowledge base regarding API usage patterns and potential security incidents. This overall approach not only highlights the importance of having a good security position but also keeps stakeholders informed of the necessity to put security aspects first in API design considerations. Over time, as the usage of APIs continues to increase across all industries, the deliberate addition of robust security solutions remains a crucial component in successful API management.

4.2. TYPES OF APIS

In software programming, Application Programming Interfaces (APIs) form important building blocks which enable various applications to communicate and behave in sync. There are primarily three types of APIs: Open APIs, Partner APIs, and Internal APIs. Open APIs or external/public APIs can be utilized by anyone. They enable broader cooperation and innovation through the facility to integrate with an external developer without any issues. For example, social networks often use Open APIs in a way that third-party applications can leverage their functionalities, thereby encouraging more user engagement and promoting their products. By contrast, Partner APIs are for a specific purpose and are opened to a limited number of developers. Such APIs facilitate strategic alliances between companies through enabling their partners to work together in a better way. Some examples are the APIs of cloud service providers, utilized by companies to integrate their services securely in an effort to deliver enhanced performance and user experience. The utilization of partner APIs often leads to rich user experiences and solid web services integrations, ultimately benefiting both the API provider as well as its partners. Internal APIs, or private APIs, are utilized within an organization and are not available for third-party developers. These interfaces enable different teams within a company to take advantage of shared functionalities without posing the risk of leaking confidential information. With Internal APIs, organizations can streamline their internal processes, increase productivity, and ensure uniform usage of their services across departments. As in research on Building Information Modeling (BIM), interoperability issues could happen where the software tools cannot pass information to each other effectively, highlighting the significance of effectively designed Internal APIs that deal with specific organizational workflows with minimal misrepresentation of data and enhanced project management (Khattra et al., 2024) (Figure 4.4).

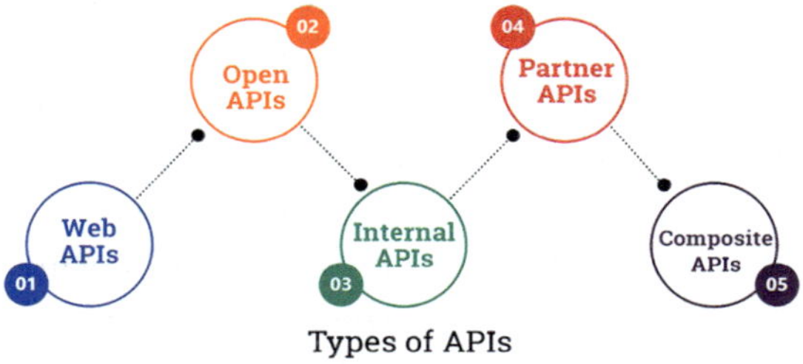

Figure 4.4. *Types of APIs.*

Source: https://www.dezven.com/images/blog/types-of-apis.jpg.

4.2.1. Open APIs vs. Internal APIs

Internal versus open APIs have the largest distinction in today's software development world. Open APIs, or external APIs, are designed to be used by third-party developers, allowing interoperability and partnerships. By making them available, the firms can create ecosystems that extend their services and products with third-party integration. For instance, a company utilizing an open API can tap the innovative capabilities of external developers to develop applications that have interactions with their data and services. Internal APIs, on the other hand, are designed primarily to be utilized in an organization. They permit different departments and teams to communicate with ease so that the data flows seamlessly among a number of different internal systems. This internal focus can promote increased efficiency and collaboration as well as safeguard sensitive data that may be exposed via open APIs (Wang et al., 2024). For API management and design, whether or not to use open or internal APIs normally hinges on the strategic objectives and resource constraints of a company. Businesses that want to innovate quickly may prefer open APIs since they can tap into a larger community of developers to expand their product landscape. The approach can be employed for quick growth and adaptability, which are necessary in competitive business environments. However, making an API available to outside developers is done under close control so that security and versioning are not compromised. Conversely, internal APIs may emphasize stability and performance since they are easier to control. These kinds of APIs allow for heterogeneous systems to be integrated, which leads to a microservices pattern that enhances the agility of a businesss internal workings. This blend of open and internal methodologies allows for access to the benefits of both (external) innovation and internal efficiencies (Wang et al., 2015). Both implementation and upkeep of open and internal APIs come with their respective sets of challenges and possibilities. Open APIs require businesses to consider what exactly it means to open their services and data to the global environment and ensure that security control is strong enough to prevent leakage of sensitive data. API documentation and support to developers become critical in order to enable external developers to access open APIs in an appropriate manner. Internal APIs, on the other hand, are often regulated through balancing the demands for flexibility with the organization's demand to adhere to organizational conventions. Organizations must come up with governance models that define usage policy, security, and performance metrics for internal APIs. Thus, a solid understanding of open and internal APIs is essential to successful API design and management so organizations can maximize their potential for increased innovation and operational efficiency (Wang et al., 2024).

4.2.2. RESTful APIs vs. SOAP APIs

In API design, RESTful APIs and SOAP APIs supply two paradigms responding to different application needs. REST, or Representational State Transfer, is reputed to be simple and easy to implement, particularly best suited to web services that require rapid development and minimal communication. On the other hand, SOAP, or Simple Object Access Protocol, is founded upon a more elaborate framework that is centered on security and reliability of transactions, thus it is appropriate for business-level solutions where significant data transactions are involved. Choosing between the two generally depends on requirements in projects, such as scalability, security needs, and complexities in operations in the API architecture (Toman, 2020). RESTful APIs rely on generic HTTP operations like GET, POST, PUT, and DELETE, making them intuitive and user-friendly for both end users and developers. Such simplicity is particularly beneficial to emerging applications that need quick iterations and agile methodologies. SOAP, in contrast, uses XML in the format of messages and provides a rich set of standards like WS-Security and WS-ReliableMessaging that cater to secure and reliable communications. These features become crucial in those applications where data integrity and process transparency are the priorities, i.e., financial and telecommunication applications. Thus, identifying the operation context and single endpoint interactions can assist developers in selecting the most appropriate API architecture for their needs (Reynolds et al., 2019). The evolution of IoT and big data has also increased the popularity of RESTful APIs due to their scalability and ability to handle large volumes of data effectively. For instance, CropSight app demonstrates the potential of REST APIs to cope with IoT devices for plant phenotyping and management of climatic data. The seamless data transfer and annotation of RESTful APIs allow for real-time tracking and comparisons of crop performance across history and present. In contrast, SOAP remains relevant in scenarios requiring secure transaction processing and frequent error correction, although with greater overhead. Lastly, the selection between REST and SOAP APIs must consider performance, development manpower, and available infrastructure to ensure overall application goals (Toman, 2020) (Figure 4.5).

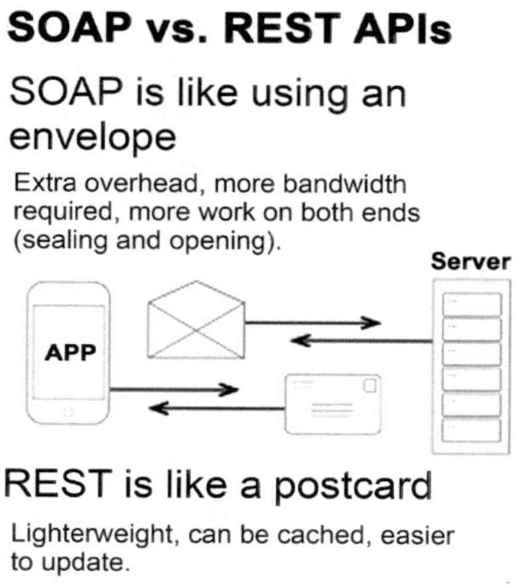

Figure 4.5. *RESTful APIs vs. SOAP APIs.*

Source: https://dz2cdn1.dzone.com/storage/temp/6632775-rest-vs-soap.png.

4.2.3. GraphQL APIs

In the ever-evolving landscape of API management and design, GraphQL APIs are a new way that is revolutionary in its promise over traditional RESTful APIs. Unlike REST, which tends to use many endpoints to retrieve different data entities, GraphQL allows clients to request precisely what they need in a single endpoint. A change like this optimizes data retrieval and reduces over-fetching, where unnecessary data is retrieved. Moreover, GraphQL's strong typing system and introspection capabilities enhance the developer experience to enable good documentation and early fault detection. Flexibility built into GraphQL APIs has also made them extremely sought after for those applications that require rapid iteration, such as the ones used in genomics studies, where access to diverse datasets is the top priority, such as in projects such as Ensemble, which are continuously being revised to support new genomic annotations and forms of data (Peter et al., 2023). GraphQL API management has unique challenges and requires careful monitoring of schema design and performance tuning. Central to GraphQL API management is schema definition, which is an agreement between the server and client for guaranteed querying of data by the clients. GraphQL's schema definition language provides precision declaration of types and relationships, allowing more collaborative development teams. But there is danger of performance bottlenecks as query complexity increases, necessitating robust backend design and efficient data fetching strategies.

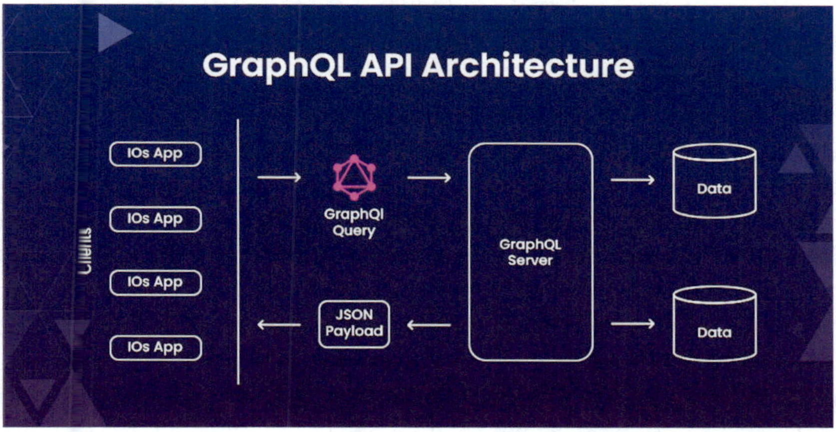

Figure 4.6. *GraphQL APIs.*

Source: https://d2ms8rpfqc4h24.cloudfront.net/what_is_graphql_f9a7e88d9c.jpg.

In order to overcome these, techniques such as batching of queries, caching, and rate limiting can be employed, which are tasked with keeping up with performance as user demand increases. These considerations are especially important for GraphQL APIs, especially in big data-intensive environments, such as in the cases under study in smart building solutions based on the merging of various systems (Chamari et al., 2023). Besides this, the implementation of GraphQL APIs has profound influences on the general development ecosystem since it impacts not only software architecture but also team dynamics and project management practices. By its developer-centric approach, GraphQL encourages a more inclusive approach to API development, as the stakeholders can be more actively involved in defining data schema that reflects end-user needs. This inclusive nature can lead to more innovative application developments where end-users directly influence the behavior of the APIs. Organizations have to overcome also the learning curve involved in deploying GraphQL, necessitating training and rebasing existing workflows.

Firms that invest in learning and governing GraphQL APIs experience increased developer morale and productivity, describing the importance of well-governed API practices in bringing out the benefits of the technology in disruptive sectors such as genomics and smart building integrations (Peter et al., 2023; Chamari et al., 2023) (Figure 4.6).

4.3. API DOCUMENTATION

Good API documentation ensures successful utilization and integration of application programming interfaces (APIs). Effective documentation serves as a guide for developers to understand the functionalities, methods, and error management of an API. When well-prepared, such documentation not only enhances the usability of the API but also reduces the time taken by developers in debugging or searching for information by a great deal. This openness creates an environment where developers can innovate without having to deal with ambiguous guidelines. Investing in a complete API documentation, therefore, is essential for organizations to ensure their APIs are put into use as required, and so satisfaction and productivity levels among the developers are enhanced. The availability and organization of API documentation also play an essential role in determining its effectiveness. Modern documentation often incorporates interactive elements, such as live code samples and integrated tools for testing API calls directly from the documentation page.

This interactivity allows developers to experiment in real time, enhancing their understanding and decreasing the steep learning curve that can accompany new technologies. Furthermore, employing a modular format can facilitate easier updates and maintenance, ensuring that documentation evolves in parallel with the API's capabilities. As APIs grow in their complexity, using a user-oriented design mindset can facilitate more lucid storytelling, hence a better overall user experience and facilitating developers to be able to do the most with the API. Aside from clarity and interactivity, ethical issues in API documentation have to be addressed. Misleading documentation or omitting complete information can result in mistakes, inefficiencies, and less trust in the reliability of the API. For this reason, organizations should do their best to see that their documents accurately represent the capabilities and limitations of their APIs and ensure their use responsibly. Fostering transparency within API documentation has the potential to not only mitigate risks and enhance user satisfaction but also lead to better-informed public discourse on ethical technologies.

Therefore, with continuous evolution in API designing and regulation, addressing these intricate aspects of API documentation remains key to facilitating long-term development and maintaining user trust in the evolving technological environments such as generative AI and robotics, which have already proved revolutionary across various fields, as illustrated in Biswas et al. (2024) and Macenski et al. (2022).

4.3.1. Importance of Comprehensive Documentation

Extended documentation plays a crucial role in designing and managing APIs since it serves as the cornerstone for effective communication among users, stakeholders, and developers. In-depth and correct documentation ensures that each of the involved parties is aware of the functions and limitations of an API, thereby reducing miscommunication and enhancing smooth integration processes. Documentation that includes elaborate endpoint descriptions, data formats, and error messages not only makes introducing new users easier but also allows for faster troubleshooting when problems arise. Also, because APIs are likely to be updated or extended, well-maintained doc setup gets everyone aligned with the latest development, which also leads to more efficient project cycles and quality products. For API design, documentation will be an essential component in creating excellent user experience and satisfaction. Users would predominantly rely on accurate documentation when they are working with an API, and it will guide them through their interactions and learn to use the API to their specific requirements. By providing ample code samples, tutorials, and use cases through documentation, developers can lower the learning barrier towards new APIs. This is particularly crucial in systems that are complicated and involve numerous services and interactions, as users can use all the potential of the API through unambiguous guidance. Therefore, spending on good documentation helps straight away in the reputation and usability of the APIs, which in turn affects its use and overall success in a competitive market. Moreover, complete documentation is not only meant for user assistance; it also plays a critical role in long-term maintainability and scalability of APIs. With changing technology environments, APIs also change that require updates and adjustments. Documentation helps to make APIs easier to handle by development teams with changes without compromising already deployed services. A robust documentation strategy has history contexts and versioning for developers to understand why things were altered over the years. It also facilitates the onboarding of new team members or inter-team collaboration by providing them with the core information to work efficiently. Without detailed documentation, projects are hindered by inefficiencies and loss of expertise and may struggle to keep up with the rapidly changing demands of the world of technology, as testified by practices in such diverse areas as healthcare and astronomy where records need to be detailed so that they may uphold quality output (Biswas et al., 2024; Team et al., 2022) (Figure 4.7).

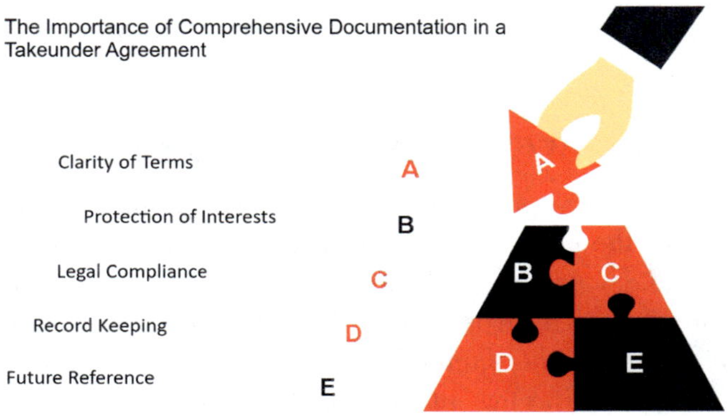

Figure 4.7. *Importance of comprehensive documentation.*

Source: https://fastercapital.co/i/The-Legal-Aspects-of-a-Takeunder-Agreement--The-Importance-of-Comprehensive-Documentation-in-a-Takeunder-Agreement.webp.

4.3.2. Tools for API Documentation

With the rapidly evolving software development landscape in today's times, effective API documentation tools play a key role in enabling seamless communication between API consumers and developers. Not only are these tools simpler to use, but they also ensure that developers can quickly understand their purposes and integration methods. Thorough documentation is a reference and guide that not only includes the API capabilities but also best practices for their use. Proper and concise API documentation significantly enhances the learning curve for developers, which translates into accelerated implementation and innovation. Inefficient investment in documentation tools can lead to ambiguity and increased development time, ultimately stifling organizational productivity as well as project success. Hence, the proper selection of documentation tools becomes a central part of the overall API design and management strategy. Of the numerous API documentation tools, Swagger stands out for its usability and versatility. Swagger provides an interactive system for documentation that allows users to see and test API endpoints in real-time. This immediacy not only enhances user experience but also helps in problem-solving for developers in case of API integrations. Further, Swagger supports OpenAPI Specification, which can generate client libraries and server stubs automatically and supports the workflow of back-end and front-end developers. Collaborative features of Swagger accommodate multiple contributors, enabling a shared understanding of API functionality in development teams. While companies struggle to enhance their APIs, investing in platforms like Swagger can significantly enhance documentation quality and developer satisfaction overall, leading to increased use of the API ecosystem. In addition to traditional documentation tools, there are many organizations that are turning to more recent technologies like Postman due to its comprehensive API testing and documentation support. Postman enables developers to write, test, and document APIs on a single platform, making it easier for them to adopt a more cohesive API management strategy. Its simplicity enables developers to generate sophisticated documentation with code examples, illustrations, and even API endpoint descriptions, which can be made available to other developers or members of the development team, or published openly to broader audiences of developers. Moreover, Postman capabilities can be used for automated testing, facilitating continuous integration and deployment practices. With such versatile tools, not only does API documentation become better, but overall operation efficiency and communication among development teams also get streamlined. Tools like Postman being included in the API development lifecycle is a perfect example of a strategic approach to designing and managing APIs, which ultimately leads to better user interaction and satisfaction.

4.3.3. Best Practices for Writing API Docs

Good documentation of APIs is essential to encouraging a solid base of application programming interfaces (APIs) knowledge among software developers. Good documentation begins with clear and brief descriptions of the purpose and functionality of the APIs, providing context for the users. The documentation should include a detailed description of the endpoints, methods, and data types utilized, enabling users to have a general overview of the architecture within a short span of time. Additionally, developers enjoy tutorial-like examples that illustrate common usage cases and illustrate the potential of the APIs in actual use. Besides facilitating easy onboarding of new users, this habit also energizes seasoned developers to revisit the documentation for how-to reasons. Therefore, adopting a scientific and user-centered approach to API documentation improves usability and engagement immensely. In building effective API documentation, the need for standardized terminology cannot be overstated. Applying standardized terminology throughout the documentation avoids any potential ambiguity to the users. For instance, employing uniform terminology in the definition of request types, error messages, and authentication schemes ensures clarity and makes the users better understand the APIs functionality. Furthermore, inclusion of diagrammatic or flowchart representations would add to text description in the form of visual context, which can further aid in demystifying complex items. A clear illustration of request and response formats, including error codes and how to fix them, aids in troubleshooting and integrating the API with greater confidence. Implementing these best practices enhances documentation clarity as well as introduces a culture of shared understanding within the developer community. In addition, periodic updating of API documentation is necessary to maintain it as relevant and useful. As APIs evolve with time, developers have to commit to maintaining the documentation to outline changes in functionality, features, or underlying frameworks. This is a critical pledge, especially in agile environments where third-party component reliance will tend to shift over time. Applying version control practices in the documentations allows developers to be compatible with previous versions while highlighting new features in the new version. Allowing user feedback on the documentations clarity and impact can also provide helpful input towards continuous improvement. This iterative process turns the API documentation into a living document that develops according to the needs of its users, ultimately leading to better integration and utilization of the API in their projects (Macenski et al., 2022; Joaquín et al., 2021) (Figure 4.8).

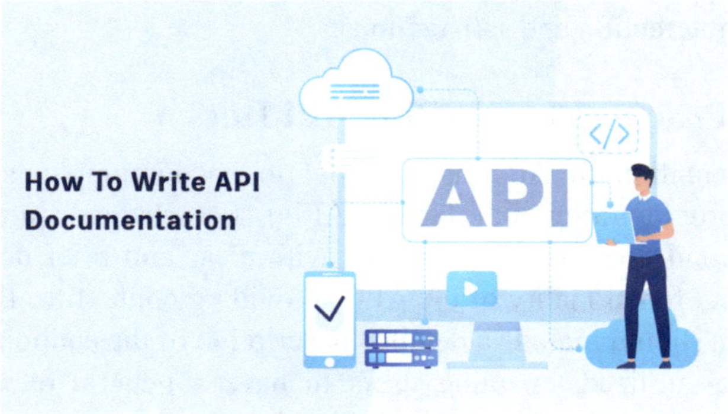

Figure 4.8. *Best practices for writing API docs.*

Source: https://technicalwriterhq.com/wp-content/uploads/2021/12/11B-How-To-Write-API-Documentation.jpeg.

4.4. API VERSIONING

In API design and management, versioning is a critical method of ensuring backward compatibility while being able to support enhancements and added capabilities. With advancing software ecosystems, the need for ease in updating becomes critical. API versioning allows developers to introduce enhancements without disturbing incumbent services consumed by partners or clients. By introducing various iterations of an API, developers can maintain legacy functionality while incrementally adding new methods or endpoints. Not only does this safeguard client integrations but also provides clear guidance for documenting changes, allowing developers to communicate modifications to end users in a clear manner. The existing debate among developers emphasizes the value of versioning, which directly impacts user experience, system stability, and software deployment process agility. A properly defined versioning scheme can take various forms, primarily in the form of URI versioning, query parameter versioning, and header versioning, which have their own advantages and disadvantages. URI versioning, for instance, involves making the version number be present in the API endpoint explicitly so that it is user noticeable and recognizable. Alternatively, query parameter versioning offers a dynamic model where clients only need to alter the parameter without having to modify the endpoint structure. Lastly, header versioning leaves it to HTTP headers such that URLs are cleaner but could complicate client-side implementations. Choosing the versioning approach generally relies on specific project requirements, the nature of the API, and the behavior of users. Regardless of the adopted approach, consistency and simplicity in documentation are critical in order to instill user trust and smooth rollover from version to version. With evolving trends in APIs, a good versioning meaning transcends functionality to strategic business consequences. Companies such as Elevate, employing newer technologies such as natural language processing (NLP) for enhancing user engagement, must handle API versions with great caution to achieve the highest user satisfaction and system performance, as pointed out in Roshini et al. (2025). Even the farm AI system as detailed in Varma (2025) is an example regarding versioning enabling farmers' use of timely and context-related information through their platforms. In either case, being backward compatible by employing judicious versioning techniques not only helps the developers innovate but also builds a healthy relationship with the end users, reducing the likelihood of disruptions caused by shifting in the API landscape. API versioning is hence important so that enhancement is beneficial for user-centric applications and enhances the user experience across sectors.

4.4.1. Reasons for Versioning APIs

Versioning is a core practice in API management and design that serves multiple purposes. Backward compatibility is one of the primary purposes of versioning APIs. As applications are updated and additional features are developed, functionality can change, disrupting users who are on previous versions. With versioning, the developers can maintain a stable interface for existing users while the new features can be incorporated into the new version. This minimizes the risk of breaking changes and promotes the introduction of a smoother experience for clients when they upgrade to updates, ending up in increased user satisfaction and trust in the API. Because organizations are increasingly depending upon APIs to drive third-party system integration, this strategic decision can be the deciding factor between retaining users' loyalty and losing valued customers. The second reason why API versioning is needed lies in the nature of technology itself, which is to constantly change, necessitating quick adaptation to new requirements and standards. The continually evolving software development environment leads to APIs being constantly altered by the addition of new industry standards, a need to enhance the number of security features, or a performance improvement. Managing such changes appropriately with versioning allows API providers to effectively inform their users what has been changed, what is being deprecated, and what is newly introduced. This openness not only lets users know what they have at their disposal but also encourages them to upgrade to more recent versions, where they can take advantage of the most recent enhancements and security updates.

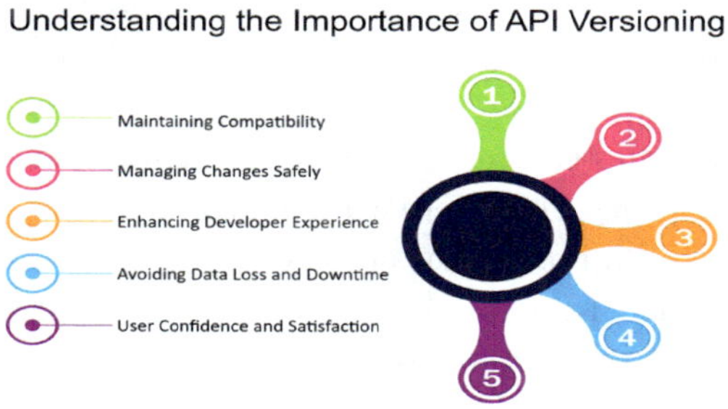

Figure 4.9. *Reasons for versioning APIs.*

Source: https://fastercapital.co/i/Versioning--API-Versioning-Strategies--Navigating-Compatibility-Challenges--Understanding-the-Importance-of-API-Versioning.webp.

As APIs become more primary drivers of operational success, this future-oriented versioning can facilitate smooth management throughout the API lifecycle to the benefit of both developers and users in the long term. In addition, API versioning can be a foundational element of organization-level strategic planning. As highlighted in API management platform arguments, businesses must consider keeping their existing infrastructure at hand when consolidating new technologies (Addagalla, 2025). By implementing a versioning strategy with organization, businesses can harmonize their API development with broader business objectives, allowing them to scale efficiently. Additionally, the adoption of cloud-native strategies highlights the importance of controlling API versions to enhance application responsiveness and performance. This is particularly true for Small and Medium-sized Enterprises (SMEs) that may not be able to maintain systems efficiently (Samira et al., 2024). In this situation, versioning not only makes it easier to operate but also enhances resource use, allowing organizations the kind of flexibility to respond to changing market demands. Emphasis on strategic API versioning is thus crucial in ensuring competitive advantage in a fast-changing digital economy (Figure 4.9).

4.4.2. Strategies for Versioning

In API design and management, employing effective techniques in versioning is critical in order to maintain service integrity along with accommodating shifting user requirements. Versioning allows the introduction of newer features and improvements without disrupting the applications that exist and are based on prior API versions. There are several approaches to versioning, including URI versioning, query parameter versioning, and header versioning. Each approach has its own advantages and limitations. For instance, URI versioning is recognizable and identifiable; however, it produces numerous endpoints which may make handling complicated. Header versioning, by contrast, can minimize endpoint clutter but conceals versioning to the end-users, which is quite unclear. The application of the correct versioning strategy plays an important part in achieving balance among flexibility, clarity, and user-friendliness in API handling. As vital as it is to develop effective versioning methods is consideration for backward compatibility. New versions of an API not breaking client applications that are already in use is a fundamental requirement to provide a stable development environment. Backward compatibility allows developers to support new features on an incremental basis and lessens the disruption to user experience. The impact of non-backward compatibility is high, where applications relying on earlier versions of an API may cease to function correctly and evoke user frustration, which in the long run discourages them from using the service. Versioning schemes prioritizing backward compatibility not only facilitate smoother migration but also extend the lifespan of API integrations. Hence, having good documentation in place along with versioning procedures is required in order to easily communicate changes to developers so that they can implement them seamlessly on various user platforms. In addition, the use of versioning mechanisms has to be accompanied by a clear communication plan and deprecation plan. Since APIs usually form the essence of web services, transparency of changes is important. Developers not only need to document existing functionalities but also notify the users about future deprecations and change timelines. Such forward-looking practices build trust among users and provide sufficient time for clients to switch to newer versions without any disruptions. As claimed in various studies, a proper communication plan is one of the biggest influencers of user engagement and lowers the chances of unfavorable reactions to version changes. Besides, organizations must utilize user feedback, assessing the impact of versioning strategies in real application to continually enhance the versioning process. By implementing adequate communication and feedback mechanisms, organizations are able to enhance API reliability alongside user satisfaction, for the good of the overall software ecosystem health (Nyambane et al., 2025; Tyagi et al., 2025).

4.4.3. Impact of Versioning on Users

Users' influence by versioning in API management and design is a multi-faceted issue encompassing stability, usability, and flexibility. Adopters of an API can benefit from good versioning practices that not only ease the transition across updates but also maintain user faith in systems' integrity. Proper versioning standards, by having architects maintain them at all times, allow users to know what to expect in terms of changes to their applications and processes. As is shown in the Astropy Project, having a core package in addition to version updates facilitates interoperability among a variety of specialist tools, which can contribute significantly to user experience. Successful versioning is hence paramount in guiding users through the complications of API evolution and supporting expansion without compromising compatibility (The Astropy Collaboration et al., 2022). Another consideration in the impact of versioning is the potential fragmentation of the user base. As APIs are developed, inconsistencies between versions can be problematic for both developers and end-users. If users are still tied to an older version due to compatibility issues or investment in the sense of upgrade procedures, fragmentation can result in variations of functionality that complicate the ecosystem. This observation highlights the importance of a good versioning strategy with a focus on backward compatibility. UCSF ChimeraX, for instance, has a design that facilitates the use of different types of data and sources with ease, which is important to enable scientists, who rely heavily on the software, to seamlessly combine their findings. By offering frequent updates and support, ChimeraX is an example of how positive versioning can handle numerous user needs and reduce the danger of fragmentation (Thomas et al., 2017). In addition, versioning considerations extend as far as being able to be flexible in the future in APIs, which is essential in a constantly changing technological landscape. Good versioning, in addition to supporting improvements and new features to be incorporated into an API, also includes user input and long-term requirements. Consequently, when good version control exists through API designers, not just do they enhance current user experiences but they also create an environment friendly to innovation in the future. Such foresight is important for projects that are community-driven and rely on such collective contributions to advance with user needs in the future. With user demands further advancing, APIs like those in the Astropy Project realize the importance of embracing user-focused design practices using cautious versioning techniques, ensuring stability without hindering innovation (The Astropy Collaboration et al., 2022) (Figure 4.10).

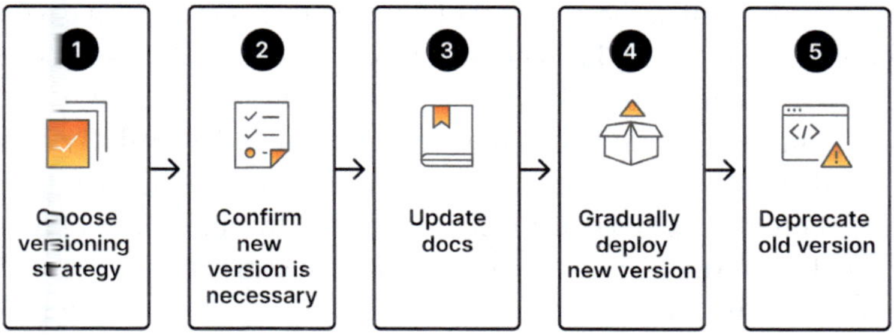

Figure 4.10. *The impact of versioning on users within API design and management.*

Source: https://voyager.postman.com/illustration/how-do-you-version-an-api-postman-illustration.svg.

4.5. API TESTING

The meticulous API Testing process is important in API Design and Management, ensuring application programming interfaces function as intended across various platforms and applications. The stage involves systematic testing of the APIs behavior under varied conditions to identify any performance degrading or bug issues before deployment. Effective API Testing employs a number of methodologies, including unit tests, integration tests, and end-to-end tests, each targeting specific aspects of the functionality of the API. To perform successful testing, teams occasionally include automated testing frameworks that execute multiple test cases quickly, thus enhancing efficiency and reducing human mistakes. Moreover, continuous integration practices enable fault detection early on in a manner that both reliability and performance levels are kept intact at all times, thereby enhancing the APIs overall efficiency during actual usage. An integral aspect of API Testing is to test security controls, which are very important for safeguarding sensitive data as well as for users' trust in systems. With the rise of digital interactions and increasing cyber threats, API security testing measures, such as authentication and authorization checks, are crucial for identifying vulnerabilities. By simulating various attack vectors, such as SQL injection or cross-site scripting, developers can ascertain the robustness of their APIs against potential breaches. Furthermore, employing security best practices across the API's lifecycle can mitigate risks significantly. By exploring the relationship between data sharing and potential threats, teams can positively address security loopholes, testifying to the imperative importance of robust API Testing as a line of defense. This focus on security is particularly relevant in light of increasing interconnectedness of services and needs for secure financial aggregation systems within the contemporary marketplace (Eziamaka et al., 2024). Additionally, the role of API Testing also comprises a performance testing component so that APIs do not collapse under load. With apps increasing and usage by users changing, there is a requirement to compare the response time of APIs, throughput, and resource consumption under load. By employing those tools that simulate large volumes of user requests, one can detect performance bottlenecks and optimize performance from the development stage itself. Normal performance testing needs to be incorporated into continuous integration and delivery paradigms so that teams are able to maintain both robustness and responsiveness in their focus. Troubleshooting of performance issues not only raises the user satisfaction but also aids the overall application sustainability within a competitive space. Finally, API Testing is a cornerstone of API Design and Management that guarantees harmonious interaction among components, information safety, and effortless user experience among merged services (Nutalapati, 2024).

4.5.1. Types of API Testing

API testing is important to test that application programming interfaces perform as anticipated and meet specified requirements. There are several types of API testing, each of which addresses different aspects of API performance and behavior. Functional testing is perhaps the most fundamental because it verifies that the API performs the functions it is intended to do in accordance with specifications. These tests verify the endpoints, request/response format, and whether the outputs are correct as a function of inputs. Focusing on functional elements, the development teams can perform early issue detection, thereby enhancing overall software quality. Conversely, non-functional testing like performance, security, and load testing verifies how effectively the API is able to handle heavy traffic, respond to security attacks, and be reliable under various conditions so that APIs are efficient and reliable in practical scenarios. In particular, performance testing is an essential type of API testing that examines the speed, scalability, and stability of an API at varying levels of loads. It involves emulating several simultaneous requests to observe how the API performs when subjected to high traffic levels and monitoring metrics such as response time, throughput, and resource consumption. Load testing is a subset of performance testing focused on the APIs behavior under heavy traffic conditions, while stress testing goes a step further by pushing the API beyond its normal operation capacity. Such tests ensure APIs can endure performance levels and respond to user demand. In unison with continuous integration and deployment practices, combining performance testing may assist in the early identification of potential bottlenecks, encourage optimization activity, and ultimately enhance user experience by ensuring APIs react well when deployed to production environments.

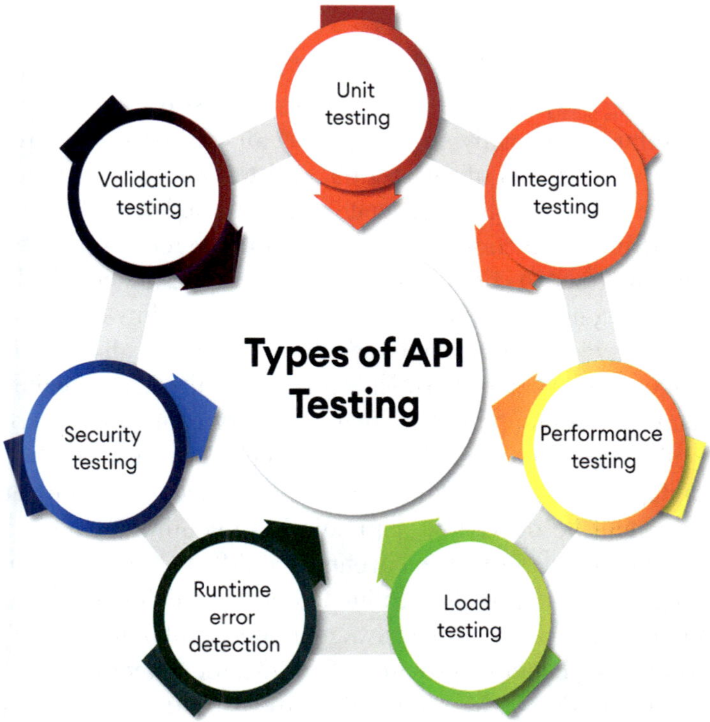

Figure 4.11. *Types of API testing.*

Source: https://www.devsecopsnow.com/wp-content/uploads/2024/07/image-20.png.

Another significant portion of API testing is security testing, which deals with vulnerability detection and safeguarding of data processed by APIs. As businesses begin using APIs more for data sharing, they emerge as natural targets for cyber-attacks. Security testing verifies several vulnerabilities such as authentication faults, threats of data exposure, and inappropriate access controls that could result in inappropriate access to sensitive data. Practices of testing may include penetration testing, where simulated attacks against the API are carried out, and static analysis, where the code is scanned for vulnerabilities. As highlighted in current research, for example, serverless app design and implementation with API Gateway, the adoption of good security testing principles is paramount in ensuring secure APIs are developed for cloud-native systems, with functionality and security as top priority as cardinal aspects of API design and management (Rasmi, 2025; Janakaraj, 2025) (Figure 4.11).

4.5.2. Tools for API Testing

Proper API testing plays a crucial role in ensuring software applications are reliable and robust, especially in the context of microservices architecture, where APIs serve as points of interaction. API testing tools facilitate various techniques like unit, integration, contract, and end-to-end testing, each addressing specific verification needs. Among the top tools are Postman, with its easy-to-use interface to conduct manual testing, and JMeter, which supports performance testing under a load scenario. These tools allow developers to test requests and observe responses so that deployed APIs actually pass functional and performance tests. This shift to microservices has also hastened the necessity for end-to-end validation approaches that span service interactions, hence the importance of strong API testing frameworks in modern software development trends (Dhandapani, 2025). In addition, the significance of adopting automated testing tools cannot be overstated, particularly in continuous integration and continuous deployment (CI/CD) environments. API test automation leads to quicker testing cycles and minimizes human error, which could be crucial as application iterations become faster. Swagger and SoapUI are two of the tools that make API testing better by providing facilities for generating and verifying API documentation side-by-side with testing processes. Besides, contract testing toolkits such as Pact enable development teams to be assured that the services they have designed follow expected behaviors defined by their contracts, thus enabling more collaboration between development teams and greater stability of composite services. Organizational demand highlighted here is the need for testing solutions that not only validate functionality but also enable the general effectiveness of the software delivery process (Dhandapani, 2025). Real-world application of API testing tools extends to functional tests, such as essential areas like monitoring and observability. Quality API testing tools generally feature real-time observation of APIs' health, ensuring round-the-clock performance and service-level agreement (SLA) compliance. Feature-rich frameworks also facilitate configuration management and error detection, thereby finding problems preemptively before they become production problems. This future-oriented mindset is increasingly becoming essential in the contexts of mobile app development where user experience is based on seamless interactions. One instance of creative thinking in interactive testing is evident in the user interface frameworks like Jetpack Compose, which emphasizes the responsive UIs. With the consideration of user interface behavior alongside backend API interactions, more dynamic and interactive applications can potentially be created that respond to user performance and reliability expectations in order to raise the general efficacy of testing methods being employed within the software development lifecycle.

4.5.3. Importance of Automated Testing

Automated testing is one of the critical elements of functionality in the context of API design and management to enhance the quality and performance of software applications. Greater sophistication of software systems necessitate a systematic process for testing, where manual testing will no longer be adequate. Automated testing not only saves time spent on testing but also facilitates continuous integration and delivery pipelines essential in delivering high-quality APIs. By leveraging automated tests, developers can rapidly spot functional, performance, and security issues, hence minimizing the chances of disruptions in deployment. Furthermore, as the demand for rapid iteration cycles increases by the day, automated testing provides an essential safety net, where modifications do not introduce regressions or upset existing functionality, and faith in the deployment process is therefore enhanced. Moreover, the scalability of automated testing significantly lightens the load of development teams to focus on higher-order responsibilities rather than time-consuming test repeatability. As organizations increasingly adopt agile methodologies, where speed and responsiveness are paramount, automated testing facilitates the shifting from clumsy manual checks toward a dynamic testing domain. This change not only increases test coverage but also increases resource utilization, so that teams can innovate without compromising quality. Additionally, integrating automated testing tools and continuous integration pipelines ensures that any defects that begin to arise are caught and resolved quickly. As technology continues to evolve, the capability to execute end-to-end test suites on demand provides organizations with the resilience to maintain sound API designs, thus contributing to improved user satisfaction and retention. The automated testing role extends much beyond naked efficiency advantages; it directly touches ethical connotations behind software quality in a hyper-digitized era. In a scenario where the potential for bias and frailty in AI-driven applications is being questioned, developers must put top premium on diligent testing procedures as an insurance against vulnerabilities behind software crashes. Automated testing is the mechanism through which such risks are mitigated by systematic verification of various aspects of APIs against given criteria, thus facilitating transparency and accountability in the life cycle of software. As termed in discussion of the implications of generative AI technologies, companies have to deal with the intricate environment of matters pertaining to security and ethical design. Therefore, robust automated test frameworks are capable of serving as a bulwark to these issues, not just ensuring APIs work as they should but also keeping ethics in mind during design and handling, thus fortifying the trust of stakeholders in digital solutions (Yogesh et al., 2023; Jürgen et al., 2023) (Figure 4.12).

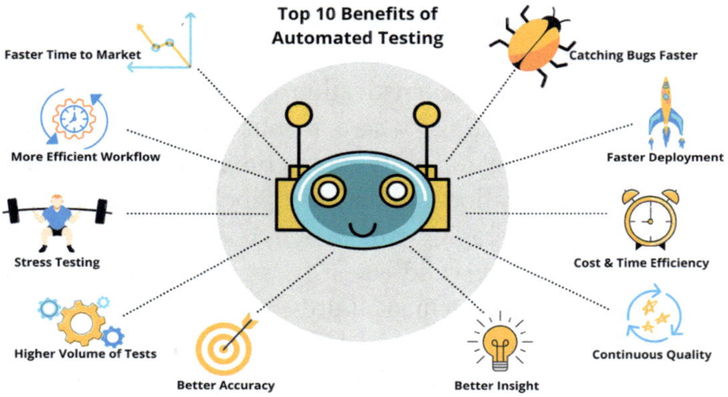

Figure 4.12. *Importance of automated testing.*

Source: https://product.testinium.com/wp-content/uploads/2021/03/MVP.png.

4.6. API MANAGEMENT TOOLS

API management software is critical infrastructure for designing, publishing, monitoring, and analyzing application programming interfaces (APIs). Such software enhances the developer experience by providing seamless processes for designing and deploying APIs and hence ensuring services are scalable and resilient. API management software makes it easier to be efficient and productive through easy integration and workflow automation. They also assist with guaranteeing the security of APIs via authentication, authorization, and rate limiting to avoid unauthorized access to sensitive information. The growing necessity for interoperability between various systems also emphasizes the central role played by API management tools in current software design, allowing various services to communicate with each other agilely and effectively. Behind it is the ability to monitor usage and performance metrics, something that can be done using various analytics tools built into API management systems. The analytics provide feedback on user trends, enabling developers to make data-driven decisions regarding the evolution and optimization of APIs. Based on real-time analytics, organizations can identify trends and points of potential bottlenecking, which enables them to make proactive improvements in their solutions. Furthermore, effective logging and monitoring functionality also ensures that any problems or inconsistencies are rectified immediately for uninterrupted performance. The collaboration of design and monitoring tools facilitates the provision of real-time feedback to allow for environments where APIs can evolve according to user needs and technological advancements, thus enhancing interoperability and resilience of overall systems. As industries increasingly embrace APIs, the need for management tools is further underscored. The tools enable organizations to establish governance frameworks for maintaining standards both internally and externally through adherence to regulatory bodies. By ensuring end-to-end documentation and version control, API management tools improve consistency and readability throughout the API lifecycle. This is particularly important in sectors like finance and medicine, where security and data integrity are paramount. Furthermore, the emergence of standards like REST and GraphQL has compelled API management solutions to evolve in line with shifting architectural patterns and facilitate smooth upgrades from one version to another of the API. Adopting next-gen API management solutions ends up placing organizations in a position to innovate rapidly without risks of API integration and use, eventually leading to business success and customer satisfaction (Macenski et al., 2022; Jones et al., 2020).

4.6.1. Overview of API Management Platforms

The API ecosystem has totally transformed with the evolution of API management platforms, which cater to the whole life cycle of APIs, from design and deployment and many more. These platforms play a very significant role in facilitating the development of APIs as fast as possible while maintaining security, scalability, and efficiency. The deployment of API management platforms allows developers to publish, build, and govern APIs with simplicity, fostering a streamlined workflow that facilitates the rapid response of organizations to market demands. To this effect, API management solutions are not merely operational tools but strategic assets whose purpose is to align the development process with business requirements, which in turn results in enriching the user experience and engagement with digital products. API management platforms are characterized by their feature-laden solutions, such as security features, analytics, and user administration, which enable teams to continuously optimize their API services. Security is given a high priority in API management, as these interfaces are likely to be exposed to external threats. Platforms may have authentication frameworks, traffic management, and data encryption to secure sensitive information. In addition, incorporating analytics provides organizations with the power of deriving meaningful insights from API usage in order to make well-informed decisions, with an optimized performance and utilization of resources. Smooth integration among various services highlights the importance of adopting a robust API management platform with the ability to handle multiple technologies and frameworks that are widespread in today's software ecosystem. As businesses come to rely increasingly on APIs for innovation and integration, the necessity for solid documentation is felt. An API management platform typically includes functionalities to create and maintain documentation, which is instrumental in onboarding and learning users. Good documentation helps internal developers as well as external partners learn API functions and use cases. For instance, comprehensive user role manuals such as the ones used in online auction system project reports ensure all have knowledge of the working workflow and security aspects embedded (Gentena, 2025). Effective API management, therefore, involves not only the technical details of API design and distribution but also creating collaborative ecosystems through readable and concise documentation materials, which are critical for effective operations (Kumar et al., 2025) (Figure 4.13).

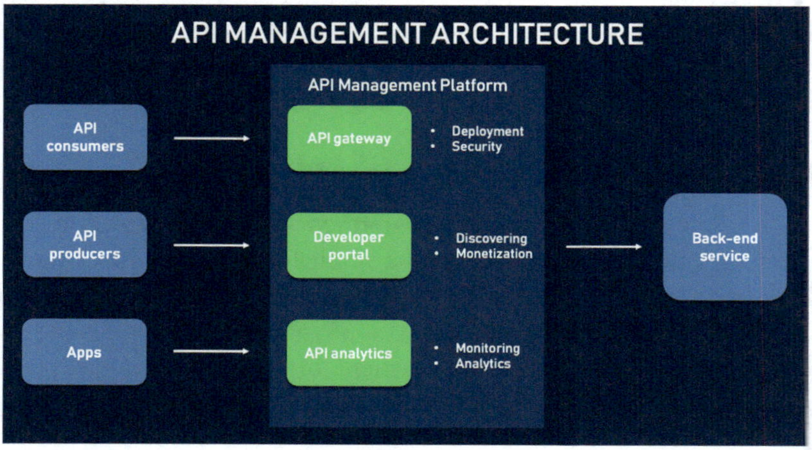

Figure 4.13. *Overview of API management platforms.*

Source: https://www.altexsoft.com/static/content-image/2024/6/26d22fa1-891d-46bc-8e00-b52e581a9e2a.jpg.

4.6.2. Features of Effective API Management Tools

Good API management tools are characterized by their ability to make API creation, deployment, and management easier, which are at the heart of modern software development. Among the most important are robust analytics and monitoring capabilities. By these capabilities, organizations can track API usage patterns, performance, and response times in ways that enable proactive improvements and adjustments. By using in-depth analytics, developers can identify bottlenecks and optimize resource usage, which continues to turn into better user experience and system performance. More importantly, a quality API management tool should be able to plug seamlessly into many data stores and services, breaking silos and enhancing interoperability—traits behind the success of microservices patterns where APIs are central (Sigala, 2025). Security is another critical requirement in API management. Efficient tools offer the enforcement of secure measures, including API authentication, authorization, and encryption methods.

Figure 4.14. *Features of effective API management tools.*

Source: https://www.techtarget.com/rms/onlineImages/whatis-api_management-f.png.

These capabilities protect confidential information against external access and minimize the possibility of cyber attack, which is of prime concern in the interconnected digital environment of the modern age. Role-based access controls (RBAC) are a significant aspect of permission management, allowing organizations to define access permissions for different user roles in the API system. In addition, the inclusion of threat detection functionalities within API management platforms allows organizations to respond in a timely manner to likely security risks, upholding data integrity and customer trust and adhering to best practices for cybersecurity, especially in sophisticated settings like ICS (Jeyaprakash, 2025). Last but not least, clean and minimal documentation and developer portals are essential features of excellent API management platforms. Well-organized and complete documentation provides developers with the ability to work effectively with APIs, reducing onboarding time and adoption. High-quality documentation will contain brief instructions, example requests and responses, and how-to-troubleshoot, enabling developers to share ideas and fix issues together. Not only is a quality developer portal a set of resources, but it also enables companies to track user feedback, track changes to the API, and foster community engagement. By prioritizing usability, organizations can create a strong developer ecosystem for their APIs and therefore ensure that the APIs evolve in terms of user needs and market demands, ultimately assisting in managing API ecosystems effectively (Sigala, 2025) (Figure 4.14).

4.6.3. Comparison of Popular API Management Solutions

When looking at popular API management platforms, it is important to look at their operational abilities and how these cater to the needs of today's businesses. Platforms like Apigee, AWS API Gateway, and MuleSoft offer end-to-end features like traffic management, security, and analytics. Apigee, for example, stands out in API analytics, where businesses can monitor usage patterns and user behavior. This feature is particularly beneficial to businesses that want to optimize their API services using statistical data. AWS API Gateway, on the other hand, provides native integration with other AWS products and hence stands as a robust choice for companies using cloud resources. MuleSoft, on the other hand, emphasizes connectivity, which enables business organizations to link APIs to many legacy systems, a feature that is valuable in hybrid deployments. This diverse functionality by popular solutions highlights the necessity of owning the right API management tool based on organizational needs. Security features are most critical in API management, particularly as organizations fall victim to increased cyber attacks. Popular solutions like Apigee and MuleSoft possess native security features that protect APIs from unauthorized access and potential data exposure. Apigee employs OAuth 2.0 for secure authentication, combined with rate limiting to avoid abuse, so only legitimate requests are delivered. MuleSoft, by contrast, provides complete security policies that can be configured at very granular levels, and companies can have specific access processes in place based on their business requirements. This is not only a technical distinction; it has profound business implications for firms that must safeguard sensitive data and yet make API services readily available. With growing worries about data privacy, the ability of API management tools to enhance security measures in turn directly impacts their use across industry segments, particularly those that deal with personal or financial information. API management tool integration features also merit close examination, as it is vital that these tools can interoperate as the world becomes more digitally connected. Tools like Postman and Azure API Management facilitate not only the design and governance of APIs but also seamless integration with other services and tools. Postman, popularly known for its ease of use, allows developers to rapidly design, test, and iterate on APIs to guarantee deployment flexibility. On the contrary, Azure API Management offers extensive integration with Microsofts cloud service platform, thus being appealing to organizations that have their origins in the Microsoft world. Integration capacity, therefore, enhances business agility through efficient development as well as through the capability of attaining rapid time-to-market for new services. Such choices between API management platforms should, however, consider these integration factors most directly related to overall operational performance as well as strategic alignment within an organization's digital framework.

SUMMARY

It is evident that strategic implementation of APIs plays a significant role in ensuring operational efficiency and organizational growth. With the use of best practices for API development, businesses not only achieve effortless integration into various software platforms but also spur innovation in their service creation. Such integration with contemporary technological tendencies indicates the need to embrace robust API frameworks able to adapt to rapidly changing market demands. Moreover, as in the case of sports management scenarios, these frameworks are also such enablers and have established that by leveraging a solidly designed API, an organization can enhance its brand reputation and its competitive edge within an ever-changing environment (Brovina et al., 2025). Furthermore, embracing an agile approach to the management of APIs continues to be topmost for reasons of staying strong even amidst unforeseen setbacks. Agile development's flexibility allows organizations to rapidly shift direction in accordance with a changing digital economy, facilitating faster deployment cycles and continuous improvement. This is a continuation of a larger trend toward management, where responsiveness and agility are key to sustaining success. As highlighted by agile resilience literature, integration of such paradigms in API management not only heightens organizational agility but also maximizes the innovation potential of service delivery. Therefore, it is crucial for organizations to focus on building agile principles-friendly culture to enhance realization of the maximum potential of their API strategies (Isabirye et al., 2025). Lastly, the conclusion of API design and management analysis is that integrating successfully is not merely a matter of technical specification but also strategic vision and awareness of user needs. Organizations should approach API management with an overall vision that tackles the operational, technical, and strategic dimensions of such interfaces. This holistic approach allows organizations to perfect the nuances of the digital world, with growth sustained and innovation ensured. The pearls of knowledge gleaned from these analyses encourage investment in training and technology because these are the essential variables in creating a solid foundation for future success with APIs. Hence, continuously iterating and evolving API strategies remains crucial to achieve long-term organizational objectives and remain current in a competitive marketplace.

REFERENCES

1. Addagalla, S. R. D. (2025). Optimizing API management: Choosing between APIM and Apigee. World Journal of Advanced Engineering Technology and Sciences. https://www.semanticscholar.org/paper/858155b36d4416e8858314eacb272a961f659eef (accessed on 11th September 2025).
2. Ahmad, M., Macvean, A., Karger, D. R., & Ma, K. L. (2024). AI-enhanced API design: A new paradigm in usability and efficiency. Extended Abstracts of the CHI Conference on Human Factors in Computing Systems. https://www.semanticscholar.org/paper/639992ef714428b91176842d42301d4177efd825 (accessed on 11th September 2025).
3. Al Badi, M., AL Yarubi, M. S., Ba Omar, S. M., Al Sinani, I. S., AL Subhi, W. N., AL Balushi, A. S., Al Dafai, H. A., et al. (2025). Improved oil recovery of viscous tertiary UeR oil reservoir through water flooding in Block 5, North Oman: Challenges and successes. SPE Conference at Oman Petroleum & Energy Show. https://www.semanticscholar.org/paper/a9dda4c2d8591509d7f1548d5797f9185a0cee33 (accessed on 11th September 2025).
4. Bhatnagar, S., Castro, S., Donovan, J. L., Emonts, B., Garcia, E., et al. (2022). CASA, the Common Astronomy Software Applications for Radio Astronomy. Publications of the Astronomical Society of the Pacific, 134, 114501–114501. https://doi.org/10.1088/1538-3873/ac9642 (accessed on 11th September 2025).
5. Biswas, A., & Talukdar, W. (2024). Intelligent clinical documentation: Harnessing generative AI for patient-centric clinical note generation. International Journal of Innovative Science and Research Technology (IJISRT). https://doi.org/10.38124/ijisrt/ijisrt24may1483 (accessed on 11th September 2025).
6. Brovina, F., Reka, I., & Latifaj, J. (2025). Embracing excellence: The imperative of best practices in sports management systems. Edelweiss Applied Science and Technology. https://www.semanticscholar.org/paper/c9d71fc48550531a366111cb961d0ede10194e39 (accessed on 11th September 2025).
7. Chamari, L., Petrova, E., & Pauwels, P. (2023). An end-to-end implementation of a service-oriented architecture for data-driven smart buildings. IEEE Access, 11, 117261–117281. https://doi.org/10.1109/access.2023.3325767 (accessed on 11th September 2025).
8. Dhandapani, A. (2025). Automated testing in microservices environments: A comprehensive approach. Global Journal of Engineering and Technology

Advances. https://www.semanticscholar.org/paper/3097c23e49f77cf725be242215fd2ca255bc0bac (accessed on 11th September 2025).

9. dos Santos, E., & Casas, S. (2025). A catalog of API Gateway metrics and its quantitative evaluation. DYNA. https://www.semanticscholar.org/paper/91ac06562590cab3f4a17b64a4d311746d497eec (accessed on 11th September 2025).

10. Dwivedi, Y. K., Ismagilova, E., Hughes, D. L., Carlson, J., Filieri, R., Jacobson, J., Jain, V., et al. (2020). Setting the future of digital and social media marketing research: Perspectives and research propositions. International Journal of Information Management, 59, 102168–102168. https://doi.org/10.1016/j.ijinfomgt.2020.102168 (accessed on 11th September 2025).

11. Dwivedi, Y. K., Kshetri, N., Hughes, L., Slade, E., Jeyaraj, A., Kar, A. K., Baabdullah, A. M., et al. (2023). Opinion paper: "So what if ChatGPT wrote it?" Multidisciplinary perspectives on opportunities, challenges and implications of generative conversational AI for research, practice and policy. International Journal of Information Management, 71, 102642–102642. https://doi.org/10.1016/j.ijinfomgt.2023.102642 (accessed on 11th September 2025).

12. Eziamaka, N. V., Odonkor, T. N., & Akinsulire, A. A. (2024). Developing scalable and robust financial software solutions for aggregator platforms. Open Access Research Journal of Engineering and Technology. https://www.semanticscholar.org/paper/252fbabfb0eab0c049c8e251aa7f0e842d84cd4e (accessed on 11th September 2025).

13. Gentena, V.K.C. (2025). Design and implementation of online auction system project documentation using the WPM method. International Journal of Cloud Computing and Supply Chain Management. https://www.semanticscholar.org/paper/fc927cc8a3b22d342445b0f34800d0e440455ab3 (accessed on 11th September 2025).

14. Goddard, T. D., Huang, C. C., Meng, E. C., Pettersen, E. F., Couch, G. S., Morris, J. H., & Ferrin, T. E. (2017). UCSF ChimeraX: Meeting modern challenges in visualization and analysis. Protein Science, 27, 14–25. https://doi.org/10.1002/pro.3235 (accessed on 11th September 2025).

15. Hale, T., Angrist, N., Goldszmidt, R., Kira, B., Petherick, A., Phillips, T., Webster, S., et al. (2021). A global panel database of pandemic policies (Oxford COVID-19 Government Response Tracker). Nature Human Behaviour, 5, 529–538. https://doi.org/10.1038/s41562-021-01079-8 (accessed on 11th September 2025).

16. Harrison, P. W., Amode, M. R., Austine-Orimoloye, O., Azov, A. G., Barba, M., Barnes, I., Becker, A., et al. (2023). Ensembl 2024. Nucleic Acids Research, 52, D891–D899. https://doi.org/10.1093/nar/gkad1049 (accessed on 11th September 2025).

17. Isabirye, A. K., & Mampuru, M. P. (2025). Agile resilience for the future human resource management profession: Methodologies, strategies, and best practices. Edelweiss Applied Science and Technology. https://www.semanticscholar.org/paper/f47d044570bd878d61dd667dba250b2f313b7f0b (accessed on 11th September 2025).

18. Jain, A. K., & Prasad, M. (2025). API design principles for financial services: Best practices and principles for designing APIs in the financial services sector. International Journal of Research in Modern Engineering & Emerging Technology. https://www.semanticscholar.org/paper/cf27555b100b260037cc6a4da9054a0860bdbcca (accessed on 11th September 2025).

19. Janakaraj, M. (2025). Architecting shared logic with Kotlin Multiplatform Mobile: Benefits, challenges, and ecosystem positioning. European Journal of Computer Science and Information Technology. https://www.semanticscholar.org/paper/d96359681480b60cd51b51aa34e97d4a9563a6b9 (accessed on 11th September 2025).

20. Jeyaprakash, S. (2025). Cyber threat intelligence for industrial control system. International Journal of Scientific Research in Engineering and Management. https://www.semanticscholar.org/paper/8037d909d0ab2b9c74133cf367cb01a498dffa32 (accessed on 11th September 2025).

21. Jones, D., Snider, C., Nassehi, A., Yon, J., & Hicks, B. (2020). Characterising the digital twin: A systematic literature review. CIRP Journal of Manufacturing Science and Technology, 29, 36–52. https://doi.org/10.1016/j.cirpj.2020.02.002 (accessed on 11th September 2025).

22. Karyono, F. A. (2025). Factors influencing the compliance of Person in Charge (PIC) in the accreditation documentation management system at Pelita Insani Hospital. Care: Jurnal Ilmiah Ilmu Kesehatan. https://www.semanticscholar.org/paper/168a65f2731680e52f027a2a051641590a3f9c3c (accessed on 11th September 2025).

23. Khattra, S. K., & Jain, R. (2024). An interoperable analysis of Building Information Modeling for structural design purposes. Asian Journal of Current Research. https://www.semanticscholar.org/paper/e68cd423a78a428158b51644d1d3d5fb22e86c6a (accessed on 11th September 2025).

24. Koers, H., Bangert, D., Hermans, E., van Horik, R., de Jong, M., & Mokrane, M. (2020). Recommendations for services in a FAIR data ecosystem. Patterns, 1, 100058. https://doi.org/10.1016/j.patter.2020.100058 (accessed on 11th September 2025).

25. Kumar, N., & Nandhini, A. (2025). Social media application using ReactJS. International Journal of Scientific Research in Engineering and Management. https://www.semanticscholar.org/paper/c1c8d5be0e062a1cd6edf8f865092470a4c6afc1 (accessed on 11th September 2025).

26. Kumar, S. P. A., & Kunte, R. S. R. (2023). SWOT analysis of parallel processing APIs–CUDA, OpenCL, OpenMP and MPI and their usage in various companies. International Journal of Applied Engineering and Management Letters. https://www.semanticscholar.org/paper/de87254cba49842c23ed8a4577dd9a641a06d7be (accessed on 11th September 2025).

27. Macenski, S., Foote, T., Gerkey, B., Lalancette, C., & Woodall, W. (2022). Robot Operating System 2: Design, architecture, and uses in the wild. Science Robotics, 7. https://doi.org/10.1126/scirobotics.abm6074 (accessed on 11th September 2025).

28. Muñoz-Sabater, J., Dutra, E., Agustí-Panareda, A., Albergel, C., Arduini, G., Balsamo, G., Boussetta, S., et al. (2021). ERA5-Land: A state-of-the-art global reanalysis dataset for land applications. Earth System Science Data, 13, 4349–4383. https://doi.org/10.5194/essd-13-4349-2021 (accessed on 11th September 2025).

29. Nutalapati, V. (2024). Essential Security Practices for Fortifying Mobile Apps. https://www.semanticscholar.org/paper/404e0897c1cce017e6d46db6fe1941a65f5f51b1 (accessed on 11th September 2025).

30. Nyambane, T., & Botha, R. J. (N.). (2025). Boards of Management Capacity Building Strategies for Effective School Governance in Wajir County, Kenya. International Journal of Research and Innovation in Social Science. https://www.semanticscholar.org/paper/42ca439f83842eb74b3e721b8ab6c4cadfc530b2 (accessed on 11th September 2025).

31. Omata, S., & Kondoh, S. (2022). Evaluation of the application of Seq2Seq towards the automatic derivation of a set of APIs that satisfy requirements from only ambiguous requirements. 2022 23rd Asia-Pacific Network Operations and Management Symposium (APNOMS). https://www.semanticscholar.org/paper/04a713571f18dc92b3774d24b7ce835fddeb3184 (accessed on 11th September 2025).

32. Petrovsky, A. A., & Rysin, M. L. (2025). Implementation of Drag&Drop behavior in an Android application based on the gesture processing API. Программные системы и вычислительные методы. https://www.semanticscholar.org/paper/3bf61edf5856a2a5c4e49fbc7567e82b8c6ef881 (accessed on 11th September 2025).

33. Pillutla, M. K. V. S. P. S. (2025). Enterprise-scale microservices architecture: Domain-driven design and cloud-native patterns using the Spring ecosystem. European Journal of Computer Science and Information Technology. https://www.semanticscholar.org/paper/036fa49a46cfaa35f77c7be987a3df320720de51 (accessed on 11th September 2025).

34. Poggio, L., de Sousa, L. M., Batjes, N. H., Heuvelink, G. B. M., Kempen, B., Ribeiro, E., & Rossiter, D. G. (2021). SoilGrids 2.0: Producing soil information for the globe with quantified spatial uncertainty. Soil, 7, 217–240. https://doi.org/10.5194/soil-7-217-2021 (accessed on 11th September 2025).

35. Pratama, S. C., Firdaus, E. A., & Adha, R. I. (2025). Web-based assignment management system application design to increase personnel productivity and effectiveness in product documentation division. Nuansa Informatika. https://www.semanticscholar.org/paper/d6e05063055a70c1edd3b02e62fd5a3e7d1ee8b4 (accessed on 11th September 2025).

36. Price-Whelan, A. M., Lim, P. L., Earl, N., Starkman, N., Bradley, L., Shupe, D. L., et al. (2022). The Astropy Project: Sustaining and growing a community-oriented open-source project and the latest major release (v5.0) of the core package. The Astrophysical Journal, 935, 167–167. https://doi.org/10.3847/1538-4357/ac7c74 (accessed on 11th September 2025).

37. Rasmi, A. (2025). Serverless application deployment using AWS Lambda and API Gateway. International Journal of Scientific Research in Engineering and Management. https://www.semanticscholar.org/paper/3b0d0c3f34cdc2dd32d0dadc1cab245ed947dd67 (accessed on 11th September 2025).

38. Reynolds, D., Ball, J., Bauer, A., Davey, R. P., Griffiths, S., & Zhou, J. (2019). CropSight: A scalable and open-source information management system for distributed plant phenotyping and IoT-based crop management. GigaScience, 8. https://www.semanticscholar.org/paper/c8e2610457912053ad78ae951132c0d58b793c78 (accessed on 11th September 2025).

39. Roshini, S., Sajith, M. A., Shasti, M., & Angeline, R. (2025). Elevate – An intelligent companion for mental wellness. 2025 International Conference on Data Science, Agents & Artificial Intelligence (ICDSAAI). https://www.semanticscholar.org/paper/538bfaf51442fcaa810b676f388d7bafafebb750 (accessed on 11th September 2025).

40. Rudolph, J., Tan, S., & Tan, S. (2023). ChatGPT: Bullshit spewer or the end of traditional assessments in higher education? Journal of Applied Learning & Teaching, 6. https://doi.org/10.37074/jalt.2023.6.1.9 (accessed on 11th September 2025).

41. Sigala, N. S. (2025). Microservices architecture in cloud computing: A software engineering perspective on design, deployment, and management. International Journal of Research and Innovation in Social Science. https://www.semanticscholar.org/paper/711ee2a15ac10e36b6be6e24e50c68a09f553433 (accessed on 11th September 2025).

42. Tholoniat, P., Caulfield, A., Cavicchioli, G., Chen, M., Goutzoulias, N., Case, B., Cidon, A., et al. (2025). Big Bird: Privacy budget management for W3C's privacy-preserving attribution API. ArXiv, abs/2506.05290. https://www.semanticscholar.org/paper/1450b84ee1788eb7408627d2c2877909c623965d (accessed on 11th September 2025).

43. Toman, S. H. (2020). Review of web service technologies: REST over SOAP. Journal of Al-Qadisiyah for Computer Science and Mathematics. https://www.semanticscholar.org/paper/544ec9c5df1a5b9630e50a5b4ac73c22eefc9448 (accessed on 11th September 2025).

44. Tyagi, M., & Venu, N. (2025). An RSI-based algorithmic trading system using Angel One Smart API: Design, implementation and performance evaluation. International Journal for Multidisciplinary Research. https://www.semanticscholar.org/paper/36b254b6802100d31316aceebad3273ae3f7ac99 (accessed on 11th September 2025).

45. Varma, J. V. A. (2025). YOLOv8-enabled real-time crop health monitoring with conversational diagnosis and geospatial support. International Journal of Scientific Research in Engineering and Management. https://www.semanticscholar.org/paper/15bafdd4371db94b3a99baa25da4cdb5ff816c01 (accessed on 11th September 2025).

46. Wang,B.,Bin,Z.,Yao,M.,&Wang,W.(2015).Virtualtenantnetworkresearch basedonpricemechanisminSDNarchitecture.https://www.semanticscholar.org/paper/d16e403238d008dfe9964a0d417bf224ce7971bd (accessed on 11th September 2025).

CHAPTER 5

CLOUD-NATIVE DATA MANAGEMENT

Contents

INTRODUCTION

The cloud-native data management trend is an innovative paradigm change in organizational data use and processing. The methodology focuses on the utilization of cloud computing architecture and technology for the optimization of data processing, storage, and analysis. Cloud-native systems differ from traditional data management systems, which are monolithic and rigid. Cloud-native systems are designed to be scalable, flexible, and dynamic. As commercial organizations continue to succeed in an age of perpetual growth in data and shifting technological landscapes, the ability to properly manage and analyze data in near real-time is crucial to maintaining competitive advantage. In this essay, the principles and practices that are at the base of cloud-native data management are discussed, illustrating its inherent role in enabling organizations to properly harness the power of data. One of the key characteristics of cloud-native data management is its inherent flexibility and scalability, allowing organizations to scale resources according to changing needs. This flexibility becomes a must in an era where the data keeps on growing exponentially, driven by a multitude of sources like IoT devices, social media, and digital transactions. Cloud-native architecture also supports the microservices architecture, which allows teams to develop, deploy, and scale applications independently. Thus, firms are capable of innovating and responding to market changes rapidly, enhancing their agility. According to experts, cloud-native practices not only streamline functions but also in effect turn the manner in which organizations approach data usage and enterprise strategy upside down, putting data squarely at the forefront of achieving strategic business objectives (Yogesh et al., 2023). However, transitioning to cloud-native data management does have challenges. Organizations have to handle issues pertaining to data security, compliance, and governance as they shift their operations to cloud environments. The increasing pace of cyber attacks demands robust security models to protect critical data from breaches and ensure regulatory compliance. Companies have to handle the complexities of multi-cloud strategies, including managing data among various cloud providers and maintaining consistency and interoperability. Solving these problems requires strategic data management that balances not only technological solutions but also considers the sociocultural implications of digital progress. Highlighted in existing research, the focus on institutional logics and change as a result of digitalization emphasizes the importance of organizations balancing their data management with broader organizational norms and ethics (Schildt, 2022).

Definition of Cloud-Native Data Management

Cloud-native data management refers to a collection of practices and technologies designed to take advantage of the agility and extensibility of cloud computing environments. It is defined by its ability to facilitate the management of data scattered across different cloud platforms and services. Unlike the conventional data management, which in most instances leans on monolithic data solutions and infrastructures that are static in nature, cloud-native data management promotes a more agile and dynamic response. By the use of microservices architecture, organizations can achieve modularity that supports ever-integrating and deploying, hence enhancing responsiveness to evolving data requirements and workloads. Central to the understanding of this paradigm is the role played by automation and orchestration tools that emphasize operational efficiency and maximizing resources. Central to cloud-native data management is the emphasis on making the data available and sharable across scattered teams. With many of the world's businesses being global in nature today, the geographical boundaries of the traditional data warehousing become insufficient to meet the timely needs for analytics and decision-making.

Figure 5.1. *The concept of cloud-native data management.*

Source: https://solutionsreview.com/data-management/files/2022/07/Microsoft-Teams-image-18.jpg.

Cloud-native architectures render data streaming and processing real-time, effectively allowing companies to make use of data from numerous sources, e.g., IoT sensors and mobile applications, in a harmonious fashion. Timeliness is essential in today's fast-paced digital world, where data-driven decision-making can radically influence competitive edge. Cloud-native architectures also often include hardened security protocols built into their frameworks, which enhance compliance and risk management related to processing sensitive data. In addition, cloud-native also describes its complementary nature to modern software development paradigms, namely the shift towards DevOps and agile methods. Since companies strive to have rapid cycles of innovation, cloud-native data management belongs comfortably within these processes, promoting a collaborative culture of continuous improvement. This convergence is vital in environments like high-energy physics studies, where computational requirements for data are rising exponentially, with the urgency of strong handling of problems spurred by software efficiency and infrastructure advancements (Asai et al., 2015). Furthermore, service-oriented architectures, such as developing Service Oriented Interactive Media (SOIM) engines, illustrate how these principles apply to varied applications beyond traditional data contexts (Aly et al., 2016). This convergence of application development and data management is central to organizations hoping to take full advantage of cloud-native technologies (Figure 5.1).

Importance in Modern Data Architecture

Future data architecture is the backbone of the efficiency and adaptability of cloud-native data management systems. As organizations strive to maximize data processing capacity, the convergence of scalable and adaptive architectures is unavoidable. Cloud-native infrastructures enable organizations to place their assets close to where data creation and consumption take place, maximizing responsiveness while ensuring high availability. This approach reduces latency issues and offers robust data-sharing capability between various applications and users. It also facilitates the quick deployment of advanced analytical tools and services using the flexibility of cloud-native architectures, thereby increasing innovation and decision-making capabilities. The necessity of modern data architecture is underscored by the increased amount and velocity of data being generated on multiple platforms, as highlighted by recent arguments among tech-focussed communities (Asai et al., 2015). Moreover, the applicability of modern data architecture is increasingly illustrated in alignment with revolutionary technologies like machine learning and artificial intelligence. Such technologies are greatly reliant on quality input data and efficient processing capabilities. A well-architected cloud-native data architecture, in addition to enabling the storage and processing of large data, also offers an environment in which real-time analytics can be enabled, which is something that is critical to making informed decisions in fast-changing markets. Data pipelining as well as streaming operations are methodologies that can be embedded within architecture such that organizations are able to act instantly to user requirements and market changes. The ability to handle significant amounts of data effectively is the foundation for the competitive advantage that many firms are seeking under the data age economy today, echoing the centrality of modern data architecture in cloud-native data management practices (Bohez et al., 2018). Finally, it is important to recognize the significance of modern data architecture in the facilitation of data governance and security. As more companies transition to cloud environments, safe handling of sensitive data becomes a top priority. A good architecture possesses inherent security features that comply with data protection law and regulations, thus effectively limiting threats from data breaches and illegal access. Moreover, modern-day architectures facilitate better data lineage and auditing capabilities, allowing organizations to track data flows and transformations throughout their life cycle. Transparency is paramount in ensuring trust and accountability, especially in industries dealing with sensitive data. The emphasis on governance in cloud-native data management systems illustrates the intricate relationship between architecture and compliance, where organizations are able to gain the benefits of cloud computing while satisfying the needed regulations to safeguard their data assets (Asai et al., 2015; Bohez et al., 2018).

Overview of Key Concepts and Technologies

Within the evolving landscape of cloud-native data management, several key concepts and innovations provide the basis for effective data governance and operational success. Supporting this structure is the application of containerization and microservices architecture, which allows applications to be developed, deployed, and scaled independently. With the use of light containers through frameworks such as Docker, organizations can offer consistent environments across development and production cycles, improving reliability and speed. Besides, the adoption of orchestration platforms like Kubernetes supports automated deployment, scaling, and orchestration of containerized applications. The transition from the traditional monolithic application to microservices encourages an agile development cycle that supports teams to innovate and adapt rapidly to changing users' requirements and technology, which is crucial in the current competitive digital landscape as cited in Nayan (2023). Data security and integrity are also of paramount importance in cloud-native environments, which reflects the position of contemporary security architecture in managing access and protecting sensitive information. These involve advanced techniques like Identity and Access Management (IAM) and Security Information and Event Management (SIEM), which have transformed the protection of organizational cloud areas. IAM ensures access to specific data resources by approved users alone, while SIEM provides a real-time analytic approach to managing security threats and data breaches. Furthermore, the migration of data to cloud systems needs in-depth understanding of best practices like data validation and integrity checks that must be adopted to authenticate accuracy and punctuality of information. These evolving security building blocks and technologies are applied directly to the overall authenticity and integrity of cloud-native designs, which prove their applicability in applications at an enterprise scale, as discussed in Nayan (2023). The integration of cloud-native technologies is also supplemented by innovations such as data orchestration and cloud automation, which enhance workflow efficiency. Automation technologies are becoming more popular as organizations are using them to automate repetitive tasks to enable more strategic initiative and complex problem-solving. Such tools not only facilitate data movement and transformation between different environments but also present data in a consumable and actionable form at scale. In addition, the advent of high-quality public cloud platforms, including Microsoft Azure, Google Cloud Platform, and Amazon AWS, provides organizations with the option to select proper services that best fit their specific needs. This changing world triggers more investigation into the relationship between cloud-native technologies and newer concepts such as the metaverse, which represents a step towards immersive, integrated environments that blur the lines between physical and virtual worlds, as explained in.

5.1. CHARACTERISTICS OF CLOUD-NATIVE DATA MANAGEMENT

Cloud-native data management is characterized by its inherent flexibility and scalability, the sheer necessity of which in the modern fast-evolving digital era. Such an architecture enables enterprises to handle variable workloads smoothly without being bogged down by the restrictions that are otherwise encountered with traditional data management platforms. Containerization and microservices support offered by cloud-native environments enable modular data services to be deployed independently to enable fast iteration and innovation. This adaptability is essential for businesses looking to maintain competitiveness as it allows them the ability to respond quickly to market demands and user needs. On top of that, automatic scaling of resources ensures that data processing can be balanced against growth trends of modern applications, providing a fault-tolerant foundation for operation as user levels fluctuate. One of the most significant features of cloud-native data management is that it relies on distributed computing principles, and this enhances performance and reliability. Data gets spread over a group of nodes, allowing optimized resource utilization and minimizing downtime. Parallel processing, enabled by the distributed architecture, can significantly improve data retrieval and processing times, which is a crucial factor in real-time analytics applications. Besides, with robust data replication, cloud-native systems ensure data integrity and availability even in the event of failure. With companies adopting cloud-native architectures at a scale, it is becoming increasingly important to include data management solutions that are able to operate well in distributed environments. Through the combination of distributed computing and cloud-native design, businesses are in a position to harness lots of data without compromising predictable performance. The utilization of advanced analytical solutions is a revolutionary shift in cloud-native data management, enabling organizations to leverage insights extracted from large datasets to their full potential. Through the adoption of machine learning and artificial intelligence on cloud-native platforms, businesses can significantly enhance the quality of their decision-making. For instance, predictive analytics may be utilized to establish user behavior trends and reallocate resources. Furthermore, the ability to use AI-powered data management systems provides for automatic data cleansing and data organization to improve data quality and make it more usable. Additionally, the momentum towards smart data governance ensures that organizations comply with not just regulatory standards but also data-focused cultures. As shown in studies of new paradigms for data management, the co-action between AI technologies and cloud-native infrastructures facilitates an affirmative approach of data stewardship, that is increasingly important in today's data-intensive age, well captured by ongoing research initiatives (Intergovernmental Panel on Climate Change, 2023; Zeb et al., 2021) (Figure 5.2).

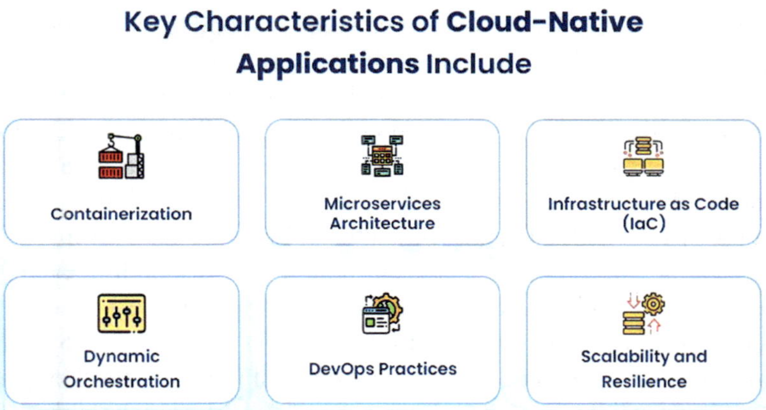

Figure 5.2. *Characteristics of cloud-native data management.*

Source: https://www.mtractionenterprise.com/blog/wp-content/uploads/2023/05/Key-characteristics-of-cloud-native-applications-include.png.

5.1.1. Scalability and Flexibility

In the rapidly changing context of cloud-native data management, scalability and flexibility are the required traits organizations need to keep in mind. Scalability refers to the ability of the systems to scale up and accommodate growing workloads without losing performance or stability. This is particularly important in cloud environments because usage is apt to change sharply based on varying user activity or processing requirements for data. Scaling. These solutions cause organizations to maximize resources and expenditure without sacrificing seamless user experiences. Furthermore, cloud-native architectures tend to use microservices, hence various components of an application scale autonomously. This modularity, besides facilitating scalability, also enhances flexibility, thereby allowing organizations to innovate and adapt changes quickly according to changing business needs (Oyeniran et al., 2024). Flexibility, on the other hand, is how a cloud-native design can accommodate varied deployment models, technologies, and frameworks based on organizational requirements. Through flexibility, businesses are able to make a transition to new methods, adopt future technologies, and blend various sources of data without the limitation of legacy systems or rigid infrastructure. Cloud-native platforms are created to enable such dynamism, and as a result, they can support tools that increase productivity, better analytics of data, and make decision-making even more advanced. Notably, the use of cloud-native technology can bring increased agility in the deployment and administration of applications, which has a direct impact on overall performance. Thus, organizations can respond to market changes and evolving customer needs on an active basis, ensuring a sustainable competitive edge in their respective areas (Yogesh et al., 2023). In addition, scalability and flexibility collectively play a crucial function in building resilience in cloud-native data management systems. Resilient architectures are able to survive disruptions and provide levels of performance in the case of stress conditions using methods such as load balancing, auto-scaling, and failover mechanisms. Using these strategies, applications keep running and responding even in high usage scenarios or unforeseen technical issues. Applying best practices such as proper monitoring and continuous integration/continuous deployment (CI/CD) also reinforces resilience so organizations can maintain service quality in the presence of outside forces. Lastly, the use of flexible and scalable solutions in cloud-native environments enables organizations not just to survive but to thrive in an increasingly complex and competitive digital landscape (Oyeniran et al., 2024).

5.1.2. Microservices Architecture

Microservices architecture adoption is a paradigm shift in how application development and deployment is being governed by organizations, particularly for cloud-native environments. Microservices architecture decentralizes applications into loosely coupled, independently deployable services that run about some business capability. Each microservice is coded to offer a specific function so that teams can innovate and scale independently, which is particularly useful for changing market demands. Besides, microservices allow continuous deployment of new features and improvements, significantly enhancing an organization's responsiveness and responsiveness towards change, hence optimizing the utilization of cloud resources. However, the resulting complexity involved in sustaining numerous microservices needs to be appreciated because it necessitates robust inter-service communication and orchestration mechanisms to encourage seamless integration and operational performance in cloud systems. Microservices adoption promotes decentralization and independence in development teams, leading to improved productivity and innovation. In this setup, different teams can develop different services simultaneously using different programming languages and technologies that fit each services requirement best.

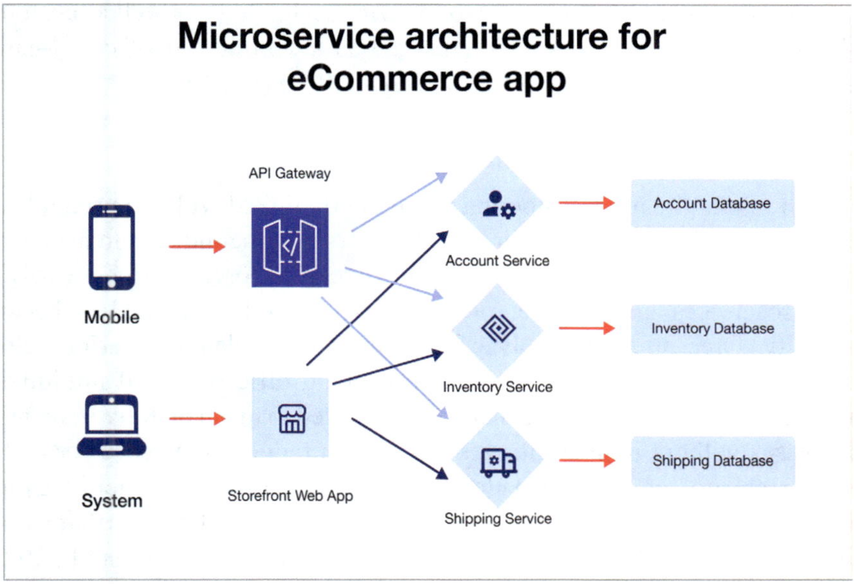

Figure 5.3. *The adoption of microservices architecture.*

Source: https://www.simform.com/wp-content/uploads/2023/12/Microservices-Architecture-for-an-eCommerce-App.png.

This provision inspires the use of the best tool for the job, which leads to more efficient solutions tailored to users. However, with this decentralization comes challenges, particularly in data management. Ensuring consistency and integrity across services requires effective mechanisms, such as event sourcing and eventual consistency models, to synchronize and update data across independently managed microservices. Therefore, organizations must thoughtfully design their data management strategies to leverage the advantages of a microservices architecture while mitigating potential pitfalls. Also, the integration of microservices architecture with cloud-native data management practices enhances performance and scale. In this case, data can be managed across distributed systems more effectively since microservices are not hindered from using different databases optimized for their needs, like NoSQL for unstructured data or SQL for transactional data. Cloud providers typically offer a selection of managed database services that facilitate simple scaling of data storage and retrieval operations, facilitating ease of meeting diverse needs. The diversity prevents vendor lock-in and promotes the use of polyglot persistence in which data is stored in multiple forms across different services (Walia, 2023). By embracing such architectural flexibility, organizations are able to render their applications flexible and responsive to evolving technology as well as customer needs, thereby microservices have emerged as a central part of cloud-native data management strategies nowadays (Walia, 2023) (Figure 5.3).

5.1.3. Automation and Orchestration

Evolution of cloud-native computing is inherently linked with the principles of orchestration and automation, being core drivers of dynamic data management in complex cloud environments. With increasing organizations evolving into microservices architecture, orchestrating several services has become a necessity. Orchestration involves controlling and balancing various cloud services to function in synch, thereby enhancing efficiency and minimizing latency. Automation, on the other hand, is employed to mean effective execution of processes without human intervention, which reduces the space for errors. When the two are put together in cloud-native applications, they facilitate rapid deployment and scaling, particularly critical for modern applications that require agility as well as resilience in a volatile market scenario (Kasım et al., 2023). Consequently, the shift towards automated orchestration frameworks maximizes the use of resources as well as promotes a more adaptive infrastructure that can respond to fluctuating demand. Apart from that, automation has its own place other than service provisioning; it represents the broader area of operational efficiency across data management processes. Cloud-native platforms utilize artificial intelligence and machine learning capabilities to forecast performance demands, optimize resource allocation, and enhance decision-making. Through automation, organizations can achieve zero-touch networking and service management that minimize human errors and improve the network configurations' reliability. As advocated for in the current body of research, such a method through automation enables attention to be diverted from day-to-day management tasks to higher-level planning and innovation, ensuring close alignment between data management and organizational objectives (Kasım et al., 2023). The key technological advancements in the network technologies such as Software-Defined Networking (SDN) and Network Functions Virtualization (NFV) facilitate this endeavor more, enabling end-to-end integration and management of different services effectively along with meeting the evolving needs of the telecoms market. Automation and orchestration together become increasingly relevant in the future, particularly in the context of upcoming technologies such as 5G and the future advancements in 6G. When businesses move to take advantage of the greater capabilities of these next-generation communication systems, network asset orchestration will be key to coping with the projected rise in connected devices and data traffic. These technologies will not only need to be deployed but also need to be provisioned efficiently using strong automated models of orchestration that learn in real-time to adapt to changing conditions and user requirements. In managing these challenges, it will be critical for organizations to develop robust strategies that integrate orchestration with automation, whereby data management systems are not merely efficient but also robust and able to accommodate future technological changes. This visionary approach will allow organizations to take advantage of opportunities posed by rapid development of cloud-native infrastructure and associated communication technologies.

5.2. BENEFITS OF CLOUD-NATIVE DATA MANAGEMENT

The rapid pace of cloud-native data management has introduced paradigm-shifting innovation in the manner in which organizations store, process, and analyze information. Using cloud platforms, businesses can scale their data management infrastructures cost-effectively to handle variable workloads and growing amounts of data with limited capital expenditure. Scalability is critical in todays real-time data economy, where timely analytics and responsive decision-making are critical to success. Moreover, the cloud-native design of the solutions also consists of built-in agility to allow organizations to rapidly roll out new applications and data services so that they can maintain faster innovation cycles. As more industries are shifting towards digital transformation, effective and efficient data management is not only desirable but inevitable in order to maintain competitive advantage as well as address customer requirements in a rapidly evolving environment. Cloud-native data management also enhances collaboration by having a centralized platform for accessing data. Cross-teams residing across different geographic locations can now access and share information comfortably, fostering a standardized approach towards data-driven initiatives. Central in its design, this not only destroys the silos but also fosters the culture of collaboration so that data scientists and analysts can interoperate dynamically. Moreover, cloud-native environments typically come with advanced security features, which not only make the data accessible but also secure against breaches. Further security features in the guise of encryption, identity management, and regular audits help foster stakeholder confidence building, as it guarantees that the sensitive information is secured. The combination of ease and security makes it beneficial for organizational processes and allows businesses to achieve a greater balance between regulatory compliance and industry standards. The unification of these various technologies for data management through a cloud-native infrastructure further adds to its value. A leading one is the development of polystore systems that enable organizations to collaborate with multiple data stores designed to excel at a particular task. As data volume keeps on rising exponentially, polystore solutions enable organizations to have optimal query ability as well as federated data across heterogenous systems. With emerging query languages like CloudMdsQL, organizations can overcome traditional data management limitations to enable successful and efficient handling of complex processing while maintaining expressiveness of queries. This technique allows companies to take advantage of parallel processing capabilities and maximize performance levels significantly. These innovations highlight the capacity of cloud-native data management systems to reduce complexity and offer flexibility in a dynamic data landscape, thus giving rise to greater productivity and operation efficiency (Kolev et al., 2018).

5.2.1. Cost Efficiency and Resource Optimization

In cloud-native data management, cost optimization and resource utilization are highest on the priority list for organizations that want to leverage the complete value of their data. With cloud-native technology, organizations can dynamically provision resources based on their needs at the moment, saving operational costs in a significant way. This kind of flexibility allows organizations to scale applications effortlessly, and this frees them from the norms that on-premises infrastructure enforces. Also, the pay-as-you-go pricing model common in cloud services helps businesses only to pay for the resources that they consume. Therefore, businesses can optimize their budgeting better and focus on innovation without the inconvenience of spending money on costly hardware. Advanced analytics within cloud-native systems are instrumental in propagating the optimization of resources. Through data-driven intelligence, companies can discern patterns of resource usage, allowing them to make effective choices on provisioning and scaling. For example, predictive analysis can anticipate demand spikes, and hence businesses can align their cloud resources to meet the requirements in advance, reducing wastage. Furthermore, the deployment of artificial intelligence tools has been found to boost productivity in cloud environments, and thus organizations have the chance to automate their operations. As companies step into these technologies, they must also be aware of the ethical and practical considerations built into their usage, which can be challenging to traditional processes and must be merged with careful thought, as investigated by Yogesh et al. (2023). As the digital transformation environment continues to evolve, the function of cost-saving, resource optimization, and novel technologies such as 5G and, in due course, 6G networks plays an increasingly crucial role. These advancements are going to augment cloud-native data management systems with increased interconnectivity as well as real-time data processing support in remote areas. The increased bandwidth and reduced latency that define 5G technology allow for faster decision-making as well as data sharing, reducing expenses even more. Organizations also need to address challenges associated with being 6G ready based on deliberations in order to still maintain competitive edge in the marketplace. Proactively embracing these developments guarantees that organizations not only optimize their resources but remain at the forefront of technological progress, as emphasized in Cheng-Wang et al. (2023) (Figure 5.4).

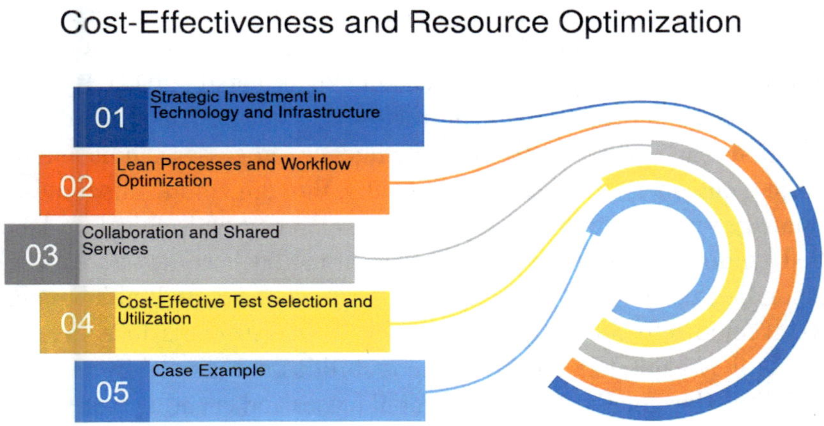

Figure 5.4. *The cost efficiency and resource optimization.*

Source: https://fastercapital.co/i/Clinical-laboratory-collaboration-Enhancing-Patient-Care--The-Role-of-Clinical-Laboratory-Collaboration--Cost-Effectiveness-and-Resource-Optimization.webp.

5.2.2. Enhanced Data Accessibility and Collaboration

The evolution of cloud-native data management has significantly enhanced data accessibilities and transformed the manner in which organizations interact with and utilize their data. The transformative change is primarily brought about by the migration of data resources to the cloud, providing room for centralized storage and easy access across diverse platforms. Modern cloud architectures support multi-user access, with teams being able to collaborate in real-time despite geographical distances. With the use of hybrid and multi-cloud models within organizations, connected relationships among multiple data sources become more evident, providing enhanced reliability and faster data retrieval times. This is followed by, through enhanced accessibility, groups being able to use data-driven intelligence to promote innovation and data-driven decision-making, ultimately translating to enhanced efficiency in operations as well as competitiveness within their respective markets. Enhanced collaboration is also facilitated with sophisticated tools to operate within cloud-native environments. Better data availability not only allows users to read and manipulate data easily, but also provides integration capabilities with advanced analysis tools that facilitate team collaboration. The emergence of generative AI is a classic example of how innovative tools can augment this collaborative process. As depicted in the current debates regarding developments in AI, these types of tools are able to significantly increase productivity, particularly in sectors such as information technology and management (Yogesh et al., 2023). By enabling interactive environments in which real-time data exchange is the norm, organizations can enhance collective intelligence, processes can be automated, and project outcomes improved. Additionally, through embracing cloud-native data management, there is a culture of transparency and ethical co-laboring instilled within organizations. As more information becomes accessible, the corresponding discussions of data privacy, governance, and ethical concerns are what come into focus. It is essential for organizations to address these matters as they capitalize on the new possibilities occasioned by greater data accessibility. This entails averting potential biases and ensuring that generative AI adoption adheres to ethical standards legitimized through ongoing scholarly discourses (Yogesh et al., 2023). As the distinctions between the physical and virtual environments continue to be minimized, understanding these effects requires strategic frameworks that can provide innovation and compliance simultaneously, facilitating balance in the utilization of cloud as a platform for collaborative enterprise across industries.

5.2.3. Improved Disaster Recovery and Data Resilience

In the cloud-native data management ecosystem, improved disaster recovery and data resilience are critical components in the safeguarding of organizational data. Unlike traditional data management systems, cloud-native architectures inherently improve recovery support via distributed infrastructure as well as automated processes. These platforms ensure data availability in spite of localized failures, with minimal disruption on unexpected events. Coupled with efficient backup systems, companies can recover operational capabilities and retrieve critical data in a timely manner, promoting continuance and sustainability. This resilience is more and more essential as companies face the increasing threats of cyber attacks and natural disasters, which call for proactive data protection. By integrating recovery solutions that are adaptive, organizations can develop an end-to-end strategy that not only controls near-term exposures but also enhances their overall operational efficiency. Moreover, the ability to leverage real-time data replication in cloud-native infrastructure enhances disaster recovery significantly. This diminishes data loss by making sure that data is always synchronized across sites in such a manner that faster recovery of the latest state of data becomes feasible. Such mechanisms provide organizations with a buffer, whereby they are in a position to utilize stored copies of data alongside real-time data feeds. Such a two-pronged approach not only makes recovery easy but also facilitates arduous compliance with data governance stipulations that require organizations to keep sensitive data under lock and key. Harmonizing data resiliency efforts with business continuity strategies forms a unified platform that fosters trust and reliability among stakeholders. Organizations can thus create a robust infrastructure that ensures continued operations even in the face of disaster. Moreover, the evolution toward improved disaster recovery reads harmoniously with the recent advances in machine learning and AI in cloud-native infrastructure. Such technology advancements make predictive analytics possible to determine probable sites of failure, programmatically adjusting resources and alerting administrators of the potential for imminent risk before it escalates into an outsize disturbance. Through implementation of these smart systems, organizations have greater situational awareness, hence their defenses against surprise events are strengthened. This anticipation is a shift from reactive recovery processes towards more dynamic, anticipatory approaches that emphasize data integrity and business continuity. By integrating resilience into the core of their data management processes, organizations can cope with an increasingly complex threat environment while being resilient and responsive. By this strategic alignment, growth potential through sustainability is enhanced as organizations can rely on strong infrastructure in achieving their ambitions without sacrificing data security and accessibility.

5.3. CHALLENGES IN IMPLEMENTING CLOUD-NATIVE DATA MANAGEMENT

The rollout of cloud-native data management introduces a set of challenges, particularly that of scalability and performance. As businesses transition to cloud environments, they may find it difficult to handle massive amounts of data in an effective way with the demand for immediate access and processing speed. Traditional methods of data management are unable to succeed when employed in cloud-native systems due to their inherent complexity and dynamic demands. Second, performance optimization can become increasingly complicated and need advanced tools and methodologies that a business may not be able to handle. Therefore, the transition from conventional database management systems to cloud-native data management systems might compel businesses to reconsider their existing infrastructure and invest in new technology, which can be cost- and resource-heavy. Security concerns are another critical challenge in deploying cloud-native data management systems. Since information is being migrated to cloud platforms, organizations are forced to contend with various vulnerabilities of distributed systems, including data breaches and unauthorized access. The shared responsibility model of cloud infrastructure complicates security further, where companies are required to ensure regulatory compliance and entrust cloud service providers with securing their infrastructure. The use of advanced security practices, such as encryption and identity and access management, is critical but challenging for the majority of firms to implement. Furthermore, security is ever-changing to keep up with evolving cyber threats, which means requiring continuous updates and trained personnel, thus placing an additional burden on organizations transitioning to cloud-native solutions. Finally, cultural shift in an organization is one of the biggest impediments to cloud-native data management. Employees accustomed to traditional data management methods may resist adopting new ones, fearful of disruptions to workflows or unfamiliarity with cloud technologies. Organizations must create a culture of ongoing learning and flexibility to overcome such resistances. This shift typically requires significant training and investment to equip personnel with the knowledge to utilize cloud-native tools effectively. Furthermore, leadership must help drive the change through showcasing the benefits of cloud-native data management, such as improved collaboration and data access. As companies surf these cultural changes, developing a supportive culture can lead to less bumpy transitions and ultimately enhance the overall performance of cloud-native systems in data management (Intergovernmental Panel on Climate Change, 2023; Yogesh et al., 2023).

5.3.1. Data Security and Compliance Issues

As businesses increasingly move to cloud-native environments, they are confronted by numerous data security and compliance challenges. One of them is the possibility of sensitive information exposure to cyber threats such as data breaches and unauthorized uses. Such attacks could lead to significant economic loss, reputation damage, and legal penalties. Organizations should therefore implement end-to-end security policies that involve encryption controls, strong identity and access management (IAM) controls, and multifactor authentication. By implementing these controls, organizations are able to safeguard their digital assets from potential attacks. Also, regular security audits and active monitoring are essential elements of a successful security plan. These processes not only help in identifying vulnerabilities but also help in following industry norms, thereby preserving the integrity and privacy of information stored in cloud infrastructure.

Hence, these security issues are a high priority for long-term cloud-native data management practices (Akinade et al., 2024). Following regulatory compliance is another area of complexity while handling cloud-native data management. Firms are required to function within a paradigm of shifting legislations, such as GDPR, HIPAA, and PCI DSS, which entail rigorous data storage and handling norms. Non-compliance can result in hefty penalties and lawsuits, thus further complicating the functioning of firms that have operations in multiple geographies. Firms must be mindful of compliance models relevant to their vertical and actively deploy measures aligning with these standards. This also entails acknowledging the cloud service providers' responsibility in the shared responsibility model of compliance, considering that organizations must verify that their providers meet required regulations as well. Furthermore, application of compliance-driven technologies, such as automated compliance monitoring software, can mechanize the process of maintaining the requirements of regulations and lower the threat of human intervention in the compliance processes (Akinade et al., 2024).

The ethical concerns with data protection and compliance in cloud-native environments cannot be sidestepped, particularly as artificial intelligence technology continues to gain more traction in such environments. Tools like ChatGPT bring added capabilities but raise basic issues regarding privacy and security, not least the risk of discriminatory results and misuse of generated data. While organizations leverage these technologies for greater operational efficiency, it is critical to assess the ethical implications and consequences on affected stakeholders. Strong governance structures must be in place to guarantee the use of generative AI and other digital technologies aligns with ethical guidelines, promoting transparency and accountability. This emphasis on ethical practice will not only assist with establishing trust with partners and clients but also ensure compliance with newly enacted laws that regulate the use of AI technologies. Ethical consideration is thus pivotal in effective data management practices in cloud-native environments (Figure 5.5).

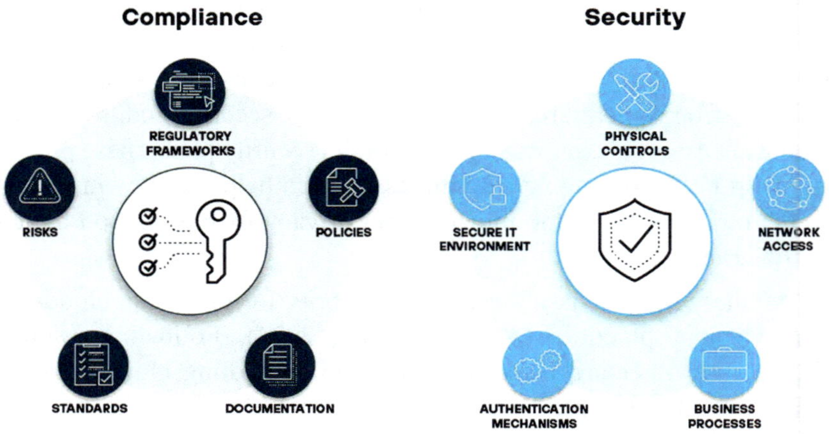

Figure 5.5. *Data security and compliance issues.*

Source: https://www.paloaltonetworks.com/content/dam/pan/en_US/images/cyberpedia/data-compliance/compliance-security.png?imwidth=1366.

5.3.2. Integration with Legacy Systems

In cloud-native data management, interoperability with traditional systems is a key issue that organizations need to address while transitioning to new architecture. Traditional systems, which are likely to be built on outdated technologies and constrained by structured infrastructures, can prove to be counter-productive to the agility and elasticity that cloud-native platforms provide. As companies shift to cloud platforms, the need for a hassle-free integration solution emerges so that data moves between legacy applications and newer apps. Integration is not just important for business continuity but also for accessing valuable data in these legacy systems. With the application of techniques such as APIs and data synchronization tools, organizations can harness the power of legacy systems while enjoying the scalability of cloud-native applications to ease the transition to digital transformation. Complexity in legacy system integration is also augmented by challenges of compatibility and data silos, which might be experienced during migration to cloud-native architectures. Organizations must address such issues to make efficient data sharing and interoperability of applications possible. For instance, embracing microservices, according to the architectural patterns analysis, can be used to dissect monolithic systems into smaller, manageable units that can effectively communicate with legacy systems. Besides promoting loose coupling, it allows teams to develop individual pieces incrementally, which makes it easier to migrate. Moreover, with methods such as the Strangler Fig pattern, organizations can migrate legacy pieces gradually, realizing a gradual transition with less disruption and ongoing operation while migrating, as emphasized by Oyeniran et al. (2024). Security and compliance are priorities when combining legacy systems and cloud-native applications. The propagation of sensitive data in legacy systems necessitates caution regarding data governance and security architecture. Organizations need to adopt full security controls that safeguard data at rest and in transit, especially as they move towards more decentralized cloud-native architectures. That involves ensuring that data access controls and encryption are strong enough to protect legacy data being consumed by newer applications. As Yogesh et al. (2023) posits, the ethical implications of data usage and disclosure become even more important in this integration effort, particularly in regulated sectors. Thus, strategic alignment of cloud-native approaches with legacy system security standards is significant, justifying the need for a comprehensive framework with scope for innovation and risk management as organizations start their journey of digital transformation.

5.3.3. Skills Gap and Training Requirements

The rapid evolution of cloud-native data management has uncovered a profound gap in skills in the workforce, triggering the need for a re-evaluation of training requirements. Organizations are increasingly migrating their data architectures to cloud infrastructure, which necessitates not only an understanding of cloud technologies but also an appreciation of agile principles and contemporary data strategies. However, many of the current staff lack the critical skills for effectively handling, analyzing, and securing data within these new-generation systems. This deficiency in skills can impair an organization's ability to maximize cloud-native data management, hence bringing inefficiency and unrealized potential. Thus, active training and reskilling initiatives are required to give the employees the appropriate skills to cope with this digital world so that they remain relevant and are capable of contributing towards the success of the organizations in a cloud economy. To support the emerging skill deficit, organizations must develop tailored training courses with a focus on both core and specialized skills in cloud-native data management. These training initiatives need to emphasize not just technical skills but also how to mix soft skills such as critical thinking and problem-solving, essential in a fast-paced cloud setting. Also, organizations can leverage continuous improvements in generative AI and machine learning to enhance their training initiatives. By combining these technologies, organizations can expose employees to more relevant, real-time situations and simulations reflecting the real issues they might face when it comes to cloud management. These rigorous training practices will ensure that the workforce is constantly able to mitigate risks associated with data management while harvesting opportunities brought by cloud solutions, ultimately creating a culture of continuous learning and flexibility. The growing reliance on advanced technologies, further understood as generative AI, emphasizes the need for a shift in organizational training models. With cloud-native data management becoming increasingly complex, the organizations are forced to realize that the traditional training methods may not be sufficient anymore. Rather, they must invest in creating dynamic learning environments, combining next-generation platforms and collaborative tools to exchange information. Such a strategy not only gains from filling the skill gap but also raises employee engagement and retention. Moreover, as noted by industry specialists, the revolutionary nature of generative AI is like that of earlier technological revolutions, compelling relentless change in job roles and work in data handling. By investing in end-to-end training tailored for these new technologies, organizations can position themselves at the forefront of cloud innovation, paving the way for a future-oriented workforce capable of thriving in an ever-changing digital landscape (Figure 5.6).

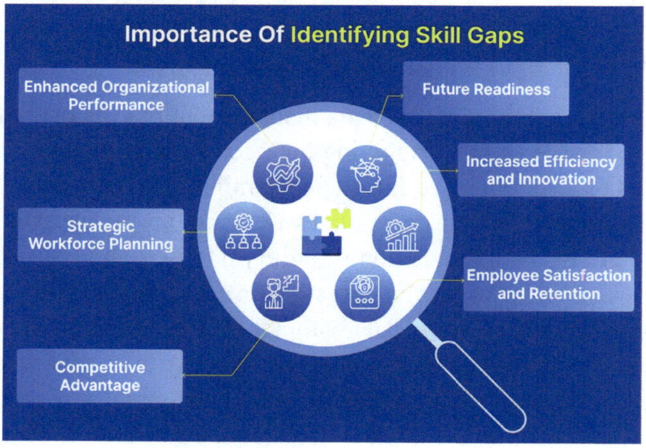

Figure 5.6. *Skills gap and training requirements.*

Source: https://cdn.prod.website-files.com/6484144ee6dda9d4b9ab7f57/6777a306693cd5814ace78e9_6777a2c299e3be052d65ba40_Importance20Identifying-20Gaps.webp.

5.4. KEY TECHNOLOGIES IN CLOUD-NATIVE DATA MANAGEMENT

One of the significant advances in cloud-native data management is the embedding of distributed ledger technologies, such as blockchain. This offers a counterpoint to the challenges posed by centralized data systems, such as data silos, that negate free sharing and access to information among various stakeholders. With the application of blockchain technology in health care service systems, for example, organizations can transform the handling of large sets of data, like electronic medical records (EMRs). The on-chain ledger and off-chain storage (OLOS) model used in the novel provides secure management through the maintenance of indexes on a public blockchain while maintaining actual data on private servers. The use of the hybrid method minimizes public ledger burdens and maximizes data protection, which is an important feature of cloud environments. Besides, the emergence of secure keyword-searchable attribute-based encryption not only encourages data secrecy but also guards against emerging attack types such as quantum attacks, addressing some of the principal challenges in current cloud-native applications (Li et al., 2022). Cloud-native databases represent a significant shift from the legacy approach that organizations use to handle data, particularly in the case of evolving needs in cloud applications. These databases are optimized to fully leverage the capabilities of hardware in contemporary systems, accepting features such as Remote Direct Memory Access (RDMA) and Non-Volatile Memory (NVM) to provide speed and efficiency. Cloud-native databases offer shared storage architecture by separating computation from storage, thus not only enhancing scalability but also providing high availability through the use of distributed consensus protocols. This flexibility of architecture enables cloud-native databases to host various workloads, particularly those that require horizontal scaling. With corporations increasing their use towards these new data management solutions, never before has there been a higher demand for effective design methodologies that embrace these evolving demands, predicating the need for ongoing technological innovation within the field (Li, 2019). Also the history of cloud-native database management is marked with innovation in real-time analytics and self-governing database systems. These technologies address the need for more real-time insights from big data, enabling organizations to compete effectively in rapid decision-making environments. For instance, technologies like PolarDB and AnalyticDB have been developed to provide high-capacity transaction processing capabilities along with real-time interactive data analysis. These systems not only provide impressive performance but also enable smart database management and autoscaling capabilities. By optimizing the use of advancements in algorithm design and architecture, these systems improve read as well as write throughput, thereby enhancing user experience and operational efficiency. With more organizations embracing such new advancements in cloud-native data management, it is clearer than ever before that where innovation and utilitarianism meet is the answer to how a data-driven culture can be achieved (Li, 2019).

5.4.1. Containerization and Orchestration Tools

The application of containerization and orchestration technology has completely revolutionized the environment of cloud-native data management. Containerization enables developers to bundle applications and their dependencies as a self-contained package known as containers that can be executed uniformly across various computing environments. Not only does this bundling ease the deployment of applications, but it also enhances scalability and resource utilization. Furthermore, by minimizing variations between development and production environments, containerization mitigates the infamous it works on my machine syndrome. As more businesses develop agile operations, the role of orchestration tools is eminent. Such tools, such as Kubernetes, automate scaling, management, and networking of containerized applications so that resources are assigned optimally and applications remain resilient in case of failure. The green effects of data management practices have also been subject to widespread examination in the recent past.

As highlighted in current discussions on cloud computing, data center energy consumption is predicted to double exponentially by 2030, necessitating action with an eye towards sustainability and efficiency (Katal et al., 2022). Containerization promotes this aim positively through its very nature of utilizing resources more efficiently. With the running of multiple containers on one host operating system, organizations are able to reduce energy usage, thus addressing the issue of performance as well as environmental sustainability. That containers are lightweight results in their deployment with less demanding physical hardware, which not only reduces energy usage but also limits the generation of e-waste, which aligns with overall green computing efforts. Moreover, the advent of 5G networks offers a unique opportunity towards enhancing cloud-native environments through the use of containerization and orchestration technologies for integration. Network Function Virtualization (NFV) implements container-based deployments aimed at dynamically scaling network functions according to real-time traffic demands, thereby optimizing resource utilization (Kuranage et al., 2022).

This is especially significant in emerging 5G applications, where dependable and versatile data management solutions are required. With telecom operators increasingly adopting Kubernetes due to its ease of use and effectiveness as an orchestration platform, the fusion of deep learning and containerization offers potential for sophisticated resource management solutions. With the assistance of predictive analytics, organizations can enhance their organizational capabilities to the extent that their infrastructures become agile, efficient, and responsive to evolving network dynamics.

5.4.2. Serverless Computing

Serverless computing represents a core cloud-native data management paradigm shift that offers developers a new architecture that hides the legacy server infrastructure management complexity. By eliminating provisioning, scaling, and server maintenance, serverless computing allows organizations to focus on coding and deploying functions in a more agile and cost-effective manner. This dynamic capability is particularly important in use cases that require rapid iterations and deployment, addressing high-speed requirements of next-generation software development. As companies increasingly adopt microservices architecture, serverless computing is a complementary pattern that accommodates scalability as well as reduces operational overhead, thereby paving the way for an agile environment to manage workloads of data. Additionally, the integration of serverless computing and edge technologies further strengthens its position in newer data management paradigms. The EdgeServe platform, for instance, illustrates how serverless architectures can be extended to the edge devices to serve the particular requirements of low-latency, high-data-usage applications such as those found in smart cities and industrial IoT.

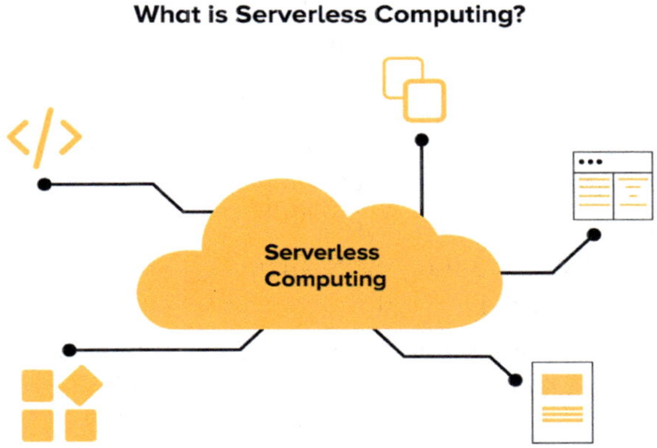

Figure 5.7. *The serverless computing.*

Source: https://appinventiv.com/wp-content/uploads/2022/05/Why-Should-Enterprises-Move-to-Serverless-Computing-03-scaled.webp.

The ability to process data close to the source mitigates latencies while improving the performance of the overall system. Practical implementations have realized phenomenal breakthroughs like a reduction of up to 82% in response time for time-critical functions and average cost savings of 43% over the traditional cloud-based architectures (Gangwani, 2024). Such progress attests to the capability of serverless computing to transform the way data is being processed and processed in distributed systems. The integration of machine learning (ML) with serverless computing also highlights its revolutionary role in cloud-native data management. Bundling ML models with a serverless framework enhances scalability as well as ease of use, making it possible for enterprises to leverage cloud infrastructure in an optimal manner. By utilizing cloud-native services, organizations can optimize ML models for improved predictive analytics without worrying about the inconvenience of managing underlying infrastructure clusters. Techniques such as auto-scaling and containerization may be employed to boost performance in real-time, making data-driven apps significantly more cost-efficient as well as dependable. As cloud adoption accelerates, particularly in countries like India, serverless computing perfects these models for finance to healthcare industries (Tirupati et al., 2022). The convergence of ML and serverless solutions puts companies in a position to facilitate drastic enhancement of operational efficiency and effectiveness of decision-making within their data management environments (Figure 5.7).

5.4.3. Data Lakes and Data Warehouses

In the cloud-native data management world, it is necessary for businesses to understand what sets data warehouses and data lakes apart in order to properly use data. A data warehouse follows a schema-on-write strategy, in which data is prepared, normalized, and transformed before being stored. This approach offers greater speed and performance when retrieving data, for which data warehouses are better suited as well as efficient for complicated querying. But whereas the rigid schema structure may complicate flexibility, particularly in environments where data types and formats differ, data lakes take a schema-on-read approach. Thus, organizations may store raw, unprocessed data in its native form. This adaptability makes it easier for organizations to handle evolving data requirements more easily, facilitating innovation and exploratory analytics increasingly important in today's changing data landscapes. Despite their own strengths, both data warehouses and data lakes have their disadvantages, particularly in terms of data security and management. Data lakes, as well as they can make it easy to access multiple datasets, typically get overwhelmed with issues around data governance and quality. Their open nature tends to have data swamp when not properly managed, making it difficult to derive insights from them. Moreover, the integration complexities inherent in bringing multiple data sources together may be enormous. Conversely, data warehouses offer powerful analytics but may be less agile at coping with rapidly changing data landscapes, potentially missing out on real-time insight opportunities. As businesses increasingly seek to leverage big data technologies, understanding such complexities is integral to effective cloud-native data management. The convergence of emerging technologies such as cloud computing and artificial intelligence with traditional data management strategies signals the start of a revolution for both data warehouses and data lakes. Sophisticated data management systems are being adopted by banking institutions and other stakeholders in order to transform decision-making capabilities and operational effectiveness. This trend is also observed in the increasing embedding of AI-powered analytics, which can potentially bring immense depth to predictive analysis and live risk assessment in financial use cases. With more companies linking data lakes and data warehouses with their cloud-native planning, caution must be exercised to remain aware of the evolving landscape of technologies and methodologies that can affect the success of these solutions. This merge emphasizes the importance of continued research and innovation to develop systems that minimize today's constraints while taking full advantage of data lakes and warehouses in a cloud-native era (Ionescu et al., 2023; Hai et al., 2023).

5.5. BEST PRACTICES FOR CLOUD-NATIVE DATA MANAGEMENT

In contemporary data management practices, embracing cloud-native architecture has been the need of the hour for those organizations that need to be efficient and scalable. A shift towards a cloud-native strategy in data management involves recreating conventional data practices by embracing best practices based on being agile and adaptive. API optimization is at the core of this since they are the binding elements which enable heterogeneous systems and cloud services to interact with one another. By redesigning APIs according to cloud-native principles, including serverless and microservices, organizations can improve flexibility and scalability. This refactoring simplifies the ability to maintain performance across varied workloads while reducing costs associated with traditional server-based systems. Therefore, API integration and management as an imperative is a fundamental practice of modern cloud-native data management that enables organizations to utilize cloud capabilities effectively (Samira et al., 2024). Apart from API optimization, the usage of continuous integration and continuous deployment (CI/CD) practices is essential in enhancing the data management lifecycle in a cloud-native ecosystem. CI/CD pipelines allow for seamless updates and comprehensive testing, reducing significantly the time required to roll out new fixes and features. This speed allows rapid innovation while keeping data secure and well-governed throughout its lifespan. Adding automated analytics and monitoring capabilities, organizations can obtain real-time insights on the data processing stage, making it simpler to optimize beforehand and offer transparency. By following a culture of continuous improvement from real-time data insights, organizations can increase operational efficiency and reduce data management risks. Hence, embracing CI/CD along with robust monitoring practices is yet another best practice important to effective cloud-native data management (N/A, 2023). Lastly, data governance and security cannot be overlooked under cloud-native data management. When organizations transition to cloud-native architecture, they must adopt stern data governance policies that ensure data quality and compliance with privacy legislation. Additionally, adopting advanced security solutions is essential to protect confidential information from burgeoning cyber attacks. This involves applying encryption, access management, and ongoing audits to enhance data integrity and confidentiality. A unified data governance and security strategy coupled with cloud-native concepts empowers companies to not only enhance their working capability but also build stakeholder confidence. With these critical areas being covered, businesses are able to realize the complete potential of cloud-native data management, prioritizing business goals and the development of long-term progress in a more digital world (Samira et al., 2024) (Figure 5.8).

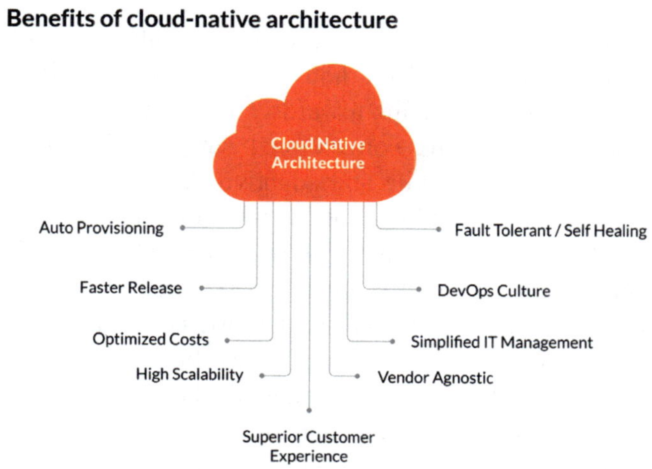

Figure 5.8. *Best practices for cloud-native data management.*

Source: https://src.n-ix.com/uploads/2024/06/14/bfe0d263-b66a-4e06-b4cd-7e5cd2e701b9.webp.

5.5.1. Establishing a Robust Data Governance Framework

In cloud-native data management, the existence of a good data governance program is crucial for organizations that wish to protect their critical information assets and achieve compliance with regulations. It is a ruling framework that specifies roles, responsibilities, and policies that lead in managing data during its life cycle. Data quality, security, and accessibility must be prioritized to effectively harness the power of their cloud assets. The robust governance framework, not only responds to risks associated with data breaches and compliance, but also facilitates sound decision-making by providing stakeholders with timely and accurate information. As companies increasingly rely on information derived from data, the proper governance approach helps the organization develop a culture that honors data integrity and encourages trust among users, hence enhancing the performance and credibility of the company at large. Also, using a data governance framework involves convening various stakeholders, including IT professionals, data stewards, and business leaders, to agree on data management. Through combining various perspectives and expertise, organizations are able to detect data management problems better and develop comprehensive policies for addressing such problems. This collaboration can lead to the implementation of standard operating procedures for data treatment, which will ensure uniformity among departments and enhance adherence to regulatory and legal mandates. Training and communication on a regular basis by all stakeholders are vital in sensitizing employees on data governance policy so that they can manage the complexity of data handling and reduce the risk of human error leading to data breaches. This partnership not only confirms the organizations credibility but also enhances overall operational efficiency. Furthermore, with continuous technological revolutions changing the data management landscape, organizations must enhance their governance policies to encompass new instruments and techniques such as artificial intelligence (AI) and machine learning (ML). These disruptive technologies can improve data governance processes by applying ML to automate data quality checks and detect abnormalities that could be an indicator of possible security threats (Yogesh et al., 2023). However, the use of AI and ML also raises ethical concerns, requiring constant assessment and updating of governance policies. By actively combating such challenges, organizations ensure their models of data governance are current and effective to contain the associated risks. Synchronization of robust governance with emerging technologies can ultimately put organizations in a place where they can leverage their data more effectively while maintaining compliance and ethics standards, providing them with long-term competitive advantage in the cloud-native era (Figure 5.9).

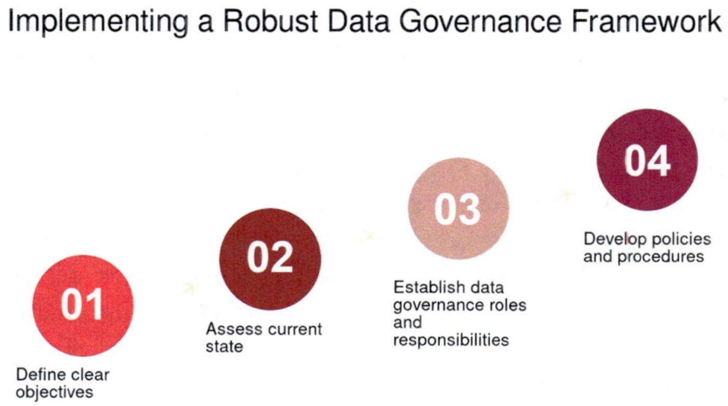

Figure 5.9. *The establishing a robust data governance framework.*

Source: https://fastercapital.co/i/Data-Governance--Ensuring-Integrity-and-Compliance-in-BD-Usage-update--Implementing-a-Robust-Data-Governance-Framework.webp.

5.5.2. Continuous Monitoring and Optimization

Continual monitoring and optimization remain crucial to make sure that cloud-native data management systems operate efficiently and effectively. The dynamic nature of cloud environments necessitates the use of adaptive measures that allow businesses to move quickly to respond to changes in the conditions. By employing robust monitoring tools and performance analytics, companies are able to acquire valuable insights regarding the system behavior, thereby identifying cases of system performance bottlenecks and inefficiencies. This preventive measure not only ensures containment of issues when they are still manageable but also assists with data-driven decision-making. A systematic performance metric check furnishes organizations with the information critical to optimize resource usage and facilitate scalability, thereby making their cloud-native infrastructure more robust. Such continuous monitoring aligns with ideas outlined in models that focus on API management and cloud integration, thereby justifying the strategic implication of constant optimization in the current IT environment (Samira et al., 2024). Incorporation of cutting-edge technology has also revolutionized the landscape of continuous monitoring and optimization in cloud-native data administration. Artificial intelligence and machine learning-driven products can filter through vast volumes of data at record speeds, identifying patterns and anomalies at scale with minimal manual intervention. This allows for greatly reduced manual management, enabling IT personnel to allocate resources towards more strategic initiatives rather than performing maintenance in-house. In addition, such smart systems can predict failures or performance degradations of a system before they become critical in nature, which allows organizations to take preventive measures effectively. As noted by existing studies from scholars, the related benefits of such technologies are extensive, particularly in areas like information technology and business administration, where efficient work and rapid response to market demands are critically crucial (Yogesh et al., 2023). Thus, the application of such innovative monitoring techniques not only enhances existing system performance but also makes companies more resilient in the face of uncertainty to come. To reap maximum benefits from continuous monitoring and optimization, companies must embrace a holistic approach that harmonizes technology with best practices. This involves having concise governance structures, defining key performance indicators (KPIs), and cultivating a culture of innovation and responsiveness. By making their monitoring strategy a top priority, with alignment against business objectives, organizations can ensure that their cloud-native infrastructures not only survive but thrive too alongside changing market facts and technological improvements. Furthermore, collaboration across departments can render optimization attempts more efficient, where insights from everyone contribute towards an integrated understanding of system performance and user experience. Lastly, continuous monitoring and tuning need to be made a core part of a larger strategy for unleashing the true potential of cloud-native data management to drive both efficiency and competitiveness in a fast-digitalizing economy (Samira et al., 2024).

5.5.3. Leveraging Cloud-Native Tools and Services

The integration of cloud-native tools and services has changed the face of data management to allow organizations to tap into scalability, flexibility, and cost-effectiveness. Cloud-native architecture allows for a microservices approach, with companies able to deploy applications as individual components that connect via APIs. This architecture allows for continuous deployment and continuous integration (CI/CD) to allow teams to innovate faster and respond to market demands quickly. As a result, organizations can minimize effort and time spent on infrastructure management and focus on core business activities. Second, cloud-native services enable data management methods to be transitioned seamlessly, with businesses having the capacity to respond in an agile way to varying data workloads and user demands while providing high reliability and performance on all applications. Cloud-native tools promote collaboration and productivity among businesses. With cloud services like serverless and container orchestration, teams can work on different parts of an application simultaneously, removing bottlenecks from the pipeline. This is crucial in today's speed-based business environment, where time-to-market might prove to be a significant competitiveness differentiator. Cloud-native data management applications also have analytics integrated into them, through which organizations can get insights out of data in real-time. This real-time analytics visibility allows decision-makers to make strategic decisions from accurate, up-to-the-minute information, resulting in better business outcomes. Overall, the cloud-native tool ecosystem not only automates processes but also creates a data-driven culture within organizations, which is key to achieving success in an information-based world.

Figure 5.10. *Leveraging cloud-native tools and services.*

Source: https://www.guavatrees.com/wp-content/uploads/2024/12/cloud-native-application-development-.jpg.

Though there are gargantuan benefits of cloud-native applications and services, one needs to be cognizant of the challenges and ethical implications that come with them. When businesses open their arms to the technologies, they must confront issues such as data privacy, security, and even tech-deployment-borne prejudices. For instance, use of artificial intelligence in data management, as evidenced by the creation of tools like ChatGPT, has significant productivity advantages and ethical considerations relating to transparency and precision in content (Yogesh et al., 2023). Furthermore, organizations must ensure that their cloud strategies are friendly to compliance legislations in order to shield against breaches of data or misuse. By addressing these challenges head-on, companies will be in a position to create an integrated framework for leveraging cloud-native technology while promoting responsible and ethical data handling practices that not only benefit their operations but also maintain the trust of their stakeholders (Figure 5.10).

5.6. CASE STUDIES OF SUCCESSFUL CLOUD-NATIVE DATA MANAGEMENT

The transition to cloud-native data management has made it possible for a number of organizations to enhance their capacity to manage data. An example is how a large retail organization employed a microservices-based approach in managing its large data landscape. Decomposing its data architecture into independent, individually scalable services helped the organization gain higher modularity, enabling teams to deploy changes without breaking the whole system. This transformation facilitated seamless interoperability with other data sources and facilitated real-time processing of transactional data, leading to enhanced customer experiences and operational efficiency. This architecture is a demonstration of the robustness of utilizing microservices in cloud-native applications, showing better performance, reliability, and agility when managing complex data workflows (Oyeniran et al., 2024). Yet another large financial institution is also a great case study of successful cloud-native data management, particularly regulatory compliance and risk management. By leveraging cloud-native solutions, the institution built a distributed ledger technology (DLT) framework that provided real-time visibility into data and transaction transparency. Not only did this innovative solution ease regulatory reporting but also minimized the potential for discrepancies with regard to older data reconciliation activities. With horizontal scalability ability, the organization succeeded in reducing its reaction time to regulations by changing data management practices to respond to emerging compliance requirements effectively. This illustration captures how cloud-native data management contributes to enhanced data governance and business resilience and lays a good foundation for reliable financial behavior (N/A, 2023). Another compelling case involves the healthcare sector, as a leading medical center transformed its patient data management using cloud-native technologies. By migrating its electronic health record (EHR) system to the cloud, the center dismantled information silos previously interfering with patient care coordination. The utilization of cutting-edge analytics and AI enabled the better utilization of data and supply of healthcare professionals with detailed views of patients and tailored care plans. Moreover, this step facilitated collaboration between specialists, improving the quality of care while maintaining stringent security for data. The achievement of this healthcare center is a classic example of the substantial value addition provided by cloud-native data management in enhancing patient outcomes and operations efficiencies, demonstrating its pivotal role in redefining healthcare delivery platforms (Oyeniran et al., 2024).

5.6.1. Company A: Transformation and Outcomes

As businesses go on competing in an increasingly digital era, Company A is an example of how company evolution can be achieved through cloud-native data management. Initially relying on legacy data infrastructure, the firm came to understand that it must be agile and scalable to accommodate evolving market demands. With its architecture migration to cloud-native, Company A has significantly increased the processing capacity of its data, allowing it to take advantage of enormous amounts of data. This transformation is consistent with the broader pattern under which businesses within the majority of industries leverage cloud technologies to innovate and redefine the effectiveness of operations. The transformation, in addition to facilitating real-time analytics and decision-making, also serves to establish spaces of collaboration where cross-functional teams can build insights around data, resulting in overall organizational performance. The implications of Company As shift to cloud-native data management are substantial, both in performance gains and market competitiveness. With an emphasis on deploying generative AI tools within its cloud stack, Company A has quantifiably seen productivity and workflow gains. As highlighted by the research of various experts in their fields, these advancements have placed the company well to leverage artificial intelligence towards better business operations, specifically in the management and marketing sectors (Yogesh et al., 2023). However, it is crucial to focus on the ensuing threats and risks, including the risk of bias in AI systems and data protection concerns. These complexities call for a strategy that aims to balance innovation with morality, where the benefits of transformation are realized without the unintended effects. Against this backdrop of these trends, Company As' march towards cloud-native data management also pose questions regarding the future of digital spaces, particularly in the case of immersive technologies like the metaverse. The ongoing evolution of data management and emerging frameworks emphasizes the need for scalability, interoperability, and security in digital ecosystems (Wang et al., 2022). As Company A faces this complexity, it is essential to decide the skills and capabilities needed to fully leverage these innovations. The focus of the company on continuous improvement and adaptability in the face of change will not only make it more robust as a business entity but also result in more experimentation with new business models in an increasingly globalized digital world. Ultimately, Company As transformation can serve as a model study for other firms that wish to embark on the same path, with takeaways serving far beyond short-term gain to include long-term sustainability and ethical considerations in cloud-native environments (Figure 5.11).

Figure 5.11 *Transformation and outcomes.*

Source: https://d1krbhyfejrtpz.cloudfront.net/blog/wp-content/uploads/2024/08/14185811/Industries-Leveraging-Cloud-based-Digital-Transformation.jpg.

5.6.2. Company B: Challenges Faced and Solutions Implemented

With weathering the complexity of data management of cloud-native data, Company B had immense challenges that tested the operational efficiency of the company. The rapid data growth imposed needed efficient data governance systems to avoid the most prevalent dangers associated with data mismanagement. Moreover, the integration of disparate systems introduced complexities in offering impedance-free data access and homogeneity across platforms. These issues not only compromised data integrity but also increased the likelihood of compliance issues with stringent regulations. As a countermeasure to these risks, Company B launched a strategic initiative to bolster its data governance processes, including the implementation of standardized data handling practices, thereby creating an integrated architecture that provided data reliability and security. To address its infrastructural shortcomings, Company B realized the essential need for technology improvements that would support its cloud-native strategy. Company B was badly in need of improvement of its legacy systems that were not cloud-ready and hampered its capacity to analyze. The process of transformation included a thorough analysis of existing technologies and potential dangers of their use in a cloud-native system. Using more advanced artificial intelligence, such as generative AI technologies, Company B could automate part of its data processes, becoming more effective and enabling quicker response to the demands of the market. Use of these technologies not only facilitated alleviating part of the constraints of operation but also laid the foundation for innovative shifts in practices of handling data according to industry standards and optimized productivity overall (Yogesh et al., 2023). In addition to this, leveraging innovative communication technologies like plans for next-generation 5G networks was also a critical element in addressing operational challenges faced by Company B. With the advent of 5G, the company anticipated faster data transmission rates and higher connectivity required for real-time data processing and decision-making. However, the transition also introduced excessive challenges, such as rigid compliance to new standards and identification of relevant usage scenarios that capitalized on 5G capabilities. In an effort to facilitate a smooth transition, Company B actively participated in collaborative research for the next 6G standards with the aim of remaining ahead of technological curves as well as overcoming probable challenges to effective adoption. This proactive stance not only gave Company B a clearer view of upcoming trends but also established a competitive advantage within the dynamic realm of cloud-native data management (Cheng-Wang et al., 2023).

5.6.3. Company C: Innovations and Future Directions

In looking at the innovations of Company C in cloud-native data management, consider the revolutionary potential of new technologies such as artificial intelligence (AI). Company C has been able to integrate AI tools with their ability to enhance processes and boost productivity. This assistance using advanced technology not only makes it easier to analyze data but also makes for a more informed decision environment. For example, through AI-based data management tools, the organization can complain against the dangers of biases or misinformation while enhancing transparency. Further, the adaptability of generative AI across different industries—covering marketing to management—indicates the Company Cs emphasis on being ahead of technology trends. The businesses in these innovations capture the dynamic interplays between strategic leadership and technology, propelling Company C into the frontline of the cloud-native era (Yogesh et al., 2023). Company C will be basking in the future on technologies in telecommunications, specifically the deployment of 5G and subsequent 6G technologies, to strengthen its data management capabilities. These advances do not only offer greater connectivity but also increased data transmission speeds, invaluable for cloud-native applications. Consequently, with industries beginning to embrace 5G, Company C stands to gain from richer experiences and the new plethora of services that this technology enables. However, the future is not without obstacles since the transition to 6G brings new requirements and application cases that must be researched by Company C. Proactiveness in this rapid world will help the company effectively deal with these challenges and advance its position in the data management infrastructure (Cheng-Wang et al., 2023). In addition, the strategic focus on ethical concerns in the application of generative AI is an indication of Company C's commitment to socially responsible positioning in its innovation. As organizations embed more of AI within their operational frameworks, maintaining users' privacy and mitigating threats from disinformation are crucial issues. The ethical concerns of cloud-native data management prompt Company C not only to innovate technologically but also to take into account the regulatory structures that regulate the application of AI. Engagement in expert dialogue regarding the transparency of knowledge and ethics, which are central to applying generative AI, will guarantee the development of a solid organizational strategy. As the company adjusts to these evolving challenges, developing a culture of continuous learning and adaptation will be crucial to its competitive edge in the ever-evolving landscape of cloud-native data management (Yogesh et al., 2023) (Figure 5.12).

Figure 5.12. *Innovations and future directions.*

Source: https://media.licdn.com/dms/image/v2/D5612AQEVGFLH6ctT9g/article-cover_image-shrink_720_1280/article-cover_image-shrink_720_1280/0/1715922298508?e=2147483647&v=beta&t=DKI-weolHlse0L4hHjUUdUPAPH26wOl-ChfFsdVEJ21A.

SUMMARY

In Summary, cloud-native data management is a paradigm shift in how organizations store, process, and analyze data. With the use of cloud technologies, companies are able to advance their operational efficiency, scalability, and responsiveness. Moving to cloud-native architectures makes it possible to utilize advanced data management tools that can handle large volumes of information efficiently. This is in line with the modern demands of real-time processing and analytics of data, which are essential for decision-making. Nevertheless, there are challenges that remain, especially in maintaining data security and privacy as organizations move their data to the cloud. A careful analysis of these forces, such as the one done by Yogesh et al. (2023), highlights the imperative for organizations to implement total strategies that balance innovation with responsible governance of data. Furthermore, the influence of cloud-native data management goes beyond corporations to impact broader societal and economic frameworks. The increasing reliance on cloud infrastructure raises its own essential ethics and legal issues regarding ownership, utilization, and protection of data. As technology advances, organizations must be proactive in addressing issues of bias in handling data as well as the spreading of misinformation. The discussion concerning these matters has been enriched with multidisciplinary insight, placing a premium on the demands of ongoing research and debate, particularly in fields that intersect with technology, law, and ethics, based on Souza et al. (2020). This multidisciplinary strand highlights that in order to reach the full potential of cloud-native data management, cross-disciplinary partnerships are essential. Lastly, the future of data management being cloud-native will continue on an ongoing basis with the majority of the developments being driven by advancements in artificial intelligence and machine learning. Leveraging AI tools within data management systems has the potential to greatly enhance automation processes to help organizations gain insights sooner. Nevertheless, such integration should be done carefully to help prevent algorithmic bias and misinterpretation of data. Ongoing research and appraisals, suggested by Yogesh et al. (2023) and Souza et al. (2020), are essential to understanding these problems and designing frameworks that optimize ethical and effective usage of information. In the end, cloud-native data management is a success or failure depending on organizations' commitment to building not only technological competence but ethical practices that are part of a broader social responsibility in the construction of digital futures.

Within the realm of cloud-native data management, several crucial aspects prevail that highlight its significance to modern businesses. The paradigm shift to cloud-native approaches allows companies to adopt scalable and elastic data architectures that lead towards operational effectiveness. Decoupling processing from data storage is the central idea behind this paradigm and hence brings with it more flexibility towards handling data. This flexibility is particularly important in an age where organizations are increasingly reliant on real-time analytics to guide decision-making processes. Secondly, bundling cloud-native solutions generally results in reduced costs and fewer overheads on infrastructure, providing a compelling business rationale for organizations to streamline their data management processes while embracing innovation and technological advancements. Another important characteristic of cloud-native data management is that it integrates seamlessly with next-generation technologies, such as artificial intelligence and machine learning. These technologies can effectively analyze massive volumes of real-time data generated, thus allowing companies to make decisions based on information not previously available. As has been shown by the deployment of revolutionary technologies like ChatGPT, cloud-native systems can utilize artificial intelligence to enhance productivity across a range of industries like marketing and information technology. With these advantages, though, also comes the necessity of addressing the ethical consequences and challenge of generative AI in the form of bias, disinformation, and potentially being privacy-violating. This dual focus on opportunity and challenge is a key part of the dialogue surrounding cloud-native data management. Finally, the implications of cloud-native data management extend beyond operational efficiencies and impact organizational culture and personnel dynamics as well. As companies adopt these next-generation principles, they must ensure their employees are adequately trained with the skills necessary to deal with evolving technologies. This aligns with the bigger vision of digital transformation, as enterprises look to integrate generative AI and cloud-based technologies into their infrastructures. The future of work involves not just the creation of technical competency but also a deep sense of ethics and openness of data usage. Thus, the cloud-native data management landscape is dynamic and continually evolving, and there has to be a focus on where technology, ethics, and workforce readiness intersect, ensuring that organizations are able to effectively navigate the complex issues of the digital era.

REFERENCES

1. Akinade, A. O., Adepoju, P. A., Ige, A. B., & Afolabi, A. I. (2024). Cloud security challenges and solutions: A review of current best practices. International Journal of Multidisciplinary Research and Growth Evaluation, 6, 26–35. https://doi.org/10.54660/.ijmrge.2025.6.1.26-35 (accessed on 11th September 2025).
2. Aly, M., Franke, M., Kretz, M., et al. (2016). Service oriented interactive media (SOIM) engines enabled by optimized resource sharing. https://core.ac.uk/download/55823013.pdf (accessed on 11th September 2025).
3. Asai, M., Bauerdick, L., Borgland, A., et al. (2015). High Energy Physics Forum for Computational Excellence: Working Group Reports (I. Applications Software II. Software Libraries and Tools III. Systems). https://arxiv.org/abs/1510.08545 (accessed on 11th September 2025).
4. Bohez, S., Daneels, G., De Geyter, M., et al. (2018). The crowd as a cameraman: On-stage display of crowdsourced mobile video at large-scale events. https://core.ac.uk/download/147049977.pdf (accessed on 11th September 2025).
5. Budhwar, P., Chowdhury, S., Wood, G., Aguinis, H., Bamber, G. J., Beltran, J. R., Boselie, P., et al. (2023). Human resource management in the age of generative artificial intelligence: Perspectives and research directions on ChatGPT. Human Resource Management Journal, 33, 606–659. https://doi.org/10.1111/1748-8583.12524 (accessed on 11th September 2025).
6. Dwivedi, Y. K., Hughes, L., Baabdullah, A. M., Ribeiro-Navarrete, S., Giannakis, M., Al-Debei, M. M., Dennehy, D., et al. (2022). Metaverse beyond the hype: Multidisciplinary perspectives on emerging challenges, opportunities, and agenda for research, practice and policy. International Journal of Information Management, 66, 102542–102542. https://doi.org/10.1016/j.ijinfomgt.2022.102542 (accessed on 11th September 2025).
7. Dwivedi, Y. K., Kshetri, N., Hughes, L., Slade, E., Jeyaraj, A., Kar, A. K., Baabdullah, A. M., et al. (2023). Opinion paper: "So what if ChatGPT wrote it?" Multidisciplinary perspectives on opportunities, challenges and implications of generative conversational AI for research, practice and policy. International Journal of Information Management, 71, 102642–102642. https://doi.org/10.1016/j.ijinfomgt.2023.102642 (accessed on 11th September 2025).
8. Dwivedi, Y. K., Kshetri, N., Hughes, L., Slade, E., Jeyaraj, A., Kar, A. K., Baabdullah, A. M., et al. (2023). Opinion paper: "So what if ChatGPT wrote it?" Multidisciplinary perspectives on opportunities, challenges and

implications of generative conversational AI for research, practice and policy. International Journal of Information Management, 71, 102642–102642. https://doi.org/10.1016/j.ijinfomgt.2023.102642 (accessed on 11th September 2025).

9. Gangwani, N. (2024). Serverless computing in the edge-cloud continuum: Challenges, opportunities, and a novel framework. International Journal of Scientific Research in Computer Science Engineering and Information Technology, 10, 337–344. https://doi.org/10.32628/cseit241051010 (accessed on 11th September 2025).

10. Hai, R., Koutras, C., Quix, C., & Jarke, M. (2023). Data lakes: A survey of functions and systems. IEEE Transactions on Knowledge and Data Engineering, 35, 12571–12590. https://doi.org/10.1109/tkde.2023.3270101 (accessed on 11th September 2025).

11. Intergovernmental Panel on Climate Change. (2023). Climate Change 2022–Impacts, Adaptation and Vulnerability. https://doi.org/10.1017/9781009325844 (accessed on 11th September 2025).

12. Ionescu, S. A., & Diaconița, V. (2023). Transforming financial decision-making: The interplay of AI, cloud computing and advanced data management technologies. International Journal of Computers Communications & Control, 18. https://doi.org/10.15837/ijccc.2023.6.5735 (accessed on 11th September 2025).

13. Jayasuriya Kuranage, M. P., Nuaymi, L., Bouabdallah, A., Ferrandiz, T., & Bertin, P. (2022). Deep learning-based resource forecasting for 5G core network scaling in Kubernetes environment. https://doi.org/10.1109/netsoft54395.2022.9844056 (accessed on 11th September 2025).

14. Katal, A., Dahiya, S., & Choudhury, T. (2022). Energy efficiency in cloud computing data centers: A survey on software technologies. Cluster Computing, 26, 1845–1875. https://doi.org/10.1007/s10586-022-03713-0 (accessed on 11th September 2025).

15. Kolev, B., Levchenko, O., Pacitti, E., Valduriez, P., Vilaça, R., Gonçalves, R. C., Jiménez, R., et al. (2018). Parallel polyglot query processing on heterogeneous cloud data stores with LeanXcale. 2021 IEEE International Conference on Big Data (Big Data). https://doi.org/10.1109/bigdata.2018.8622187 (accessed on 11th September 2025).

16. Li, C., Dong, M., Li, J., Xu, G., Chen, X. B., Liu, W., & Ota, K. (2022). Efficient medical big data management with keyword-searchable encryption in Healthchain. IEEE Systems Journal, 16, 5521–5532. https://doi.org/10.1109/jsyst.2022.3173538 (accessed on 11th September 2025).

17. Li, F. (2019). Cloud-native database systems at Alibaba. Proceedings of the VLDB Endowment, 12, 2263–2272. https://doi.org/10.14778/3352063.3352141 (accessed on 11th September 2025).
18. N/A. (2023). 2023 Alzheimer's disease facts and figures. Alzheimer's & Dementia, 19, 1598–1695. https://doi.org/10.1002/alz.13016 (accessed on 11th September 2025).
19. Ooi, K. B., Tan, G. W. H., Al-Emran, M., Al-Sharafi, M. A., Căpățînă, A., Chakraborty, A., Dwivedi, Y. K., et al. (2023). The potential of generative artificial intelligence across disciplines: Perspectives and future directions. Journal of Computer Information Systems. https://doi.org/10.1080/08874417.2023.2261010 (accessed on 11th September 2025).
20. Oyeniran, O. C., Adewusi, A. O., Adeleke, A. G., Akwawa, L. A., & Azubuko, C. F. (2024). Microservices architecture in cloud-native applications: Design patterns and scalability. Computer Science & IT Research Journal, 5, 2107–2124. https://doi.org/10.51594/csitrj.v5i9.1554 (accessed on 11th September 2025).
21. Öztoprak, K., Tuncel, Y. K., & Butun, İ. (2023). Technological transformation of telco operators towards seamless IoT edge-cloud continuum. Sensors, 23, 1004–1004. https://doi.org/10.3390/s23021004 (accessed on 11th September 2025).
22. Ruparelia, N. B. (2023). Cloud Computing. The MIT Press eBooks. https://doi.org/10.7551/mitpress/14821.001.0001 (accessed on 11th September 2025).
23. Samira, Z., Weldegeorgise, Y. W., Osundare, O. S., Ekpobimi, H. O., & Kandekere, R. C. (2024). API management and cloud integration model for SMEs. Magna Scientia Advanced Research and Reviews, 12, 078–099. https://doi.org/10.30574/msarr.2024.12.1.0148 (accessed on 11th September 2025).
24. Samira, Z., Weldegeorgise, Y. W., Osundare, O. S., Ekpobimi, H. O., & Kandekere, R. C. (2024). API management and cloud integration model for SMEs. Magna Scientia Advanced Research and Reviews, 12, 078–099. https://doi.org/10.30574/msarr.2024.12.1.0148 (accessed on 11th September 2025).
25. Schildt, H. (2022). The institutional logic of digitalization. Research in the Sociology of Organizations. https://doi.org/10.1108/s0733-558x20220000083010 (accessed on 11th September 2025).
26. Souza, C., Shimbo, J. Z., Rosa, M. R., Parente, L., Alencar, A., Rudorff, B. F. T., Hasenack, H., et al. (2020). Reconstructing three decades of land

use and land cover changes in Brazilian biomes with Landsat archive and Earth Engine. Remote Sensing, 12, 2735–2735. https://doi.org/10.3390/rs12172735 (accessed on 11th September 2025).

27. Tirupati, K. K., Mahadik, S., Khair, M. A., Goel, O., & Jain, A. (2022). Optimizing machine learning models for predictive analytics in cloud environments. International Journal for Research Publication and Seminars, 13, 611–642. https://doi.org/10.36676/jrps.v13.i5.1530 (accessed on 11th September 2025).

28. Walia, C. (2023). Mastering Cloud-Native Microservices. BPB Publications. https://play.google.com/store/books/details?id=jv3EEAAAQBAJ&source=gbs_api (accessed on 11th September 2025).

29. Wang, C. X., You, X., Gao, X., Zhu, X., Li, Z., Zhang, C., Wang, H., et al. (2023). On the road to 6G: Visions, requirements, key technologies, and testbeds. IEEE Communications Surveys & Tutorials, 25, 905–974. https://doi.org/10.1109/comst.2023.3249835 (accessed on 11th September 2025).

30. Wang, Y., Su, Z., Zhang, N., Xing, R., Liu, D., Luan, T. H., & Shen, X. (2022). A survey on metaverse: Fundamentals, security, and privacy. IEEE Communications Surveys & Tutorials, 25, 319–352. https://doi.org/10.1109/comst.2022.3202047 (accessed on 11th September 2025).

31. Zeb, S., Rathore, M. A., Mahmood, A., Hassan, S. A., Kim, J., & Gidlund, M. (2021). Edge intelligence in softwarized 6G: Deep learning-enabled network traffic predictions. 2022 IEEE Globecom Workshops (GC Wkshps). https://doi.org/10.1109/gcwkshps52748.2021.9682131 (accessed on 11th September 2025).

CHAPTER 6

DEVOPS AND CI/CD PIPELINES

Contents

INTRODUCTION

With the accelerating pace of technology in the current era of digitization, software development and deployment have become increasingly complex. Organizations are compelled to adopt practices that not only facilitate quicker release cycles but also align development and operations teams. DevOps, a set of practices bridging the divide between the two worlds, has become an integral framework to deliver quality software on a regular basis. Under this program,

CI/CD pipelines are important components that enable teams to automate the process of software development stages, from the actual coding to the final deployment. Because of the speed and efficiency that is needed, understanding the principles and best practices around CI/CD pipelines is necessary for organizations that intend to remain competitive in the market. However, when businesses implement CI/CD pipelines to automate their deployments, they need to also confront the native security risks around such high-speed development methodologies. Cyber attacks have come a long way, hitting software supply chains and revealing weaknesses in the CI/CD ecosystems. As established by recent reports, integrating security into CI/CD methodologies is no longer an option but a necessary requirement. Application of supply chain security best practice, such as provenance metadata, is essential to ensure the integrity and authenticity of the software being deployed. This intersection of security and DevOps innovation points to an essential challenge that practitioners must navigate through, the need to adopt a global mindset that includes security as part of the full development lifecycle. In an attempt to meet the real potential of CI/CD pipelines regarding complexity and security issues, organizations must adopt standardized platforms and robust architectural systems. This is achieved by optimizing CI/CD workflows, particularly in multi-cloud platforms such as AWS and Azure, as organizations have a tendency to utilize various cloud solutions to meet their operational needs. Interoperability between numerous tools and technologies not only makes deployment simpler but also enhances monitoring and security controls. By the practice of end-to-end deployment best practices and interoperability, businesses are able to achieve significant reductions in deployment speed, cost, as well as infrastructure reliability. As evidenced through recent studies, optimizing these processes leads to reduced operational complexity as well as resource optimization, ultimately converting into effective DevOps culture that is extremely responsive and resilient in a uncertain digital landscape.

Definition of DevOps

The DevOps definition refers to a particular cultural and professional evolution in software development and IT operations toward more collaboration and efficiency. DevOps seeks to merge development (Dev) and operations (Ops) teams to enable flows and engendered common responsibility to deliver software and operate infrastructure. It centers on the desire to eliminate the silos that historically have hindered cross-functional collaboration. By encouraging a shared goals and continuity culture between teams, DevOps enables organizations to deliver more quality software at higher velocity. For CI/CD pipelines, DevOps supplies the structural foundation necessary to facilitate seamless automation and improve iterative development cycles, strengthening the ideal that collaboration enhances the software lifecycle. Additionally, the implementation of DevOps is just as much about tools and processes as it is cultivating a change culture and innovation.

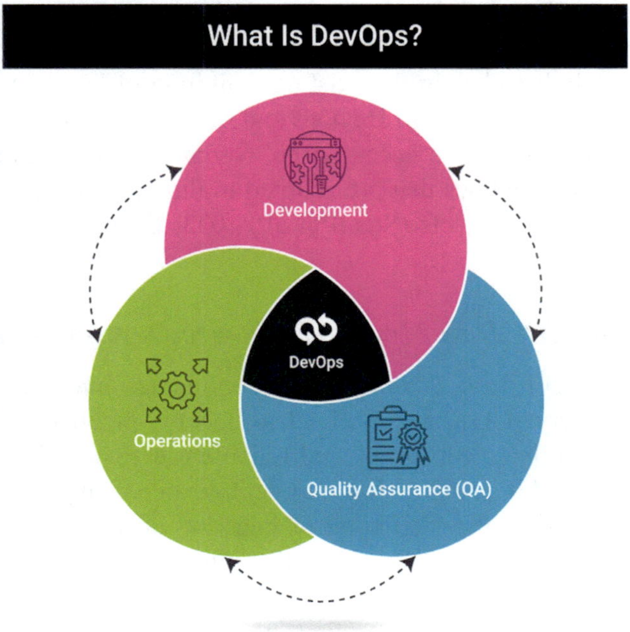

Figure 6.1. *The definition of DevOps.*

Source: https://zd-brightspot.s3.us-east-1.amazonaws.com/wp-content/uploads/2021/08/10123612/DevOps-Philosophy.png.

This is where the value of CI/CD can be realized, as these practices embody the spirit of DevOps in enabling teams to deploy code more reliably and with more confidence. CI/CD pipelines integrate and test automatically, enabling quick feedback loops. Therefore, these pipelines facilitate the identification and fixing of software bugs early during development, hence improving quality as a whole and risk mitigation. The DevOps and CI/CD intersection emphasizes the need for end-to-end methodologies that encompass best practices in automation, monitoring, and collaboration throughout the software development life cycle to ensure dynamic and effective response to changing customer needs. Besides, applying DevOps presents particular challenges in the instance of Machine Learning Operations (MLOps), which extends the practice of DevOps to include machine learning pipelines. Companies are likely to experience difficulties in automating and deploying Machine Learning models into production, leading to failed projects and unfulfilled expectations. MLOps seeks to address these issues through integrating the most effective practices from DevOps implementation and domain-specific ML processes, establishing an environment amenable to rapid experimentation and incremental optimizations. A close examination of MLOps offers the necessary principles and components for integration success, ultimately broadening the existing definition of DevOps. Through an understanding of the subtleties of DevOps and MLOps, organizations can more effectively assemble the tools necessary to overcome challenges and develop streamlined CI/CD pipelines that are adapted to the sophisticated needs of AI and machine learning projects (Steidl et al., 2023; Kreuzberger et al., 2023) (Figure 6.1).

Importance of CI/CD in Modern Software Development

In contemporary software development, Continuous Integration (CI) and Continuous Delivery (CD) have evolved to become practices which cannot be done without in the event of fast and reliable processes. Their application is such that they enable teams to test and deploy code changes automatically, which not only reduces the likelihood of bugs but also accelerates the cycle of feedback. In a CI/CD pipeline, code is continuously merged into a central repository, which enables one to detect integration issues in real-time. This iterative process promotes collaborative interaction between team members and guarantees that software is continually aligned to satisfy user demands. Minimizing the time invested in manual testing and deployment enables development teams to work more time on innovation, thereby developing a more agile reaction to pressure from the marketplace. Moreover, application of CI/CD practices guarantees ease of integration with the DevOps practices, resulting in enhanced productivity and streamlined workflow. CI/CD breaks down the silos long inherent in software engineering and operations and thereby builds a culture of collaboration and joint responsibility among members. Such coming together has the potential to shorten the deployment turnaround time for features and fixes. With greater development velocity, however, comes to the forefront the need to incorporate security controls into these processes. As discussed in existing studies, organizations need to address issues such as vulnerability management and compliance in high-speed DevOps practices, and that points to the significance of adopting CI/CD pipelines not only in terms of efficiency but security too (Tatineni, 2023). Addressing the issues of security in CI/CD is of top priority, especially as software becomes more inclined towards cloud-native environments. With the growing rise of distributed infrastructures, cloud-native services bring new cybersecurity challenges, and it is therefore imperative to highlight security in the CI/CD pipeline. The necessity for robust security solutions comes to the forefront with the extensive array of threats that cloud-native architectures are vulnerable to, ranging from malware and DDoS to others. With the inclusion of security controls throughout the entire CI/CD pipeline, organizations can more effectively address these risks. This forward-thinking approach ensures that security is not an afterthought but an integral part of the development process, further strengthening the software deployment process (Θεόδωρος et al., 2023). At its core, with CI/CD shaping software development today, the requirement for an active security strategy can't be stressed enough.

6.1. THE EVOLUTION OF DEVOPS

DevOps evolution has been marked by a distinct shift from traditional software development methodologies towards more integrated and collaborative approaches that emphasize cross-functional collaboration. Initially, the operations and development teams operated in isolation, and it led to inefficiencies and sluggish delivery of the software. The implementation of Agile methodologies provided a more collaborative environment within the development team but did not bridge the gap with operations. This gap influenced the need for DevOps as a unified practice that unites development, quality assurance, and operations. Through the encouragement of mutual responsibility, DevOps produces quicker iterations and an increased software delivery cycle, thereby aligning with the emerging need for rapid deployment in today's quick-paced digital environment. As DevOps evolved, embracing Continuous Integration and Continuous Deployment (CI/CD) pipelines became the center of attention in streamlining software development. CI/CD practices automate key phases of testing and deployment, reducing the time it takes for code changes to reach production. Automation reduces human errors and increases code reliability, thus boosting overall productivity. The utilization of CI/CD pipelines is in keeping with the DevOps principle of establishing a culture of experimentation and ongoing improvement, enabling teams to deploy smaller, more regular updates that have less risk. Furthermore, CI/CD's incremental methodology is in keeping with the foundations of Agiles, further ensuring the status of DevOps as a front-runner in current software development processes, as businesses aim to bring high-quality products to market more rapidly. The union of AI and Machine Learning with DevOps practices is a revolution in the development evolution of the same. By implementing AI-driven workflows as part of CI/CD pipelines, organizations can enhance efficiency and productivity and address difficult problems in software development. For instance, through the use of machine learning algorithms, possible vulnerabilities or performance problems may be anticipated, and teams may handle risks ahead of time. Moreover, AI solutions provide automated threat detection and incident management, thus integrating security components naturally into the development lifecycle. As organizations adopt such innovative solutions, they also have ethical considerations regarding algorithm transparency and privacy of personal data. By leveraging the insights of new studies, it is evident that strategic use of AI in DevOps can facilitate not only the agility and efficiency of software release but also help companies maintain competitiveness within an accelerating market landscape, evidenced from the findings of Dhruvitkumar (2025) and Camacho (2024) (Figure 6.2).

Figure 6.2. *The evolution of DevOps.*

Source: https://intellimindz.com/wp-content/uploads/2023/10/6.-Evolution-of-Devops.webp.

6.1.1. Historical Context of Software Development Practices

Historical settings requiring methodology and collaboration model shifts have supported the evolution of software development practices in an essential capacity. The late 1950s and the 1960s saw the peak of classic waterfall models, which were purely linear and progressive via very structured phases of building. This was often resisted in permitting changes or feedback integration, considering that the design and coding were sequentially rigid. As systems grew more complex, there was growing awareness of the need for more flexible frameworks. This revolution gave way to agile methods at the turn of the late 1990s, which encouraged iterative development, open participation of stakeholders, and flexibility to fit changing requirements, an era of change in software development methodologies. The emergence of agile techniques brought about a paradigm shift in software development by changing the process of how design and implementation are developed by teams. The agile techniques, such as Scrum and Extreme Programming, emerged as a response to the limiting traditional techniques with an emphasis on collaboration, iterative planning, and quick delivery of working software. With increasing emphasis on delivering high-quality software within compressed time frames, the practices became ingrained with the evolution of automation tools. The evolution of Continuous Integration (CI) and Continuous Delivery (CD) solutions was a part of this shift, enabling development and operations to easily shift from one to the other through the facilitation of frequent integration of code changes and automated tests. As these paradigms evolved, they gave rise to the DevOps phenomenon, which sought to bridge the divide between development and operations and ushering in an enhanced software delivery strategy that was more unified and in response to user needs and technical subtleties. Looking at the trajectory of past advances leading to the current practices presents forefront the role of cooperation and automation as the twin pillars of contemporary software engineering. The emphasis on performance-aware practices, particularly in cloud and big data environments, indicates a growing need to integrate performance engineering into DevOps practices, as highlighted in more recent seminars aimed at fostering inter-disciplinary collaboration (Jamshidi et al., 2017). Besides, the implementation of automation tools such as Jenkins and Docker has given processes efficiencies through the reduction of manual efforts and the shortening of deployment cycles, hence enhancing efficiency and reliability in software delivery systems (Aiyenitaju et al., 2024). Such historical background enriches our body of knowledge regarding DevOps and CI/CD pipelines, showing how historical innovations inform contemporary practices and pave the way for future innovations in software development.

6.1.2. Key Milestones in the Development of DevOps

The evolution of DevOps has been marked by a succession of significant milestones that have signaled its growing significance in software development. The term “DevOps” entered usage around 2009 as a response to the cultural and operational challenges presented by siloed work teams. This initial school of thought was predicated on increasing cooperation among operations and development teams, aiming to streamline processes and condense software delivery timelines. The development of Agile methods played a central role within this endeavor, accentuating iterative software development and customer feedback. When businesses began adopting Agile methodologies, they felt the need for an end-to-end approach including all stages of software development, and hence the first formal DevOps events such as the DevOps Days of 2010. This marked a drastic shift towards innovation through collaboration and more open lines of communication among stakeholders of the software life cycle. With the principles of DevOps becoming increasingly popular, automation was the central theme, introducing a new revolution in the software development cycle. With the advent of Continuous Integration (CI) and Continuous Deployment (CD) techniques, how teams operated actually saw a significant change. This paved the way for Infrastructure as Code being implemented, which allowed teams to automate provisioning and configuring resources, thereby making the process more streamlined and reducing human intervention errors.

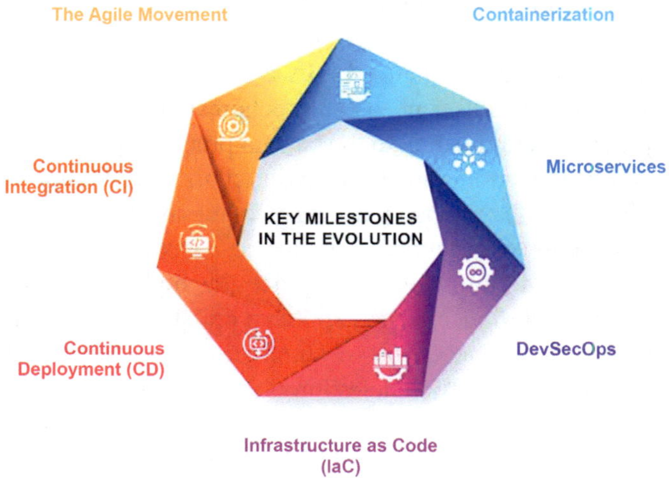

Figure 6.3. *Key milestones in the development of DevOps.*

Source: https://media.licdn.com/dms/image/v2/D5612AQG_q1UKqAZ7xg/article-inline_image-shrink_1500_2232/article-inline_image-shrink_1500_2232/0/1695363344853?e=1761177600&v=beta&t=hcTXfpEIV9C8Q44uyRaE06pBCeC1daFq7ppkaH_qymA.

The integration of CI/CD pipelines into DevOps practices not only accelerated software delivery speed but also product quality delivered. These paradigms became core to the DevOps process because they created a more responsive and agile software development environment. Consequently, more interest in automating CI/CD pipelines has led to extensive scholarly work and industrial application of standardized software to make these processes more efficient (Tonnarelli et al., 2023). Another major advancement in the evolution of DevOps is the creation of MLOps, which integrates machine learning operations into the existing system. Since businesses are now more and more adopting machine learning technologies, they understood that data and model management had issues that were not being managed properly by the traditional DevOps practices. It resulted in the development of MLOps as a new collaboration paradigm that combines DevOps ideas with machine learning-specific practices. The resulting pipeline centers on the continuous integration and delivery of machine learning models, thus enabling agility and responsiveness in data-driven applications. Additionally, MLOps has spurred the development of specialized tools that streamline the end-to-end process of machine learning, further magnifying the DevOps ecosystem as well as demonstrating its vibrant characteristics in regard to technological advancements (Bacig, 2024). With such progressive developments, the DevOps framework has emerged as a vital methodology within the modern software development arena (Figure 6.3).

6.1.3. The Role of Agile Methodologies in Shaping DevOps

The intersection of Agile practices is the central element influencing DevOps practices and principles, particularly within Continuous Integration and Continuous Delivery (CI/CD) pipelines. Agile endorses a culture of collaboration, flexibility, and iterative improvement, which aligns perfectly with the fundamental pillars of DevOps. By bridging the communication divide between development and operations teams, Agile practices facilitate the quick recurrence of software features, allowing organizations to quickly respond to user feedback as well as changing market demands. Not only does this quick responsiveness speed up the development process, but it also sensitizes operations to ongoing developmental modifications, thus cutting down on process bottlenecks. With the aim for more team-based workplaces, the Agile principles provide an underlying structure in which teams will be able to work in concert toward common objectives, ultimately making CI/CD pipelines more responsive. Besides this, Agile practices contribute a lot towards making CI/CD pipelines more efficient by emphasizing continuous development along with regular releases. This framework allows for releasing smaller, incremental updates rather than huge, monolithic ones that are prone to errors during deployment. Sprints and prioritization of the backlog in agile facilitate early identification and resolution of problems, leading to the resulting stable production environment. Agile's iterative nature is also complementary to DevOps's intrinsic continuous testing and feedback loops, enabling timely responsiveness to real-time performance feedback. Merging of Agile practices and performance engineering is critical, as highlighted in the recent controversy surrounding performance-savvy DevOps, to maintain software quality in adaptive environments where system performance must be continually monitored and optimized to keep pace with user expectations (Jamshidi et al., 2017). Finally, the adoption of Agile methodologies fortifies the security position of DevOps practices, especially due to the increasing evolutionary speed of software development. Traditional security practices typically falter under agile and fast-paced environments; hence, integrating security within the development cycle, referred to as DevSecOps, has become unavoidable. Agile processes facilitate real-time threat modeling and risk analysis throughout the software lifecycle, allowing teams to detect threats early on and adjust their defenses in response. The use of frameworks such as STRIDE and LINDDUN within Agile environments allows for close threat analysis that can engage security threats without stopping the development process. By incorporating these security frameworks into Agile methodologies, organizations can gain substantial risk mitigation with the agility and efficiency necessary for successful CI/CD operations (Sonar et al., 2025). Not only does this end-to-end strategy fortify the software development process, but it also puts the onus of security squarely on the shoulders of every stakeholder, further solidifying the DevOps collaborative nature.

6.2. UNDERSTANDING CI/CD

The phrase Continuous Integration and Continuous Deployment (CI/CD) is also a mainstay of modern software development practices, particularly with DevOps. CI refers to the process of integrating code updates on a regular basis into a shared repository, where testing is automated to ensure that new additions do not develop any faults in the already set functions. Such integration without pauses promotes collaboration between development teams towards ensuring error detection early and accelerating iteration. Meanwhile, Continuous Deployment extends the integration scope by deploying tested changes into production environments continuously, thereby streamlining the delivery process. Recent studies indicate that organizations applying CI/CD practices realize enhanced software quality and reliability, reflecting its critical role in today's fast-paced digital landscape (Babar et al., 2018). Understanding CI/CD entails the significance of software architecture in enabling these practices to be grasped. When organizations are heading towards Continuous Delivery and Deployment, the software system architecture must be able to handle high-frequency release requirements. Some of these include adopting principles such as microservices, where smaller, independent deployment units can be built, tested, and deployed individually. The implications of such an architecture have wide-reaching effects; a good CI/CD pipeline, for instance, must incorporate resilience and operational aspects to avoid system failure during deployment. As research shows, the inclusion of quality attributes in the software architecting process enables operations-focused architectures that eventually lead to more efficient deployment processes (Babar et al., 2018). In addition, the convergence between performance engineering and DevOps processes enhances the importance of CI/CD. Modern debates among research communities emphasize the relevance of performance-focused DevOps practices to detect and address performance issues throughout the CI/CD process. By including performance metrics at the development stage and run phase, organizations are not only in a position to enhance the performance of their applications, but also address performance anomalies ahead of time, before they affect users. Such an inter-disciplinary strategy sets up a stage for interaction, where teams can share knowledge and correct problems together. As more firms adopt CI/CD pipelines, the concern for performance-awareness is likely to become one of the cornerstones of effective DevOps adoption, underscoring the need for cross-community collaboration in software engineering (Figure 6.4).

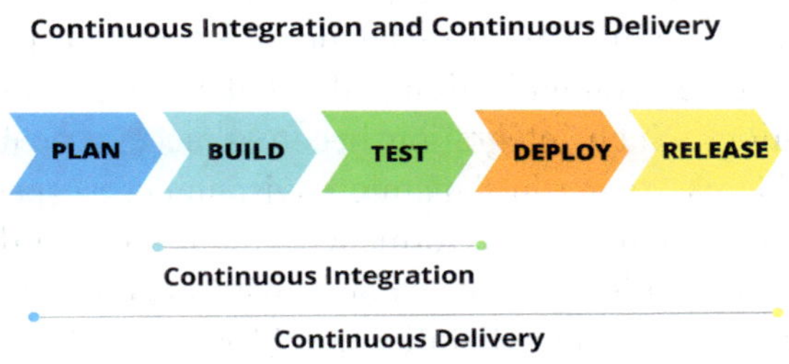

Figure 6.4. *The concept of continuous integration and continuous deployment (CI/CD).*

Source: https://razorops.com/images/blog/Arrow%20Timeline%20Process%20Diagram%20Infographic%20Brainstorm.png.

6.2.1. Definition and Components of Continuous Integration (CI)

Continuous Integration (CI) is a software development practice that emphasizes frequent integration of the code changes in the common repository. Thus, integration errors will be found earlier by the developers, there will be enhanced collaboration, and there will be a stable codebase. CI is powered by the concept of automating the building, testing, and deploying procedures so that teams can easily identify bugs and inconsistencies that may be introduced by new changes. The key components of CI are automated testing, version control systems, and build automation tools. Leveraging these components, development teams can continually test code changes against a baseline, making it easier to progress to subsequent stages of the CI/CD pipeline. This well-structured process not only enhances the quality of software but also facilitates agile response to changing project requirements. Automated testing is perhaps the most essential part of the CI philosophy, and the reason is that it can verify whether new code inserts flaws into the present system. Unit tests, integration tests, and functional tests execute automatically whenever a commit is made to the repository. With the inclusion of automated tests right at the start of the development cycle, teams create a quality assurance culture and are in a position to detect issues that would otherwise hinder deployment schedules. Moreover, as the complexity of software architecture increases, so does the requirement for an effective testing strategy. As recent studies discover, designing applications to enable Continuous Delivery (CD) demands adequate planning regarding quality properties, and for this reason, the integration of automated testing within CI practices is essential (Babar et al., 2018), hence enhancing the overall resiliency of software delivery. Coordination of CI practices within a DevOps culture also demands adequate communication and collaboration among development teams and operations. Such integration becomes necessary for dealing with performance problems arising in dynamic environments, especially for cloud and big data systems. Analyzing performance irregularities at the development and deployment stages allows teams to anticipate operational issues that can otherwise compromise system reliability. Besides, cross-disciplinary seminar talks have highlighted the need for ongoing communication between software and performance engineering communities, paving the way for performance-centric DevOps practices (Jamshidi et al., 2017). This cross-communication enables development teams to construct robustly designed systems that not only deliver functionality but also excel in terms of performance, yielding a holistic view of software quality that is vital in the current competitive world.

6.2.2. Definition and components of Continuous Deployment (CD)

CD is one of the DevOps key practices with automated software change deployment to production without human interference. The practice tries to minimize the cycle time from code change to deployment in a bid to foster an environment where software can be delivered rapidly and reliably. Essentially, CD unifies various tools and processes where CI can be converted to deployment pipelines. This seamless conversion allows developers to focus on coding while automatic testing and deployment procedures handle the complexities of code verification and release (Babar et al., 2018). With automation of these processes, organizations can experience faster feedback loops, enhance the synergy between development and operations teams, and reduce the chances of introducing bugs into the production environment. The aspects of Continuous Deployment entail several key aspects, which in combination make it work. First and foremost, version control systems are a fundamental part of version control and collaboration among developers.

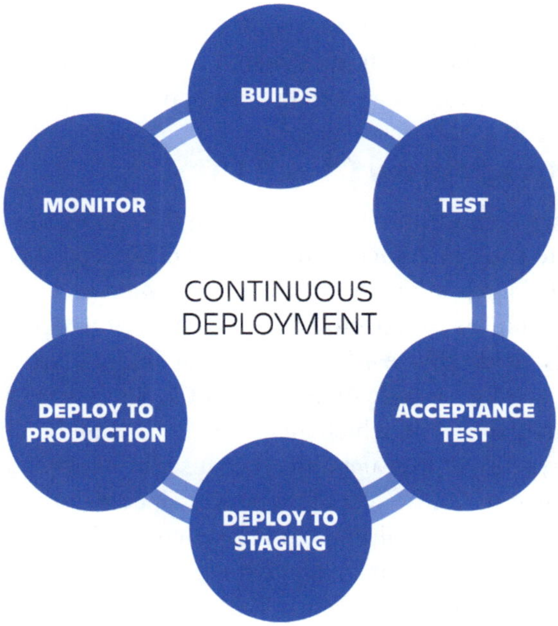

Figure 6.5. *Definition and components of continuous deployment (CD).*

Source: https://wac-cdn.atlassian.com/dam/jcr:1ebe6373-ebd0-46f4-9b76-791ea-2be9d56_cd-diagram@2x.png?cdnVersion=2928.

These systems enable teams to track changes, create branches, and merge code in a straightforward manner. Along with version control, test automation plays an important role, such as unit tests, integration tests, and end-to-end testing to ensure new code does not introduce defects (Jamshidi et al., 2017). More importantly, the deployment pipeline itself, including build, test, and release stages, is at the center of CD practices. Adding infrastructure as code (IaC) further enhances CD by allowing teams to provision and administer infrastructure through code so that it becomes reproducible and consistent across environments. To implement Continuous Deployment effectively, organizations must also consider the software system's architecture. How an application is designed has a strong influence on whether it can embrace CD practices effectively. For instance, systems built on microservices are more conducive to CD, allowing teams to deploy in small decoupled pieces of functionality and tackle the complexity risks that come with monolithic applications. Adopting principles such as resiliency and operational efficiency allows teams to structure their systems to support the demands of CD (Babar et al., 2018). The CD iterative methodology not only accelerates the deployment but also requires a shift in culture with teams, enabling them to encourage a culture of collaboration, communication, and shared accountability to drive ongoing improvement in software delivery and operating performance (Figure 6.5).

6.2.3. Differences Between CI and CD

The distinction between Continuous Integration (CI) and Continuous Delivery (CD) is essential to decide the success of DevOps practices. CI primarily focuses on automating the integration in development, wherein code changes from different contributors are merged into a shared repository at regular time intervals. This makes bugs detectable earlier, since each integration is automatically tested, thereby maintaining code quality. With CI, the issues in their code can be easily detected by the team, which gives timely fixes and reduces integration hell, where delays grow exponentially because of unforeseen conflicts or bugs. In the absence of CI, projects fare poorly since merging different codes increases with time and size, ultimately impacting the development cycle and leading to increased deployment cycles. On the contrary, Continuous Delivery enhances the practices of CI by making the software deployable at any time. While CI allows for code integration, CD is concerned with automating the delivery process. This means that after successful integration, code changes are prepared automatically for release to production environments. This feature of CD provides flexibility to deployments such that deployments can be made at any time, giving developers the freedom to deploy changes without much manual effort. Therefore, CD not only reduces the release window but also maximizes the capability of the organizations to respond to market dynamics or user feedback instantaneously. By automating the integration and delivery process, teams are then capable of increasing their deployment frequency in order to stay competitive in an environment that demands responsiveness as well as agility. In the end, uncovering differences between CI and CD reinforces the importance for organizations to adopt the practices collectively towards an efficient DevOps strategy. Whereas CI is tasked with maintaining good code quality and early bug detection, CD takes the process further to enable quick release cycles. This dual approach works to maximize efficiency, minimize downtime, and improve user experience since releases occur effortlessly and successfully. As organizations and businesses embrace digital transformation, it is imperative that one understands and implements both CI and CD to achieve operational excellence and maintain a competitive advantage. Further research on some of the use cases and success factors in CI and CD practices can further clarify their impacts on the success of projects and interactions of teams, which can create next-generation innovations in software development practices.

6.3. BENEFITS OF IMPLEMENTING CI/CD PIPELINES

The use of Continuous Integration and Continuous Delivery (CI/CD) pipelines is an essential innovation in the history of software engineering, particularly under the DevOps framework. It is one of the major benefits of CI/CD pipelines that speed up the software delivery process. Organizations mechanize much of the development lifecycle, and the window of time for code changes to being deployed to production environments is reduced. This high-speed delivery not only speeds up release cycles but also facilitates quicker response to user and market needs. Additionally, incorporating testing into CI/CD practices ensures that issues are identified earlier during the development cycle, which significantly minimizes the chance of bugs reaching the user, thereby enhancing overall product quality and user satisfaction. Consequently, CI/CD pipelines are the cornerstone of agile practices since they facilitate a culture of continuous improvement and innovation (Koneru, 2025). Besides accelerating delivery, CI/CD pipelines facilitate teamwork between development teams, an important aspect in today's complex software ecosystems. Using CI/CD, developers are free to share and integrate their code changes, thus creating better team collaboration and communication. The centralization nature of CI/CD systems makes everyone on the team aware of the status of the projects, creating transparency and accountability. The collaborative environment minimizes the possibilities of miscommunication and code conflicts, leading to an integrated development process. Also, by using standardized tools and workflows, organizations can adopt a standardized operation procedure across various teams, enhancing productivity and reducing operation complexity. Since groups work according to a common pattern, they can give more time to innovation and less time to logistical issues (Patel, 2025). Last but not least, the security benefits of employing CI/CD pipelines cannot be underestimated. While the tremendous advancement in terms of speed and cooperation is a significant benefit, CI/CD environments also have specific security issues, especially associated with software supply chains. Secure practices built into CI/CD pipelines, such as provenance metadata and supply chain security models, are crucial in combating cyber-attacks. Not only do these practices provide depth of security to code being deployed, but they also foster a culture of security awareness among developers. Where teams lock down security in their CI/CD, they will be able to develop more secure applications that are better suited to defend against potential adversarial attacks. Since CI/CD is more integrated into DevOps, emphasis on security best practices is to make sure that the speed of development does not sacrifice reliability and safety, thereby justifying its value in contemporary software engineering (Patel, 2025) (Figure 6.6).

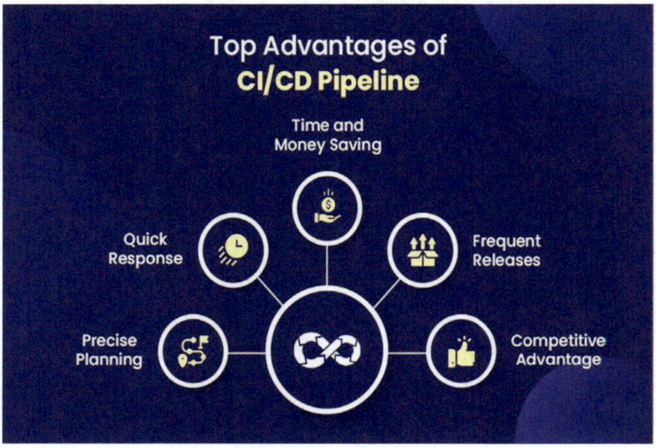

Figure 6.6. *Benefits of implementing CI/CD pipelines.*

Source: https://d2ms8rpfqc4h24.cloudfront.net/top_advantages_of_CICD_pipeline_5cfa073b1d.jpg.

6.3.1. Increased Deployment Frequency

In modern software development, the paradigm shift to DevOps and Continuous Integration/Continuous Deployment (CI/CD) pipelines has significantly enhanced deployment frequency. The rationale behind the shift is the merging of development and operations teams to form collaboration that reduces bottlenecks normally seen in software release cycles. Increased frequency of deployment enables organizations to respond quickly to market demands and customer feedback, making software solutions timely and competitive. In addition to this, organizations adopting this model can take advantage of incremental improvements, which not only make the process simpler but also improve overall software quality being delivered. As seen in recent research, the effect of this higher frequency is not limited to technical measurements, having an impact on organizational culture and operational efficiency too. The correlation between deployment frequency and architecture is a very important element in the context of CI/CD. Empirical evidence shows that software architecture is paramount to allow for frequent deployment, particularly as companies contend with the imperative of agility. New techniques, such as adopting microservices architectures, facilitate developing small, isolated deployment units, hence eschewing the complexity of monolithic systems. These tiny units not only enhance deployment speed but also support continuous delivery practices that deal with resilience and operational challenges in development cycles. New research clarity suggests that firms must strategically plan their architecture to allow for greater deployment rates, realizing that successful deployments usually rely on architected solutions that adhere to CI/CD best practices (Babar et al., 2018). Frequent deployment also brings opportunities for improved measurement of response time and performance for incidents. With more frequent changes released by organizations, they are able to obtain real-time feedback on performance that is utilized to drive future development cycles. This feedback loop is important to the identification of anomalies in performance and optimization of the software product, especially in cloud and big data environments. Empirical evidence indicates that through the establishment of a performance-aware DevOps culture within organizations, monitoring and correcting flaws is more ingrained and leverages learning acquired from operational data to make wise development decisions in the future (Jamshidi et al., 2017). In the end, the resultant cycle of intensified frequency of deployment creates a dynamic environment where software not just grows at a faster pace but does so under a fuller understanding of both user demand and operating optimality.

6.3.2. Improved Software Quality and Reliability

The use of DevOps methodologies, particularly in the form of Continuous Integration and Continuous Deployment (CI/CD) pipelines, has proven to be crucial for enhancing the quality and dependability of software. Software delivery automatically allows organizations to continuously test and observe code changes, significantly reducing the chance for defects to propagate through the system. Updates on regular integration ensure errors are detected early, and quick fixing becomes achievable. Qualitative results of a mixed-methods project show that successful implementation of CD practices demands intentional re-architecting of software systems with a focus on small, independent deployment units in order to mitigate risks associated with monolithic architectures. Such tactical realignment not only streamlines deployments but also helps focus on resilience and operations at the cost of reliability and robustness of software (Babar et al., 2018). Moreover, the convergence of DevOps with performance engineering highlights the importance of preserving software quality during an environment that favors high-speed deployment cycles. Performance anomaly recognition is vital, especially in cloud environments where software has to be dynamic enough to respond to a wide range of operating loads. The seminar's emphasis on understanding what are important performance metrics and getting these reflected back to developers quickly is insightful in this regard. The information shared among researchers is that there is a requirement for an integrated approach in software engineering, performance engineering, and cloud computing in order to improve quality as well as reliability.

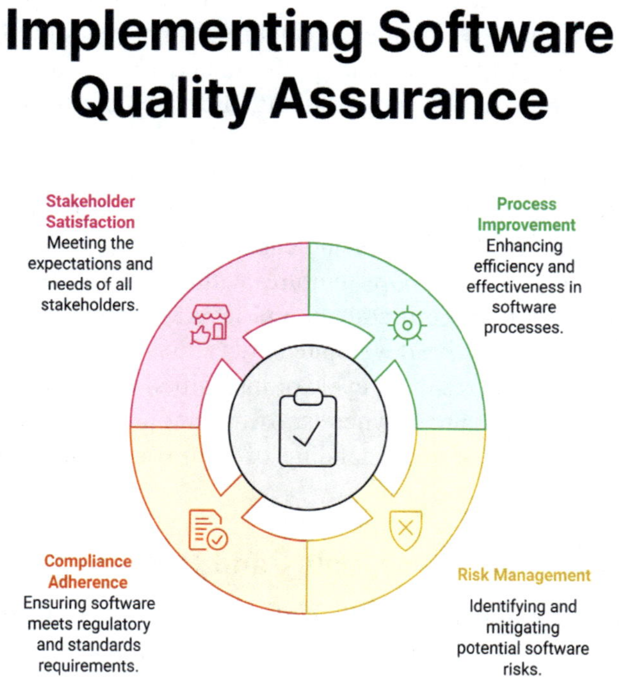

Figure 6.7. *Improved software quality and reliability.*

Source: https://www.6sigma.us/wp-content/uploads/2024/11/implementing-software-quality-assurance-1024x900.webp.

When the companies embrace such approaches, development teams can create solutions that are not just functional but also efficient and maintainable under high-demand scenarios, thus enhancing overall software performance (Jamshidi et al., 2017). Furthermore, the deployment of CI/CD pipelines demands rigorous testing frameworks and constant observation to support software quality. Built-in automated testing processes in pipelines allow teams to validate code modifications systematically. This provides a culture with quality assurance inherent in development and not something added afterward. Through embracing a cultural transformation that gives rise to feedback loops, the developers' culture becomes one of responsibility and continuous improvement. By integrating metrics of quality into development life cycles, organizations achieve higher standards of reliability while reducing downtime and enhancing user satisfaction. Ultimately, the constant upgrading of processes via a DevOps framework ensures software products meet not just user expectations but exceed them through efficiency and reliability (Babar et al., 2018) (Figure 6.7).

6.3.3. Enhanced Collaboration Among Development Teams

In today's software development environment, greater collaboration among development teams presents itself as the pillar upon which effective DevOps and CI/CD pipelines are built. Through such collaboration, there is an open communication culture in which cross-functional teams of developers, operations staff, and quality assurance professionals work more intimately together. Such interaction is essential to establish early on areas that would be problematic during the development process and therefore save time on revisions and corrections down the line. By breaking down silos and enabling teams to work together, organizations are able to leverage different skill sets and perspectives that enable more innovative solutions and an improved level of deliverables. Enhanced collaboration not only creates a sense of shared ownership but also yields accountability, which directly contributes to overall performance toward project objectives. Unifying tools and technologies that support frictionless communication is paramount in enhancing collaboration among development teams. For instance, integrating Azure Bot with tools like Slack offers real-time interaction, which makes it much easier to deal with the complexity of workflow management within DevOps pipelines. Automations offered through such integrations notify teams immediately of modifications, automatically execute tasks, and respond to incidents promptly, thus minimizing interruptions to development. Apart from that, the transparency of these tools ensures that team members regardless of their geographical location are able to work efficiently, fostering a climate conducive to agile principles. More transparency through such channels also helps facilitate quicker feedback loops, an imperative when it comes to iterative development, ultimately birthing a cleaner, more responsive software product. Automation of CI/CD processes cannot be overstressed when it comes to collaboration among distributed development teams. As highlighted by recent studies, the application of automation tools automates continuous integration and delivery processes to achieve significant testing and deployment time reductions as well as better system stability and overall quality of the product (Jeeri, 2025). Correct automation not only lowers human error but also forms a stable environment that facilitates continuous workflow among scattered teams. This is particularly important because organizations increasingly adopt distant working practices, which can stimulate synchronization and communication challenges. Through focus on the basis of CI/CD pipeline automation, development teams can implement a good foundation that supports collaboration, i.e., intentional integration of technology is a critical factor in overcoming challenges caused by today's distributed environments.

6.4. TOOLS AND TECHNOLOGIES FOR CI/CD

Implementation of the CI/CD pipeline highly relies on a collection of sophisticated tools and technologies that enable efficient software development and deployment. Among the principal tools utilized in the CI/CD pipelines are version control systems, build servers, and test automation frameworks. Version control systems like Git are core to the team's workflow as they allow teams to track code modifications, work in harmony, and keep track of the entire project history. Build servers like Jenkins and CircleCI automate code compilation and testing, enabling rapid feedback on the code quality. Automated testing environments check that whatever changes are happening in the codebase do not bring in new bugs, hence keeping the software reliable. With the addition of these tools, organizations are able to automate their development cycles, permitting rapid and reliable releases of updates and new features within their software products. Even more, the landscape of CI/CD tools has expanded leaps and bounds with the advent of cloud technologies, further simplifying deployment strategies. AWS and Azure, for example, offer plug-and-play CI/CD services, simplifying automation of deployment processes. Based on recent studies, companies face substantial challenges handling CI/CD processes across different cloud infrastructures, including AWS and Azure. Such challenges should be addressed by adopting standardized CI/CD platforms, Infrastructure as Code (IaC), and full-fledged monitoring tools to ensure successful deployment. This integration destroys not just the complexity of handling multiple cloud services but also encourages scalability, security, and cost savings. The effectiveness in utilizing CI/CD pipelines through cloud technology is evident from case studies that show higher rates of deployment and significant cost reductions, which point to the significant role such tools play in the modern software development environment (Koneru, 2025). Finally, the integration of versioning tools like GitHub with DevOps practices has changed the way developers manage CI/CD. GitHub is also a core platform for team coding, which allows teams to use features such as GitHub Actions to automate processes with ease. This makes it possible for developers to maintain high software quality while keeping time-to-market in check. Companies that use GitHub together with DevOps practices such as automated testing and agile release cycles enjoy enhanced operational efficiency. Interestingly, metrics like build success ratios and change lead time are metrics of such success, pointing towards the necessity of cooperation and automation. Companies can respond faster to customers' needs and scale their solutions effectively, thus ensuring system integrity. The findings emphasize that the evolution of CI/CD is not just dependent on technological tools but also on establishing a culture of collaborative development and operation teams (Agarwal, 2025) (Figure 6.8).

Figure 6.8. *Tools and technologies for CI/CD.*

Source: https://axify.io/hubfs/20%20Best%20CICD%20Tools%20Features%2C%20Benefits%2C%20and%20Selection%20Tips.webp.

6.4.1. Overview of Popular CI/CD Tools (e.g., Jenkins, GitLab CI)

In DevOps, the CI/CD tools are the masters of automating the software development cycle. Out of all the heavyweight tools available in this field, Jenkins stands out as a powerhouse due to its pluggability and robust community support. Jenkins is an open-source automation server that allows building, testing, and deployment of applications through various plugins.

By enabling teams to manage sophisticated pipelines and connect with many other tools, Jenkins facilitates support for a broad range of programming languages and platforms. This flexibility increases developer collaboration, allowing for faster releases and feedback cycles, which is crucial in today's fast-paced software development environment. CI/CD plugins like Jenkins not only help to automate mundane work but also act as cornerstones in achieving high availability and resiliency needed for modern applications (Naga, 2023). GitLab CI has grown to be a favorite since it is an all-in-one tool that merges the version control system and CI/CD pipelines in a beautiful way. Built into the GitLab system, GitLab CI shares the same repository as code and pipeline definition, which makes it simpler for development teams to work. This internal linkage helps facilitate transparency and responsibility because every modification is tracked and traceable back to corresponding pipeline activity. Secondly, pipeline definition as code enhances reproducibility and reduces the intricacy in managing multiple environments. GitLab CI also includes out-of-the-box monitoring and analytics features, allowing teams to assess software performance and quality in real time. These integrations mark a trend toward more agile software development practices, highlighting the growing importance of CI/CD tools toward fostering collaboration and efficiency in DevOps practices (Asfour et al., 2020). aside from Jenkins and GitLab CI, there are other tools emerging to augment continuous integration and delivery pipelines. CircleCI and Travis CI, for example, provide cloud-based solutions that allow teams to execute automated builds and tests in a very scalable manner. These solutions meet the requirement of obtaining quick feedback with minimal infrastructure overhead, hence making the DevOps process smoother. Moreover, tools like Azure DevOps and Atlassian Bitbucket CI offer smooth integration with project management tools, which further enhances developers' ability to monitor their activities effectively. As more organizations rely on automated processes to maintain the quality of code high and deployment cycles quick, the presence of these services becomes more significant. Lastly, the evolution of CI/CD tools is a reflection of broader industry trends towards automation, config management, and agile practice development, as businesses look to remain competitive in the context of accelerating technological advances and rising customer expectations (Naga, 2023).

6.4.2. Comparison of Cloud-Based vs. on-Premises CI/CD Solutions

In looking at the landscape of Continuous Integration and Continuous Deployment (CI/CD) solutions, there is a stark divergence when comparing cloud-based versus on-premises solutions. Cloud-based CI/CD solutions provide unmatched flexibility and scalability that enable organizations to dynamically resize resources based on varying project demands. This flexibility delivers increased efficiency in deployment schedules, as observed with GitHub-hosted runners whereby convenience is usually more expensive for bigger workflows. Alternatively, on-premises solutions provide enterprises complete control over their infrastructures, something that is essential for companies with strict compliance and data protection requirements.

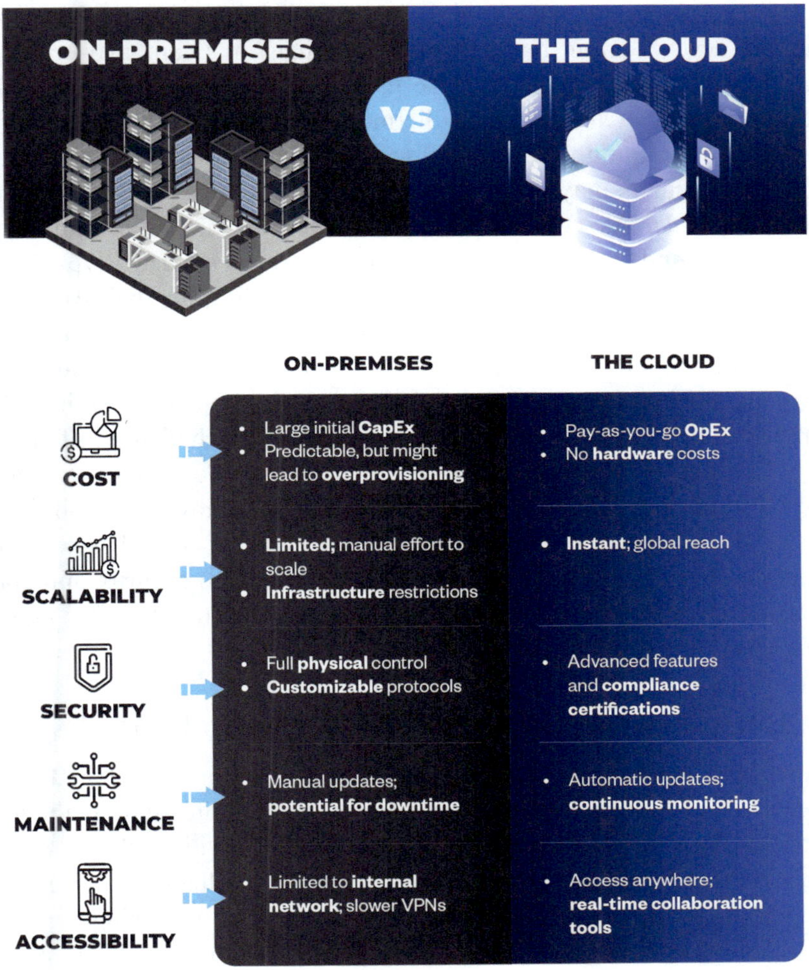

Figure 6.9. *Comparison of cloud-based vs. on-premises CI/CD solutions.*

Source: https://mainstreetitsolutions.com/wp-content/uploads/2025/06/Comparing-On-Premises-Servers.jpg.

As valuable as this control is, however, it exacts a price in maintenance and resource management burdens. It could also jeopardize overall operational efficiency within high-speed development cycles. The cost-related implications of selecting a cloud-based versus on-premises CI/CD solution are significant and multifaceted. While cloud services may be less expensive upfront—typically pay-as-you-go—they have operational expenses that add up quickly in the long run, particularly under heavy usage conditions. Conversely, on-premises typically requires significant one-time investments in hardware and extended operational costs. Current research estimates that firms can save in the long run using self-hosted runners because they can efficiently optimize resource utilization (Kozlov et al., 2025). Furthermore, companies will need to balance cost with need for uptime and security within high-stakes situations, where on-premises data centers may be a compelling choice in areas such as healthcare (Ali et al., 2024). As companies decide about CI/CD, the complexity of implementation and the specific demands of each project need to drive decisions. Cloud-based CI/CD tools are becoming more appealing for their ease of use, ease of deployment, and scalability, especially for teams that do not have large infrastructure support. However, as reported in recent research, Kubernetes-based runners offer a strong argument for demanding projects involving a lot of resource optimization as well as dynamic scaling. The challenges of applying CI/CD solutions in healthcare environments point towards the necessity of hybrid solutions that can leverage both cloud and on-premises capabilities (Ali et al., 2024). Therefore, all organizations need to make a critical assessment of both options, weighing the benefits of scalability against security and control imperatives, in order to arrive at more tailored and effective DevOps practices (Figure 6.9).

6.4.3. Integration of CI/CD Tools with Version Control Systems

The integration of Continuous Deployment and Continuous Integration (CI/CD) software with version control systems (VCS) is an inherent methodology in modern-day software development, particularly within the context of DevOps. Version control systems such as Git facilitate collaboration in software development by allowing different contributors to work on a single codebase while tracking revisions in a clear manner. When combined with CI/CD tools, the integration provides automated deployment and testing cycles that reduce development-to-production time by a significant margin. By automating build, test, and deployment phases, companies can optimize efficiency, deliver better-quality software, and eliminate errors, leading to a more consistent pipeline for software delivery that can support speedy iterations and innovation. Also, such synergy fosters a culture of collaboration where developers do not have to worry about experimenting in case of destabilizing the main branch, thus cultivating an active problem-solving and improvement strategy. Moreover, the effortless correlation of CI/CD tools with version control acts as a catalyst for best practices such as Infrastructure as Code (IaC) that standardizes and automates infrastructure management. This comes in very useful in multi-cloud environments where disparate systems and services have to work in harmony with each other. As more and more organizations adopt multi-cloud deployments for optimal performance and returns on investment, handling disparate resources is too complicated without advanced orchestration tools. Version-controlled CI/CD pipelines enable teams to establish infrastructure requirements alongside application code within the same repository, thus consistency and scalability. The result is not only improved operational efficiency but reduced risk as infrastructure changes can be versioned and tested in the same manner application code is. This end-to-end visibility allows proper compliance and security procedures while allowing agile response to changing business demands, thus improving the organizations overall resilience. Real-world implementation of the integration of CI/CD tools with version control systems sees intense emphasis in the fields of cloud computing and service delivery. Through the usage of GitHub and its CI/CD capabilities, developers are in a position to automate workflows, realizing quicker feedback loops as well as enhanced deployment strategies across environments. Organizations utilizing these capabilities are likely to observe enhanced deployment rates without sacrificing on quality. According to a qualitative case study, performance metrics such as deployment success rates rise significantly with the use of version control combined with CI/CD tools, forcing organizations to react faster to customer demands. These findings underscore the necessity of cultivating a culture that embraces CI/CD practices not as mere technical adjustments but as organizational development initiatives that enable innovation and responsiveness to ultimately enhance the business stance in competitive environments. Such a linkage between CI/CD and version control systems provides a recipe for achievement and sustainability in software development practices, leading industries towards future innovation.

6.5. CHALLENGES IN ADOPTING DEVOPS AND CI/CD

The implementation of DevOps and Continuous Integration/Continuous Deployment (CI/CD) practices is challenged by several issues that organizations have to overcome. To begin with, cultural resistance among teams tends to be a major challenge. This can be due to existing mindsets, where roles and responsibilities have been traditional and can hinder teamwork necessary for DevOps success. Organizations tend to have challenges bringing their development and operations teams on the same page, resulting in disjointed processes and communication issues. The cultural transformation to a DevOps culture demands dynamics changes in team dynamics where the ownership of software delivery is shared. Therefore, constructing a collaborative culture is time-consuming, demanding leadership dedication, and extensive training to familiarize all members with the DevOps philosophy. Besides, the technical complexities involved with the utilization of CI/CD pipelines should not be underestimated.

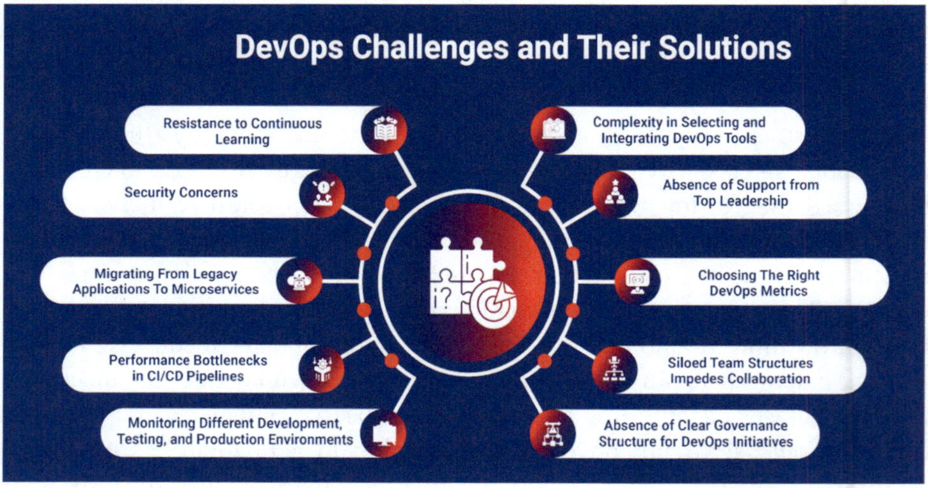

Figure 6.10. *Challenges in adopting DevOps and CI/CD.*

Source: https://www.rishabhsoft.com/wp-content/uploads/2024/06/Top-DevOps-Adoption-Challenges-Image.jpg.

The synergy of newer technologies and tools is critical in the automation of test, build, and deployment activities. However, most organizations lack the proper tools, which are adaptable to their unique environments and needs. Without a suitable framework and architecture supporting these tools, development processes fall apart, as they compromise software quality and speed of delivery. The concept of small and independent deployment units is important here, as indicated by recent research that investigates software architectures contribution to Continuous Delivery (CD). For companies that are embracing CI/CD, it is important to make sure that their software architecture accommodates the same to facilitate successful automation and stable releases (Babar et al., 2018). Lastly, the incorporation of performance engineering concepts into DevOps frameworks brings in greater levels of complexity. While both DevOps and performance engineering are now among the top priority domains, their convergence is yet to be realized in its full potential. It is normally challenging for organizations to fix performance anomalies that may arise in cloud and big data environments during deployment. Aligning operations and development teams to enable monitoring and feedback loops becomes central to success. This interdiscipline collaboration is necessary to create a performance-aware DevOps environment that identifies and responds to performance issues early in the development phase. Accessing research and seminars specific to this intersection can provide valuable information and develop collaborations between software engineering, performance engineering, and cloud computing teams (Jamshidi et al., 2017) (Figure 6.10).

6.5.1. Cultural Resistance Within Organizations

Organizational cultural resistance manifests itself as a main hindrance to DevOps and CI/CD pipeline adoption success. Despite the operational efficiency that these practices ensure, most organizations are faced with entrenched mindsets that prefer working in traditional ways as opposed to novel methods. Frequently, the change resistance is fear-based, particularly from the employees accustomed to ingrained processes. Moving to continuous integration and delivery requires a cultural shift, that is, not just changes in tools but also restructuring team cultural norms. Organizations are hence stuck in a paradox where the anticipated benefits of DevOps are not being realized because of unwilling labor forces that are opposed to new workflows and collaboration among teams that are required for agile development and operations. Furthermore, recent study findings point to the resistance culture as one of the greatest impediments to the adoption of DevSecOps by small and medium enterprises (SMEs). While the majority of the leaders within such companies recognize the necessity of integrating security within their culture of development, the articulated resistance at 38% by respondents indicates that there is greater organizational resistance against it. It is this cultural resistance that is felt most strongly when security practices are perceived to cut across established development cycles. Organizations will have to address these cultural attitudes head-on, establishing a culture that allows experimentation and exposure, one in which members feel comfortable reporting issues without fear of backlash. It is this type of strategy that is key to making the strategic value of DevOps a reality and creating a strong CI/CD pipeline. Effective management of cultural resistance to DevOps requires effective leadership and strategic plans to foster collaboration and new tool adoption. Since more organizations are embracing DevOps practices and CI/CD, the leaders need to set a strong security culture as indicated by research that indicates 73% of leaders think security is crucial in their development workflows. This requires not only training and education but the development of cross-team dynamics that can bridge knowledge gaps and common purposes. With the deployment of best practices such as automated security shields and ongoing feedback loops, businesses can minimize resistance and streamline. Ultimately, cultural resistance recognition and response facilitate a more resilient organization capable of leveraging technological advancements in order to maintain competitive edge amidst a dynamic technological landscape (Cheenepalli et al., 2025; Rongali, 2025).

6.5.2. Technical Complexities and Integration Issues

Part of the deeper aspect of employing DevOps and Continuous Integration/ Continuous Deployment (CI/CD) pipelines is the inherent technical complexity and integration issues that businesses will have to contend with. As infrastructure becomes decentralized, the challenges related to issue-free communication between various microservices increase. These are added upon when combining various tools and platforms that do not natively align for collaboration. Inconsistent versioning, configuration issues, and diverse deployment environments could contribute to long integration cycles, finally undermining the velocity and efficiency that CI/CD pipelines promise to enhance. These issues are addressed by strict standards for standardization and configuration management such that all the components of the pipeline co-operate and do not work in isolation. In addition, incorporation of higher-order technologies like artificial intelligence into CI/CD processes is promising as well as threatening. Using AI can enable predictive maintenance through the detection of potential problems ahead of time before they turn into catastrophic failures, hence improving system robustness. For example, companies are able to use machine learning algorithms to track application performance and ensure that any anomalies are quickly fixed. Nevertheless, as noted in the example of a large retail company, the implementation of AI gets complicated in a microservices architecture with many components needing to coordinate smoothly. An ill-integrated AI solution can lead to alert overload for engineers and frustrate the aims of predictive maintenance, thus the need for careful planning and execution in the integration phase – one made even more complex by available technical complexities that come with CI/CD pipelines (Baswareddy, 2025). In addition to technical integration complexities, security matters also top the list in deciding the overall performance of CI/CD pipelines. While corporations are adopting automation, the automated testing infrastructure (IAT) becomes a vulnerability of high concern. More particularly, the rise of malicious open-source software (OSS) packages and critical vulnerabilities in CI tools further aggravates the threat landscape. To make CI/CD pipelines secure, an amalgamated solution needs to be developed on the basis of many threat vectors that can compromise the software supply chain. Existing studies emphasize the importance of ensuring an end-to-end security mechanism that incorporates continuous monitoring and auditing, as well as cryptographic security to protect artifacts. Incorporating these steps addresses not just the technical complexities of CI/CD but also strengthens the stability and maturity of deployment and development cycles, ultimately safeguarding against future threats (Yevhenii, 2025) (Figure 6.11).

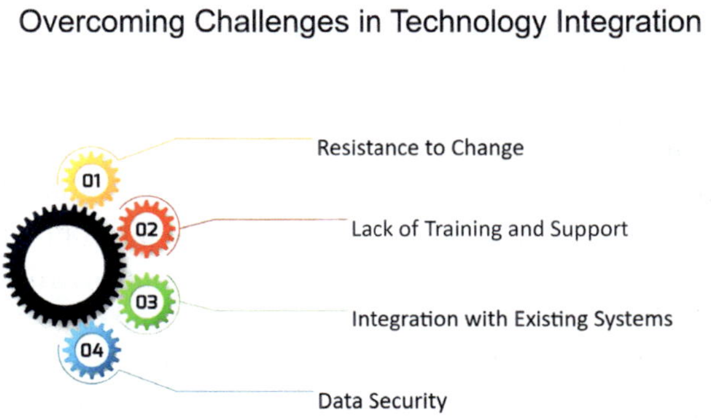

Figure 6.11. *Technical complexities and integration issues.*

Source: https://fastercapital.co/i/Embracing-Technology-Integration--Enhancing-STIF-Operations--Overcoming-Challenges-in-Technology-Integration.webp.

6.5.3. Security Concerns in Automated Deployments

The rapid development of DevOps practices and CI/CD pipelines has indeed transformed software delivery practices significantly but also has amplified security concerns in automated deployment. As more organizations move towards cloud-native CI/CD platforms, vulnerabilities are typically amplified by the intricate relationship between development and operations. This complexity typically leads to gaps in adherence to security processes, which is crucial in a high-level cyber threat environment. The deployment rate and frequency, while good, can often result in speeding up security deficits, and hence the compromise between agility and secure coding needs to be questioned. To overcome this, organizations must ensure that security tests are included in every phase of the CI/CD pipeline in order to safeguard against vulnerabilities that are capable of destroying software integrity and organizational trust (Miriyala et al.,

2025). Moreover, security automation being part of CI/CD pipelines has also become a necessary response to the increasing need for automated deployment. Specifically, policy-as-code and automated security scanning implementations have been essential in providing having robust security postures. Aside from accelerating vulnerability discovery, these practices also help maintain compliance throughout the whole deployment cycle. By incorporating these security controls into deployment workflows, organizations are offered greater visibility and an active defense posture against threats. This dynamic security model allows companies to constantly review their security position for deployments and implement custom risk mitigation controls. This makes development teams able to maintain operational velocity without sacrificing the aggressive security controls needed in today's digital world (Bondalapati et al., 2025). Finally, co-location of development and security teams is critical to solving security problems in automated deployments. Mutualism between the two groups keeps security problems integrated into the cultural DNA of the development process rather than being marginalized as an afterthought. With a holistic approach that balances speed and security, organizations can build an environment where deployment speed does not compromise risk management. Designing such coordination facilitates better vulnerability detection and quicker remediation time, yielding a better workflow that collectively enhances the security of CI/CD practices. Integrating agile techniques with robust security frameworks not only guards against software integrity but also helps in building an organization's overall resilience against relentless cyber attacks in an increasingly automated world (Miriyala et al., 2025; Bondalapati et al., 2025) (Figure 6.12).

Figure 6.12. *Security concerns in automated deployments.*

Source: https://www.workfusion.com/wp-content/uploads/2019/08/data-security-in-automation-1.jpg.

6.6. BEST PRACTICES FOR SUCCESSFUL CI/CD IMPLEMENTATION

A successful deployment of Continuous Integration and Continuous Delivery (CI/CD) relies on sustaining open communication and collaboration across development teams. This entails a shift in culture where openness and open communication among team members are more likely to dominate, essential to the rapid velocity of DevOps. Daily stand-up meetings and frequent code reviews can assist in guaranteeing improved understanding of project status and potential concerns. Furthermore, utilizing collaboration tools becomes easier to communicate in a way that everyone understands as far as the projects goals and timelines are concerned. Through a platform where employees can relax enough to share ideas and talk about problems, organizations can significantly enhance efficiency and innovation in their CI/CD pipeline, leading to an agile and responsive software development process. The evolving interaction between constant feedback and collaboration is the cornerstone upon which CI/CD succeeds, and it is the component driving the overall success of DevOps practice. Merging sound testing methodologies is the second cornerstone of successful CI/CD implementation. Automated testing systems like unit tests, integration tests, and end-to-end tests are key mechanisms by which the code changes will neither add new faults nor cut down functionality. Incorporating these testing steps within the CI/CD pipeline gives immediate feedback that can enable developers to detect and correct problems early on in the development lifecycle. This proactive measure not only reduces the risk of releasing buggy code but also enhances code quality and reliability. It also fosters a culture of collective responsibility for software quality among the team. Emphasizing testing, too, along with immediacy of CI/CD processes places organizations in a good position to act quickly on changing requirements and user feedback, ending up causing more successful product releases (Patel, 2025). Last but not least, building comprehensive monitoring and logging procedures is key to maintaining CI/CD pipelines in effective condition. Real-time monitoring of applications and infrastructure allows teams to see performance problems, security problems, or deployment problems in real-time so diagnosis and resolution can be done quickly. Logging needs to not only catch errors, but also performance statistics and user activity, providing a complete view of application health. In addition, the creation of key performance indicators (KPIs) and the use of analytics tools to gauge these indicators allow teams to qualify the impact of CI/CD efforts on business objectives as a whole. By performing in-depth analysis on this data, businesses can gain insights that enhance the CI/CD process such that not only is deployment frequent, but also consistent. Emphasizing monitoring and logging, therefore, encapsulates an anticipatory strategy for adding security as well as performance to the CI/CD pipeline (Adebayo, 2025).

6.6.1. Establishing a Robust Testing Framework

In DevOps and CI/CD pipelines, a good testing framework plays an essential role in ensuring the quality of software and accelerating delivery. A well-structured testing framework comprises various types of testing like unit, integration, and end-to-end tests, which enable complete verification of the software at every stage of development. This systematic approach, along with early defect detection, also encourages a quality assurance culture throughout teams. By integrating automated testing into the CI/CD pipeline, organizations are able to gain a faster feedback loop, which is essential for rapid iteration and deployment. As has been suggested in some recent conversation in the software performance engineering community, tying testing strategies to performance measures helps bridge the gap between development and operations and make the entire system more reliable and responsive as stated in Jamshidi et al. (2017). Moreover, a solid testing framework should leverage appropriate tools and technologies to the needs of infrastructure and application. Automation is also the core of scaling testing activities, particularly in continuous integration contexts where quick verification of code changes is crucial. Jenkins, Kubernetes, and containerization technologies simplify automating throughout the pipeline.

The smooth integration of these tools not only improves efficiency but also minimizes human error, which translates to significant cost savings in the long run. In addition, the successful implementation of these systems heavily relies on continuous monitoring and real-time feedback mechanisms to ensure functional and non-functional requirements are captured through tests. Understanding these toolsets and their interaction is essential to gaining a high level of test efficiency and reliability, as underscored by observations of automation of DevOps practices (Aiyenitaju et al., 2024). Lastly, establishing a good testing framework is only achievable if there is an organizational commitment to creating a culture of ongoing improvement and tight operation-deployment team collaboration. Training and upskilling team members on optimal testing practices, and encouraging cross-functional collaboration, are essential elements for success. When teams learn the importance of testing and have the right set of skills, they are in a better position to adopt automated processes and add value to the testing framework. Furthermore, infusing performance awareness into test culture can facilitate the identification of performance problems early in the development lifecycle, thereby increasing the robustness of applications deployed on complex environments. Fostering knowledge exchange channels and ongoing learning not only strengthens the test framework but also enhances the inherent DevOps principles, with the ultimate goal of achieving CI/CD pipeline success (Jamshidi et al., 2017) (Figure 6.13).

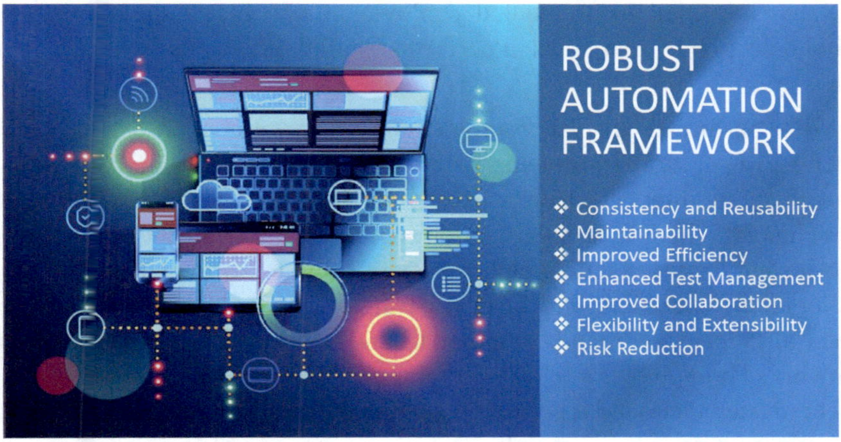

Figure 6.13. *Establishing a robust testing framework.*

Source: https://www.matryxsoft.com/new/wp-content/uploads/2024/08/Framework_New.png.

6.6.2. Automating the Deployment Process

Automated deployment is one of the most important components in the DevOps model, facilitating seamless integration and delivery of software applications. With the advent of microservices architecture, traditional methods of deployment have proved to be insufficient, necessitating a sound, predictable, and scalable process. Automated deployment not only reduces the chances of human errors but also accelerates the release cycles, allowing businesses to deliver operational updates to end-users more quickly. Through the use of continuous integration and continuous deployment (CI/CD) pipelines, teams are able to standardize their workflows, ensuring that any code changes are automatically tested and deployed. Automated testing enhances productivity as a whole and encourages the culture of continuous development amongst development teams. Successful automation of deployment processes further enables smarter resource allocation and risk management. With end-to-end CI/CD pipelines, the whole software life cycle from coding to deployment is tracked by the teams effectively. Insight into the project status facilitates identifying bottlenecks at an early stage, and based on that, proactive reforms are brought about for optimizing resource utilization. Because of this, performance engineering takes the forefront in such a situation, as it bridges the DevOps ecosystem ensuring application reliability and efficiency. The complementarity of performance monitoring software embedded in automated deployment systems is the driving force behind detection of anomalies in performance and thereby optimal deployment strategy.

With performance-aware automation, organizations are better able to respond to operational problems without impairing quality of software. The game-changing impact of automating the deployment phase is not in technical gains alone; it is in mutual collaboration among stakeholders. CI/CD automation offers a shared understanding and consistent communication channels between development, operation, and business teams. This interconnection advances greater alignment to organizational goals and thus enhances collaboration and teamwork. Through research, greater alignment is shown to increase success in project management and a culture of joint responsibility. Additionally, placing emphasis on automation not only streamlines procedures but also elevates the productivity of resource allocation and risk management.

Through faster time-to-market and deployment frequencies, automated deployment practices benefit business stakeholders in terms of achieving a competitive edge amidst the dynamic market environment. In this regard, familiarity with the implementation and upkeep of such automated frameworks is critical in ensuring long-term success and sustainability for software development projects, as offered by Jamshidi et al. (2017) and Vu et al. (2024) (Figure 6.14).

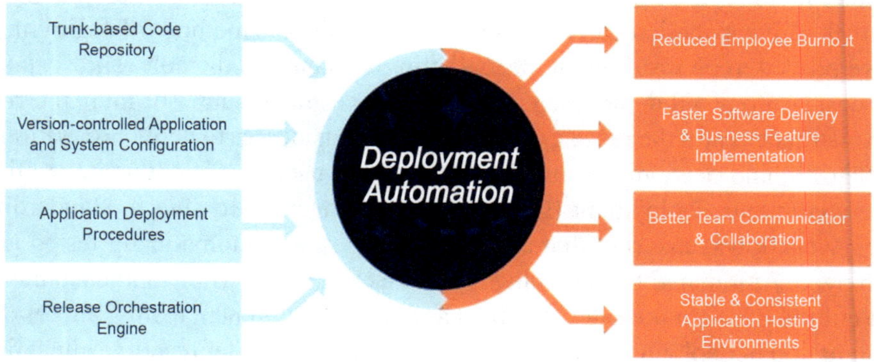

Figure 6.14. *Automating the deployment process.*

Source: https://www.aemcorp.com/hs-fs/hubfs/AEM%20Micro%20website/Devops/Development%20Automation/deployment.jpg?width=650&name=deployment.jpg.

6.6.3. Continuous Monitoring and Feedback Loops

In DevOps and CI/CD pipelines, continuous monitoring is the essential building block that ensures application health and performance throughout its lifecycle. The monitoring allows early identification of any bottlenecks and issues with performance before they would ultimately cause catastrophic failure. Using real-time monitoring tools and solutions, teams can collect vital metrics around application performance, resource consumption, and end-user experience. Real-time monitoring gives development and operations teams the power to act immediately on anomalies, ensuring an uninterrupted user experience. Additionally, the insights provided by constant observation enable data-driven decision-making, foster accountability and a culture of improvement across the development cycle.

The integration of continuous monitoring practices into CI/CD pipelines not only enhances the stability of applications but also contributes to improved resource utilization, eventually contributing to the success of software delivery initiatives as a whole. The feedback loop is a fundamental part of the DevOps system as it enables organizations to learn from their monitoring and enhance their software products in an iterative manner. By generating a feedback loop of learning through performance data and customer feedback, teams are able to identify areas of improvement at every stage of the development pipeline. These feedback loops actually unite development and operations so that both teams can collaborate in addressing issues before they happen and optimizing procedures. To illustrate, incorporating user feedback can lead to actionable information that can be used to drive feature enhancement or bug fixes, hence making software more in line with customer needs. Second, automated feedback tools simplify the collection of feedback such that teams can focus on analysis and not on data collection. Feedback loops thus not only establish a culture of continuous improvement in CI/CD pipelines but also enable the agility of the organization as a whole. Synergism between constant monitoring and feedback loops in DevOps practices is further entrenched on contemplation regarding the inclusion of Site Reliability Engineering (SRE) and Platform Engineering. These two disciplines further enunciate a robust mechanism that connects constant improvement practices and performance awareness, and this has become even more imperative in cloud infrastructures. For instance, performing Service Level Objectives (SLOs) during performance management allows teams to define attainable performance targets, while error budgets provide insight into reliability vs. release velocity trade-offs. The combined effort of DevOps teams and SRE practices ensures that rapid deployment of software is not at the cost of stability. With the increased use of more sophisticated architectures by companies, such as microservices, the addition of continuous monitoring and feedback loops increases the necessity in optimizing the CI/CD pipelines, leading to faster and more reliable software releases, and developing an environment of shared accountability (Jamshidi et al., 2017; Devan, 2022).

SUMMARY

Briefly, the implementation of DevOps culture and CI/CD pipelines has totally transformed the software development environment by making it efficient, collaborative, and dependable to ship software. Organizations that implement these practices are able to react faster to market changes and customer needs and thus become one up from others. It requires a deep understanding of technical as well as organizational dynamics for a transition from traditional development practices to a DevOps culture. This transformation is not only procedural but also cultural and requires all the stakeholders to embrace CI as a natural cycle of development. Establishing a supportive climate for collaboration can significantly maximize the benefits derived from CI/CD strategies and tools. Also, the use of software architecture in making effective CI/CD practices cannot be overstressed. A thoroughly designed pattern for (re-) architecting applications enables organizations to implement Continuous Delivery and Deployment more effectively. Through research, it has been proven that improving software architecture with the idea of small and autonomous deployment units can actually reduce the complexity of monolithic systems. The quality attributes, i.e., resilience and ease of operation, need to be prioritized highly to reinforce the CI/CD process. By adequately managing these architectural pieces, organizations can hold up against the challenges of rapid deployment cycles without compromising high levels of software quality and performance (Babar et al., 2018). Finally, automation is an imperative facilitator in raising the efficiency of DevOps, particularly through tools like Jenkins, Docker, and Kubernetes, which normalize Continuous Integration and Delivery mechanisms. Automation minimizes human interaction tremendously, improves deployment cycles, and facilitates effective interaction between development and operations teams. However, the practitioners should also be conscious and address the challenges that accompany this transformation, including integration problems and potential resistance from the teams. Future research in this field needs to explore new automation approaches, including the application of AI and ML paradigms, to further enhance the efficiency of DevOps processes (Aiyenitaju et al., 2024). With the discovery of the socio-technical impact of automation, organizations can cultivate resilient practices that not only maximize processes but also enhance resilience in software delivery.

REFERENCES

1. Adebayo, A. O. (2025). Securing financial transactions: DevSecOps best practices for banking applications. International Journal of Science and Research Archive. https://www.semanticscholar.org/paper/c5dadb810fcd470e46143bc91fa96d7e901d88d9 (accessed on 11th September 2025).
2. Agarwal, G. (2025). Optimizing cloud deployments using GitHub-driven DevOps and continuous integration. International Journal of Advanced Research in Science, Communication and Technology. https://www.semanticscholar.org/paper/56048ee808c8baeabaf28e4a80826bb1db4c254a (accessed on 11th September 2025).
3. Aiyentaju, K. (2024). The role of automation in DevOps: A study of tools and best practices. https://core.ac.uk/download/638725565.pdf (accessed on 11th September 2025).
4. Ali, Z. (2024). NLPOps: A case study on automation and integration of Norwegian medical entity recognition model in clinical environment. https://core.ac.uk/download/654484785.pdf (accessed on 11th September 2025).
5. Asfour, M. (2020). Desenvolvimento e manutenção de pipelines de integração contínua para aplicativos móveis. https://core.ac.uk/download/344683557.pdf (accessed on 11th September 2025).
6. Babar, M. A., Shahin, M., Zahedi, M., et al. (2018). An empirical study of architecting for continuous delivery and deployment. https://core.ac.uk/download/161850887.pdf (accessed on 11th September 2025).
7. Bacigâl, M. (2024). Design and implementation of machine learning operations. https://core.ac.uk/download/643428419.pdf (accessed on 11th September 2025).
8. Baswareddy, J. P. R. (2025). Intelligent CI/CD pipelines: Leveraging AI for predictive maintenance and incident management. European Journal of Computer Science and Information Technology. https://www.semanticscholar.org/paper/74eebd4bb235d815d9024654316b338978c384e6 (accessed on 11th September 2025).
9. Bondalapati, R., & Malaraju, S. K. (2025). Enhancing secure deployment automation in cloud environments: A risk-driven approach to CI/CD pipelines. European Journal of Computer Science and Information Technology. https://www.semanticscholar.org/paper/40971571f0a1493158443e23d469c5165b3f377e (accessed on 11th September 2025).

10. Camacho, N. (2024). Unlocking the potential of AI/ML in DevSecOps: Effective strategies and optimal practices. Deleted Journal, 2, 79–89 https://doi.org/10.60087/jaigs.v2i1.p89 (accessed on 11th September 2025).
11. Cheenepalli, J., Hastings, J. D., Ahmed, K. M., & Fenner, C. (2025). Advancing DevSecOps in SMEs: Challenges and best practices for secure CI/CD pipelines. 2025 13th International Symposium on Digital Forensics and Security (ISDFS). https://www.semanticscholar.org/paper/773c37d10205113c2b1306fa98827906d2738d15 (accessed on 11th September 2025).
12. Dasari, H. (2025). Infrastructure as code (IaC) best practices for multi-cloud deployments in enterprises. International Journal of Networks and Security. https://www.semanticscholar.org/paper/8ce1d9fe6cafbf32705a232eec0a4dd480677c7d (accessed on 11th September 2025).
13. Devan, K. (2022). Streamlining CI/CD pipelines with DevOps, SRE and platform engineering. https://core.ac.uk/download/654637385.pdf (accessed on 11th September 2025).
14. Ivanchenko, Y. (2025). Security issues in automated testing infrastructure. International Journal of All Research Education and Scientific Methods. https://www.semanticscholar.org/paper/a63150374692439140b807af03cc7cb6bd125c59 (accessed on 11th September 2025).
15. Jamshidi, P., Leitner, P., van Hoorn, A., et al. (2017). Report from GI-Dagstuhl Seminar 16394: Software performance engineering in the DevOps world. https://core.ac.uk/download/pdf/141718346.pdf (accessed on 11th September 2025).
16. Jeeri, K. (2025). Approaches to automating CI/CD processes in distributed teams. The American Journal of Engineering and Technology. https://www.semanticscholar.org/paper/5045407561333212a5846f1a2f515f5b9e695959 (accessed on 11th September 2025).
17. Koneru, N. M. K. (2025). Optimizing CI/CD pipelines for multi-cloud environments: Strategies for AWS and Azure integration. The Eastasouth Journal of Information System and Computer Science. https://www.semanticscholar.org/paper/ea5d97b16eea728ecb56461fa39059cc30258101 (accessed on 11th September 2025).
18. Kozlov, I. (2025). A comparative study of GitHub-hosted, self-hosted, and Kubernetes-based GitHub Runners for web applications GitHub Actions workflows. https://core.ac.uk/download/657101011.pdf (accessed on 11th September 2025).

19. Kreuzberger, D., Kühl, N., & Hirschl, S. (2023). Machine learning operations (MLOps): Overview, definition, and architecture. IEEE Access, 11, 31866–31879. https://doi.org/10.1109/access.2023.3262138 (accessed on 11th September 2025).

20. Lovén, H., Erichsen, R., Tøttrup, A., & Bisgaard, T. (2025). Long-term outcomes after elective inguinal hernia mesh-repair in patients with inflammatory bowel disease. Hernia, 29. https://www.semanticscholar.org/paper/2f8e30d77818408d088e23b423824d9336389e0f (accessed on 11th September 2025).

21. Miriyala, N. S., Bandaru, B. K., Mittal, P., Macha, K. B., Venkat, R., & Rai, A. (2025). Impact of cloud-native CI/CD pipelines on deployment efficiency in enterprise software. International Journal of Computational and Experimental Science and Engineering. https://www.semanticscholar.org/paper/ef5585995c44bb615a3e095aef7a99cbd8a750d4 (accessed on 11th September 2025).

22. Patel, D. G. (2025). Enhancing CI/CD security with provenance metadata and supply chain best practices. World Journal of Advanced Engineering Technology and Sciences. https://www.semanticscholar.org/paper/8d5257ce280b75b90d49d7ef9af31981d9258afb (accessed on 11th September 2025).

23. Rasmussen, N. F., Moos, C., Gregersen, L., Hikmat, Z., Andersen, V., Green, A., Jess, T., et al. (2024). Impact of sex and socioeconomic status on the likelihood of surgery, hospitalization, and use of medications in inflammatory bowel disease: A systematic review and meta-analysis. Systematic Reviews, 13. https://www.semanticscholar.org/paper/a7ceabe073c020eb60b6f3b7797a4aa50dc00964 (accessed on 11th September 2025).

24. Rongali, L. P. (2025). Continuous integration and continuous delivery (CI/CD) pipelines: Explore how DevOps practices ensure seamless integration and delivery of AI models. International Journal of Advanced Research in Science, Communication and Technology. https://www.semanticscholar.org/paper/f6c04c017ece5661f6c2112829e33edcd7fdb83b (accessed on 11th September 2025).

25. Sonar, A. J. (2025). Bridging the gap: Enhancing DevOps security through comprehensive threat modeling. https://core.ac.uk/download/660328827.pdf (accessed on 11th September 2025).

26. Srinivas, S., & Renuka, A. (2025). Integrating Azure Bot with Slack for enhanced communication and automation in DevOps pipelines. International Journal for Research Publication and Seminar. https://www.

semanticscholar.org/paper/652e5e2bfa845b556152ceee8ed5dac40647d6a3 (accessed on 11th September 2025).

27. Steidl, M., Felderer, M., & Ramler, R. (2023). The pipeline for the continuous development of artificial intelligence models—Current state of research and practice. Journal of Systems and Software, 199, 111615–111615. https://doi.org/10.1016/j.jss.2023.111615 (accessed on 11th September 2025).
28. Talati, D. V. (2025). AI-driven cloud workflows: Enhancing efficiency in CI/CD pipelines. International Journal of Latest Technology in Engineering Management & Applied Science, 14, 124–129. https://doi.org/10.51583/ijltemas.2025.14020015 (accessed on 11th September 2025).
29. Tatineni, S. (2023). Compliance and audit challenges in DevOps: A security perspective. International Research Journal of Modernization in Engineering Technology and Science. https://doi.org/10.56726/irjmets45309 (accessed on 11th September 2025).
30. Tonnarelli, M. (2023). Fallacies and pitfalls of large-scale DevOps pipelines: An industrial proof-of-concept study. https://core ac.uk/download/650040415.pdf (accessed on 11th September 2025).
31. Vedanbhatla, N. V. K. A. (2023). Pipeline to production: Modern CI/CD strategies with Docker, Kubernetes, and cloud-native tooling. https://core.ac.uk/download/666027033.pdf (accessed on 11th September 2025).
32. Vu, D. T. (2024). CICD automation's impact on microservices project management. https://core.ac.uk/download/638724859.pdf (accessed on 11th September 2025).

CHAPTER 7

OBSERVABILITY AND MONITORING IN CLOUD COMPUTING

Contents

INTRODUCTION

The rapid development of cloud computing has transformed the landscape of information technology, profoundly altering the way in which organizations deploy and manage applications. With organizations relocating resources and services to the cloud, observability and monitoring capabilities are of critical need. Observability refers to understanding the internal state of a system through data it generates, enabling proactive identification of issues prior to becoming critical. This proactive approach is critical to smooth application operation and service quality in complex cloud systems. With distributed architectures becoming increasingly sophisticated, it is critical for organizations to adopt sophisticated observability frameworks to interpret performance, security, and operational metrics so as to lay a solid foundation for a resilient cloud infrastructure. In observability and monitoring, one needs to observe the broad array of methodologies and tools that are utilized in inspecting cloud environments. These technologies utilize data analytics, machine learning, and automation to provide end-to-end visibility into system health and activity. Using these technologies, companies can best map performance metrics into related application behaviors, illuminating relationships previously unknown. Also, with the ongoing development of cloud infrastructure, the integration of artificial intelligence in observability tools has opened up opportunities for predictive analytics and anomaly detection. This development not only fosters operational efficiency but also keeps pace with the growing demands for security and compliance in cloud operations. These are challenges met at the center of building a robust observability plan that suits the requirements of current cloud computing. The observability is not only relevant to the resolution of issues but rather a broader commitment to continuous improvement and innovation. As organizations navigate the turbulence of hybrid and multi-cloud environments, the ability to draw real-time insights into how the system operates is a competitive edge. This necessitates ongoing investment in observability practice and technology with a sense of emphasis on the significance of cloud-native solutions that augment monitoring and provide seamless integration across platforms. Further, the development of observability culture within organizations can enhance cooperation between development and operations teams even more to ensure optimal response to incidents and enable even more agile development. In the long term, the commitment to adequate observability and monitoring of cloud computing not only defends operational integrity but also guides organizations towards gaining the complete potential of the cloud, enabling strategic goals.

Definition of Observability in Cloud Computing

In cloud computing, observability is a system's capacity to provide insight into its internal workings through the information it generates. This goes beyond monitoring because it is tied up with gathering, analyzing, and graphing diverse metrics, logs, and traces that identify how programs and services are operating in real time. Observability allows engineers to be aware of the state of a system not just from its outputs but also from its behavior at runtime under varied conditions. With observability, organizations can detect anomalies, debug issues, and tune performance in intricate cloud environments. These capabilities are important as cloud infrastructures become increasingly complex, where conventional monitoring solutions may not be sufficient to deliver the level of detail needed to ensure effective incident response and system optimization. Moreover, observability as a practice in cloud computing is important to foster resilience and enhance proactive incident management. By having a firm understanding of system behavior, teams are able to identify performance hotspots and foresee imminent failures before they turn into significant events. An observability system that is well constructed consolidates disperse sources of data to render an entire picture of cloud operation and user experience.

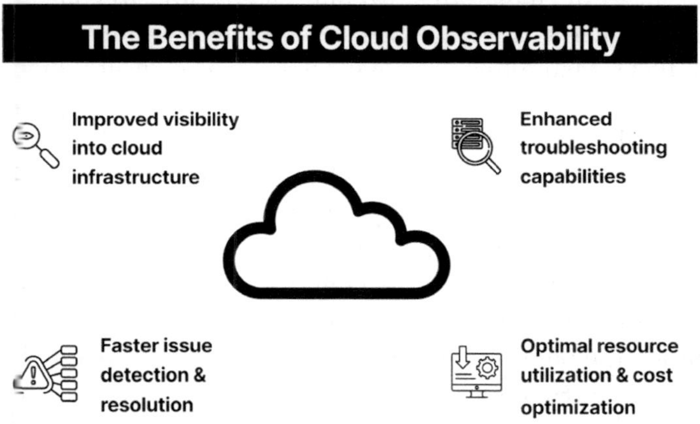

Figure 7.1. *The observability in cloud computing.*

Source: https://cdn.prod.website-files.com/626a25d633b1b99aa0e1afa7/64c7996c6e2115e7b41fea0d_CPqUmpLmHLObnQohOgSYoMPoe38O-vnPSRdNe-BRkoiZSG-46CccdTrbI6vM9lfXj-aZijURIZguX1EumMUX8lxY-R5qeidE8nNt-V3eql8X-N-ChEqRLC3E4GdT3CgKHT7plkTQyNCUc7gqXFKIBc1Ps.png.

This is particularly important when organizations are rolling out microservices-based architectures where service dependencies tend to obscure the underlying issues of problems. Consequently, high observability results in improved decision-making. The ability to correlate data across layers raises situational awareness, facilitates effective troubleshooting, and ultimately speeds up the development cycle by allowing teams to iterate and innovate quickly. Further, as cloud computing continues to develop, the importance of observability becomes apparent in business intelligence as well as regulation compliance. Organizations need to be transparent and accountable for their data behavior, and thus observability is a core component of their operational strategy. By employing observability tools, businesses are able to demonstrate straightforward compliance with industry standards while eliminating waste and increasing business efficiency. This dual benefit solidifies the relevance of observability as not just a technical imperative, but also as a tactical enabler of greater business ambitions. By ingraining a culture that is observability-focused, firms can better manage the complexities of the cloud environment, hence being able to dynamically adapt to changes in technology, user requirements, and market forces (Kodheli et al., 2020; Rose et al., 2020) (Figure 7.1).

Importance of Monitoring in Cloud Environments

The significance of monitoring within cloud infrastructures cannot be overstated, particularly as organizations increasingly turn to cloud computing for its operations. Monitoring is a vital component in ensuring the reliability, performance, and security of cloud services. By observing system statistics and logs in real time, businesses are able to obtain valuable insights on resource usage, system health, and application performance. Such proactive strategy enables the identification of problems that can be detected before they actually evolve into full-scale critical failures. Having effective monitoring mechanisms in place also guarantees high levels of service, as companies are better equipped to cater to user needs and operational concerns in real-time. Last but not least, monitoring fosters a sense of responsibility and continuous improvement, required for maintaining a competitive edge in today's fast-paced digital landscape. In addition, efficient monitoring in cloud environments also helps in compliance with security policies and regulatory requirements. Since organizations keep sensitive information stored in the cloud, it becomes important to have visibility into data interactions and user access. Monitoring tools are able to monitor anomalies, detect unauthorized access attempts, and send alerts for probable security violations, thus helping with data protection measures. For instance, the integration of machine learning and analytics within monitoring frameworks allows auto-detection of patterns that are representative of security problems. By the use of such sophisticated technologies, companies can enhance the practice of risk management and assist in ensuring that their cloud infrastructure is in compliance with industry regulations. Its role as a preventive measure is what makes monitoring emphasize its role in the protection not only of the data but also of the reputation and credibility of the organization among stakeholders. Beyond performance and security benefits, monitoring in cloud environments significantly impacts resource optimization and cost management. Awareness of resource utilization patterns allows organizations to make informed decisions on scaling infrastructure, translating directly into optimal usage of the cloud. Vision acquired by monitoring can recognize wasted resources and help eliminate wastage, thereby reducing the expense of over-provisioning. Further, constant monitoring of application performance helps detect opportunities for improvement and optimization, enabling improved efficiency of operation. Monitoring plays more than a mere watchdog role; it becomes a vital feedback loop for organizations looking to be agile and constantly deliver on their cloud transformation efforts. Through having a robust monitoring strategy, organizations can remain responsive to changing business requirements while deriving the most value from their cloud investment.

7.1. THE CONCEPT OF OBSERVABILITY

The concept of observability in cloud computing is an absolute requirement for effective monitoring and management of large systems. Observability has been described as the capacity to infer the internal state of a system from its external outputs. In cloud systems, where services execute dynamically and have the potential to scale very rapidly, it is absolutely necessary to know how a system behaves in order to achieve reliability and performance. Through the application of observability practices, companies can capture traces, logs, and metrics that provide a qualitative view of system behavior. Not only does this information help diagnose issues in real time, but it also enables proactive measures to be taken to prevent failures. The goal of observability is eventually to gain a holistic view of system behavior, which further contributes to better decision making and performance tuning in cloud infrastructure. Moreover, the integration of observability with microservice systems validates its increasing relevance in modern cloud computing. With companies adopting microservices as a consequence of their flexibility and scalability, it becomes more complex for systems to interact. Observability acts as a vital mechanism to decimate the mystery because it enables the monitoring of various components interacting together with high precision. Here, achieving observability requires a paradigm shift in how monitoring has been handled in the past because microservices generate gigantic amounts of data that must be well-provided and understood. An improved understanding of microservitization noted in the literature indicates a greater emphasis on achieving maximum service granularity and understanding the interactions between microservices. Through observability, companies can access the intelligence needed to traverse such complexities, resulting in efficiency and resilience in their cloud operations (Andrawos et al., 2019). Further, the role played by emerging technologies in enhancing the concept of observability cannot be overstated. The development of IoT systems for monitoring surroundings, such as educational buildings, is a good example of how technology can be used to achieve energy efficiency and behavioral change among users. By utilizing several sensors and applying advanced analytics, these systems can track real-time data that enhances the observability of energy consumption as well as resource distribution in schools. These installations are particularly emphasized to indicate the payoff involved in deploying ICT with observability in terms of helping stakeholders make observable data usable as actionable information. In such scenarios, user interaction becomes critical as fluctuations in the behavior of students and instructors have a direct bearing on energy usage patterns. Thus, the adoption of advanced observability paradigms becomes necessary for ensuring efficiency in all dimensions, which makes this idea even more crucial for contemporary cloud computing applications (Akrivopoulos et al., 2017).

7.1.1. Key Components of Observability

In-depth understanding of cloud computing observability relies on knowing its most important elements, which include metrics, logs, and traces. Metrics provide quantitative data about system performance, such as response time and error rate, allowing for real-time monitoring and measurement of the system's health. Logs are in-depth records of events in a system, such as error messages and transaction records, and contain information used to fix errors. Finally, traces enable monitoring the requests flow between various services, providing an overview of service interaction and latency. Together, these pieces of information provide an overall picture of the systems activity, allowing teams to correct issues beforehand and optimize performance, thus underlining their untold value within the context of maintaining healthy cloud environments. Another important aspect of observability is ensuring support for employing advanced analytical techniques to yield meaningful insights from gathered data through the means of metrics, logs, and traces. Utilizing machine learning models and visualization abilities provides more opportunities for identifying patterns or anomalies in huge amounts of data generated as a result of cloud operations. For instance, anomaly detection can be applied to discover potential security threats or performance bottlenecks beforehand before turning into more severe issues. These holistic analytical tools not only facilitate proactive decision-making but also facilitate root cause analysis on complex systems. Therefore, the efficient application of these analytical methodologies effectively elevates the observability framework, turning raw data into strategic intelligence facilitating improved cloud system management. Last but not least, creating a culture of observability in organizations is paramount to attaining the utmost efficacy of its components. This change of culture involves inspiring developers and engineers to incorporate observability into their process, inspiring them to develop systems with built-in abilities of gathering and forwarding observability information that is relevant. Emphasizing collaboration among development, operations, and security teams also ensures that each has a stake in the process of observability. Fostering transparency and shared accountability for system performance has the effect of disintegrating silos that typically get in the way of timely incident response. In this way, organizations can establish a stronger cloud infrastructure that is responsive to conditions and demands quickly, ultimately resulting in better overall service delivery and customer satisfaction (Figure 7.2)

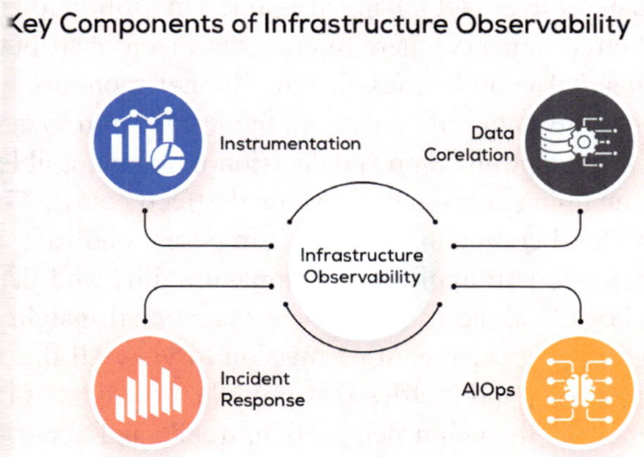

Figure 7.2. *Key components of observability.*

Source: https://www.inspirisys.com/uploads/blog_image/Key-Components-of-Infrastructure-Observability.jpg.

7.1.2. Differences Between Observability and Monitoring

The distinction between monitoring and observability is a fundamental concept in the realm of cloud computing because they are both essential but distinct capabilities. Monitoring refers to collecting and analyzing metrics, logs, and events from apps and infrastructure to ensure consistent and reliable performance. Monitoring is primarily interested in known bounds, alerting operators when issues occur based on anticipated parameters. In this sense, monitoring is a response mechanism that captures system failures or performance degradation by pre-defined indicators. Observability is different from mere monitoring as it helps to better understand complex systems through analyzing internal states. By using strong data analysis practices, observability allows teams to ask and answer critical questions concerning the behavior of the systems under unforeseen circumstances. This transition from monitoring to comprehension paves the way for improved troubleshooting and stability of the system. The most important difference among these concepts lies in their treatment of analysis of system behavior. Monitoring operates within a bounded paradigm, actually providing snapshots of system performance at predetermined intervals. It gives responses to What happened? in the case of problem noticed, with little significance of the root cause. Conversely, observability focuses on the ability to investigate the inner mechanisms of a system with more agility so that teams can respond to questions such as Why did this occur? and What needs to be done in order to not let it happen again? This ability to investigate is essential for cloud environments where microservices and distributed systems can result in unintended complexities that traditional monitoring might not detect. Thus, observability not only enhances the insight into system behavior but also makes proactive optimization and decision-making possible, which are most critical in maintaining sustained operational effectiveness. The inclusion of observability in cloud computing strategies imposes a holistic approach to system management. Modern applications demand agility and dependability, where monitoring bounds alone can introduce operational insight gaps. With observability built in, companies gain permission to view all the information in the form of logs, traces, and metrics that provide a complete picture of the system's performance. With such a perspective, trends and abnormalities can be detected, and therefore, faster responses to issues prior to becoming massive failures. Moreover, with systems growing up and with increasingly complex cloud architectures, evolving from monitoring to observability enables teams to constantly optimize their approach by using advanced tools and methods to learn. Lastly, the partnership of observability and monitoring fosters a culture of continuous improvement, enabling cloud environments to be strong, optimized, and prepared to address emerging challenges in a dynamic world.

7.1.3. Role of Observability in System Performance

The concept of observability plays a key role in enhancing system performance, particularly in cloud computing systems wherein intricate frameworks are the standard. Monitoring is merely one component of observability, which is the comprehensive ability to understand the internal states of a system through its external outputs. In cloud computing, it means that administrators can detect performance bottlenecks, service outages, and even predict impending failures by analyzing data such as logs, metrics, and traces. This proactive stance enables organizations to realize better availability and reliability with optimal use of resources. As technology gets more complicated, the requirement for good observability grows stronger, highlighting its value in enabling effective functioning and responsiveness to altering circumstances. Moreover, observability is also necessary in facilitating rapid development cycles with Agile and DevOps methodologies, both of which play essential roles in the software era now. Using continuous integration and continuous deployment (CI/CD) processes, teams must be aware of their app's performance in real-time. Observability tools achieve this by providing developers with the capability to easily identify problems when and after deployment so that they can do iterations faster. These results are not just of critical importance for solving immediate problems but also for longer-term optimizations that ensure that applications do not only operate as intended but evolve in harmony with user needs and advances in technology. By integrating observability practices into their work processes, organizations can build an environment of continuous improvement that fuels performance and innovation. Finally, the push toward emerging technologies such as sixth-generation networking and satellite communications increases the demand for robust observability frameworks. The emerging systems will tend to introduce complexity in the technological landscape, with special performance requirements and specifications. As has been noted in discussions pertaining to (Tataria et al., 2021; Kodheli et al., 2020), the new-age systems call for precise real-time monitoring and analytics to manage their inherent complexities successfully. Observability will play a central role in managing and optimizing these dynamic environments with the emergence of new applications that require high bandwidth and low latency. The ability to take advantage of huge amounts of data and still be able to separate actionable insights will be central to maintaining levels of performance and making sure that organizations can react quickly to change and capitalize on evolving capabilities as they happen (Figure 7.3).

Figure 7.3. *Role of observability in system performance.*

Source: https://cdn.vidyard.com/thumbnails/42409050/DHEDRGoTOTJ-4f_i93uBqKpGxPO8FWKP.jpg.

7.2. TYPES OF MONITORING IN CLOUD COMPUTING

In cloud computing, various types of monitoring are important to service reliability, efficiency, and performance. Infrastructure monitoring is one of them, being a fundamental piece that focuses on the physical and virtual components that comprise cloud infrastructure. The type of monitoring looks at the health of the servers, usage of resources, and system metrics such that the administrators are able to identify prospective bottlenecks and optimize resource assignments. The significance of infrastructure monitoring cannot be overstated since it makes the key insights into the operational state of cloud services and their infrastructure, thereby enabling proactive management and maintenance. By continuous monitoring of such metrics as CPU usage, memory consumption, and disk I/O, cloud service providers can enhance system stability and accommodate evolving needs while minimizing downtime, thereby conforming to best practices for cloud observability. Application performance monitoring (APM) is another critical component of cloud monitoring aiming to assess and optimize end-user quality for cloud applications. APM solutions aim to analyze application performance across various stages of the user experience, monitoring response times, transaction completion rates, and error detection. With the ability to accept real-time input and present representations of application performance metrics, APM solutions enable early detection of issues that might delay user satisfaction. Besides, the tools enable developers to fix bottlenecks and analyze application dependencies to make sure that there is seamless user experience. The employment of APM within a cloud monitoring system not only assists in guaranteed application health but also prompts constant improvement in performance, which is of paramount importance to businesses to sustain user needs and achieve competitive advantage in an increasingly digital environment. Last but not least, network monitoring is an integral part of holistic cloud monitoring solutions, addressing the measuring of data flow and performance of networking components in clouds. This type of monitoring checks parameters such as bandwidth utilization, latency, and packet loss, enabling organizations to maintain optimal network performance and security. With advanced network monitoring software, administrators can gain knowledge about network traffic behavior, detect anomalies, and take action against potential security breaches. Furthermore, the necessity for monitoring networks is brought forth by increased reliance on cloud service integrations that mandate good and effective communication between various cloud services and external apps. As organizations navigate the complexities of cloud infrastructures, good network monitoring is necessary, avoiding connectivity issues from interfering with service delivery or jeopardizing the overall system performance (Grigorescu et al., 2019). This inclusive cloud monitoring strategy ultimately stimulates an adaptive and resilient cloud infrastructure that is capable of handling dynamic operational needs and problems (Kocher et al., 2019).

7.2.1. Infrastructure Monitoring

Infrastructure monitoring is a key component of cloud computing observability, including real-time data gathering, processing, and visualization of operational data across cloud infrastructures. Well-operating monitoring infrastructure enables organizations to uncover performance bottlenecks, identify anomalies, and predict resource needs in advance. Organizations can enhance their infrastructure monitoring capabilities by employing cloud-native tools such as microservices and event-driven architectures. For instance, container orchestration tools like Kubernetes can bring automated deployment and governance of microservices while enabling robust monitoring tools that give valuable information regarding application and infrastructure health. This aligns with the need for flexibility in rapidly changing environments, giving infrastructure resilience to surprise challenges, as seen in the evolution of architecture patterns for scalable systems (Berezin, 2025). Observation tools integration also allows teams to exercise control over cloud infrastructure. These offer comprehensive monitoring by collecting metrics, logs, and traces from multitudes of sources with the ability to perform in-depth analysis. The employment of services like AWS CloudWatch or third-party tools allows deeper knowledge of application performance and infrastructure up-time, as the monitoring is more data-based and automated. The shift to serverless architecture and microservices encourages a dynamic environment that calls for sophisticated observability processes. Thus, organizations are adopting more mature monitoring approaches, such as those involving in-memory caching and event streaming, to attain better overall system performance and reliability. The demand for insight into infrastructure components is now unprecedented, which is encouraging innovation in monitoring practices that mature in today's cloud environments (Katta, 2025). Moreover, monitoring efficiency of infrastructure is largely dependent on smart scaling capability and automation. Smart automated monitoring technologies make resource allocation easier in order to provide optimal performance and value for money when utilizing the cloud. Autoscaling types of approaches help to guarantee that infrastructure adjusts dynamically as demand changes, thus guaranteeing user experience and operational efficiency. Incorporating real-time monitoring within cloud strategy helps businesses compare performance and avoid potential overloading infrastructure bottlenecks. As organizations are more and more adopting cloud-native architecture, the emphasis on observability increases, highlighting the importance of integrating advanced monitoring tools. This holistic approach addresses not just the pressing operational concerns but puts companies strategically in a universe marked by rapidly developing technologies and an increased amount of complexity in data (Berezin, 2025; Katta, 2025) (Figure 7.4).

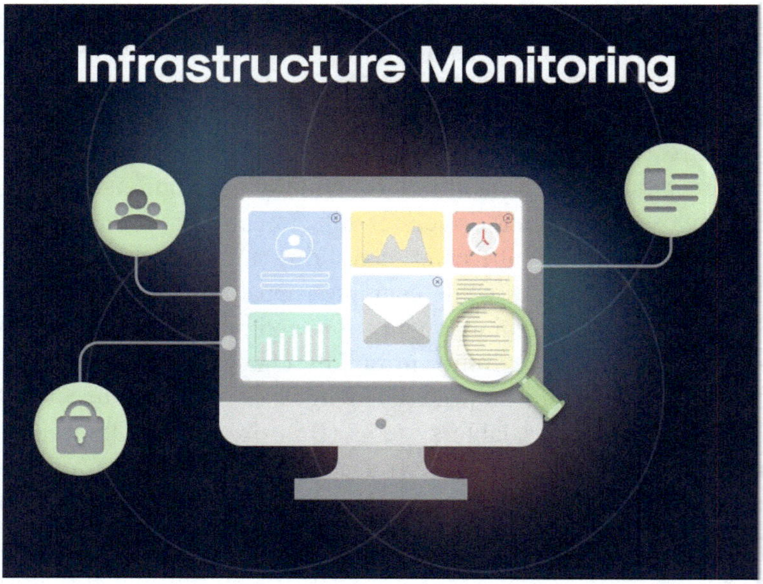

Figure 7.4. *Infrastructure monitoring.*

Source: https://cdn.prod.website-files.com/5ff66329429d880392f6cba2/65f4465b0dfda05e33c7eb73_397-min.jpg.

7.2.2. Application Performance Monitoring (APM)

APM is essential in ensuring that cloud-based applications perform at their best. As enterprises increasingly depend on microservices architectures for improved scalability and flexibility, the intricacy of monitoring application performance increases drastically. APM tools are created to offer visibility into application behavior, allowing developers and operators to identify bottlenecks, excessive latencies, and other performance issues. Through their use of metrics, logs, and distributed tracing functionality, these products collect data that provide end-to-end visibility across different components of application performance. Of significance is the fact that contemporary APM products need to seamlessly integrate with cloud orchestration platforms in order to provide actionable insight, hence enabling timely interventions that can improve application reliability and user satisfaction. At the center of effective APM is mapping performance markers to business outcomes, something that serves to underscore the significance of observability in cloud computing. Legacy monitoring strategies have no place in distributed systems where microservices exchange data among different systems. It is imperative, therefore, that there be a move toward greater complexity in observability practices. By utilizing frameworks that bring together performance information, businesses can gain a clearer picture of how their programs work and identify issues more accurately. Emerging research suggests that data fusion performance can be improved by using a combination of signals from various monitoring frameworks and ultimately lead to more effective root cause analysis. This approach enables organizations to sense microservice delays better, enabling performance optimization to be both broad-based and targeted (Tzanettis et al., 2022). The evolution of APM also suggests the growing importance of continuous monitoring in agile development environments, where deployment cycles demand instant awareness of application performance. This not only encompasses the correlation of real-time statistics but also the utilization of predictive analytics to forecast future performance issues in advance before they start influencing end users. With cloud infrastructures growing, precise and flexible monitoring tools to accommodate dynamic loads are necessary. The integration of APM into larger observability environments allows organizations to have a more reliable application delivery pipeline. In addition to addressing immediate performance challenges, this holistic monitoring strategy gives teams the intelligence necessary for enhancing overall service quality and operational efficiency, thus promoting innovation and gaining competitive advantage in a digitally advanced and more complex environment (Grigorescu et al., 2019).

7.2.3. Network Monitoring

Monitoring networks is an essential role in ensuring the performance and reliability of cloud computing infrastructures. With companies shifting operations to the cloud, network interactions become a lot more intricate. Robust monitoring tools are a necessity in providing real-time data regarding the well-being and performance of a network so administrators can recognize anomalies and troubleshoot issues effectively. Effective network monitoring can help identify bottlenecks in data flows, misconfigurations, or possible security vulnerabilities. On top of that, through proactive management instead of reactive, organizations will be able to minimize risks related to service disruptions and data leaks. As considered by Zhou, secure monitoring capabilities have evolved to allow for recording dependencies of system state, which enhances the ability to detect changes over time and overall enhances cloud infrastructure security postures (Jajodia et al., 2020). In addition to performance monitoring, network observability is also critical to identify hidden issues that may affect service delivery.

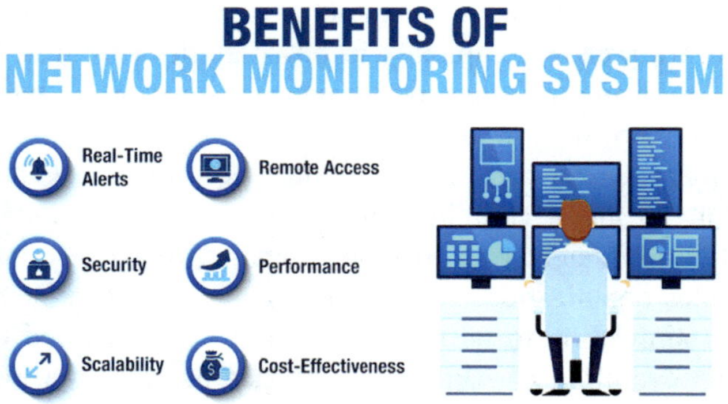

Figure 7.5. *Network monitoring.*

Source: https://www.extnoc.com/learn/wp-content/uploads/2022/08/Benefits-of-Network-Monitoring-System-2.jpg.

This requires a multi-modal solution, leveraging varied tools and techniques monitoring not only network traffic but also application activity and resource utilization. Integrating telemetry data from various layers in the cloud stack offers end-to-end visibility for developers and also for IT operations. Furthermore, observability frameworks can leverage machine learning models to predict potential failures or inefficiencies based on patterns in past data. Through traffic flows and user behavior analysis, organizations can optimize resources more effectively and improve the quality of service. Such efforts align with security monitoring frameworks like those provided by Wu et al., which aim at ongoing verification of system integrity through concurrent checks for violation (Grigorescu et al., 2019). The challenges of monitoring in cloud platforms are numerous and must be addressed holistically. With heightened architecture complexity like hybrid and multi-cloud environments, monitoring strategies must evolve. Traditional tools will get outpaced by dynamic setups and fluctuating levels of traffic, necessitating more responsive and dynamic monitoring strategies. Security threats are also augmented by the increased attack surface that follows cloud connectivity, and it is important that network monitoring technologies align security protocols effectively. As noted in high-level research, orchestration of monitoring and observability platforms can potentially lead to better system resilience and more informed decision-making, ultimately leading to improved cloud service delivery while safeguarding sensitive data (Jajodia et al., 2020; Grigorescu et al., 2019) (Figure 7.5).

7.3. TOOLS AND TECHNOLOGIES FOR OBSERVABILITY

In the cloud computing ecosystem, observability technologies and tools have come to be of most significance in ensuring system performance and reliability. Observability refers to the capacity to understand the internal status of a system from the external signals of the system, and the success of observability tools relies on their capacity to generate actionable information. These critical observability technologies include logging, monitoring, tracing, and metrics collection, which all work in conjunction with each other to create an end-to-end picture of the systems behavior. Organizations can use these tools to rapidly detect anomalies and performance issues, enabling them to solve problems proactively prior to becoming significant outages. This constant visibility into system health fuels improved user experience and increases operational efficiency across cloud environments, establishing observability as one of the building blocks of modern digital infrastructure. Among the numerous platforms for observability, open-source platforms are the primary drivers of flexibility and scalability. These types of platforms are best suited for organizations that seek to minimize expenditure without being vendor-locked, as they allow them to customize it to very specific requirements. For instance, the implementation of Infrastructure as Code (IaC) with monitoring solutions can deploy observability tools in distributed environments with reliability and consistency. In addition, applications of tools such as Grafana, Prometheus, and OpenTelemetry support real-time data visualization, metrics collection, and distributed tracing respectively. Such technologies are not only helpful in diagnosing complex issues but also helpful in historical analysis of data, which is a great advantage for debugging as well as forecasting performance trends. Hence, bringing in such open-source technologies can lead organizations to have a strong culture of observability, thereby improving their cloud computing infrastructure in the long run. Also, incorporating tools of observability in cloud infrastructures requires a knowledge of testing techniques to work effectively. The contribution made by cloud-specific test tools cannot be overstated; they ensure that the observability infrastructure is running optimally under varied loads. Cloud testing, as per Lněnička et al. (2013), encompasses multi-layer testing and SLA-based testing, which ensure observability tools can meet predetermined performance benchmarks under varied conditions. This calls for massive-scale simulations that mimic real traffic and behavior, enabling organizations to decide potential points of failure or bottlenecks in their observability stack.

Ensuring the observability tools are strong and function as intended during peak usage hours is essential for service continuity. With ongoing maturity of cloud infrastructure, test tool creation and specialization will play a crucial role in the larger context of observability, ultimately contributing to operational success.

7.3.1. Popular Observability Tools (E.g., Prometheus, Grafana)

Within the evolving world of cloud computing, adoption of observability tools is essential in sustaining robust system performance and reliability. Perhaps the most outstanding tool is Prometheus, an open-source monitoring and alerting tool designed specifically to be utilized in cloud-native environments. Prometheus allows effective time-series data collection and storage, with seamless compatibility across various applications. Through its multi-dimensional query language, PromQL, developers are able to extract valuable information from big datasets, thereby encouraging data-driven decision-making in organizations. As things get more complex in systems, being able to analyze real-time becomes increasingly more important, and that's why such observability tools become so central to maintaining clarity of operations and mitigating the effects of system failures, particularly in cloud environments that are always in motion (Nerella et al., 2019). In addition to Prometheus, Grafana is a stable visualization software employed to read data better through comprehensive dashboards and alerts. With the capacity to create usable graphical representations of metrics collected by various data sources, Grafana helps teams identify trends and outliers within cloud infrastructure readily. This feature is vital because it enables companies to respond ahead of time to performance degradation, hence actually minimizing downtime while enhancing user satisfaction. In addition, Grafana's extensive plugin universe also adds to its value in differing cloud offerings and data solutions, further cementing its position as the foundation of observability practice. By combining Grafana and Prometheus, companies can leverage the strengths of each tool, maximizing their observability solution and reaffirming commitment to service reliability and operational excellence (Perumal et al., 2025). While multi-cloud environments continue to gain traction, so does the need for high-level observability tools. As new levels of sophistication arise, such as in hybrid layers and various providers, accurate visibility into the systems is something that needs to be tackled by organizations. Prometheus and Grafana are not merely tools for being able to monitor individual pieces, but they pull data from multiple platforms in order to have a comprehensive view of performance metrics. This blended approach supports efficient incident management and root cause analysis, which are imperative for high performance and availability in cloud systems. Moreover, the incorporation of artificial intelligence into these tools enhances their capability by allowing them to automate monitoring and incident management. While companies seek operational efficiency through their cloud projects, investments in advanced observability tools will be paramount to their achievement (Nerella et al., 2019; Perumal et al., 2025) (Figure 7.6).

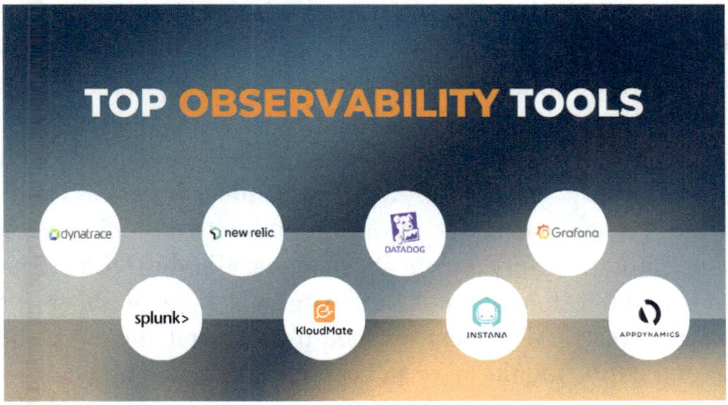

Figure 7.6. *Popular observability tools.*

Source: https://framerusercontent.com/assets/ZasTz0jYxlULr4vUOMRolUaMQk.png.

7.3.2. Cloud-Native Monitoring Solutions

Cloud-native monitoring tools have revolutionized the way companies monitor and observe their cloud infrastructures. Conventional monitoring tools are more focused on infrastructure measurements, but cloud-native monitoring tools are architected to provide profound observability of distributed systems structures. As applications are decomposed into microservices, the complexity increases, and thus the monitoring frameworks need to be capable of handling dynamic scaling, different technology stacks, and different deployment environments. These solutions leverage newer techniques such as automated instrumentation and service mesh technology, enabling developers to observe, troubleshoot, and fix issues in real time. This level of visibility not only emphasizes performance optimization but also contributes to overall stability and dependability to cloud-native applications. Moreover, cloud-native monitoring solutions also gel very well with continuous integration and continuous deployment (CI/CD) practices that are prevalent among modern software development. By integrating monitoring into the CI/CD pipeline, teams can establish observability early in the application development lifecycle. It aids in foreseeing potential issues before they turn into severe failures. Real-time monitoring provides actionable metrics and traces that allow performance tuning and problem diagnosis, leading to improved user experience. In addition, the capability to monitor application health in dashboards and notifications empowers teams to make data-driven decisions, responding rapidly to variations in system behavior. In contrast to traditional monitoring approaches, cloud-native tools enable collaboration between development and operations teams, or DevOps, by creating shared views of application performance. By providing rich metrics and logs, the tools enable cross-functional teams to respond cohesively in real time. This collaboration is also supplemented by being integrated with incident response and management solutions, which streamline workflows and help with successful crisis management. The use of cloud-native monitoring also helps organizations embrace agility and responsiveness, aligning with industry trends such as Industry 4.0 technology integration and machine intelligence evolution (Morgan et al., 2021). Additionally, since the demand for 6G technology is evolving, cloud-native monitoring can keep up with increasing complexities of new applications and services so that businesses can remain competitive in the rapidly evolving digital world (Tataria et al., 2021).

7.3.3. Open-Source vs. Commercial Tools

In cloud computing observability and monitoring, the open-source versus proprietary choice is a strategic one for businesses. Open-source solutions have the advantage of flexibility and customization by which users can tailor solution fit to meet individual monitoring needs. They foster community collaboration that brings rapid iterations and improvements driven by collective feedback. Such software, such as platforms like Prometheus and Grafana, allows organizations to establish high-strength observability systems without paying the hefty license costs. These benefits, however, have their counterparts, such as possibly complicated installation and maintenance procedures, which might demand specialized expertise in order to overcome them. Therefore, while open-source solutions can make novel monitoring strategies possible, organizations will need to balance these advantages against the operational burden of installing and maintaining such systems. On the other hand, commercial solutions offer a different perspective that enjoys simplicity and expert customer support. Commercial solutions are known to have easy-to-use user interfaces and integrated functionalities that support the deployment of observability and monitoring infrastructure. Organizations can leverage established solutions like Dynatrace or New Relic and back their monitoring with fewer resource investments towards training staff and system maintenance. However, the financial implications of license fees and vendor lock-in problems can be significant concerns for planning within organizations. Further, commercial products naturally limit the extent to which they can be modified against their open-source alternatives, leading to the risk of incompatibility between some organizational requirements and provision capabilities. Therefore, while commercial tools provide a convenient option, the cost and flexibility constraints of these tend to cause organizations to evaluate their long-term monitoring plan with care. In the final analysis, the decision to utilize commercial or open-source tools is based on the specific needs and priorities of the respective organization. Budget, technical skill set, and long-term vision for cloud monitoring are principal determining factors in making this choice. Organizations should also consider adopting the trend towards hybrid solutions that utilize both commercial and open-source solutions, leveraging the best features of each. By integrating adaptable open-source functionality with commercial-grade security and support, organizations can craft an end-to-end observability strategy that offers resilience and responsiveness for their cloud environments. This blended strategy appropriately dialogues with the evolving sophistication of cloud architectures and applications, for instance, the innovative developments in edge AI technologies enhancing observability capacities and addressing specific latency and performance concerns relevant to diverse applications (McEnroe et al., 2022). In the evolving environment of cloud computing, the deliberate exploration of these toolsets will ultimately determine the effectiveness of monitoring systems (Figure 7.7).

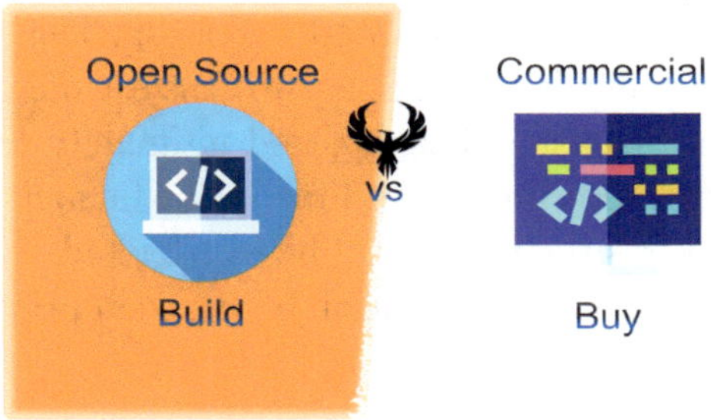

Figure 7.7 *Open-source vs. commercial tools.*

Source: https://phoenix.security/media/Screenshot-2021-10-11-at-01.35.46.png.webp.

7.4. CHALLENGES IN IMPLEMENTING OBSERVABILITY

Cloud computing's use of observability is filled with challenges that may make monitoring and troubleshooting ineffective. One of the principal problems is the temporary nature of cloud environments, particularly serverless environments where applications are made up of diverse microservices. The services are able to be scaled dynamically and act in an unstable manner, making it difficult for traditional monitoring systems to capture effective information. The lack of stable states complicates it further to track performance degradation or track anomalies over time. This situation is compounded by vendor lock-in problems, in which specific tools and services lock organizations into specific providers, restricting flexibility and their observability capabilities. Thus, organizations must deal with these complexities while striving to deliver a high quality of service. Thus, the need for elastic observability solutions is critical in addressing the special challenges posed by the cloud environment's dynamic nature. In addition to the technical problems, the human aspect of adopting observability practices poses a significant barrier. Most teams lack the required experience to successfully put cutting-edge observability methods into action, leading to improper application or insufficient mastery of available tools.

The subtlety of deploying observability solutions typically results in inconsistencies between teams, developing information silos that make it hard for groups to debug together. Such information fragmentation can prevent an organization from having a bird's eye view of their cloud environments required for effective monitoring. Additionally, cultivating observability culture within teams requires leaders to learn and commit to establishing observability practices as a priority and facilitate knowledge sharing. This cultural shift will require money and time, but it is necessary to harvest the long-term benefit of an observability system that is healthy, and ultimately leads to improved system resilience and operation efficiency. Finally, the financial cost of applying observability to cloud infrastructure cannot be overlooked. Sophisticated tools of observability, by nature, come with a high cost, comprised of integration, upkeep, and training fees.

Firms may be deterred by the steep price of setting up extensive observability solutions, especially if they are operating on tight budgets. This frustration would do nothing but keep them from implementing necessary tools and practices needed for quality monitoring, creating a vicious cycle of missed possibilities for optimization and issue-solving. Secondly, as business ventures increase their cloud functionalities, there is greater potential for heightened complexity, thus compounding the necessity to invest in observability tools to guarantee performance and reliability. Under such circumstances, it becomes a top priority for companies to understand the worth of enhanced observability in the long term because this directly grows proportionally with less downtime and improved operational efficiency, thus validating the necessity to make judicious financial choices in that respect.

7.4.1. Data Volume and Complexity

The exponential growth of volume and complexity of data is a very serious observability and monitoring challenge for cloud computing environments. As more businesses move operations to the cloud, they will be faced with huge amounts of data from myriad sources like user interactions, system logs, and external services. Such a deluge forms an information web of complexity that needs to be monitored so that the systems can perform optimally and securely. The traditional methods of managing data also fall behind in dealing with such complexity and need the development of advanced observability solutions to handle real-time data streams without undue delay. Advanced data analytics and visualization capabilities are required to understand patterns and anomalies in this enormous body of data to facilitate anticipatory decision-making as well as simplify resource allocation.

The combination of the volume and complexity of data also bears a close relationship to technology sophistication. For instance, advancement in artificial intelligence and machine learning allows organizations to utilize enormous volumes of data effectively, which results in better understanding of system behavior. As observed in recent studies, the use of deep learning algorithms facilitates accurate detection of problems in massive data structures compared to conventional methods. With increasingly complex cloud environments where many services and platforms are integrated, the need for proper observability is even more apparent. Interspersing tools that are able to leverage these technological advancements, while adding to real-time observation, also adds to better understanding of systemic relationships that are present in cloud architectures so as to act quickly on change. Data complexity is further exaggerated by the dynamic nature of cloud offerings where flexibility and scalability are of topmost concern.

Continual innovation in services and the availability of new technologies make organizations more used to processing differentiated types and formats of data. This variety makes complexity greater in the task of ongoing observation and analysis of data on multiple platforms. As organizations embrace cloud-native architectures, the observability toolset that can harmonize heterogeneous streams of data becomes necessary to integrate. Effective observability solutions must not only handle large amounts of data but also provide actionable output that accounts for the intricate interdependencies among services. The challenge presented by data volume and complexity dictates ongoing research and development of observability practices as organizations strive to build reliability into their cloud computing infrastructures, with attention directed to holistic monitoring (Figure 7.8).

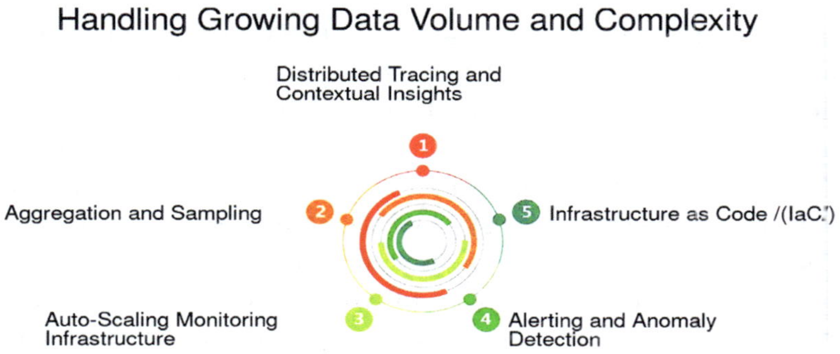

Figure 7.8. *The exponential growth of data volume and complexity.*

Source: https://fastercapital.co/i/Pipeline-monitoring--How-to-monitor-your-pipeline-health-and-troubleshoot-issues--Handling-Growing-Data-Volume-and-Complexity.webp.

7.4.2. Integration with Existing Systems

The integration of observability and monitoring tools within the current systems is one of the major challenges in cloud computing environments. As more and more organizations move their infrastructure to the cloud, it is important that these monitoring solutions are integrated into existing systems and applications seamlessly. Seamless integration not only helps in providing clear images of dynamic cloud assets but also provides continuous views of system performance. For example, a good observability model must be able to accommodate different data sources ranging from legacy to newer cloud-native applications in a manner that allows relative metrics to be collected and analyzed consistently. This interoperability enables companies to maintain a harmonized method for managing systems, hence enabling them to enjoy continuous monitoring and constant optimization of their operational effectiveness while growing their cloud infrastructures. In addition, the versatility of monitoring systems is required for accommodating various kinds of scenarios most likely to arise in various organizational settings. In this regard, the use of open-source and proprietary technologies can facilitate integration much more easily, as attested by the case study of an educational building utilizing IoT solutions. The ability to combine several hardware and software platforms supports efficient management of data from diverse sources that facilitates better decision-making and energy-saving initiatives. Evidence indicates that developing an information and communication technology system that is innovative and region-specific facilitates behavior change and maximizes the utilization of resources (Akrivopoulos et al., 2017). The replicability and extendibility of these types of systems demonstrate their value in various industries beyond the initial point of utilization, showing their usage in creating sustainable practices across the industry. Additionally, the Future Internet development aligns with the need for enhanced management and monitoring capabilities in cloud computing. With the global race to expand Internet capabilities speeding up, activities like Future Internet Forum Korea and European Union Future Internet Assembly are meant to address complexities of multiplexing multiple networks and services. At the center of activities like these is the issue of service-aware network architectures that can offer seamless integration with legacy systems (Abramowicz et al., 2009). By adopting these progressive paradigms, organizations are able to maximize their observability and monitoring strategy, ultimately providing greater system resiliency and agility within an increasingly digital society. This crossroads of leading-edge networking research and real-world application emphasizes the necessity for a strategic integration approach, positioning businesses for success within a cloud-centric operational model.

7.4.3. Skills and Knowledge Gaps in Teams

In cloud computing, the performance of monitoring and observability relies to a great extent on the skills and knowledge base of team members involved in these activities. As organizations increasingly use cloud-based infrastructures, the skills needed to manage such systems have risen exponentially. This change is particularly evident in the need for competency in newer technologies, such as the Internet of Things (IoT), that demand team members to follow technological developments in data management as well as decision-making functions. Deployment of these technologies generates complexities that pose impending skills gaps among teams, requiring that companies make competency building and training a foremost priority. By developing a culture of continuous learning and knowledge sharing, teams can heighten their capability to implement effective monitoring practices that ultimately lead to operational efficiency in the cloud environment. Further, knowledge gaps management within teams is not all about remedial technical skills; it also involves the building of soft skills needed for effective team collaboration and communication. Cloud computing observability teams often consist of a blend of individuals who possess varying skills and backgrounds, hence posing the potential for conflict and misunderstandings. Communication is critical to ensuring that everyone on the team is in accord regarding goals and methods. Additionally, as teams engage in complex problem-solving tasks, the ability to communicate knowledge and information is critical. Leadership must recognize these interpersonal skills as key components of team functionality and therefore invest in training workshops based on collaboration and communication. Emphasis on enhancing these soft skills can build a more cohesive unit, better able to face the complexities that come with cloud observability. Confluence of skills and knowledge gaps can also be the impetus for out-of-the-box thinking in cloud teams. Since individuals encounter challenges related to implementing observability frameworks, they may be able to identify how existing procedures can be improved. Solving problems generally forces team members to utilize their individual perspectives and experience, resulting in innovative thinking and innovation. However, without the proper skills and knowledge, such innovation chances would not be realized. By an organized analysis of available workforce capacities, organizations can actually establish training needs that cater to current and future demands. This proactive approach not only enhances teams with the necessary equipment to maximize cloud monitoring practice but also equips businesses to be competitive in a continually evolving technology world, thereby guaranteeing their success in the long run (Figure 7.9).

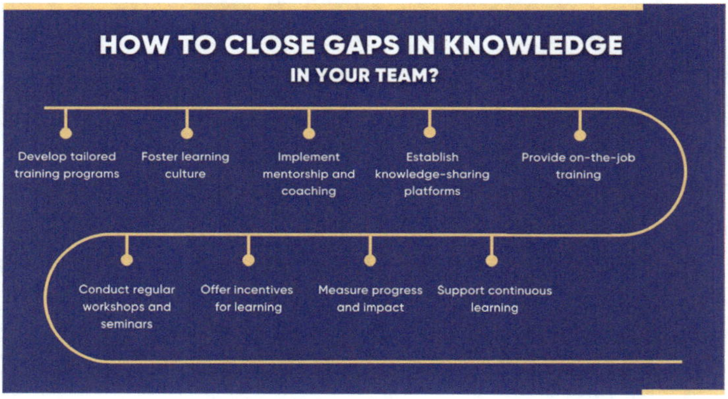

Figure 7.9. *Skills and knowledge gaps in teams.*

Source: https://blog.smart-tribune.com/hs-fs/hubfs/How%20to%20Close%20Gaps%20in%20Knowledge%20%20in%20Your%20Team.webp?width=1920&height=1080&name=How%20to%20Close%20Gaps%20in%20Knowledge%20%20in%20Your%20Team.webp.

7.5. BEST PRACTICES FOR EFFECTIVE MONITORING

Effective monitoring in cloud computing is essential in ensuring the system's reliability, performance, and satisfaction. An excellent approach to monitoring begins with establishing goals that align with the business strategy. Companies should outline the most important key performance indicators (KPIs) that are most crucial in measuring the health of their cloud infrastructure. This helps teams focus on meaningful measures rather than being bogged down by immense amounts of data. Critical parameters like response time, resource utilization, and failure rates have to be kept under constant observation. Furthermore, with a layered monitoring approach, there is enhanced visibility into various segments of the system so that deterioration in performance can be easily tackled. Including synthesis and granularity in their monitoring model, organizations create an even more effective and reliable means to respond reactively towards any issues, effectively avoiding potential downtimes that could affect business operations. Apart from identifying the pertinent KPIs, organizations also need to choose the right monitoring tools and technologies that complement their own needs. The inclusion of automated monitoring technologies can go a long way towards alleviating the burden of manual monitoring, hence enabling teams to concentrate on higher-level tasks. These tools ought to offer real-time feedback as well as support historical data analysis to identify trends. A future-proof monitoring solution needs to feature components like application performance monitoring (APM), infrastructure monitoring, and user experience monitoring to embrace the whole picture of cloud operations. With changing cloud structures, support for microservices and serverless computing in tools is required. This ensures that monitoring practices remain up to date with technological advancements, such as those coming with the 6G technologies requiring adaptive and agile monitoring paradigms outlined in Tataria et al. (2021) and Kodheli et al. (2020). Lastly, establishing a culture of continuous improvement in monitoring practices is necessary for sustainable success in cloud systems. The companies have to reassess their monitoring strategies regularly so that they can adapt them according to changing business demands and technology landscapes. This could involve establishing feedback loops that bring learnings from incidents or performance reviews to enhance existing monitoring frameworks. Facilitating collaboration between development and operations teams can lead to better insights and innovation in the domain of monitoring. Second, employee training in the optimal use of monitoring tools promotes optimal usage and expertise with accessible resources. By emphasizing an active strategy and leveraging the group mind within a firm, companies gain improved monitoring efficiency that not only maintains system integrity but also increases business flexibility as a whole.

7.5.1. Setting Clear Objectives and KPIs

In cloud computing, having clearly stated goals and key performance indicators (KPIs) is the foundation of effective observability and monitoring. The goals create a model that guides the deployment and management of cloud applications. They assist in aligning the monitoring efforts with the business objectives at the enterprise level, in a way that the technological advancements find direct expression as an advantage to the firm. This alignment helps teams focus on what matters, such as response times, user engagement levels, and resource utilization. Furthermore, setting specific KPIs allows teams to measure performance in an objective manner, identify bottlenecks, and prevent issues from spiraling into severe ones, hence enhancing the reliability and efficiency of the systems. The inclusion of KPIs in the monitoring strategy facilitates it for organizations to develop a culture of continuous improvement and accountability. Regular monitoring of such indicators can reveal trends and patterns, enabling teams to make informed decisions on infrastructure investments and application optimization.

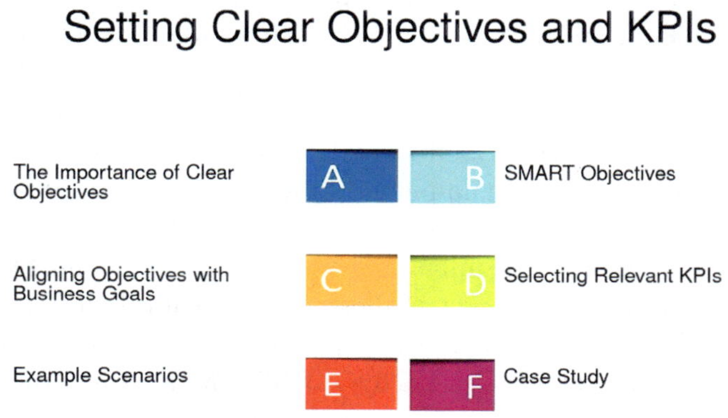

Figure 7.10. *Setting clear objectives and KPIs.*

Source: https://fastercapital.co/i/Influencer-marketing-strategy-differentiation-Influencer-Marketing-Strategies-to-Drive-Business-Growth--Setting-Clear-Objectives-and-KPIs.webp.

For example, if an application on the cloud is failing to meet performance expectations, the issue can be traced back by stakeholders to certain operation parameters that are being tracked by the KPIs. As a result, having quantifiable and actionable KPIs available is important not only to track success but also data-driven optimization to customize performance and scalability of cloud services. The procedure is a bit akin to performance testing in software development, whereby regular testing against established measures is essential in ensuring application efficiency (Bahrami et al., 2024). Furthermore, the efficient use of transparent objectives and KPIs allows for a transition from legacy data management to cloud-native. In the modern cloud ecosystem, scalability and resource efficiency are vital, particularly with increasing data workloads. Transparent objectives guide the re-engineering of legacy systems to enable companies to rescale infrastructure to meet fluctuating business needs. As companies shift to cloud-native technologies, scalability, reliability, and performance as KPIs become top priority. Through the support of high-quality analytics capabilities inherent to cloud technology, organizations can monitor such KPIs in real-time, therefore facilitating insights to drive rapid iterations and cloud service delivery optimization (Lenartavicius et al., 2024). Thus, establishing clear goals and KPIs is not merely a procedural necessity; it is a strategic imperative that governs the effective observability and monitoring processes in cloud computing systems (Figure 7.10).

7.5.2. Implementing Automated Alerting Systems

In the cloud computing environment, use of automated alerting mechanisms is a fundamental aspect of monitoring and observability. They act as live sentinels, which notify stakeholders of performance anomalies, potential failures, or significant shifts in resource consumption. With the use of sophisticated algorithms that track system parameters and user behavior, organizations receive immediate alerts whenever certain thresholds are breached. This proactive approach enables teams to address issues early on before they develop into critical failures, ultimately safeguarding service availability and user experience. Notably, automated alerting systems make processes involving event management easier, which enhances operational efficiency in dynamic cloud environments. IoT technologies incorporated assist in enhancing the effectiveness of automated alerting systems within cloud computing environments. As companies increasingly rely on IoT devices, data volume and complexity generated are unprecedented and necessitate real-time monitoring technologies. Automated alert systems can cope best with, and scrutinize, the deluge of data, making stakeholders aware of relevant events and trends. Studies emphasize the necessity of developing suitable IoT infrastructures that are adaptable to meet evolving requirements, thus enhancing overall operational and decision-making efficiencies (Allioui et al., 2023). With organizations embracing such architectures, automated alerting is essential in the attainment of system stability and performance. Additionally, the need for innovation in automated alerting systems is brought about by the contemporary challenges in various industries. The latest innovations in areas such as precision agriculture and big data analytics show the potential of automated alerts in raising productivity levels while minimizing negative environmental effects

(Karunathilake et al., 2023). As organizations struggle with issues like data management and technology acceptance, the deployment of efficient automated alerting solutions is critical towards enhancing responsiveness and utilization of resources substantially. Properly setting up alerting processes in specific operating environments ensures that applicable information effectively reaches those who are concerned so that it initiates timely interventions to maximize performance and minimize risks in ever-more complex cloud landscapes.

7.5.3. Regularly Reviewing and Updating Monitoring Strategies

With the evolving environment of cloud computing, revisiting and updating monitoring strategies on a regular basis cannot be overstressed. Monitoring processes and tools need to be periodically assessed to enhance observability and also for optimal optimization of resource usage. Cloud environments being dynamic by nature and heterogeneous in configuration, organizations must reconsider their monitoring frameworks to account for the complexities of their services properly. Through regular reviews, organizations can identify performance bottlenecks, trend analysis, and how changes or updates to systems impact overall performance. It is a preventive method that prevents failures from occurring before they turn into catastrophic failures, ensuring service availability and reliability are ensured in a more competitive market scenario. Moreover, the integration of new technology into monitoring plans is crucial for a robust cloud infrastructure. With the spread of Internet of Things (IoT) and smart technologies, organizations must refresh their observation frameworks to include the voluminous data generated by these gadgets, which can dramatically enhance observability. For example, applying opacity verification tools ensures privacy is addressed in real-time, as it goes on, when sensitive information transmitted by IoT devices is secured (Bourouis et al., 2017). This is particularly significant in areas where the integrity of data is of the highest priority, such as in healthcare, where monitoring strategies must adequately manage not only the performance statistics but also the privacy elements typical of IoT systems. Revising monitoring strategies at regular intervals also involves engaging various stakeholders from various fields to achieve their respective needs and expectations. With regard to smart grids, for instance, detailed monitoring must consider regulators' interactions with consumers and energy producers. Regulatory compliance, data security, and the use of new technology must be incorporated into monitoring activity (Axon et al., 2014). Through encouraging collaboration between most influential stakeholders, organizations can make sure that their monitoring approaches are technically accurate as well as complementary to the overall societal and regulatory forces. Such a synergistic strategy emphasizes the essentiality of regularly re-examining monitoring frameworks in order to effectively combat the changing issues of cloud computing (Figure 7.11).

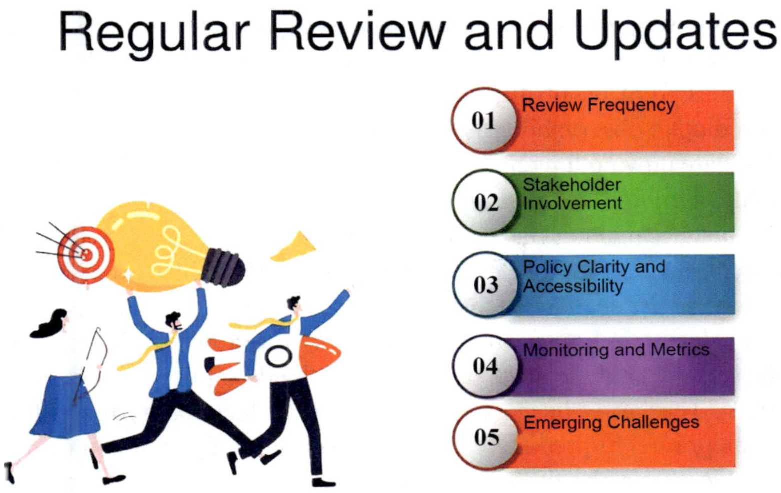

Figure 7.11. *Regularly reviewing and updating monitoring strategies.*

Source: https://fastercapital.co/i/Intellectual-property-policy--How-to-Create-and-Implement-an-Intellectual-Property-Policy-for-Your-Organization--Regular-Review-and-Updates.webp.

7.6. THE FUTURE OF OBSERVABILITY IN CLOUD COMPUTING

Cloud computing observability evolution is directly related to the issues faced by modern-day microservices architectures. While applications are increasingly being deployed in distributed systems, complexity in being observable has grown. This is because monitoring and inspecting interactions among numerous microservices that offer varying aspects of functionality is needed. Observability tools will be required to evolve to provide end-to-end visibility into application behavior while addressing the sheer volume of data being generated due to these interactions. Service meshes that facilitate inter-microservice communication have been touted to make observability easy. They introduce a purpose-designed infrastructure layer that enhances visibility and management over service interactions and solves problems related to inter-service communications and overall system reliability (Sedghpour et al., 2022). The future of observability is most likely going to be about leveraging such technologies in order to get a better understanding of distributed system health and performance. Together with technological advancements, the increased focus on operational efficiency in cloud computing also calls for out-of-the-box approaches to observability. Companies want to not only detect anomalies but proactively predict and prevent possible issues from occurring before they become critical issues. This shift towards predictive observability is transforming the functionality of monitoring tools, which are now no longer mere data collection tools but advanced systems that leverage machine learning algorithms for anomaly detection. These tools can review historical trends of data in order to offer insight into the expected state of the system, making it more possible to respond to incidents in a timely and effective way. As the need for such predictive capabilities intensifies, embedding real-time analytics and autonomous responses within observability platforms will be instrumental in defining the future of cloud computing (Friedlingstein et al., 2022). Therefore, businesses must invest in technology that allows for seamless integration of predictive analytics to ensure they maintain operational resilience. Moreover, the future of cloud computing observability will greatly rely on the increasing emphasis on security and compliance within distributed systems. With various regulatory models rising and awareness of data privacy increasing, organizations must ensure that their observability initiatives do not threaten security. This calls for the development of observability tools that, besides providing operational insights, incorporate compliance tests and security verifications into their architectures. The marriage of observability and security systems, referred to as security observability, will enable organizations to improve their ability to detect malicious activity and vulnerabilities. Besides, as the market transitions towards the use of service meshes and technologies like eBPF to enhance performance and security, it is critical that these technologies support observability work rather than hindering it (Sedghpour et al., 2022). In the long term, the future of observability will be based on delivering end-to-end solutions that find a balance between operational efficiency, security, and compliance in cloud computing environments.

7.6.1. Trends in Observability Technologies

With the advancement of cloud computing, observability technologies are increasingly being at the forefront of managing complex systems. New paradigms driven by artificial intelligence (AI) and machine learning are determining the latest trends in the sector. For instance, predictive analytics are employed to predict system failures and performance bottlenecks ahead of time so that they cannot impact service delivery. By integrating AI into observability platforms, businesses can combine high volumes of telemetry data and turn it into action-insights. This new way not only enhances the potential of application monitoring in an efficient manner but also empowers developers and operations teams to create more resilient architectures. In consequence, businesses can enhance performance and restrict downtime while being nimble in a competitive market, which makes the adoption of cutting-edge technology within observability frameworks essential. Another significant trend in observability technologies is the growing usage of distributed tracing and metrics-based monitoring. These methods provide greater insight into the more prevalent microservices architecture found in modern cloud environments. Distributed tracing enables developers to follow requests across many services, giving them information on latency and potential failure points.

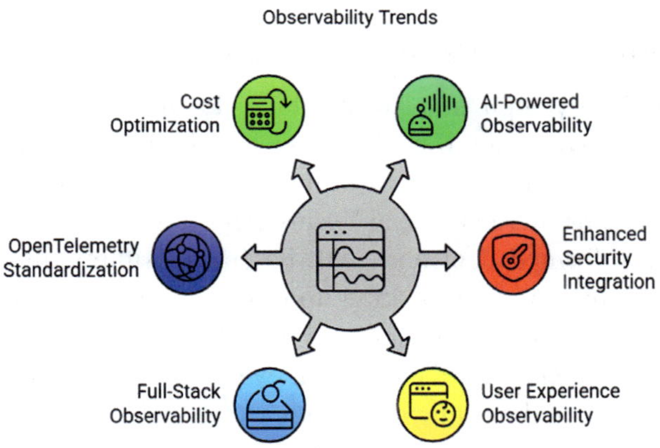

Figure 7.12. *Trends in observability technologies.*

Source: https://www.motadata.com/wp-content/uploads/2025/04/Key-Observability-Trends-for-2025.png.

When this is augmented with metrics-based monitoring, it provides greater insight into system performance, leading to improved troubleshooting capabilities. As businesses adopt such practices, they stand to gain from better collaboration between development and operations teams, or better known as DevOps. The convergence of such approaches is a reflection of the speeding up of efforts towards more sophisticated observability tools for better-informed decision-making and operational efficiency, enabling businesses to quickly address problems brought about by evolving technologies. Further, the advent of open-source observability tools is changing the way organizations adopt and implement monitoring practices. These kinds of tools, which are normally contributed by communities and focused on collaborative innovation, allow businesses to customize observability solutions to meet their unique needs. Such openness of observability technology makes cutting-edge tools accessible to small companies and startups without the exorbitant price tag of proprietary software. Furthermore, open-source projects are known to share collective attention, which results in rapid developments and a diverse array of features to be tailored for different applications. With regard to trends in observability technology, the trend towards open-source solutions reflects the broader trend towards openness and adaptability within cloud architecture which ultimately enables users to more effectively monitor and manage application performance, ultimately keeping organizations agile and competitive within an ever-changing marketplace (Figure 7.12).

7.6.2. The Impact of AI and Machine Learning

The exponential developments in machine learning (ML) and artificial intelligence (AI) have a significant impact on observability and monitoring in the cloud computing paradigm. With more companies moving to the cloud, data explosion means there is a need for efficient tools to analyze data in real-time and make informed decisions. ML-based algorithms allow systems to process huge volumes of data, picking up trends and anomalies which cannot be detected using conventional approaches. This functionality is critical to securing cloud architectures and ensuring they run optimally, saving companies money on downtime and optimizing resource use. Incident response times and operations can be improved by stakeholders through the implementation of AIs predictive analytics, which can ultimately translate to enhanced user satisfaction as well as greater trust in cloud-based applications, making it crucial their integration into observability platforms so that their potential can be optimized. To comprehend even more deeply the overbearing impact of AI and ML, it is important to delve into how they help in the field of big data analytics. Big data has transformed the way organizations think and utilize information, particularly in power systems, where the volatility can be overwhelming for traditional methods of analysis. According to available research, big data analytics powered by AI and ML allows for extraction of necessary insights from vast amounts of datasets. Such techniques grant decision-makers the ability to handle large and complicated information and facilitate smart grid implementations and battery storage management scenarios (Gharehpetian et al., 2019). The result is not just enhanced operational efficiency but also the creation of breakthrough innovations that mature in anticipation of the changing demands of cloud platforms. Thus, their application in observability platforms can aid in creating more efficient decisions, enabling a healthy and robust cloud platform. In addition to enhancing operational performance, AI and ML also aid in the creation of more sophisticated observability solutions through the support of new AI agent stacks. These stacks involve the integration of various components, such as vertical agents and observability tools, that facilitate effective deployment and management of AI systems in various applications (Siramgari, 2024). Integration enhances scalability and decision-making policies to facilitate anticipatory maintenance and cloud resource optimization. Also, the incorporation of memory components and sandboxes facilitates continuous learning and experimentation, which are essential in addressing shifting business needs. Finally, it is this multi-faceted strategy towards monitoring and observability that adds to the general integrity and efficacy of cloud computing, making AI and ML necessary in navigating the complexity of today's technology landscapes.

7.6.3. Evolving Standards and Practices

The cloud computing ecosystem is evolving at a rapid pace, necessitating responsive practices and standards in observability and monitoring. Among the stand-out characteristics that are driving this transition is increasing complexity in cloud architectures based on distributed systems and microservices. With the migration to such kinds of environments by organizations, traditional monitoring strategies are inadequate because they were premised on central infrastructures. Accordingly, contemporary standards are transitioning to decentralized principles that prioritize end-to-end observability. This transformation includes not only the implementation of advanced monitoring technologies but also the establishment of practices supplemented by flexible methodologies. By building a culture that encourages continuous integration and feedback, organizations are able to develop their flexibility and resilience to the shift in technology. Over time, these emerging practices establish an innovation culture that conditions teams to respond proactively to system failure and performance issues, hence limiting the downtime of operations. With advances in cloud computing technologies, so do their standards when applied to data management and processing. This change is best understood in the integration of artificial intelligence and machine learning into cloud services, which necessitates new models of observability. For instance, distributed data from edge nodes can be trained on machine learning algorithms, and practice allows for resource efficiency and consideration of privacy issues (Wang et al., 2019). This paradigm shift compels organizations to develop practices that not only highlight real-time analytics but also adopt newer standards of data management. With the implementation of these newer standards, businesses are able to optimize their functions, making data-driven decisions that improve customer experience and operational efficiency. With this, the integration of evolving standards into observability strategies not only supports the technical capabilities of cloud infrastructures but also supports overall organizational objectives. Furthermore, cloud computing industry norms are increasingly influenced by demands for robust security procedures in the context of observability. The hazards actualized through cyberattacks advance along with cloud platforms, and hence the necessity for organizations to institute thorough monitoring procedures encompassing security metrics and performance measurements is increasingly urgent. Current practices necessitate an end-to-end observability strategy, with security events being logged and analyzed with the same gravity as application metrics (Grigorescu et al., 2019). Having this two-pronged operational and security monitoring capability, an organization is in a better position to detect anomalies early and respond in due time to potential threats. By incorporating security practices into the observability model, organizations not only address evolving regulatory compliance, but also establish greater trust among stakeholders. The creation of standards and practices within observability and monitoring thus serves to acknowledge the symbiotic relationship between security and performance in current cloud environments (Figure 7.13).

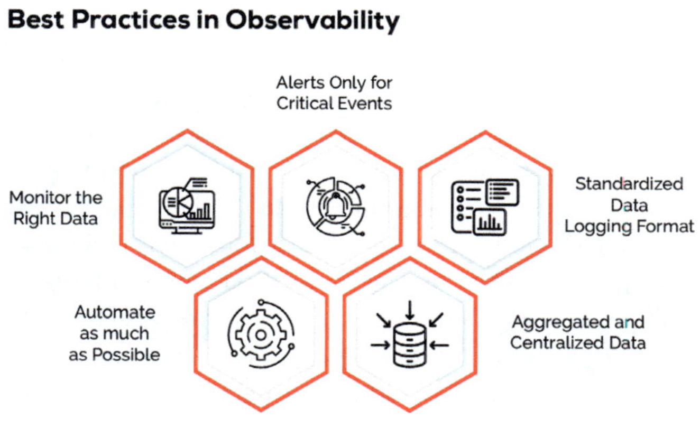

Figure 7.13. *The landscape of cloud computing is rapidly transforming, necessitating evolving standards and practices in observability and monitoring.*

Source: https://www.inspirisys.com/uploads/blog_image/Best-Practices-in-Observability.png.

SUMMARY

The abstract of this foray into observability and monitoring in cloud computing captures the imperative nature of these words in the resiliency and functionality of modern digital infrastructure. With companies increasingly relying on cloud services for scalability and flexibility, demand has exponentially risen for far-reaching observability. Robust monitoring frameworks enable organizations to gain actual-time visibility into application performance and user experience, thus enabling them to intervene proactively in resolving issues before they scale into large problems. This proactive approach not only optimizes operations but also aids cost savings and efficient resource utilization. Hence, a robust observability framework is fundamental in guaranteeing service reliability alongside organizational success amid fast-evolving cloud environments. In addition, the observability issues of the cloud cannot be minimized. The very complexity of multi-cloud setups, in addition to a vast amount of data generated, necessitates advanced analytical functionalities. Organizations are tasked with maintaining data integrity, processing different data sources, and merging monitoring tools from disparate service models. This is the type of complexity one would also encounter in new technologies in which there is a requirement to come up with functional architectures that address safety and computational hardware limitations (Grigorescu et al., 2019). As this study further highlights, effective application of observability practices can indeed lower threats and enhance decision-making capability, thereby optimizing operations and customer satisfaction in cloud systems. Briefly, cloud computing growth continues to require a sophisticated approach to observability and monitoring. Outcomes produced from studies such as those conducted by the Planck satellite indicate the importance of accuracy and responsiveness in obtaining useful insight into complex systems (Aghanim et al., 2019). As organizations embrace cloud technology, the application of sophisticated monitoring methods will be imperative in achieving excellence in service and reliability. Lastly, the future of cloud computing depends on the harmonious integration of observability practices that will allow organizations to navigate the intricacies of their digital realms with confidence, thus driving innovation and long-term expansion.

REFERENCES

1. Abramowicz, H., Brunner, M., Chemouil, P., Galis, et al. (2009). Management and service-aware networking architectures (MANA) for future internet position paper: System functions, capabilities and requirements. https://core.ac.uk/download/pdf/11476514.pdf (accessed on 11th September 2025).

2. Aghanim, N., Akrami, Y., Arroja, F., Ashdown, M., Aumont, J., Baccigalupi, C., Ballardini, M., et al. (2019). *Planck* 2018 results. *Astronomy and Astrophysics, 641*, A1–A1. https://doi.org/10.1051/0004-6361/201833880 (accessed on 11th September 2025).

3. Akrivopoulos, O., Amaxilatis, D., Chatzigiannakis, I., Mylonas, et al. (2017). An IoT-based solution for monitoring a fleet of educational buildings focusing on energy efficiency. https://core.ac.uk/download/158327961.pdf (accessed on 11th September 2025).

4. Allioui, H., & Mourdi, Y. (2023). Exploring the full potentials of IoT for better financial growth and stability: A comprehensive survey. *Sensors, 23*, 8015–8015. https://doi.org/10.3390/s23198015 (accessed on 11th September 2025).

5. Andrawos, M., Aßmann, U., Bass, L., Behara, D. G. K., Betts, T., Bianco, P., Bryant, D., et al. (2019). Microservice transition and its granularity problem: A systematic mapping study. https://core.ac.uk/download/426749569.pdf (accessed on 11th September 2025).

6. Axon, C., Balta-Ozkan, N., Cipcigan, L., et al. (2014). Scenarios for the development of smart grids in the UK: Literature review. https://core.ac.uk/download/155776124.pdf (accessed on 11th September 2025).

7. Azimi, M., Eslamlou, A. D., & Pekcan, G. (2020). Data-driven structural health monitoring and damage detection through deep learning: State-of-the-art review. *Sensors, 20*, 2778–2778. https://doi.org/10.3390/s20102778 (accessed on 11th September 2025).

8. Bahrami, S. (2024). Automated performance testing in ephemeral environments. https://core.ac.uk/download/613697324.pdf (accessed on 11th September 2025).

9. Berezin, S. (2025). Architecting scalable AI-CRM systems: Design patterns, infrastructure, and performance optimization. *International Journal of Engineering and Computer Science.* https://www.semanticscholar.org/paper/80bb2698525d6d0ebea9d65af93b875a0422200c (accessed on 11th September 2025).

10. Bourouis, A., Saboori, A., Lin, F., Lowe, G., Bryans, J. W., Atzori, L., Li, M., et al. (2017). Checking and enforcing security through opacity in healthcare applications. https://arxiv.org/abs/1710.00011 (accessed on 11th September 2025).
11. Dwivedi, R., Dave, D., Naik, H., Singhal, S., Rana, O., Patel, P., Qian, B., et al. (2022). Explainable AI (XAI): Core ideas, techniques, and solutions. *ACM Computing Surveys, 55*, 1–33. https://doi.org/10.1145/3561048 (accessed on 11th September 2025).
12. Friedlingstein, P., Jones, M. W., O'Sullivan, M., Andrew, R. M., Bakker, D. C. E., Hauck, J., Le Quéré, C., et al. (2022). Global carbon budget 2021. *Earth System Science Data, 14*, 1917–2005. https://doi.org/10.5194/essd-14-1917-2022 (accessed on 11th September 2025).
13. Gharehpetian, G. B., Marzband, M., Moradi, J., et al. (2019). Attributes of big data analytics for data-driven decision making in cyber-physical power systems. https://core.ac.uk/download/305121394.pdf (accessed on 11th September 2025).
14. Grigorescu, S., Trăsnea, B., Cocias, T., & Măceşanu, G. (2019). A survey of deep learning techniques for autonomous driving. *Journal of Field Robotics, 37*, 362–386. https://doi.org/10.1002/rob.21918 (accessed on 11th September 2025).
15. Jajodia, S., Kant, K., Samarati, P., Singhal, A., Swarup, V., & Wang, C. (2020). *Secure Cloud Computing.*
16. Karunathilake, E. M. B. M., Le, A. T., Heo, S., Chung, Y. S., & Mansoor, S. (2023). The path to smart farming: Innovations and opportunities in precision agriculture. *Agriculture, 13*, 1593–1593. https://doi.org/10.3390/agriculture13081593 (accessed on 11th September 2025).
17. Katta, V. K. (2025). Leveraging AWS cloud native services for scalable application architectures. *World Journal of Advanced Research and Reviews.* https://www.semanticscholar.org/paper/ceba1bdca874f7e12b24027c6cd17ab1c9ca9bf3 (accessed on 11th September 2025).
18. Kocher, P., Horn, J., Fogh, A., Genkin, D., Gruss, D., Haas, W., Hamburg, M., et al. (2019). Spectre attacks: Exploiting speculative execution. *2022 IEEE Symposium on Security and Privacy (SP).* https://doi.org/10.1109/sp.2019.00002 (accessed on 11th September 2025).
19. Kodheli, O., Lagunas, E., Maturo, N., Sharma, S. K., Shankar, B., Mendoza Montoya, J. F., Merlano Duncán, J. C., et al. (2020). Satellite communications in the new space era: A survey and future challenges.

IEEE Communications Surveys & Tutorials, 23, 70–109. https://doi.org/10.1109/comst.2020.3028247 (accessed on 11th September 2025).

20. Lenartavicius, V. (2024). Re-engineering legacy data platforms with cloud-native technologies. https://core.ac.uk/download/636345332.pdf (accessed on 11th September 2025).
21. Lněnička, M. (2013). Cloud based testing of business applications and web services. https://core.ac.uk/download/14742035.pdf (accessed on 11th September 2025).
22. McEnroe, P., Wang, S., & Liyanage, M. (2022). A survey on the convergence of edge computing and AI for UAVs: Opportunities and challenges. *IEEE Internet of Things Journal, 9*, 15435–15459. https://doi.org/10.1109/jiot.2022.3176400 (accessed on 11th September 2025).
23. Morgan, J., Halton, M., Qiao, Y., & Breslin, J. G. (2021). Industry 4.0 smart reconfigurable manufacturing machines. *Journal of Manufacturing Systems, 59*, 481–506. https://doi.org/10.1016/j.jmsy.2021.03.001 (accessed on 11th September 2025).
24. Nerella, V. M. L. G. (2019). Observability-driven SRE practices for proactive database reliability and rapid incident response. https://core.ac.uk/download/666027074.pdf (accessed on 11th September 2025).
25. Park, S., & Kim, Y. G. (2022). A metaverse: Taxonomy, components, applications, and open challenges. *IEEE Access, 10*, 4209–4251. https://doi.org/10.1109/access.2021.3140175 (accessed on 11th September 2025).
26. Perumal, A. P., & Ahire, V. (2025). Multi-cloud observability: Tools and techniques for monitoring and troubleshooting complex hybrid cloud environments. https://core.ac.uk/download/654637540.pdf (accessed on 11th September 2025).
27. Pusukuri, M. K. (2024). Leveraging observability-driven predictive analytics for cost-effective hybrid cloud migration on AWS. *International Journal of Scientific Research in Computer Science, Engineering and Information Technology*. https://www.semanticscholar.org/paper/d19bed2352c7f9138e59737acfbdb4ed79c0f112 (accessed on 11th September 2025).
28. Rose, S., Borchert, O., Mitchell, S., & Connelly, S. (2020). Zero trust architecture. https://doi.org/10.6028/nist.sp.800-207 (accessed on 11th September 2025).
29. Sarker, I. H. (2022). AI-based modeling: Techniques, applications and research issues towards automation, intelligent and smart systems. *SN*

Computer Science, 3. https://doi.org/10.1007/s42979-022-01043-x (accessed on 11th September 2025).

30. Sathe, M. M. (2025). Serverless web development. *International Journal of Scientific Research in Engineering and Management*. https://www.semanticscholar.org/paper/b74ef717e46e1d7dd1c578678f31af938b4d1222 (accessed on 11th September 2025).
31. Sedghpour, M. R. S., & Townend, P. (2022). Service mesh and eBPF-powered microservices: A survey and future directions. https://doi.org/10.1109/sose55356.2022.00027 (accessed on 11th September 2025).
32. Siramgari, D. (2024). Building the future: Unveiling the AI agent stack. https://core.ac.uk/download/654637507.pdf (accessed on 11th September 2025).
33. Tataria, H., Shafi, M., Molisch, A. F., Döhler, M., Sjöland, H., & Tufvesson, F. (2021). 6G wireless systems: Vision, requirements, challenges, insights, and opportunities. *Proceedings of the IEEE, 109*, 1166–1199. https://doi.org/10.1109/jproc.2021.3061701 (accessed on 11th September 2025).
34. Tzanettis, I., Androna, C. M., Zafeiropoulos, A., Fotopoulou, E., & Papavassiliou, S. (2022). Data fusion of observability signals for assisting orchestration of distributed applications. *Sensors, 22*, 2061–2061. https://doi.org/10.3390/s22052061 (accessed on 11th September 2025).
35. Wang, S., Tuor, T., Salonidis, T., Leung, K. K., Makaya, C., He, T., & Chan, K. (2019). Adaptive federated learning in resource constrained edge computing systems. *IEEE Journal on Selected Areas in Communications, 37*, 1205–1221. https://doi.org/10.1109/jsac.2019.2904348 (accessed on 11th September 2025).

CHAPTER 8

SECURITY IN CLOUD-NATIVE APPLICATIONS

Contents

INTRODUCTION

The universal adoption of cloud-native applications is a characteristic shift in the way businesses approach computing resources, data storage, and application deployment. With the use of microservices architecture and containerization, these apps offer more flexibility, scalability, and fault tolerance than traditional monolithic systems. Though this shift introduces the complexity of security threats to be addressed comprehensively,. The constant evolving nature of cloud environments yields a rich soil for vulnerabilities to emerge at a fast pace, necessitating robust security controls that are well equipped to deal with ongoing alteration of application architecture and infrastructure. Thus, being aware of the intrinsic security risks introduced by cloud-native applications is essential for companies seeking to protect sensitive data and maintain system integrity. Perhaps one of the largest cloud-native application security concerns is their inherent reliance on coupled services and components. Although each microservice is meant to be modular, it does increase the attack surface and could expose organizations to every type of threat that includes unauthorized access and data breaches. Furthermore, the multi-cloud and hybrid cloud models that businesses implement make the security model more complex because they call for homogenous security controls on multiple platforms. The need for real-time monitoring and incident response capabilities becomes downright indispensable in this kind of environment, where detection and remediation can significantly mitigate potential damages. To this end, an end-to-end solution incorporating proactive security controls like continuous threat analysis and vulnerability management is downright imperative to securing cloud-native applications in this new digital landscape. Other than security technology concerns, organizational culture is a key determinant of the successful implementation of security practice in cloud-native environments. Successful implementation of security best practices not only requires the integration of advanced technologies but also a shift of mind by developers, operations personnel, and stakeholders. Security awareness training and education are important in order to get all employees cognizant of possible threats and informed of new security trends in the cloud industry. Moreover, collaboration across departments might lead to more holistic security plans spanning the entire application life cycle. Empowering these blended teams can build a culture of shared accountability and vigilance, critical to the long-term security and success of cloud-native applications in an increasingly networked world.

Definition of Cloud-Native Applications

Cloud-native applications are a new leap in software development that is designed to execute optimally within cloud computing environments. Cloud-native applications leverage the native strengths of cloud platforms, such as scalability, resilience, and elasticity. Employing microservices architecture, cloud-native applications are broken down into loose, independent components that can be deployed and upgraded one by one. This modular architecture not only supports agility in development and deployment processes but also facilitates CI/CD processes. As resources are dynamically provisioned on-demand, cloud-native applications allow organizations to respond rapidly to market situations and user needs, ultimately resulting in innovation and competitiveness. Cloud-native application design principles also impact their security posture. One of the primary characteristics is their ability to integrate security controls in the application lifecycle, a procedure known as DevSecOps. Ongoing monitoring and automated security scan become second nature to the development process so that security vulnerabilities are identified and rectified in real time. Such measures are vital, given the ever-changing nature of the cloud platform, where threats will evolve much more rapidly. Secondly, the utilization of containerization technologies serves to isolate applications and their dependencies, thereby limiting the attack surface and enhancing overall security. The framework thus strengthens the security model to bring focus on the necessity of implementing good security practices into the pipeline of development. Moreover, the complex interdependencies and interactions among microservices in cloud-native applications pose particular security challenges. With many components of functionality talking to one another over networks, breaches or misconfigurations carry a much higher risk. Robust access controls, encryption of data, and strong identity management solutions have to be used to ensure the risks are mitigated. In addition, emergence of new technologies in cloud-native platforms such as machine learning and artificial intelligence brings about risks along with opportunities and calls for continuous research and development in security measures. This evolving world raises privacy, compliance, and governance questions that need to be addressed by the organizations. Knowledge of cloud-native applications is needed in order to assist in enhancing security practices and addressing concerns raised in the new technology space (Figure 8.1).

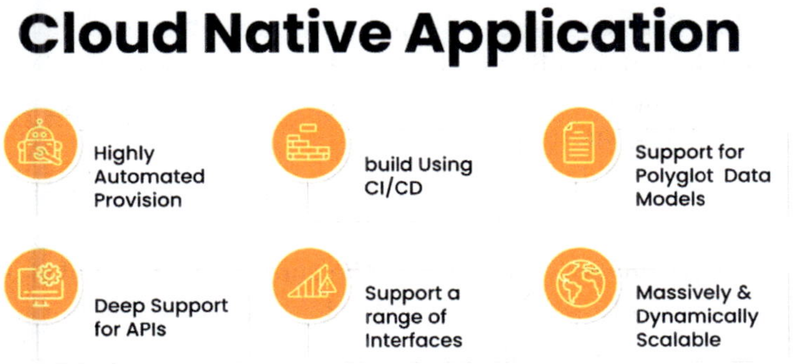

Figure 8.1. *Cloud-native applications.*

Source: https://www.moontechnolabs.com/blog/wp-content/uploads/2023/11/Cloud-Native-Applications.webp.

Importance of Security in Cloud Environments

The adoption of cloud-native applications has revolutionized the management and deployment of an organization's IT assets, but with this comes unprecedented security implications. Cloud security is critical because weakness in it will expose critical information and disrupt business operations. Cloud environments, as opposed to traditional IT structures, operate under shared resources, and this opens them up to a heightened risk of unauthorized access and data breaches. The hybrid nature of cloud services and dynamic character require robust security that is responsive and adaptive to changing threats. More confidentiality, integrity, and availability are essential, as intrusions not only compromise information but lead to financial loss, reputational damage, and legal violations. Organizations must value highly the implementation of stringent security mechanisms to safeguard their cloud-native applications. In addition to traditional security solutions, cloud platforms require advanced technologies specifically tailored to address their requirements for navigating the unprecedented challenges. Artificial intelligence and machine learning both hold promises as well as risks.

Their application has the potential to enhance security systems by identifying patterns and anomalies indicative of probable violations and enabling proactive response. However, they also introduce new avenues of vulnerability, particularly with regard to data privacy and regulatory compliances. As argued in Wang et al. (2022), the evolution of cloud technologies demands serious examination of the support frameworks to ensure they are immune to both inherited and unique threats of distributed computing environments. The implementation of a security framework, therefore, becomes an ongoing necessity rather than a one-time setting. Security issues in cloud settings are also complemented by scalability and interoperability problems. As businesses increasingly adopt multi-cloud and hybrid approaches, they must facilitate seamless yet secure consolidation across multiple platforms.

The limitations outlined in Khaled et al. (2019) for new-generation wireless communication systems emphasize the need for uniformity of security standards to operate similarly on different systems. The complexity of cloud architecture combined with rapidly advancing technology developments necessitates continuous vigilance and adaptations to security protocols. Impeccably dealing with these factors not only reduces risk but also supports operational efficacy, ultimately leading to trust from users and clients. This unflinching commitment to security, thus, not only secures assets but supports innovation and development in cloud-native applications.

8.1. UNDERSTANDING CLOUD-NATIVE ARCHITECTURE

The shift to cloud-native architecture marks a crucial leap in software design, integrating tenets that value flexibility, elasticity, and fault tolerance. In contrast to the conventional monolithic approach, cloud-native applications are architected as a group of loosely connected microservices, allowing individuals to deploy and scale components independently. Through this modularity, software development cycles are streamlined, and organizations can respond quickly to changing market needs and technological advancements. While, this change presents its own set of challenges, particularly in maintaining robust security among scattered components. As seen in the case of banks, organizations need to tread carefully between strict compliance requirements and adoption of cloud-native technology. This enables them to enhance operational responsiveness and adaptability without compromising the integrity of high-value information, which points to the dual mandate of security and innovation in contemporary cloud environments (Indukuri, 2025). Additionally, the architectural transition to cloud-native applications also necessitates embracing practices such as containerization and orchestration, which in turn encourage resource-efficient use and optimal functioning. Containers package applications and their dependencies in a standard environment throughout development and deployment phases. In the meantime, orchestration tools facilitate automated container management, facilitating easier deployment and offering transparent scaling. However, when applications are broken down into microservices, security becomes increasingly complex. Organizations will have to implement a multi-layered security strategy, addressing vulnerabilities that can happen across various levels—from network security all the way through to application-level protection. Best practice in cloud-native development, particularly in the financial technology sector, underscores the critical meeting point of architectural innovation and concerns about security to enable innovative but secure applications (Jayantha, 2025). Finally, moving to cloud-native architecture isn't solely technology; it's a revolutionary cultural transformation in organizations. Embracing agile practices, DevOps strategies, and security-first practices becomes essential as cross-silo activities work together as one team. This culture transformation enables organizations to determine what their technical capabilities can benefit the business and adopt a proactive security mindset in application development and delivery. The challenge of applying new technology with existing systems is the most critical, but successful transformations leverage iterative processes that focus on constant improvement. As businesses realign their practices to better enable a cloud-native approach, they build resilient flexibility that is ideally suited to counter security attacks. Ultimately, organizations that concentrate on both cloud-native architecture and security will be well-positioned in today's rapidly evolving digital landscape (Indukuri, 2025) (Figure 8.2).

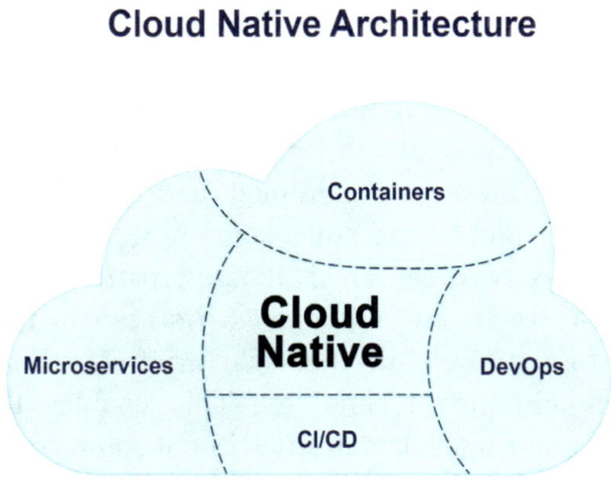

Figure 8.2. *The transition to cloud-native architecture.*

Source: https://media.geeksforgeeks.org/wp-content/uploads/20230415110023/Cloud-Native-Images-(1).jpg.

8.1.1. Key Components of Cloud-Native Applications

Cloud-native applications are a software development and deployment paradigm shift emphasizing agility, scalability, and resilience. Microservices are central to cloud-native applications that decompose complex systems into separate, independent services deployable and manageable in isolation. Such an architecture enables teams to add isolated components of an application without influencing the overall system, thereby enhancing continuous integration and delivery (CI/CD) processes. Although these have some benefits, it is imperative to keep security concerns in mind because every microservice may pose risk. Since cloud-native applications are run in dynamic environments, securing such microservices for threats demands taking strong security practices during the development phase, which in turn would affect the overall security stance of the application as a whole. Another critical cloud-native application requirement is the use of containerization technologies such as Docker and Kubernetes, which facilitate the successful deployment and orchestration of microservices. Containers encapsulate application code and its dependencies, thereby enabling consistency from environment to environment, from dev to prod. Security challenges arise, however, such as those pertaining to container image vulnerabilities and runtime configurations. It is important that development teams adopt secure coding practices, periodic security audits, and continuous monitoring of the container environments. As more and more organizations utilize cloud-native architectures, they must understand that a comprehensive security plan targeting this environment is important so as to prevent potential breaches and loss of data and align with enterprise-level organizational security policies. Lastly, the employment of cloud-native patterns such as serverless computing and service meshes comes a long way in enhancing the efficiency and flexibility of modern applications. Serverless designs eliminate server administration requirements, allowing developers to focus on coding while the infrastructure is scaled and maintained by the cloud providers. However, this convenience comes with security consequences like data exposure vulnerabilities as well as complexity in monitoring compliance in a multi-cloud environment. In the same fashion, service meshes facilitate secure communication between microservices but add complexity when it comes to traffic handling, security policy management, and observability. Organizations transforming towards cloud-native applications must recognize these components as belonging to their security frameworks so that security functionalities are integrated at every level, thereby forming a resilient and secure cloud-native ecosystem, as evidenced in the evolving paradigms of technology discussed in Yogesh et al. (2023) and Wang et al. (2022).

8.1.2. Differences Between Traditional and Cloud-Native Architectures

The transformation from traditional to cloud-native architectures is a significant paradigm shift in how software applications are designed, deployed, and maintained. Traditional approaches are based on monolithic designs, where applications are built as unbreakable single pieces. This is hard to scale because any modification must redeploy the whole application. Cloud-native designs center on microservices, allowing individual components to be built, deployed, and scaled independently. This modularity enhances resilience and facilitates continuous integration and deployment, which is critical in maintaining security in cloud-native applications. Cloud-native systems' built-in flexibility also enables organizations to quickly act on emergent security threats, thereby improving their security stance overall. The second significant difference lies in the operational patterns of the two architectures. Traditional systems are typically operating on single-purpose, on-premise hardware, which also carries risks of underutilization and increased operating costs. Conversely, cloud-native architectures leverage virtualized infrastructures in the cloud, where resources can be dynamically allocated based on need. Not only does this facilitate cost-savings, but it also makes it simpler to implement end-to-end security controls. Cloud-native applications are likely to incorporate automated security processes, such as continuous monitoring and threat response, essential to safeguard sensitive data. Furthermore, the use of serverless computing solutions, as seen in existing research, provides developers with an opportunity to focus more on code and less on infrastructure issues, adding additional layers of security built into the cloud infrastructure (Baldini et al., 2017). In addition, traditional architectures are plagued by integration and interoperability issues, which can hinder security efforts. In these kinds of systems, legacy applications are not always designed to communicate with existing technologies in an optimal way, and thus may become silos that might be exploited by malicious parties. Cloud-native architectures, on the other hand, inherently support APIs and containerization, enhancing cross-platform integration ability. This facilitates better collaboration and data sharing between services, which is critical in detecting and countering security threats. The ability to seamlessly interact with IoT devices, as acknowledged in scholarly literature, is another cloud-native framework security advantage. An interface of this kind facilitates real-time monitoring and rapid response to threats across the whole system (Copeland et al., 2019). As more organizations adopt cloud-native, such differences reinforce the demand for a viable security strategy sensitive to the unique characteristics of cloud landscapes (Figure 8.3).

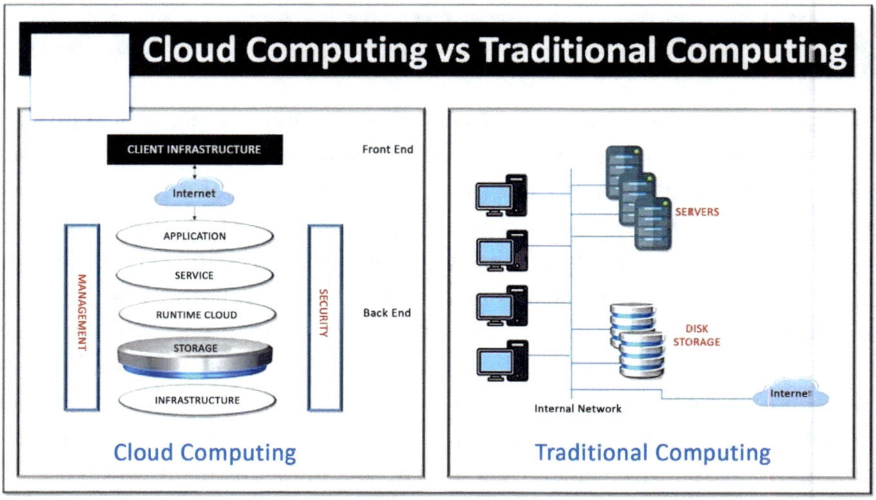

Figure 8.3. *Differences between traditional and cloud-native architectures.*

Source: https://i0.wp.com/cloudwithease.com/wp-content/uploads/2022/11/cloud-compuring-vs-traditional-computing-dp.jpg.

8.1.3. Benefits of Adopting Cloud-Native Approaches

Adopting cloud-native approaches has numerous benefits, particularly when it comes to application security. One of the notable ones is the greater scalability that cloud-native architectures have. With this scalability, the organization can respond timely to evolving needs through the dynamic scaling of resources. In terms of security, this means that organizations can incorporate additional defense features, like more monitoring or firewall capabilities, at times of higher risk, such as following a breach of data. Besides, the scalability found within cloud-native ecosystems enables rapid deployment of security patches and updates, hence minimizing loopholes that could be exploited by bad actors. By incorporating such enhancements into continuous integration pipelines through developers, there is a build-up of overall application strength to better foster a secure computing environment that is designed to effectively counter many threats, ultimately aiding organizations in safeguarding critical data (Marti et al., 2019). Another significant benefit of cloud-native approaches is that they harmonize with DevOps principles, which create a working culture of collaboration among development, operations, and security teams.

This harmony facilitates an environment which enables not only rapid deployment but greater security as well. When stakeholders from various disciplines work together, they are able to anticipate potential security risks early during the development phase, resulting in faster fixes and more secure applications. The emphasis on automation in DevOps ensures security practices such as code scanning, compliance testing, and vulnerability scans are always included in deployment pipelines. With companies utilizing these practices, they can create a more security-focused culture with a priority on the development and deployment cycle of applications, which makes it easier to adapt to new threats and ensures software released is both functional and secure (Ebert et al., 2019). With a cloud-native solution, visibility and monitoring capabilities also improve, which is beneficial in maintaining the security of the applications. With traditional deployments, the monitoring data could become siloed on multiple platforms and systems, becoming harder for the security framework. With cloud-native architecture, though, centralized logging and monitoring solutions are used, which provide real-time visibility into application performance and security states.

This integrated information prepares organizations to detect anomalies rapidly, enabling proactive prevention of risk threats. Cloud-native technology also has built-in security features, such as identity and access management, and automated compliance features that streamline security management. The combination of enhanced visibility and automation not only accelerates the speed of incident response but also encourages a more assertive security posture, making the organization an adaptive entity capable of managing the complexities of current cyber threats with assurance.

8.2. COMMON SECURITY THREATS IN CLOUD-NATIVE APPLICATIONS

As businesses migrate more and more to cloud-native applications, they expose themselves to an array of security attacks that compromise data integrity and confidentiality. High on the list of most serious is the lack of security for the underlying infrastructure, namely the graphics processing unit (GPU). Although GPUs enhance performance in dealing with large data sets and computationally intensive computations, they are also riddled with severe security flaws. Specifically, such vulnerabilities allow it to be simple for stealth malware to lie dormant, becoming the weakest point in the security chain. As a result, developers and security professionals must be taught about GPU-based vulnerabilities and implement careful countermeasures to secure these essential components (Abhinaya et al., 2018). Aside from GPU threats, container orchestration systems used in cloud-native environments present particular security threats.

For instance, flawed container setups can lead to unwarranted access, enabling critical application components to be exposed to exploitation. DevOps teams will have to adhere to best practices, such as mandating strict access controls, periodic security audits, and the use of automated software for vulnerability scanning. The transitory nature of cloud-native apps makes it even more complicated, with these apps scaling up and down on a regular basis, commonly leading to abandoned security positions. This realization allows organizations to incorporate effective security practices that can manage the dynamic environment of cloud-native systems (Dudley et al., 2020). Third-party integration in cloud-native applications is also a source of additional threats that must be closely monitored. The majority of applications are reliant on external APIs and microservices, which offer vulnerability points for hackers to exploit. For example, weak authentication systems and open connections can be used as entry points for attackers to intercept data or inject mischief into operations. These threats are best thwarted by strict security controls such as rate limiting, logging, and strict API management. By giving these security aspects high priority, application developers can create more secure cloud-native applications that are immune to common attacks and still retain the flexibility and scalability characterizing this emerging software development paradigm (Abhinaya et al., 2018) (Figure 8.4).

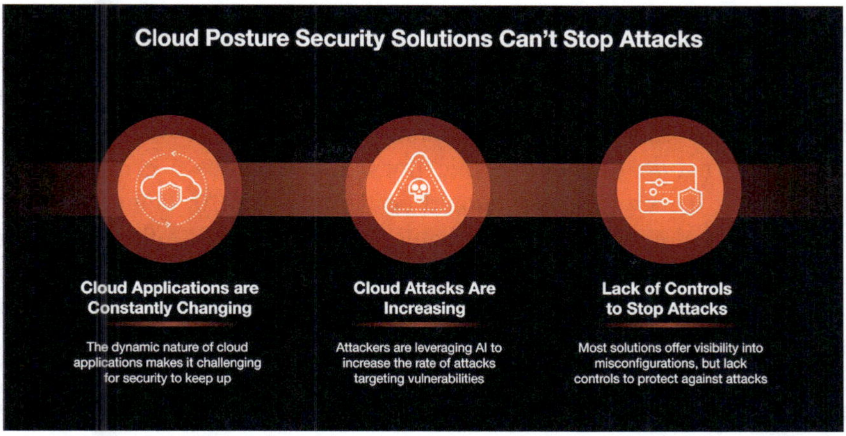

Figure 8.4. *The cloud-posture-security-solutions-cant-stop-attacks.*

Source: https://www.paloaltonetworks.com/content/dam/pan/en_US/images/cyberpedia/cloud-security-threats-detection-and-challenges/cloud-posture-security-solutions-cant-stop-attacks.png?imwidth=1366.

8.2.1. Data Breaches and Unauthorized Access

Increased use of cloud-native applications has transformed the manner in which organizations handle data, but in doing so, it has also heightened risks of data breaches as well as unauthorized access. As cloud environments store enormous amounts of sensitive information, the dangers of malicious actors taking advantage of vulnerabilities have escalated tremendously. Organizations must realize that conventional security measures utilized within on-premises settings might not be effective within cloud environments. Improper access controls and poor practices in encryption will lead to unauthorized access, which includes cybercriminals infiltrating systems to steal information or destroy application integrity. Consequences of these exposures can be disastrous, including high financial losses, loss of reputation, and potential legal proceedings against organizations lacking suitable security in their systems. Thus, an aggressive strategy towards security in cloud-native applications is required in order to fight against these attacks and protect sensitive information. Overcoming these issues requires a novel security framework paradigm that emphasizes the importance of improved technologies and methodologies. A prime example is the QP-ChainSZKP framework, which integrates Quantum-Secure Cryptographic Algorithms with Zero-Knowledge Proof Management. This visionary architecture plays a basic role in securing cloud ecosystems from both conventional and emerging quantum attacks, which are critical to preventing data breaches and unauthorized access. By enhancing existing security mechanisms, organizations can achieve rigorous compliance levels while simultaneously safeguarding their data from new cyber attacks. The scalability of the frameworks ensures that it is still capable of adapting to the ever-evolving nature of cloud applications and provides a critical layer of protection that legacy measures would be deprived of. As organizations rely increasingly on cloud-native infrastructure, the deployment of such advanced security architectures becomes necessary in the protection of sensitive data and maintenance of operational integrity. Moreover, shifting threats underscore the necessity of ongoing research and development in database and application security. The landscape of data security is not static; it is always advancing with technology, such as the proliferation of NoSQL databases and the integration of Internet of Things (IoT) devices. As highlighted in recent publications, theres a pressing need to fill gaps in terms of insider threats and resulting vulnerabilities due to hybrid cloud deployments. Existing security frameworks, although foundational in nature, must be complemented through embedding with advanced technologies such as artificial intelligence, machine learning, and blockchain to fight emerging threats. The strict regulatory compliance frameworks, such as GDPR, also challenge organizations when they attempt to align legal norms with security controls. By bridging these security control gaps and continuous innovation, organizations can develop adaptive, multi-layered security solutions, thus making their defenses more resilient to data breaches and unauthorized access in cloud-native applications.

8.2.2. Misconfiguration Vulnerabilities

For the cloud-native application universe, misconfiguration vulnerabilities represent an overarching problem, one that generally tends to compromise the integrity and security of otherwise healthy architectures. These vulnerabilities arise when services and apps are not configured correctly, leaving them open to attackers who can capitalize on such loopholes and gain unauthorized access. Misconfigurations can occur on various levels, like cloud service configurations, network configurations, and app deployments, which can lead to possible data leaks, unauthorized entry points, and even service downtime. The rapid adoption of cloud environments leaves the right security procedures behind, and thus cases of misconfigurations abound. While organizations transform to more scalable and agile forms, they will need to place highest priority on strict configuration management and security hardening to effectively combat these vulnerabilities. The arrival of such frameworks as Open RAN introduces new opportunities with additional security risk, particularly when considering misconfiguration issues. Open RAN with the added flexibility and cost-effectiveness in the open environment comes at the price of a more advanced configuration that could contribute to the likelihood of misconfigurations. Stakeholders need to be cautious since the hodgepodge of vendors could result in inconsistent configurations or overlooked security best practices. Since Open RAN redesigns how Radio Access Network components communicate with one another, flawed setups might lead to severe vulnerabilities. The security and privacy risks surrounding them, if not checked, might undermine not only single users but also the overall network infrastructure, highlighting the necessity for rigorous monitoring when deploying as well as persistent scrutiny. The incorporation of advanced technologies such as artificial intelligence and machine learning is critical in addressing misconfiguration vulnerability in cloud environments. With the employment of smart monitoring mechanisms such as those detailed within the OpenStackDP framework, organizations are able to effortlessly identify anomalies that point to misconfigurations. The capability of the framework to analyze data in motion allows for instant detection and correction of would-be vulnerability prior to exploitation. With an accuracy of 99.81% in threat identification, this technique allows cloud administrators to possess dynamically secure settings. With the rapidly evolving environment, such mechanized systems not only enhance security but also provide improved Quality-of-Service and a more robust infrastructure, demonstrating that managing misconfiguration vulnerabilities is paramount to cloud-native application integrity (Figure 8.5).

Figure 8.5. *The misconfiguration vulnerabilities.*

Source: https://qawerk.com/wp-content/uploads/2022/11/Lead_magnet.svg.

8.2.3. Insecure APIs and Their Implications

Application programming interface (API) security is now one of the priority areas in cloud-native applications. An insecure API can provide a route for unauthorized access, leading to data breaches and leaks of sensitive information. With organizations relying on APIs to facilitate communication between microservices, the attack surface expands, and therefore developers must implement good security practices. Insecure APIs usually contribute to vulnerabilities such as improper authentication, sensitive data exposure, and inadequate logging, which can be exploited by cybercriminals. The impact of such security weaknesses extends beyond data loss; they can not only damage an organization's reputation, erode user trust, but also cause severe financial losses. API security thus forms a central part of securing all cloud-native apps and needs to be given high priority across the software development life cycle. The risk of insecure APIs is particularly acute as companies transition to the Internet of Things (IoT) and mobile ecosystems leveraging real-time data. As these systems integrate machine learning and AI to enhance functionality, such as in the instance of Precision Agriculture, safe APIs are even more crucial. Recent discussions regarding future development for certain technologies, such as 5G and 6G networks, indicate that security measures must evolve parallel with enhancements in these integrated systems (Porambage et al., 2021). As these interactions become more complex, with distributed ledger and edge computing being employed, the developers must ensure that the APIs are secure from potential attacks. This includes the utilization of advanced authentication techniques, regular security audits, and utilization of frameworks that have been designed to address the particular challenges of such interconnected systems. Besides, the intersection of cloud-native applications and API security demands cross-disciplinary solutions to counter the many threats aimed at shifting dynamics. Utilization of various enabling technologies such as Software Defined Networks (SDN) and fog computing can be employed in enhancing the security of APIs through bringing computations close to the data generation sources, thus limiting latency and exposure risk (Singh et al., 2021). But deploying these solutions needs insight into the operational environment and ongoing optimization of security procedures. With the ecosystem of cloud-native applications becoming increasingly complex, organizations need to be on their guard in API security work. By instilling a culture of security awareness, continuously updating security controls, and actively pursuing vulnerabilities, organizations can significantly reduce the threat risk introduced by insecure APIs, while at the same time reinforcing their overall security position in a cloud-dominant world.

8.3. SECURITY BEST PRACTICES FOR CLOUD-NATIVE DEVELOPMENT

With the evolving climate of cloud-native application development, the best practices in security play a crucial role in ensuring protection against potential vulnerabilities. One of the key fundamentals involves the use of an efficient Identity and Access Management (IAM) framework that outlines user privilege and hence prevents unauthorized access to sensitive information. By enforcing standards like the principle of least privilege, organizations can ensure that users are granted only those privileges required to undertake the function they are about to execute. Moreover, the inclusion of improved security features such as multifactor authentication (MFA) significantly enhances access controls by providing a security level that is downright crucial in cloud environments. This applies especially in response to the additional push toward microservices architecture, which, as observed by Oyeniran et al. (2024), can be accompanied by complexity that needs careful monitoring and management of communications across services. Thus, having robust IAM policies not just protects against security breaches but also facilitates a safer cloud-native setup. Security scanning and monitoring is another key part of security best practices in cloud-native development. Vulnerability scans and penetration testing on an ongoing basis is essential to identify vulnerabilities that are sure to arise in the high-speed deployments typical of cloud-based environments. These pre-emptive measures allow organizations to preclude vulnerabilities from being exploited for ill intent before they can be used. Furthermore, employing Security Information and Event Management (SIEM) systems allows monitoring of security events in real time, providing hints which help to identify anomalies in application behavior or unauthorized access attempts, as the improvements in security fundamentals demonstrate (Nayan, 2023). Apart from reactive measures, organizations must also integrate security at every stage of the development cycle and adopt the philosophy of DevSecOps. This end-to-end approach facilitates a culture whereby security is an integral part of application design and deployment. Finally, data integrity and very robust data encryption are some of the most important best practices necessary for securing cloud-native applications. As required in the latest talks regarding new technologies, organizations must ensure that data stored or in transit, which is sensitive in nature, is encrypted according to industry standards. It reduces substantially the threat of data breaches and adhering to regulations such as GDPR and HIPAA. Moreover, maintaining copies of data updated and establishing disaster recovery plans aids business continuity in case of the event of a security breach. In combination with microservices architecture, as identified in Oyeniran et al. (2024), the implementation of container security tools and orchestration platforms like Kubernetes helps increase data security alongside an agile deployment environment. By integrating these practices, organizations can establish a secure cloud-native platform that is compliant with best practices, thus establishing trust and reliability for users and stakeholders.

8.3.1. Implementing DevSecOps Principles

Implementing DevSecOps practices in cloud-native application development is critical to enhance security without sacrificing healthy agility and efficacy. DevSecOps emphasizes ongoing collaboration among development, security, and operations teams through fostering a culture where security is shared responsibility and not assigned to a specific team. This paradigm shift allows organizations to identify and fix vulnerabilities throughout the software development lifecycle, reducing the likelihood of breaches resulting from the lag in security controls. With the utilization of automation tools and the inclusion of security tests in continuous integration and continuous deployment (CI/CD) pipelines, organizations build security into the core of application development and operation. Such a forward-looking approach addresses security problems at an early stage, in accordance with guidelines outlined in Surendranath et al. (2025), thereby facilitating a seamless move to cloud-native environments. A key part of implementing DevSecOps principles is adopting a Zero Trust paradigm of security. This is not trusting everything simply because it is inside a secure boundary but never trusting and always validating, which is something that is extremely sensitive in modern cloud environments. This model requires continuous validation of users and devices trying to access applications, limiting access to only authenticated users. In CI/CD pipelines, adopting these Zero Trust principles enforces a stronger security posture with tighter identity and access controls, reducing possible entry points for attackers. Holistic strategies for Zero Trust implementation—like the use of automated compliance checks and end-to-end monitoring—are essential to organizations that experience the transition to cloud-native infrastructure, as analyzed in Kadulla (2025). Such stealthy adoption of security processes helps build improved immunity against continuously evolving threats. Furthermore, promoting and rewarding a DevSecOps culture within an organization can play a significant role in the effectiveness of security projects in cloud-native applications. Training and engagement programs can be invested with security-first cultures, viewing security as a natural component of their processes and not a hindrance. By creating security awareness of best practices, organizations can avoid human weakness that has a tendency to violate systems. And by having metrics of security performance, it ensures teams are accountable and bound to keep security in mind throughout all stages of development. The combination of the collaborative culture and regular security training not only enhances the security of the organizations but also illustrates the advice given by Surendranath et al. (2025) and Kadulla (2025). Lastly, this holistic approach to implementing DevSecOps principles facilitates the secure application delivery while optimizing the agility and scalability of cloud-native architectures (Figure 8.6).

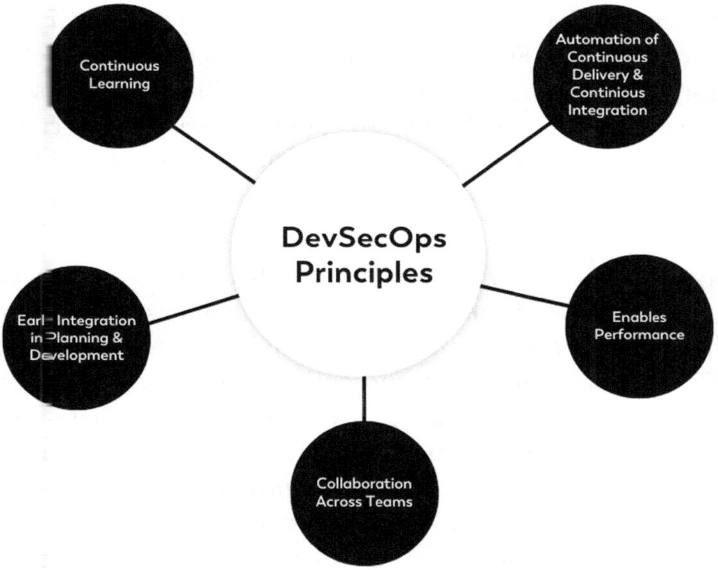

Figure 8.6. *Integrating DevSecOps principles into cloud-native application development.*

Source: https://evergreen.insightglobal.com/wp-content/uploads/2024/10/DevSecOps-Blog-Graphic-1024x768.png.

8.3.2. Utilizing Automated Security Tools

In cloud-native applications, it is important to utilize automated security tools to ensure that they have strong security postures. With more developers using microservices architectures, conventional security controls are inadequate because of the dynamic environments. The dynamic nature of these environments makes it difficult for traditional security controls to catch up. Automated security tools, including those embedded in continuous integration and continuous deployment (CI/CD) pipelines, enable organizations to spot vulnerabilities in real-time. Through automated code scans, dependency management, and threat analysis tools, developers can identify potential vulnerabilities before they are actual security breaches. The utilization of these tools constructs a perpetual feedback loop that enhances the overall security posture of cloud-native applications, facilitating an increased proactive approach to security management. Cloud-native applications must also ensure that they have streamlined observability practices to effectively monitor security vulnerabilities. Security automation tools enhance this visibility with natively integrated orchestration systems like Kubernetes, thereby enabling real-time monitoring and alerting. For instance, Prometheus and Grafana tools, coupled with security scanning tools, can not only be utilized to represent system performance graphically but also track security vulnerabilities in containerized environments. This dual function allows organizations to respond instantly on suspected threats and compromises, enabling security controls to evolve with the application life cycle.

As organizations move more towards cloud-native architectures, the deployment of integrated automated security solutions will be pivotal in safeguarding sensitive data and remaining compliant to regulatory measures. In addition, the transition from traditional application frameworks to cloud-native patterns brings unique security challenges that can be addressed by automated tools. Even more so in case of migration from Java to Go, security practices need to adapt to new patterns and paradigms of deployment. Automated security solutions can facilitate this by offering tailored solutions for API security, vulnerability scanning, and dependency management. As cloud-native applications become more advanced and microservices-based in their design, automated security testing tools are that much more relevant. Not only do they facilitate compliance processes more easily, but they also enhance the general agility of security methods, enabling organizations to protect themselves more effectively against the constantly evolving nature of cyber-attacks, as the most important findings of the examination of cloud-native security architectures highlight (Naayini, 2025; Karri et al., 2025).

8.3.3. Regular Security Training for Development Teams

Within cloud-native applications, regular security training for development teams becomes an important factor in guarding sensitive information and ensuring good application integrity. Such training facilitates the establishment of a security-focused culture within development, enabling team members to detect vulnerabilities and implement best practices throughout the software life cycle. As development teams are generally the front line defense against cyber threats, it is essential to equip them with knowledge necessary to identify, assess, and mitigate threats. Pedagogies that emphasize experiential learning, case studies, and simulations have a significant influence on remembering security protocols, thus instilling a proactive response towards tackling cybersecurity challenges. Furthermore, the rapidly evolving nature of cloud-native applications dictates that security training not only needs to be periodic but also proactive in response to emerging threats and technologies.

The dynamic nature of cybersecurity indicates that threats can potentially arise from an infinite array of sources, necessitating constant revamps of training content to handle the new attack methods and defense mechanisms. Incorporating generative AI elements, as suggested in current research, would also improve training packages by providing intelligence for advanced threat discovery and adaptive response measures (Yogesh et al., 2023). The development teams must, therefore, be equipped with ongoing training that keeps pace with technological advancement such that they can always deal with emerging and unforeseen problems that could undermine application security. Moreover, establishing a model for continuous learning and improvement has the potential to make the training program much more effective.

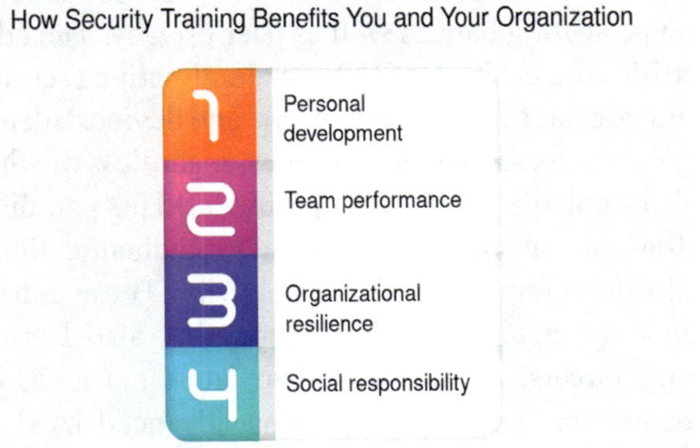

Figure 8.7. *Regular security training for development teams.*

Source: https://fastercapital.co/i/Security-Training--How-Security-Training-Benefits-You-and-Your-Organization.webp.

The members exchanging their knowledge can build a rich tapestry of learning experiences leading towards better security procedures. The performance of regular security drills and assessments helps to reinforce introduced ideas as well as identify areas where improvements can be made. This loop of iteration is crucial for maintaining the best levels of security because it fosters a culture in which security is never an afterthought, but an integral part of the development process (Huynh et al., 2023). By investing in security training as a priority, organizations can equip their development teams to not only react to existing threats but also prepare for future challenges, hence building resilience against an increasingly dynamic cybersecurity environment (Figure 8.7).

8.4. IDENTITY AND ACCESS MANAGEMENT (IAM)

IAM is central to safeguarding cloud-native applications, particularly with the increasing number of organizations embracing such environments for utilization in their operational needs. IAM systems provide a proper mechanism for managing user identities and governing access to resources, where only legitimate users obtain access to sensitive services and data. This is highly significant in cloud computing, where perimeter-based security models are not sufficient due to the dynamic and distributed nature of cloud infrastructures. Effective IAM solutions enhance not just authentication processes but also authorization controls, allowing organizations to put into place fine-grained access controls that automatically adjust to various roles and functions of users. When IAM is infused into cloud-native applications, businesses can mitigate unauthorized access and insider threats as well as simplify compliance with regulatory requirements on protecting data as well as user privacy. The adoption of a Zero Trust model fortifies the position of IAM in cloud-native security. In Zero Trust, there is a need for constant validation of users' and devices' identity and integrity before granting them access to their resources, regardless of whether the request originates inside or outside the network perimeter. This paradigm shift calls for a good IAM strategy that involves multi-factor authentication, least privilege access, and real-time monitoring of user behavior. These comprehensive IAM frameworks not only enhance access security but also learn in real time to counter changing threats. As underlined in latest research, organizations in sectors like finance are currently integrating advanced IAM procedures with other security controls to build a hardened environment which can ward off sophisticated cyber-attacks (Daah et al., 2024). By giving more importance to IAM, firms can increase their overall security position as well as support consumer trust in the protection of personal information. Besides, the integration of IAM with next-gen technologies such as artificial intelligence and machine learning is revolutionizing cloud-native security methods. The technologies allow for dynamic access control and anomaly detection by analyzing user behavior patterns to catch potential security weaknesses before they happen. Such an enhancement allows IAM systems to evolve from static setups into adaptive, intelligent structures that can respond to contextual fluctuations in the cloud ecosystem. In addition, as applications become more prevalent with the use of microservices architecture, IAM must be able to manage credentials and permissions for diverse, often fleeting services seamlessly. It is this need that leads to the necessity of organizations adopting next-gen IAM solutions that, in addition to securing access, also optimize identity management as a whole within a cloud. With the use of these technological advancements, companies are able to offer hardened security to their cloud-native applications effectively addressing the multidimensional nature of cyber threats (Usman et al., 2024) (Figure 8.8).

Figure 8.8. *Identity and access management (IAM).*

Source: https://media.licdn.com/dms/image/v2/D4D12AQEeKm8OGFu6uA/article-cover_image-shrink_600_2000/article-cover_image-shrink_600_2000/0/1708705445333?e=2147483647&v=beta&t=q5bl6MUAlbezElaKTRKRqHBxL5ouA2v9wX0eLQAMT-k.

8.4.1. Role of IAM in Cloud-Native Security

In the new cloud-native application world, Identity and Access Management (IAM) is part of security architecture. IAMs primary job is to determine what people have access to what resources within a cloud environment, to ensure users are provided with proper access with minimal security risks. As organizations shift more to cloud services, identities and permissions of users become more complicated to manage. IAM technologies make this possible by automating identification verification, provisioning, and deprovisioning of access, reducing the potential for human errors in access management. Furthermore, as microservices and serverless architectures become more and more prevalent in cloud-native applications, robust IAM mechanisms play a pivotal role in implementing strict access controls across numerous service endpoints to safeguard organizational data and enforcing regulatory compliance. The dilemma of ease of access with rigorous security measures in cloud-native environments serves to underscore the essence of IAM. With cloud services moving towards a shared responsibility paradigm, where both service providers and users contribute to security for the data, an effective IAM strategy is essential to delineate such responsibilities. Cloud service providers (CSPs) offer an array of IAM products that help organizations manage user access, like advanced features like role-based access control (RBAC) and multi-factor authentication (MFA). These features are critical in protecting sensitive data from unauthorized access while providing room for flexibility in user experiences. The extremely dynamic nature of cloud-native applications combined with the increasing sophistication of cyber threats requires the implementation of an end-to-end IAM solution as not merely desirable, but as imperative to ensure operational integrity and compliance in today's fast-paced digital landscape. Furthermore, IAM solution interlinking goes beyond mere access control; it is a part of a larger-scale Governance, Risk, and Compliance (GRC) approach across cloud infrastructures. As highlighted in the literature, IAM is pivotal in addressing data security, vendor, and compliance issues in cloud deployments (Apeh et al., 2023). IAM products, for instance, must be integrated with current frameworks like NIST or ISO in a way that organizations are placed to successfully navigate the regulatory landscape. With automated security solutions and AI-driven insights, organizations can actively prevent and mitigate risks of IAM misconfigurations and vulnerabilities. Thus, the successful implementation of IAM not only enhances security but also enhances an organization's ability to respond to changing threats and compliance requirements, hence ultimately raising the security posture of cloud-native applications (Chauhan et al., 2023).

8.4.2. Best Practices for Managing User Identities

User identity management plays a central role in the security of cloud-native applications. An effective identity management system must employ various methods, such as employing multi-factor authentication (MFA) and least privilege access principles. MFA provides robustness to security as it requires multiple factors of identification from users before permitting sensitive resources to be accessed. This largely eliminates the danger of unauthorized access based on stolen or compromised credentials. Further, enforcing least privilege access ensures that only the permissions necessary for the specific role and duties of a user are provided. This minimizes the attack surface where these security flaws can occur, thereby improving the overall cloud-native app security posture since applications operate within environments that are exposed to constant threats and vulnerabilities. These measures in tandem present a strong bulwark against identity-based attacks while allowing organizations to maintain operational efficiency. The other critical component of user identity management is to leverage advanced identity and access management (IAM) solutions, which provide centrally managed control of user access and authentication procedures. For example, Azure Entra Conditional Access enables organizations to enforce fine-grained security policies based on various user attributes such as role, device compliance, and location. With such tools, companies can dynamically modify their security controls based on the situation around the request for access, thus promoting regulatory compliance across industries including finance and health care, according to Gannavarapu (2025). Real-time monitoring is also critical, as it creates a chance to identify and address anomalous patterns of behavior that may signal impending breaches. These IAM strategies are not just implemented to secure sensitive information but also to enable companies during digital transformation projects. Lastly, ongoing user education and training is a minimum best practice in user identity administration of cloud-native applications. Human error is still one of the largest causes of security breaches; thus, a culture of cybersecurity awareness is invaluable. Organizations have to implement regular training periods that not only inform users of the necessity to protect their credentials but also demonstrate best practices in recognizing phishing attacks and other security violations. In addition, the use of automated identity management procedures with regular checks for conformance can aid efficient user provisioning and deprovisioning to ensure access rights correspond to current job functions. As identified in Halliburton's case study in Atiq et al. (2025), adoption of such comprehensive identity management practices can work towards increasing operational efficiency while providing critical data protection in cloud-based systems in an era of expedited technology change (Figure 8.9).

Figure 8.9. *Best practices for managing user identities.*

Source: https://discover.strongdm.com/hubfs/iam-best-practices.jpeg.

8.4.3. Multi-Factor Authentication as a Security Measure

As cloud-native applications continue to spread across sectors, maintaining robust security measures is imperative. Multi-factor authentication (MFA) has become a crucial part of safeguarding sensitive data and users' identities in such systems. By requiring multiple identifiers — such as passwords, biometric details, and one-time tokens — MFA renders it significantly more challenging for attackers to bypass and gain entry into the system. This is done by minimizing the threat of hijacked credentials as unauthorized access is made even more difficult. Further, MFA use can lead to greater user trust, empowering a safer ambiance for consumers and service providers. The importance of MFA is also highlighted as cloud-native applications continue to shift towards sophisticated environments that utilize technology like artificial intelligence and blockchain. For instance, MFA not only secures user accounts but also operates in synchronization with advanced technologies aimed at ensuring data integrity and confidentiality.

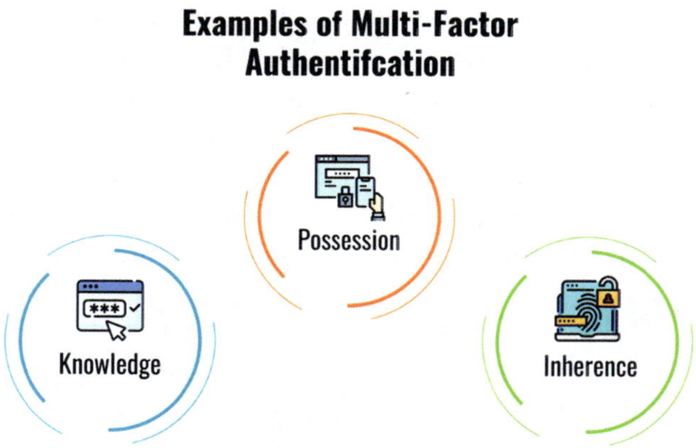

Figure 8.10. *Multi-factor authentication as a security measure.*

Source: https://www.fortinet.com/content/dam/fortinet/images/cyberglossary/MFA.jpg.

This synchronization is particularly relevant in the paradigms of the next generation, i.e., the metaverse, where virtual, multi-sensory experiences are in need of strong security provisions to protect users digital identities and assets. According to current research, a comprehensive analysis of security for such installations mirrors the possibility in merging MFA and blockchain technology, providing traceability and tamper resistance for user transactions (Huynh et al., 2023). MFAs effectiveness also relies not merely on its installation but on user awareness and interaction with security best practices. They must understand the significance of MFA and be a willing participant in implementing such security elements to avoid potential intrusions. With cloud-native applications on the rise, developers and users both bear the responsibility for using effective security tools, such as MFA. Increasing awareness of the specific threats that are prevented by MFA among the users is crucial. The risks from typical cyber threats, particularly in changing environments like the metaverse, help to further reinforce the necessity for tough security protocols that can keep pace with emerging threats (Wang et al., 2022). Overall, the addition of MFA to the cloud-native framework is a proactive measure toward making security more resilient in the face of a fast-changing threat landscape (Figure 8.10).

8.5. DATA PROTECTION STRATEGIES

In the developing ecosystem of cloud-native applications, data protection policies are critical for securing sensitive information from a myriad of cyber threats. One such critical method is the adoption of strong encryption protocols. Encryption works as an electronic fortress where, even if data is routed through, it is not accessible without the proper decryption key. In addition, applying end-to-end encryption means data is encrypted at its origin and remains secure throughout its path to the cloud. This method not only protects data en route but also addresses issues regarding data storage security. Combined with encryption, constant monitoring of network traffic is crucial in identifying unwanted access or anomalies. This proactive approach is also in accordance with the principles of a good intrusion detection system, which is essential in averting potential breaches and ensuring the integrity of cloud-native environments (Jerez et al., 2018). Aside from encryption, access control features enhance much better the protection of data in cloud-native applications. With role-based access control (RBAC), organizations are able to restrict access to certain data sets by only authorized individuals. This minimizes the risk of insider threats and information leaks because permissions are formulated based on various roles within the organization. Besides, incorporating multi-factor authentication (MFA) offers an added layer of protection by requiring the users to verify themselves through multiple channels. All these features work together in concert to create a more secure data environment, particularly beneficial within cloud computing environments, where many different users and apps exist. Because organizations continue to move to cloud platforms, addressing challenges such as data governance and compliance becomes increasingly vital, and this requires an end-to-end strategy for data protection methods that is aligned with regulatory standards and best practices (Farahbakhsh et al., 2017). Increasingly, the emergence of the Internet of Things (IoT) introduces additional complexity and challenges into the data protection methods in cloud-native applications. With devices becoming more and more interconnected, the velocity of the data generated increases, necessitating robust management and storage solutions. With the integration of IoT with cloud computing, popularly referred to as the Cloud of Things (CoT), the necessity for robust data protection is even more accentuated. Middleware solutions play a critical role through a healthy communication framework among diverse devices and applications, typically disparate in operation systems and designs. Utilizing suitable middleware will streamline data management activities and improve security controls in heterogeneous infrastructure. Amidst the challenges of IoT adoption, protection of data needs to be a primary agenda in managing to prevent dangers from an ever-expanding attack surface, to ensure data integrity and confidentiality of sensitive information in cloud-native apps (Farahbakhsh et al., 2017).

8.5.1. Encryption of Data at Rest and in Transit

Protection of sensitive information in cloud-native applications is greatly dependent on sound encryption of information at rest and in transit. Information at rest refers to information stored in physical media, whereas data in transit describes data in transit from one point to another. Both states of data are vulnerable to unauthorized access and attack and need robust encryption algorithms to secure data. Encryption transforms readable data into unreadable form and can be transformed into its original form through decryption keys only. Use of effective encryption methods not only secures sensitive data from confidentiality violations but also helps organizations comply with several regulatory requirements regarding data protection, thereby strengthening the overall security framework in cloud environments. By direct communication, weaknesses of normal network protocols therefore pose risks that must be actively mitigated by organizations in order to maintain integrity for their cloud storage technologies (Borisaniya et al., 2012). Additionally, the process of managing cryptographic material is critical towards enhancing security in cloud-native applications. An innovative mechanism uses electronic identity (eID) tokens to manage access to the cryptographic keys used to secure stored information. The strategy fortifies the process of authentication to prevent unauthorized access to sensitive information by ensuring that only approved individuals have access to the information, eliminating the possibility of unauthorized access. Secondly, applying peer-to-peer protocols for exchanging cryptographic materials eliminates maximum resistance to attacks and offers a more secure environment for information sharing. Organizations can pre-emptively respond to threats caused by simultaneous alterations and malicious manipulation under this architecture, ensuring data integrity within shared cloud storage. Such cryptographic advancements validate the actual applicability of security technologies that develop along with the dynamic world of online threats (Duarte et al., 2014). For the domain of securing cloud-native applications, both forms of encryption are the foundations for data confidentiality and integrity. Importantly, as cloud services continue to grow more complex and massive in size, there is mounting demand for hermetically sealed encryption measures. Companies must adopt diversified strategies that address both administrative and technical controls in order to sufficiently counter threats. Robust encryption not only protects sensitive data from potential exposure but also enhances customer confidence in cloud providers. Lastly, the careful application of data encryption, along with ongoing risk monitoring, enables companies to get past cloud security challenges and deliver stable and secure services. Therefore, companies that assign high importance to encryption in their cloud-native applications not only enhance their security status but also place themselves in a favorable position in the digital sphere (Borisaniya et al., 2012) (Figure 8.11).

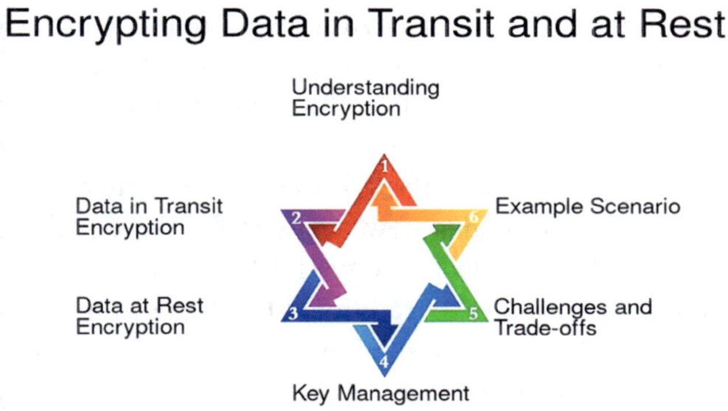

Figure 8.11. *Encryption of data at rest and in transit.*

Source: https://fastercapital.co/i/Pipeline-Security--How-to-Protect-Your-Pipeline-from-Cyberattacks-and-Data-Breaches--Encrypting-Data-in-Transit-and-at-Rest.webp.

8.5.2. Data Loss Prevention Techniques

In the security context of cloud-native applications, data loss prevention (DLP) techniques are a primary consideration in preventing sensitive data from unauthorized access and potential breaches. DLP approaches entitle several methodologies with the objective of observing, sensing, and protecting data in motion, data in use, and data at rest. By leveraging the use of such tools as content discovery and data classification, organizations can identify sensitive data within their network and enforce data handling policies in an effective manner. These measures not only assist with compliance with regulatory landscapes such as GDPR and HIPAA but are also a proactive measure in avoiding threats in the form of insider threat or external cyberattacks. Lastly, a good DLP strategy strengthens the overall security stance of cloud-native applications by minimizing the threat of data leakage or loss to the highest degree possible. Additionally, effective implementation of DLP techniques necessitates a multi-purpose solution that harmonizes technical controls with organizational policies. The twin-pronged approach not only guarantees that the users comprehend the significance of data security but also equips them with the appropriate tools to protect it. For example, the use of encryption tools for storing and transmitting data enhances data integrity while, at the same time, making unauthorized access much more difficult. On top of this, incorporating user behavior analytics (UBA) is capable of fortifying DLP by allowing systems to identify anomalies in user behavior that can indicate malicious intent. These are all the more important within environments dominated by cloud-native architecture, where the scalability and flexibility of technologies necessitate equally adaptive security solutions. Therefore, an adherence to end-to-end data loss prevention is necessary so that cloud-native applications can be trusted. Moreover, as cloud technology evolves, bringing next-generation technologies into DLP infrastructures provides new avenues for the development of data protection. Distributed ledger technology (DLT) and machine learning (ML) methods can significantly improve traditional DLP procedures by tripling real-time monitoring capabilities and predictive analytics of potential data breaches. For instance, the emergence of quantum computing has the ability to redefine encryption standards in use, something that would necessitate DLP strategies to be revamped to counter emerging technological threats. As highlighted, the anticipated impact of emergent networks such as 6G adds yet another layer of complexity to the ecosystem by introducing new threats that would have to be counteracted using proactively smart DLP approaches (Wang et al., 2022; Porambage et al., 2021). Thus, continuous innovation and responsiveness of the data loss prevention solutions are crucial to build the security of cloud-native applications against ever-evolving threats.

8.5.3. Compliance with Data Protection Regulations

In the cloud-native application world, data protection compliance is critical in protecting sensitive information from improper access and leakage. As businesses move their services to the cloud, they are being exposed to various legal regimes that dictate how data must be collected, processed, and stored.

Such legislation, e.g., the General Data Protection Regulation (GDPR) of the European Union and California Consumer Privacy Act (CCPA), is putting severe requirements in place that are meant to provide users total control of their personal information. Noncompliance will also result in large fines together with damage to an organization's reputation. While designing cloud-native applications, developers and architects need to integrate compliance right from the beginning, avoiding data mismanagement risks and establishing trust among users by addressing data encryption challenges, data storage practices, and access control.

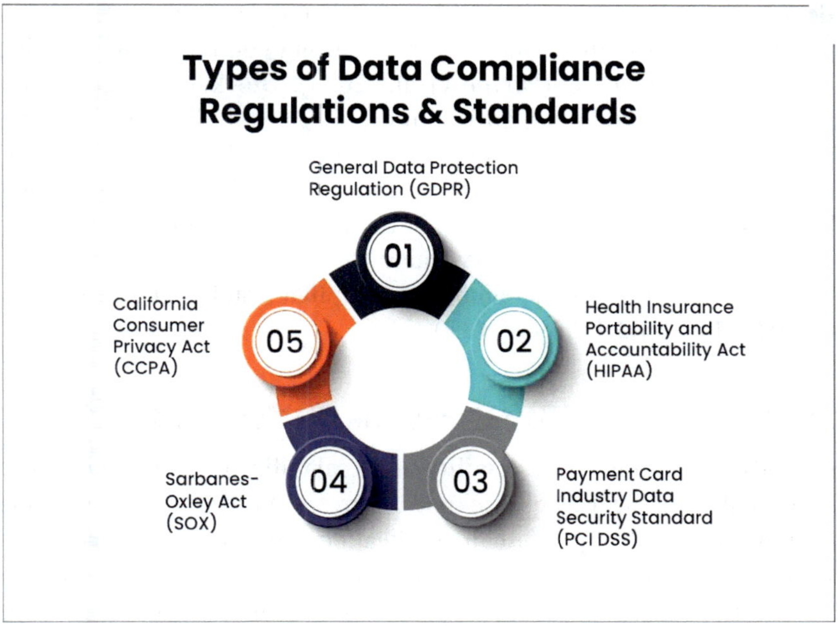

Figure 8.12. *The compliance with data protection regulations.*

Source: *https://media.geeksforgeeks.org/wp-content/uploads/20240522162152/Types-of-Data-Compliance-Regulations-and-Standards-(1).webp.*

Widespread adoption of artificial intelligence (AI) and machine learning (ML) in cloud-native environments complicates compliance. Such technologies have the tendency to require massive amounts of data in order to function effectively and therefore present challenges in remaining within regulation guidelines that set data usage thresholds. The case is that generative AI models can enhance application potential but do so with ethical issues touching on data privacy and consumer consent. The CEO of ChatGPT has spoken of the risk and potential of the technology, emphasizing the application of informed consent and open practice in AI as a way to ensure legislative compliance (Budhwar et al., 2023). Organizations therefore must not only put technical fixes in place to be compliant but also build a culture of ethical AI usage and data responsibility among their workforce, hence addressing compliance end to end. The application of blockchain technology offers a feasible solution to enhancing data security and regulatory compliance with cloud-native applications. Leveraging the intrinsic characteristics of blockchain—decentralization, immutability, and transparency—organizations can create systems that emphasize data privacy and integrity by design. In such a context as the metaverse, where user interaction and data exchange are rampant, blockchain guarantees that consumers retain their own control of digital content while ensuring compliance with stringent data protection regulations (Huynh et al., 2023). Blockchain also facilitates easier audit trail streamlining, so it is more responsible by being capable of producing auditable evidence of how data is processed. However, companies need to weave their way through the technical complexities and integration challenges that blockchain solutions introduce along with harmonizing the innovations with existing regulatory frameworks. By doing so, companies are able to build a more secure, regulatory-compliant, and user-friendly cloud-native application model (Figure 8.12).

8.6. INCIDENT RESPONSE AND RECOVERY

With cloud-native applications, agility and scalability in cloud environments can also make incident response and recovery processes more complex. Because of the tendency of such applications to rely on inter-dependent microservices, an incident in one service can quickly spread to the entire ecosystem. This interdependency requires a robust incident response process that relies on real-time monitoring and rapid threat containment. Having an overarching incident response plan implemented, encompassing detection, evaluation, and mitigation of security incidents, is crucial. With such models in place, organizations are able to enhance their resilience to potential threats, lessening impact on operations and services in addition to upholding user trust in the cloud-native system. Persistent investment in training and resources to hone incident response skills will ultimately toughen security roles within cloud-native infrastructure, allowing for proactive rather than reactive response to emerging security threats. Restoration of security incidents is as vital as incident response itself, especially in the dynamic world of cloud-native apps. In the case of an incident, organizations must not only restore services but also conduct a thorough analysis to prevent recurrence. This post-incident report has to consider vulnerabilities that were attacked and the effect of the incidents on business and data integrity. Cloud-native environments are associated with advantages that involve automated backup procedures and scalability in resource allocation, which enhance recovery processes. Disadvantages such as data integrity and maintaining continuity of services also must be considered to allow for complete recovery. Besides, integrating lessons learned from incidents into standard development cycles will also facilitate a security and resilience culture, enhancing integrity of cloud-native applications as well as overall security architecture. With emerging threats of advanced attacks, organizations applying cloud-native applications must put incident response and recovery at the top of their overall security strategy. New technologies introduce new threats and vulnerabilities to which an agile and vigilant security posture is required. For instance, expansion in virtual worlds, for example, the features of the metaverse highlighted in current studies, presents challenges that impinge on cloud-native security architectures. Issues such as user privacy, trust, and secure interactions in the virtual worlds must be addressed alongside traditional incident response methods. Moreover, organizations must consider the implications of rapid technological shifts on their recovery processes and response strategies. By developing a visionary thinking that mobilizes various perspectives and new threats, organizations can establish a robust incident response and recovery plan that effectively manages the intrinsic complexities of cloud-native applications to secure long-term security and resilience against evolving cyberattacks.

8.6.1. Importance of Having an Incident Response Plan

In the context of cloud-native apps, the presence of an effective incident response plan is not just an overture but a part of security planning and operational solidity. The extremely dynamic and often volatile nature of the cloud environment propels organizations toward the creation of a structured process to recover from security incidents and minimize their associated effects. Such a plan for incident response enables organizations to respond promptly and efficiently in the case of probable threats, ensuring that response teams are not only prepared but also aligned. Effective incident management can significantly reduce downtime and data loss, both of which are critical in maintaining customer confidence as well as business continuity in the digital era. Furthermore, incident response plans are especially important in outlining clear procedures and guidelines for identifying, examining, and responding to security incidents. By having this structured order, proactive response is enabled in identifying anomalies and potential breaches before they mature into more advanced threats. For multi-cloud environments of cloud-native applications, where complexities of handling data are further compounded by multi-cloud, procedural protocols can also ease the inherent challenges pertaining to the detection of incidents and coordinating responses. Each incident, if effectively handled, becomes an opportunity for learning and improvement that leads to the creation of better security procedures and mechanisms. Ongoing revisions of an incident response plan have the capability to make the organization more resistant to the ever-evolving threat landscape, according to industry security practitioners (Anagnostopoulos et al., 2018). Besides, ongoing testing and revisions of incident response plans are crucial for their effectiveness. The daily practice and scenario training not only cement the response strategy but also identify the areas of weakness in the current strategy. The continuous process of improvement enables organizations to maintain their cloud-native application security harmonized with the emerging best practices and threat intelligence. For instance, as cloud environments evolve, so do the tactics employed by malicious actors. Carrying out effective post-incident reviews can provide lessons learned, which influence the adaptation of existing protocols to enhance future response. In addition, having open communication channels within the organization for roles and responsibilities in case of a security compromise lays the groundwork for a readied and resilient culture. This is one of the most important considerations for maintaining up to speed on the subtleties of cloud infrastructures and, consequently, protecting organizational assets and sensitive data (Cornet et al., 2017) (Figure 8.13).

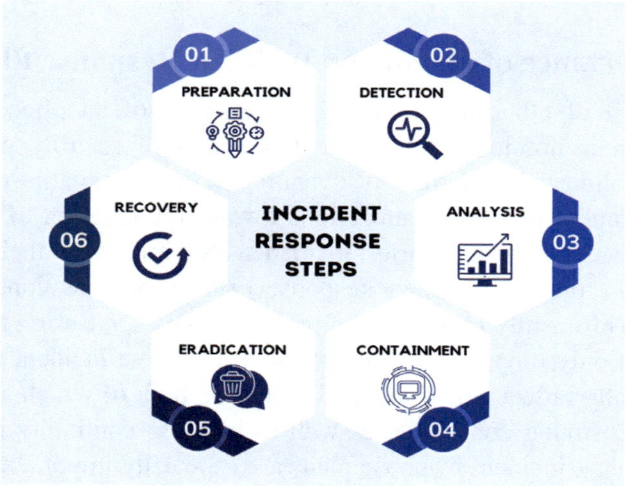

Figure 8.13. *Importance of having an incident response plan.*

Source: https://media.licdn.com/dms/image/v2/D4E12AQGRtKEPv1gIPw/article-cover_image-shrink_720_1280/article-cover_image-shrink_720_1280/0/1694101650385?e=2147483647&v=beta&t=YVTbd7RnJfRfq35wBxDmmFPT1KpP2JnS71T-o2X7q5k.

8.6.2. Steps to Take During a Security Breach

In case of a security breach, immediate and coordinated response is imperative for organizations that use cloud-native applications. The first step is detection and assessment, whereby the organizations have to identify the nature and extent of the breach. This is done through the application of monitoring technologies and security information and event management (SIEM) systems to recognize the user behavior anomalies and data access patterns. A timely response can significantly mitigate the damage; thus, incident response plan development is imperative, setting out precise roles, responsibility, and communication processes for concerned stakeholders. Through the immediate identification of the breach, organizations can prioritize their actions in light of the severity of the incident and exposed data, thus preventing unnecessary service interruption and enhancing overall security posture (Budhwar et al., 2023). Following the detection process, organizations have to implement containment procedures in order to halt further unauthorized access and data loss. This might involve isolating infected systems, deactivating compromised accounts, and resetting access controls. Organizations must also notify relevant internal and external stakeholders like legal, compliance, and public relations departments so that there is openness during the incident.

A timely report ensures stakeholder trust is maintained and reputational loss is averted. Besides, the inclusion of cybersecurity professionals may be required to carry out a forensic analysis as this helps in determining the cause of the breach and provides recommendations utilized in developing countermeasures. Using these containment procedures allows organizations to stabilize their infrastructure while developing recovery and improvement plans in the long term (Yogesh et al., 2023). The recovery and post-incident analysis is the final step and crucial in preventing future breaches. Organizations must restore hacked systems from secure backups and retool security procedures based on lessons learned from the breach. This may include patching vulnerabilities, tightening encryption, and redistributing access rights. Educating employees in best practices for cybersecurity can also assist in raising awareness and preventing human error, one common vector of breaches. Finally, there ought to be a comprehensive post-incident analysis that assesses the incident response plan and whether or not it was successful, outlining what worked, what failed, and how it can be improved. Such analyses not only improve an organization's resilience against future threats but also aid in the development of a culture of continuous improvement of security within cloud-native environments (Budhwar et al., 2023) (Figure 8.14).

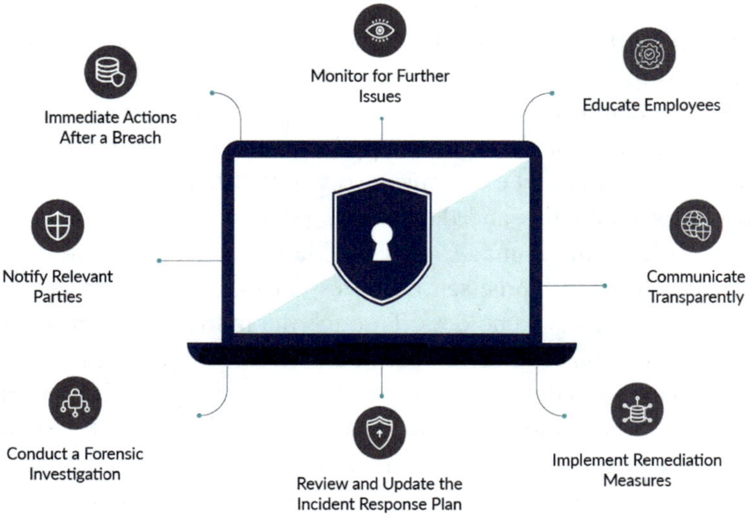

Figure 8.14. *Steps to take during a security breach.*

Source: https://www.sattrix.com/blog/wp-content/uploads/2025/01/si-28.jpg.

8.6.3. Post-Incident Analysis and Improvement

The security incident-post analysis is a critical mechanism for acquiring knowledge from vulnerabilities and improving system protection. After a security incident has taken place, teams are required to conduct a detailed study to determine the root causes, either human, software, or security policy based. By applying methods such as forensic evaluation and incident reporting, organizations have the ability to collect detailed data that highlights some of the vulnerabilities in their security infrastructure. This assessment is not an after-the-fact exercise; it actively informs subsequent policy, so that the same types of incidents do not happen again. Thus, a good post-incident analysis instills a culture of ongoing improvement among organizations, which synchronizes technical enhancements with organizational learning goals. Growth in security posture is facilitated by learning from past incidents for cloud-native applications. From the aggregation of findings through post-incident assessment, teams are in a position to focus more on enhancements addressing the most severe vulnerabilities uncovered in the course of such reviews. If, for instance, an attack exploits an established weakness on a specific cloud service, teams are motivated to apply required patches or to rearchitect to mitigate possible future risk. In addition, use of continuous monitoring functions with embedded tools to automate can tighten real-time reaction to threats and close the window of exposure to attackers. Iterative process of post-incident review not only makes each deployment more resilient but also improves overall resilience of cloud-native platform, which is directly linked with security practices within the organization as a whole. In addition, the application of post-incident analysis lessons is not contained within a single organization but inspires a wider knowledge base across the information security community. As cloud-native apps become more prominent, learning from incidents may inform best practices as well as impact the design of more secure architectures. Sharing between security practitioners can achieve great leaps in threat identification as well as response strategy. In addition, leveraging advancements in technologies such as generative AI may also enhance the analytical tools used during these post-incident reviews. While organizations continue to confront the complexities of cloud-native security, promoting a culture of shared learning and continuous enhancement continues to be essential in preventing possible future attacks (Keng-Ooi et al., 2023; Wang et al., 2022).

SUMMARY

In essence, security concerns embedded within cloud-native applications point to the need for comprehensive approaches that fuse technological controls with organizational policies. As businesses migrate more and more operations to cloud settings, they must concentrate on robust security measures to safeguard sensitive data. This becomes absolutely vital as cloud-native designs evolve towards microservices and serverless architectures, which can be potentially riskier. Organizations shall have multifactor authentication, continuous monitoring, and strict access control to mitigate the threats of these architectures. In addition, creating security vigilance among teams that are tasked with cloud applications will allow employees to recognize potential threats and respond accordingly. The pairing of robust security practices and an observant organizational attitude is a good defense against potential break-ins. In addition, the ethics of sending cloud-native applications are of supreme importance. Third-party vendors to offer cloud computing typically have to be open to data handling and regulation compliance. The capability of legal personnel and IT departments to collaborate and navigate the complicated trail of data protection law is critical. Meeting the ethical side of cloud defense can enhance the firm's public image and acquire consumer trust. Research has shown that incorporating ethics into technological innovation will have a plethora of benefits, including more active user involvement and commitment. Ultimately, the pursuit of security in cloud-native applications must extend beyond technical measures to include ethical responsibility, propelling organizations towards practices that benefit both their operations and stakeholders. Lastly, the future of cloud-native application security will be driven strongly by emerging technologies such as artificial intelligence and machine learning. These technologies are extremely promising in augmenting security controls through predictive analytics, which will enable organizations to anticipate and disable threats even before they emerge. However, reliance on such technologies introduces new vulnerabilities that must be handled carefully. Organizations will have to balance utilizing these innovations with ensuring that they have a strong security infrastructure that emphasizes human control. As cloud computing continues to expand, research into the implications of emerging technologies, including their ethics and legality, is imperative. The confluence of cloud security, AI, and user experience will certainly reshape the definition of how to secure cloud-native applications in the coming years, paving the way for a future full of opportunities and challenges.

REFERENCES

1. Abbas, R., Ahmad, I., Ali, S., et al. (2020). 6G white paper on machine learning in wireless communication networks. https://arxiv.org/abs/2004.13875 (accessed on 11th September 2025).
2. Abhinaya, S. B., Ali, I., Mittal, S., et al. (2018). A survey of techniques for improving security of GPUs. https://arxiv.org/abs/1804.00114 (accessed on 11th September 2025).
3. Aijaz, U. N., Abubakar, M., Reddy, A. C., & Pujari, A. C. (2024). An analysis on security issues and research challenges in cloud computing. Journal of Security and Cloud-Native Distributed Systems, 1, 37–44. https://doi.org/10.46610/joscnds.2024.v01i01.005 (accessed on 11th September 2025).
4. Anagnostopoulos, D., Psomakelis, E., Tserpes, K., et al. (2018). BUDAMAF: Data management in cloud federations. https://arxiv.org/abs/1805.00680 (accessed on 11th September 2025).
5. Ananthakrishna, V., & Yadav, C. S. (2025). QP-ChainSZKP: A quantum-proof blockchain framework for scalable and secure cloud applications. International Journal of Computational and Experimental Science and Engineering. https://www.semanticscholar.org/paper/1c901c168b27245a47b97a3bb02ef540b35ea9e1 (accessed on 11th September 2025).
6. Apeh, J. A., Hassan, A. O., Oyewole, O. O., Fakeyede, O. G., Okeleke, P. A., & Adaramodu, O. R. (2023). GRC strategies in modern cloud infrastructures: A review of compliance challenges. Computer Science & IT Research Journal, 4, 111–125. https://doi.org/10.51594/csitrj.v4i2.609 (accessed on 11th September 2025).
7. Baldini, I., Castro, P., Chang, K., et al. (2017). Serverless computing: Current trends and open problems. https://arxiv.org/abs/1706.03178 (accessed on 11th September 2025).
8. Borisaniya, B., Modi, C., Patel, A., et al. (2012). A survey on security issues and solutions at different layers of cloud computing. https://core.ac.uk/download/76981198.pdf (accessed on 11th September 2025).
9. Budhwar, P., Chowdhury, S., Wood, G., Aguinis, H., Bamber, G. J., Beltran, J. R., Boselie, P., et al. (2023). Human resource management in the age of generative artificial intelligence: Perspectives and research directions on ChatGPT. Human Resource Management Journal, 33, 606–659. https://doi.org/10.1111/1748-8583.12524 (accessed on 11th September 2025).
10. Chauhan, M., & Shiaeles, S. (2023). An analysis of cloud security frameworks, problems and proposed solutions. Network, 3, 422–450.

https://doi.org/10.3390/network3030018 (accessed on 11th September 2025).

11. Copeland, R., Crespi, N., Rehmani, M. H., et al. (2019). Internet of Things-aided smart grid: Technologies, architectures, applications, prototypes, and future research directions. https://arxiv.org/abs/1704.08977 (accessed on 11th September 2025).
12. Cornet, R., McCowan, C., Peek, N., et al. (2017). Addendum to Informatics for Health 2017: Advancing both science and practice. https://core.ac.uk/download/132585011.pdf (accessed on 11th September 2025).
13. Daah, C., Qureshi, A., Awan, I., & Konur, S. (2024). Enhancing zero trust models in the financial industry through blockchain integration: A proposed framework. Electronics, 13, 865–865. https://doi.org/10.3390/electronics13050865 (accessed on 11th September 2025).
14. Dokka, B. K., & Chhapola, A. (2025). Database security and hardening. International Journal of Research in Modern Engineering & Emerging Technology. https://www.semanticscholar.org/paper/9977b7712946e0810bc615237399cebf36fc106d (accessed on 11th September 2025).
15. Duarte, E., Gomes, H., Pinheiro, F., & Zúquete, P. (2014). Secure and trustworthy file sharing over cloud storage using eID tokens. https://core.ac.uk/download/32243296.pdf (accessed on 11th September 2025).
16. Dudley, N., Figgis, P., Hockings, M., & Keenleyside, K. (2020). Strengthening the global system of protected areas post-2020: A perspective from the IUCN World Commission on Protected Areas. https://core.ac.uk/download/323062336.pdf (accessed on 11th September 2025).
17. Dwivedi, Y. K., Hughes, L., Baabdullah, A. M., Ribeiro-Navarrete, S., Giannakis, M., Al-Debei, M. M., Dennehy, D., et al. (2022). Metaverse beyond the hype: Multidisciplinary perspectives on emerging challenges, opportunities, and agenda for research, practice and policy. International Journal of Information Management, 66, 102542–102542. https://doi.org/10.1016/j.ijinfomgt.2022.102542 (accessed on 11th September 2025).
18. Dwivedi, Y. K., Kshetri, N., Hughes, L., Slade, E., Jeyaraj, A., Kar, A. K., Baabdullah, A. M., et al. (2023). Opinion paper: "So what if ChatGPT wrote it?" Multidisciplinary perspectives on opportunities, challenges and implications of generative conversational AI for research, practice and policy. International Journal of Information Management, 71, 102642–102642. https://doi.org/10.1016/j.ijinfomgt.2023.102642 (accessed on 11th September 2025).
19. Ebert, C., Erich, F., Kim, G., Thomas, J., Lwakatare, L. E., & Runeson, P. (2019). DevOps in practice—A preliminary analysis of two multinational

companies. https://arxiv.org/abs/1910.07223 (accessed on 11th September 2025).

20. Farahbakhsh, R., Farahzadia, A., Rezazadeh, J., & Shams, Z. (2017). Middleware technologies for cloud of things–a survey. http://arxiv.org/abs/1705.00387 (accessed on 11th September 2025).
21. Gannavarapu, P. (2025). Best practices in implementing Azure Entra conditional access for multi-tenant environments. International Journal of Networks and Security. https://www.semanticscholar.org/paper/ecdbac843723c155b600c125958143ecd80c7f23 (accessed on 11th September 2025).
22. Huynh-The, T., Gadekallu, T. R., Wang, W., Yenduri, G., Ranaweera, P., Pham, Q. V., da Costa, D. B., et al. (2023). Blockchain for the metaverse: A review. Future Generation Computer Systems, 143, 401–419. https://doi.org/10.1016/j.future.2023.02.008 (accessed on 11th September 2025).
23. Indukuri, A. V. (2025). Cloud architecture as a catalyst for financial innovation: Design principles and implementation strategies. European Journal of Computer Science and Information Technology. https://www.semanticscholar.org/paper/a5dc68aa4b093f0e89a92e6d239d083078ab8d79 (accessed on 11th September 2025).
24. Janda, M., & Gabriel, J. (2019). Automation of the continuous integration (CI) - continuous delivery/deployment (CD) software development. https://core.ac.uk/download/286456226.pdf (accessed on 11th September 2025).
25. Jayantha, R. (2025). Decoding cloud-native architecture: Best practices for modernizing legacy applications. Journal of Computer Science and Technology Studies. https://www.semanticscholar.org/paper/fe0403f1192c102805e54cf7b0b50323f06a9128 (accessed on 11th September 2025).
26. Jerez, C. L., Zhou, J., Jungwon, K., Maxim, K., & Stolfo, S. J. (2018). Toward network-based DDoS detection in software-defined networks. https://core.ac.uk/download/188008410.pdf (accessed on 11th September 2025).
27. Kadulla, S. (2025). Zero trust in cloud infrastructure: Implementing secure CI/CD pipelines. World Journal of Advanced Research and Reviews. https://www.semanticscholar.org/paper/23cdbc1fea835b3ef1ff7e28725a6c3b12c3a77a (accessed on 11th September 2025).
28. Karri, S. B. R., Penugonda, C. M., Karanam, S., Tajammul, M., Rayankula, S., & Vankadara, P. (2025). Enhancing cloud-native applications: A

comparative study of Java-to-Go micro services migration. International Transactions on Electrical Engineering and Computer Science. https://www.semanticscholar.org/paper/14661e7d40137873098d12368124b9188b5e770 (accessed on 11th September 2025).

29. Keng-Boon, O., Tan, G. W. H., Al-Emran, M., Al-Sharafi, M. A., Căpățînă, A., Chakraborty, A., Dwivedi, Y. K., et al. (2023). The potential of generative artificial intelligence across disciplines: Perspectives and future directions. Journal of Computer Information Systems. https://doi.org/10.1080/08874417.2023.2261010 (accessed on 11th September 2025).

30. Krishnan, P., Jain, K., Aldweesh, A., Prabu, P., & Buyya, R. (2023). OpenStackDP: A scalable network security framework for SDN-based OpenStack cloud infrastructure. Journal of Cloud Computing: Advances, Systems and Applications, 12. https://doi.org/10.1186/s13677-023-00406-w (accessed on 11th September 2025).

31. Letaief, K. B., Chen, W., Shi, Y., Zhang, J., & Zhang, Y. J. A. (2019). The roadmap to 6G: AI empowered wireless networks. IEEE Communications Magazine, 57, 84–90. https://doi.org/10.1109/mcom.2019.1900271 (accessed on 11th September 2025).

32. Liyanage, M., Braeken, A., Shahabuddin, S., & Ranaweera, P. (2023). Open RAN security: Challenges and opportunities. Journal of Network and Computer Applications, 214, 103621–103621. https://doi.org/10.1016/j.jnca.2023.103621 (accessed on 11th September 2025).

33. N/A. (2017). SciTech News, 71(1). https://core.ac.uk/download/83049835.pdf (accessed on 11th September 2025).

34. Naayini, P. (2025). Building AI-driven cloud-native applications with Kubernetes and containerization. International Journal of Scientific Advances. https://www.semanticscholar.org/paper/1816c96c31fb066530caf91c2da22db0b48fb11c (accessed on 11th September 2025).

35. Oyeniran, O. C., Adewusi, A. O., Adeleke, A. G., Akwawa, L. A., & Azubuko, C. F. (2024). Microservices architecture in cloud-native applications: Design patterns and scalability. Computer Science & IT Research Journal, 5, 2107–2124. https://doi.org/10.51594/csitrj.v5i9.1554 (accessed on 11th September 2025).

36. Porambage, P., Gür, G., Moya Osorio, D. P., Liyanage, M., Gurtov, A., & Ylianttila, M. (2021). The roadmap to 6G security and privacy. IEEE Open Journal of the Communications Society, 2, 1094–1122. https://doi.org/10.1109/ojcoms.2021.3078081 (accessed on 11th September 2025).

37. Rehman, A. U., Fogat, M., & Aika, M. (2025). Navigating an E&P

operator's journey to cloud—Planning, execution, challenges and impact. International Petroleum Technology Conference. https://www.semanticscholar.org/paper/8b508236b7c3e79161c5ded4e515db2c14753ab3 (accessed on 11th September 2025).

38. Ruparelia, N. B. (2023). Cloud Computing. The MIT Press eBooks. https://doi.org/10.7551/mitpress/14821.001.0001 (accessed on 11th September 2025).

39. Singh, R. K., Berkvens, R., & Weyn, M. (2021). AgriFusion: An architecture for IoT and emerging technologies based on a precision agriculture survey. IEEE Access, 9, 136253–136283. https://doi.org/10.1109/access.2021.3116814 (accessed on 11th September 2025).

40. Surendranath, N., Basava Raju, S. A., & Ganguly, R. (2025). Migrating traditional applications to cloud-native DevOps: A framework for successful cloud migration and modernization. 2025 13th International Symposium on Digital Forensics and Security (ISDFS). https://www.semanticscholar.org/paper/188e3d65ca7ac3d86ec640ba9cc2ccef71acc505 (accessed on 11th September 2025).

41. Wang, Y., Su, Z., Zhang, N., Xing, R., Liu, D., Luan, T. H., & Shen, X. (2022). A survey on metaverse: Fundamentals, security, and privacy. IEEE Communications Surveys & Tutorials, 25, 319–352. https://doi.org/10.1109/comst.2022.3202047 (accessed on 11th September 2025).

CHAPTER 9

SCALABILITY, RESILIENCE, AND PERFORMANCE IN CLOUD-NATIVE

Contents

INTRODUCTION

The advent of cloud-native architectures has changed the way organizations practice application development and deployment. By virtue of their nature to embrace scalability, resilience, and performance, these architectures bring an aspect of responding faster to changing business demands. Cloud-native technologies, such as microservices, containers, and orchestration tools, enable organizations to build systems that can accommodate varying loads as well as never-ending outages. With the aim of furthering their digital transformation, it is now imperative to understand the fundamental role that these characteristics involve. The development not only dictates the technical direction of software development but also strives to fulfill the growing demand for efficient utilization of resources and cost-saving solutions in the competitive market. Therefore, cloud-native approaches are a revolution in how technology is involved in facilitating business operations, with the start of a new era of more innovation and demanding customers. Examining the intricacies in cloud-native architecture, scalability comes out as a central element that allows applications to scale with user growth. It allows for effortless support of workload variation, thereby ensuring continuity and performance under circumstances. This is a major capability in a world where end-users' requirements for responsiveness and dependability are at all-time highs. By taking advantage of elastic resources offered due to cloud services, organizations can scale applications horizontally or vertically, depending on their requirement. However, scalability is not simply dealing with scaling up for growth; it is also dealing with provisioning environments for the purpose of optimizing resource usage. This optimization makes a large impact on operational efficiency, as companies are able to deploy resources in a strategic manner without overexpenditure, efficiently managing costs of operations while being able to react quickly to demand variations. Another pillar of cloud-native architecture, resilience, is the capacity to uphold service continuity in spite of failures and disruptions. Microservices and containerization's design principles ensure workload distribution across multiple environments, thus reducing the effect of failures in individual components. This stern stance not only encourages an architecture that can recover from incidents swiftly but also enhances overall performance via proactive monitoring and automated recovery actions. With more and more businesses relying on integrated cloud solutions, handling possible vulnerabilities becomes a priority. The enormous investment made in cloud infrastructure obliges organizations to create effective resilience strategies that not only ensure continuous service delivery but also achieve maximum user satisfaction. With ongoing technological and infrastructural innovations, as recent studies have shown in the socio-economic dimensions of virtual environments (Yogesh et al., 2022), the argument on cloud-native resilience persists to expand, citing the significant contribution to organizational futurization strength.

Definition of Cloud-Native Architecture

Cloud-native architecture revolutionizes the manner applications are built, deployed, and run in cloud computing. Unlike traditional architectures that tend to deploy monolithic systems, cloud-native applications embrace a microservices architecture whose applications are broken down into loosely coupled, discrete pieces of services. This architecture optimizes flexibility by allowing development teams to deploy and iterate updates independently across different services. Therefore, businesses are able to react in a timely manner to changes in market conditions, satisfying the demand for continuous delivery and integration. The containers' adoption by the architectures enables this, with applications being able to run transparently across multiple cloud environments and statically contain their dependencies, rendering them more portable and consistent from development to production. Additionally, cloud-native systems are inherently scalable and resilient, which are essential aspects of computing nowadays. Cloud-native practices like automated scaling and health management are required for the continuity of services with varying loads and potential failures. According to the literature, successful cloud-native applications require continuous management to dynamically scale resources based on demand and resolve system failures immediately through self-healing mechanisms. By embracing these philosophies, cloud-native systems not only enhance operational efficiency but also minimize the need for heavy human intervention. This inherent trait of autonomous operation reduces possible threats related to resource allocation and application availability, paving the way for highly resilient systems able to adapt to failure or spikes in user requests (Blöchlinger et al., 2017). Other than scalability and high availability, cloud-native architecture is characterized by focusing on performance optimization by innovative management methods. For instance, the performance of job schedulers plays a significant role in how effectively cloud-native applications work in aggregate, particularly for big data platforms. Efficient scheduling mechanisms can translate to improved resource utilization and latency reduction, possibly elevating system performance to rates of over 90% in peak periods. These advancements show the significance of cloud-native principles that place performance management on an equal footing with software architecture to achieve a symbiotic relationship between the way applications are built and the way applications execute in the cloud. The shift to cloud-native architectures is therefore not merely about adopting new technology but constructing a performance measurement and management culture (Arcand et al., 2017). This integrated method ensures that applications stay strong, effective, and able to survive in competitive environments.

Importance of Scalability, Resilience, and Performance

In cloud-native applications, scalability is the critical pillar that enables seamless modifications in resource allocation to adapt to fluctuating demands. This malleable flexibility ensures that services never stumble, not even at unforeseen spikes in traffic. For instance, some cloud platforms are capable of scaling resources horizontally with automatic addition or removal of instances based on real-time measurements, thus optimizing performance and maintaining users contented. These capabilities do not only make operations more efficient but also boost cost-effectiveness because resources are utilized when needed. With more and more companies embracing cloud-native architecture, good scaling has become a necessity to foster innovation and ensure competitive advantage. Highlighting scalability is therefore paramount for developers and companies seeking to create dependable systems capable of sustaining growth and offering seamless user experiences. As important as scalability, however, is the concept of resilience, or the capacity of cloud-native applications to recover from failure quickly.

With the inevitability of hardware failure and network downtime, it is essential that such systems provide support for service availability. Baumann et al. (2019) highlights this requirement by outlining the resilience of containerized cloud storage, which emphasizes the need for quick recovery methods in order to provide continuous service. Cloud-native businesses must prioritize developing applications that are self-healing and will continue to run amidst unexpected issues. Not only does this protect the user experience, but it reinforces business continuity as well. Thus, it becomes a necessity to adopt models of resilience-based design since these allow applications to recover and weather failures, and thereby effectively meet the ever-increasing user expectations within the cloud-based ecosystem. Performance, the third essential column, directly influences user experience and operational performance in cloud-native environments.

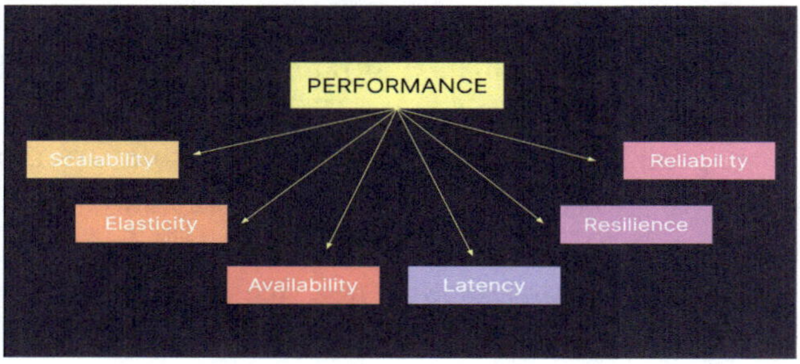

Figure 9.1. *The scalability, resilience, and performance.*

Source: https://nicolevanderhoeven.com/assets/performance-ilities.png.

High-performance systems translate into faster processing times, which enhances overall functional response times, important since users require immediate feedback. For instance, the system presented in Bohez et al. (2018) shows how a scalable approach to video upload processing can effectively manage resource assignment in times of high-demand, which is an example of fast video processing with many concurrent users. This performance improvement is invaluable for businesses that seek to leverage information based on data in real time. Therefore, businesses must invest in performance monitoring and optimization techniques to ensure their cloud-native applications not only excel at satisfying current demands but also anticipate the forming expansions. Ultimately, a concerted focus on scalability, resilience, and performance in cloud-native architecture will make it possible for businesses to thrive in an increasingly competitive landscape (Figure 9.1).

9.1. UNDERSTANDING SCALABILITY

Scalability is a key word in cloud-native applications, in effect dictating the performance and resilience of most systems. In effect, scalability is the ability of a system to accommodate increasing load without affecting performance. Such capability is necessary, particularly as companies grow their services or face fluctuations of user demand. By adopting scalable architectures, organizations can efficiently manage growth without affecting the responsiveness and resilience of applications under varying conditions. With the implementation of multi-cloud strategies by organizations, they can avail themselves of the benefits offered by various cloud service providers (CSPs) to enhance the scale of operations efficiently (Bairy, 2022). By adopting a strategic path in this manner, organizations can distribute workloads across various platforms to ensure maximum utilization of resources as well as delivery of services. Other than traditional scalability, deeper understanding of continuous management emerges in cloud-native applications. It is the concept of automated resource reallocation based on varying loads and the avoidance of temporary failures. Continuous management enables a preventative methodology towards disruptions, granting applications resilience through health management and auto-scaling functions (Blöchlinger et al., 2017). Coupling this practice with cloud-native principles allows for applications not only to scale well but to also perform critical functions independently without much human intervention. The trend towards incorporating management capabilities in-built within the applications themselves works to circumvent issues such as vendor lock-in and support natural scales, enhancing overall operational flexibility. Furthermore, the interplay between scalability and security in a cloud-native architecture cannot be ignored. As organizations increase their use cases, they increase their exposures as well, and an effective security model is required. Establishing a list of robust security practices such as converged security management and Zero Trust designs becomes crucial to maintain scalability as well as resilience in multi-clouds (Bairy, 2022). Data privacy and identity management approaches become critical to address along with supporting the complexity introduced by progressively distributed architecture. Both scalability and resilient security controls can be achieved to not only safeguard sensitive information but also to improve the overall performance of cloud-native applications, allowing businesses to map the intricate webs of today's digital landscapes with ease and efficiency.

9.1.1. Types of Scalability: Vertical vs. Horizontal

Scalability is a key parameter in cloud-native applications that characterizes the system performance and stability under a variety of loads. Vertical and horizontal scaling are two common types of scalability. Scaling up, or vertical scaling, is a technique of improving the capacity of an individual machine by adding resources such as CPU, RAM, or storage. This method is simple and usually best for scenarios where there is a central architecture. It hits a limit, though, because there is a limit to how much hardware can be added to one server. Additionally, the vulnerability of a single point of failure in vertical scaling contradicts the resiliency principles critical to cloud-native architecture, which prefers reliability and distributed operation across a system. By way of contrast, horizontal scaling, or scaling out, allows systems to bring in extra units, such as additional servers or instances, to spread the load across various hardware components evenly. This is more cloud-native-friendly because it supports the dynamic nature of cloud computing and enhances resilience and performance. By taking advantage of microservices architecture, say, applications can scale each service independently based on demand, leading to improved resource utilization and system efficiency as a whole. Antony et al. (2018) contend that automation and cloud-native approaches make this kind of horizontal scaling feasible, enabling it to be easy to distribute resources automatically as a result of varying traffic demand. This ability to self-manage decreases human interaction and accommodates more flexibility to varying loads in production. Choosing between vertical and horizontal scaling depends on a number of variables, including cost, operational complexity, and performance requirements. Vertical scaling is often provided with an easier management interface, and it is desirable to organizations that have exceeded ordinary infrastructures. However, as greater demands are placed and applications grow, organizations usually find that horizontal scaling is a more viable option. It allows them to recover from transient failures and varying workloads more effectively than its vertical counterpart (as per Blöchlinger et al. (2017)). Scalable cloud solutions need to have a properly planned strategy with both types of scalability based on emerging traffic patterns and business needs in order to make organizations realize the full potential of cloud-native architectures with high availability and steady performance (Figure 9.2).

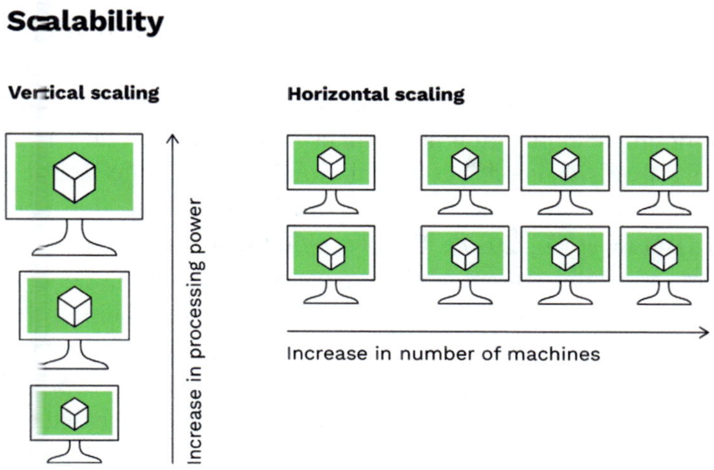

Figure 9.2. *Types of scalability: vertical vs. horizontal.*

*Source: https://miro.medium.com/v2/1*gee5Zkih2dZ7tYWRgmRbkw.png.*

9.1.2. Factors Influencing Scalability in Cloud-Native Applications

Scalability of cloud-native applications is highly reliant on storage infrastructure choice and its ability to manage varied data characteristics present in today's dynamic environments. Designing an effective system for big data necessitates key decisions in storage and computing resources that translate to some degree to specific application requirements. As cloud-native applications tend to work with multiple kinds of data, employing a NoSQL approach can prove to be particularly useful, offering the flexibility needed to accommodate different kinds of data models, such as document-oriented, key-value, graph, and wide-column stores. Each of these models has its complexities, affecting overall performance as well as total data throughput. Choosing the appropriate form of storage not only addresses application demands but also enhances the scalability feature of cloud-native applications, which in turn impacts their resilience and performance as they grow larger and more complex (Alam et al., 2019). Besides storage, the inclusion of software-defined networking (SDN) also strengthens the scalability of cloud-native applications by the use of effective traffic engineering (TE) methods. The methods involved in TE, such as congestion avoidance by advanced reservation schemes or traffic spreading over multiple routes, facilitate peak network performance. Peak performance is necessary as applications expand, so resources can adjust to increasing loads and heterogeneous traffic efficiently. By categorizing SDN protocols according to the interfaces' interactions with different kinds of interfaces in the SDN architecture, developers are better able to understand how the protocols can be used to optimize application performance. By this strategic integration, not only is scalability enhanced, but global cloud-native application resiliency is also promoted through reduced bottlenecks in communication and resource allocation (Burgo et al., 2017). Finally, cloud-native application design lies at the core of scaling them. Microservices architecture, containerization, and orchestration software are some of the factors that help with workload distribution and enabling scaling applications smoothly when there is high demand. Microservices allow developers to break down applications into pieces that are small, independently deployable, and can be scaled horizontally without affecting the entire system. Containerization extends this approach further by bundling applications and dependencies inside containers that can be deployed quickly in any cloud environment. Orchestration tools like Kubernetes orchestrate then these containerized applications, scaling up and down dynamically based on workload needs. Together, all these architectural elements create a good basis for cloud-native applications, not just providing their scalability but also reliability and performance in infinitely changing operating environments.

9.1.3. Tools and Technologies for Achieving Scalability

The quest for scalability in cloud-natives is the solution to utilizing advanced tools and technologies that aid businesses in dealing with massive amounts of data and computational workloads in an effective way. Increasingly, platforms like Apache Spark have come to the fore since they can cater to many-task applications effectively. The flexibility of Apache Spark allows scientists and developers to parallelize loads and optimize resources significantly. For instance, the Kira toolkit employs Apache Spark to process astronomy images and demonstrates that it can execute with a dazzling 2.5x speedup over traditional C implementations when dealing with big datasets. This kind of enhancement not only makes processes easier but also illustrates how big data infrastructure can supplant high-performance computing (HPC) systems and demonstrate how modern tools can significantly enhance scalability on various applications. This transformation is part of a broader pattern toward the employment of distributed frameworks to manage growing computational requirements. In addition, scalability extends beyond processing data to cover real-time functionality, particularly in instances with high densities of concurrent users. A great example is the framework for collecting and blending video shots from smartphones while covering live events, which provides a creative solution to scalability challenges in media production. This approach not only facilitates mixing amateur video with professional cam feeds but also streams video uploads based on network ability and event director requirements. With the capability of handling hundreds of inputs at a time, the system reflects a great improvement in handling large-scale media operations. Its highly successful field tests, during which over 1,183 videos were uploaded within strict time constraints, underscore the capability of cloud-native solutions to process and manage vast amounts of data in real time, delivering a better user experience and guaranteeing smooth operations. Finally, the employment of scalable tools needs a robust infrastructure that can resist performance levels and adapt to changing demands. Technologies for resilience and efficient use of resources play a vital role in cloud-native applications. Adaptive provisioning systems that monitor workload distributions and proactively deploy resources are able to significantly optimize performance during peak usage periods. By employing these adaptive systems on platforms like Apache Spark, organizations are able to optimize operational efficiency and ensure data processing continuity. This adaptability not only facilitates scalability but also increases system resilience as a whole, allowing organizations to maintain high performance under shifting conditions of load. Emphasizing the necessity to include scalable tools and technologies signifies a strategic intent to cope with the intricacies involved in meeting the rapidly evolving nature of cloud-native applications (Figure 9.3).

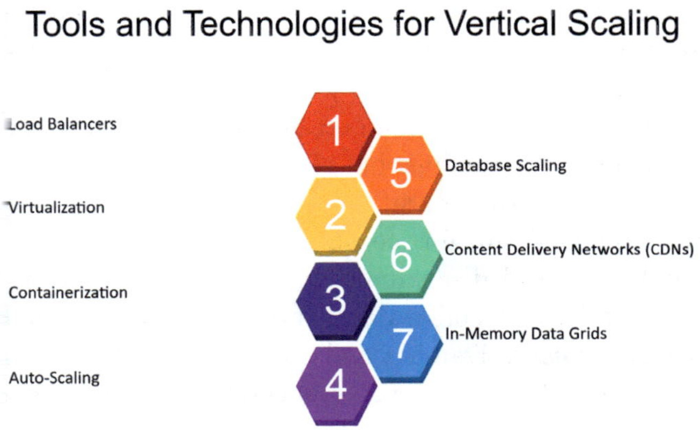

Figure 9.3. *Tools and technologies for achieving scalability.*

Source: https://fastercapital.co/i/Vertical-scaling--Vertical-Scaling--Maximizing-Scalability-Potential--Tools-and-Technologies-for-Vertical-Scaling.webp.

9.2. THE ROLE OF RESILIENCE

The concept of cloud-native resilience is a foundation for continuity of operation in the presence of unavoidable disruption. With increasing organizational designs incorporating cloud infrastructure, the ability to withstand and recover from failure becomes critical. Resilience is the practice of making provisions to ensure systems will be able to continue functioning regardless of adverse events, such as hardware crashes or network failures. A resilient cloud-native application does not merely react to failures; it actually anticipates failures occurring and incorporates fault tolerance mechanisms. In addition to minimizing downtime, this preemptive stance also ensures maximum user experience, further highlighting the necessity of incorporating resilience into design architecture. For instance, Rooks deployment in container-based storage systems illustrates how the recovery time can be enhanced by using resilience monitoring and hence application availability and reliability in a production environment (Baumann et al., 2019). Additionally, resilience also closely intersects with scalability and performance when it comes to cloud-native applications. With increasing company growth, the company is likely to experience uneven demands that necessitate rapid resource allocation adjustments. A strong architecture is paramount here, as it allows for effortless scaling with optimum performance. Not only safeguarding operations but also facilitating scaling, robust systems allow organizations to respond dynamically to shifts in the market. The focus on performance-sensitive DevOps indicates a trend for incorporating resilience into the software development lifecycle. This approach ensures that performance differences are promptly adjusted, ultimately leading to robust applications that may withstand varied environments (Jamshidi et al., 2017). Via such a technique, organizations can utilize resilience as an insurance against interruptions but also as a source of competitiveness in the agile digital age. Furthermore, establishing resilience culture requires an organizational enthusiasm for constant improvement and adjustment. Resilience should be accorded maximum priority by development teams by way of the frameworks that address both procedural and technical aspects of application management. Training and cross-team collaboration between software engineering and performance engineering teams can accelerate the adoption of resilient practices into cloud-native systems. By participating in inter-disciplinary seminars and workshops on performance engineering in the DevOps space, professionals can share knowledge and best practices leading to increased system resilience. In the long run, such cross-domain synergies assist in breaking silos so that cloud-native development may be performed as an entity with a holistic approach that enables organizations to respond best to current and future challenges (Jamshidi et al., 2017). Overall, the value of resilience is not merely a technical requirement but also a basic catalyst for long-term organizational achievement with cloud computing.

9.2.1. Definition and Significance of Resilience in Cloud-Native Systems

Cloud-native resilience refers to the ability of cloud-native systems to recover and sustain unplanned failures without losing functionality in their operations. As more businesses depend on cloud infrastructures, it became more crucial to have assurance of resilience. Resilience is defined as the system's capability to sense automatically that a failure has occurred and to reschedule failed instances' workloads to existing ones so that service delivery can be sustained. The cloud-native applications' flexibility, enabling instant deployment and constant fine-tuning, provides a nimble platform where services can be fine-tuned with minimal downtime. The fast reaction to disruptions ensures low disruption in user experience and operational efficiency, which are paramount in maintaining customer trust and satisfaction. The applicability of cloud-native resilience goes beyond mere uptime; it encompasses total business agility that results from such resilience. In a cutthroat business world, companies with the capability to quickly adapt and react to changes in demand or unforeseen events can derive substantial competitive advantage. Agility corresponds with innate scalability of cloud-native designs, where elastic resources can respond to varied demand on workload. A resilient cloud-native system that not only is good at responding to adversity but also leverages such incidents as opportunities to perform better and optimize itself. By adopting resilience as an inherent norm, companies can build systems that not only survive but thrive in the time of adversity and set the foundation for sustainable growth and innovation. Furthermore, resilience contributes to long-term cloud-native system sustainability by mitigating threats that are likely to be triggered by external pressures such as the rising rate of cyber-attacks and increasing complexity in service integrations. The fact that cloud solutions are interdependent makes them susceptible to cascading failures unless resilience is adequately addressed. Creating robust architectures that incorporate redundancy, fault tolerance, and recovery mechanisms executed through automation is critical. This investment in forward-thinking resilience ultimately translates to reduced downtime and lower costs of operation, thereby improved overall performance. In the midst of the intricacies of digital transformation, focus on resilience in cloud-native applications, anchored on future trends and potential pitfalls, is a must to ensure continuity and build stronger competitive edge (Yogesh et al., 2022; Matthew et al., 2022) (Figure 9.4).

Figure 9.4. *The significance of resilience in cloud-native syst.*

Source: https://media.licdn.com/dms/image/v2/D4D12AQFDXt5JiPNCTw/article-cover_image-shrink_600_2000/article-cover_image-shrink_600_2000/0/1725628568169?e=2147483647&v=beta&t=4_tUpMAKLQ48w0gNNaSRVBO36piqz-kFFpWqtPbxMQaM.

9.2.2. Common Challenges to Resilience in Cloud Environments

The concept of resilience in cloud infrastructures is constantly challenged by complexity in multi-provider systems. As businesses trend toward utilizing more than a single provider of cloud computing services to enhance reliability and decentralize the computing process, issues in terms of compatibility and integration arise. This is also compounded by varying service levels and operational policies by providers, which result in varying levels of performance and availability. These issues not just test the performance efficiency of applications running on multiple environments but also restrict the ubiquitous scaling required in dynamic workloads. The cloud infrastructure's dynamic nature requires organizations to develop new architectures capable of adapting to these dynamics, as reported in current literature highlighting the need for adaptive solutions to guide the changing cloud landscape (Buyya et al., 2017). Moreover, cloud environments tend to be hampered by the massive overhead of failure prevention and management. Due to the complexity of cloud services, there is a need to establish strong monitoring and automated response mechanisms to ensure system dependability, particularly in the wake of unexpected interruptions or failures. Whereas organizations deploy technologies like Software Defined Networking (SDN) and Network Functions Virtualization (NFV) to enhance their resilience, they also encounter the attendant issues of scalability and availability of service. Non-optimization of the same could result in service outages, performance degradation, and user dissatisfaction. Resolution of the issues, therefore, requires adequate analysis and innovation in service architectures, particularly as the pressure for 5G solutions intensifies (Antony et al., 2018). Finally, security vulnerabilities are also a major bottleneck in achieving resilience for cloud-native configurations. As cloud infrastructure becomes increasingly interconnected and dependent, the attack surface expands, and they become open to threats as disparate as data breaches to denial-of-service attacks. Strong security controls while maintaining agility of cloud operations is a delicate balance that organizations need to achieve. The real-time nature of cloud infrastructures often makes traditional security mechanisms useless and necessitates the use of sophisticated security architectures that can counter real-time threats. This cooperation of security in the context of resilience is necessary, as it helps organizations properly protect their resources without giving up on the scalability and elasticity provided by cloud infrastructures. Therefore, there is a need for ongoing research and development to fortify cloud systems against the upcoming security attacks (Buyya et al., 2017; Antony et al., 2018).

9.2.3. Strategies for Enhancing Resilience in Applications

In cloud-native applications, resilience needs to be enhanced in order to ensure smooth delivery of service despite failures or interruptions. One of the strategies for this is adopting microservices architecture. This enables the splitting of applications into small, independent services, each of which can be independently developed, deployed, and scaled. Modularity inherited not only satisfies operational needs but also enhances fault isolation—issues with a single microservice do not necessarily spill over to others. As emphasized by literature, the transition to microservices, which is known as microservitization, includes particular technical practices which enhance the overall dependability of cloud-native applications (Andrawos et al., 2019). Through focusing on the granularity level of these microservices, programmers can better reason about recovery and service dependencies, thus ultimately gaining greater application resilience under load. For further resilience support, organizations can implement techniques such as automatic recovery and self-healing design. Automatic recovery schemes, where restore actions for service components occur automatically upon failure, actually do reduce downtime and enhance user experience. Along with this, self-healing systems can detect and resolve issues in advance before the performance of a system is impacted. Such methodologies are highly applicable in the cloud scenario where optimal scaling and provisioning of resources is of utmost importance. With increasing cloud infrastructure complexity, leveraging decentralization and multi-provider strategies can also ensure enhanced resilience. By leveraging resources from around multiple cloud providers, organizations can avoid single points of failure and ensure service continuity even in the event of provider-level outages (Buyya et al., 2017). These deliberate architectural designs and operational practices aid in maintaining high levels of resilience in modern applications.

Another key method for enhancing resilience in cloud-native applications is the implementation of strict testing and monitoring controls. These practices are required to identify potential weaknesses and performance bottlenecks early on prior to them becoming major issues. CI/CD pipelines empowered by automated testing tools can make it simple to identify faults early, and teams can address weaknesses in steps. Additionally, with robust monitoring solutions in place, there can be real-time performance analytics and visibility into the health of the application once deployed. This pre-emptive action brings a feedback mechanism that not only enables real-time problem avoidance but also informs long-term architecture choices. Greater insight into system behavior strengthens other resiliency techniques, completing a solid framework that optimizes the responsiveness and performance of cloud-native applications in fast-changing environments (Figure 9.5).

Figure 9.5. *Strategies for enhancing resilience in applications.*

Source: https://lh7-rt.googleusercontent.com/docsz/AD_4nXcZLifj5g37rPXjxH-mcJNe2nsB9vEaXcJfd5bI440jPFz8yq8JQVpgMikyceVTd7KNXzapCRYLq5E5F1HPG1htZ-wAARbHQyPQZIyPuYa6zwc2rd3ZB-AhJn1fbDxOZ5lmK5fvLRR0TM-juD18LS_AfrUM4?key=zo0mgAUJC1TOqAXUsXjD8A.

9.3. PERFORMANCE METRICS IN CLOUD-NATIVE ENVIRONMENTS

Performance metrics in cloud-native systems are among the driving determinants of an application's efficiency and ability to endure. As organizations increasingly shift their apps to the cloud, it is crucial to understand and apply such metrics. Response time, throughput, and error rates are some of the most important performance indicators (KPIs) that show user experience and system reliability. The ability to monitor these metrics in real time allows failure and bottleneck detection to be proactive, which supports the general goal of scalable architectures. This focus on continuous monitoring can actively encourage operational resilience, such that applications remain available and responsive even when subjected to varying loads. As cloud-native applications continue to evolve, practitioners must also be performance-first in their solutions, using empirical evidence to optimize and enhance their systems based on changing usage patterns and requirements. To measure performance in cloud-native systems correctly, organizations must have appropriate monitoring solutions in place that align with their infrastructural dynamics. For instance, given the emphasis on containerized applications, it requires particular tools that can provide insights between layers of abstraction. The integration of the likes of Rook shows how strong storage structures can form the backbone of cloud-native solutions to enable trouble-free service continuity. Recent whitepaper highlighted the need for a resilience monitoring module for Rook, and it was also evaluated in a production setup and exhibited spectacular recovery times even for failure scenarios. This skill is essential as cloud infrastructures grow increasingly sophisticated, necessitating organizations to not only be aware of their performance metrics but also the environment in which they are functioning. Nuanced understanding of these interactions produces environments that are not just scalable but also resilient against the inevitable failures that occur in distributed systems (Baumann et al., 2019). Also, the emergence of decentralized computing architectures raises the need for advanced measures of performance that will capture the intricacy of multi-provider setups. With the cloud computing environment getting congested with a multiplicity of service options, organizations must struggle with having to manage heterogeneous systems in an efficient way. This movement toward decentralized and distributed setups demands constant measurement of performance between services handled by different providers. A comprehensive plan to address the next-generation cloud system performance monitoring challenges is necessary for the full realization of future cloud systems. The plans will have to incorporate addressing data-intensive computing, connection handling, and user experience across devices. By concentrating on a more holistic approach to performance metrics across such ecosystems, organizations are better able to evolve scalability and resilience features, leading to broader success and innovation across the cloud-native marketplace (Buyya et al., 2017).

9.3.1. Key Performance Indicators (KPIs) for Cloud-Native Applications

In cloud-native application evaluation, the KPIs are crucial measures to determine scalability, resilience, and performance. The performance of cloud-native designs is mainly attributed to their capacity to scale resources automatically according to changing demands on workloads. For example, response time, throughput, and error rates all reflect how well applications deal with changing levels of traffic. These KPIs not only track existing performance but are also utilized to facilitate predictive analytics, allowing companies to anticipate future capacity needs and take preventive measures. For resiliency, uptime and recovery time from failure are critical metrics that ensure business continuity by allowing applications to recover rapidly from downtime while maintaining user satisfaction.

This total measurement approach encourages an agile culture receptive to continuous optimization and improvement in cloud-native environments. Cloud-native applications also require a sound framework of use metrics to track resource efficiency and cost management. These types of KPIs include resource utilization rates, cost per transaction, and latency, which enlighten decision-makers on the overall economic impact of cloud operations. Through analyzing these metrics, organizations can better manage resource allocation and minimize waste so that their cloud infrastructure is operating at optimal levels. Apart from that, with growing services from MNOs and other operators, the position of being resource-efficient in infrastructure cannot be avoided. MNOs are reportedly seeking to utilize cloud computing technologies to best advantage so as to leverage low-cost commodity hardware for providing essential telecommunication services.

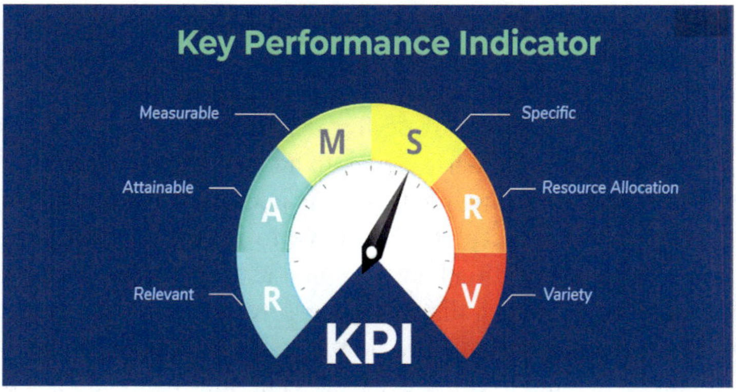

Figure 9.6. *Key performance indicators (KPIs) for cloud-native applications.*

Source: https://media.geeksforgeeks.org/wp-content/uploads/20240122163223/What-is-a-KPI-(Key-Performance-Indicator-(1).png.

Therefore, KPIs are at the core of sustaining competitive advantages because they allow organizations to continually adapt to dynamic market conditions and customers (Bohnert et al., 2016). Lastly, automation and processing of data in real-time are important in maximizing cloud-native app performance, focusing on specific KPIs that quantify these traits. Measures such as deployment frequency, change failure rate, and mean time to recovery (MTTR) indicate the success of continuous integration and continuous deployment (CI/CD) practices. Such a focus on automation allows the development teams to release updates on a regular basis and maintain applications in a stable state. In addition, metrics measuring user interaction and satisfaction allow organizations to ascertain the direct impact of application performance on end-users. Embedding these KPIs into operation builds the agile and innovation culture, thereby leading to improved service delivery and customer retention. The practical examples from various applications illustrate how cloud-native architectures, protected by value-specific KPIs, ensure operational resilience and continuous improvement (Munnangi, 2022) (Figure 9.6).

9.3.2. Tools for Measuring Performance

In the cloud-native application world, measurement tools are at the heart of performance assessment. The tools allow scalability and reliability to be tested and provide useful insights on how applications work under various loading conditions. For instance, performance monitoring tools can offer measurements such as response time, throughput, and resource utilization, allowing developers to trace inefficiencies as well as where the system is being bottlenecked. Increased understanding of system performance encourages knowledge-based decision-making about resource allocation and design optimization. Thus, selection and utilization of high-performance measurement tools can also play a determining role in the overall success of cloud-native solutions in meeting user requirements as well as operational objectives. Incorporation of tools such as VirtFogSim is a significant leap forward in the performance measurement, particularly for next-generation cloud architectures. As a comprehensive software toolkit for dynamically adjusting the delay and energy efficiency of Mobile-Fog-Cloud systems, VirtFogSim facilitates reproducible simulations across various environmental conditions. Given its ability to handle general Directed Application Graphs (DAGs), system performance in realistic cases is more comprehensively understood. Additionally, the focus on dynamic tuning aligns with the inherent variability of mobile applications, where users' requirements and available capacity might differ significantly. Through the use of such an advanced simulation tool, cloud-native app developers are able to make informed decisions based on data that maximize both scalability and resilience within their systems and thereby attain the best performance results overall. Additionally, the use of frameworks such as those outlined by the

4CaaSt project demonstrates lifecycle management and orchestration services as key in quantifying performance within cloud environments. By offering a suite of pre-configured services, 4CaaSt streamlines the process of performance evaluation to enable quicker deployment and metering of cloud applications. Its comprehensive lifecycle management features allow performance data not only to be collected but also to be treated during the entire lifecycle of an application. The proactive approach of performance measurement underscores the need for regular monitoring and fine-tuning for tackling evolving user requirements and technology advances. In summary, effective performance measuring solutions lie at the heart of optimal scalability, fault tolerance, and overall performance in cloud-native applications, as they create enduring competitive leads in a changing environment.

9.3.3. Impact of Performance on User Experience

Cloud application performance plays a major role in user experience, with direct effects on responsiveness, stability, and satisfaction. Since more people are becoming increasingly dependent on digital services, the requirement for timely and seamless interaction increases. Particularly in cloud-native ecosystems where resources are pooled and allocated, performance can prove to be an issue, causing lag and annoyance. Therefore, these systems need to be optimized to run at high performance levels, as it is directly related to user interaction and retention. Research has indicated that even subtle delays impact the behavior of users to a great extent, with most users rejecting applications that are not meeting their performance standards. Thus, organizations need to focus on performance tuning to provide an improved user experience, so applications run smoothly even at fluctuating loads. In addressing performance, cloud-native designs are able to leverage advanced frameworks and technologies that allow for scalable solutions. As a case in point, the utilization of container management platforms allows for rapid deployment of applications and avoids the resource cost associated with traditional cloud environments. Utilizing frameworks such as COMPSs allows developers to execute parallel applications, resulting in faster processing and more efficiency while developing and deploying. The benefits of this approach are evident: rapid deployment of applications enhances user satisfaction as well as encourages broader usage across disparate user bases. Scalability to develop applications easily while maintaining maximum performance ultimately enables a positive user experience and generates a competitive market advantage (Sala et al., 2018). Moreover, personalization of performance for workloads of individual applications can lead to significant enhancements in the user experience. Custom operating systems like Genesis demonstrate how highly optimized environments can give improved performance for cloud applications. By allowing per-application optimizations, these types of systems can make operations more effective, leading to reduced latency and improved responsiveness. Benchmarks of systems using such new architectures reflect substantial gains in performance metrics like web service 99th percentile latency reduction. As performance directly influences how users perceive and interact with applications, these tailor-made strategies are critical to ensure that cloud-native applications surpass and fulfill users' expectations. The continued evolution of performance via advanced systems not only offers superior instant user experiences but also facilitates long-term user loyalty and satisfaction (Appavoo et al., 2015) (Figure 9.7).

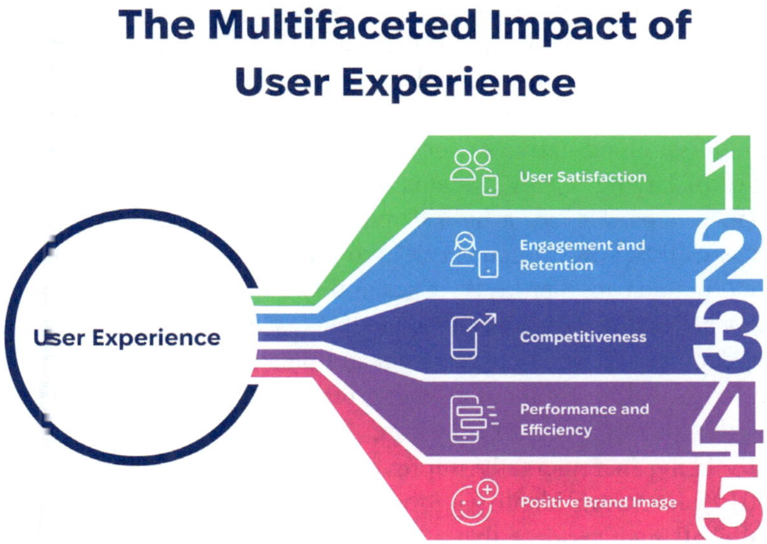

Figure 9.7. *Impact of performance on user experience.*

Source: https://attractgroup.com/wp-content/uploads/2023/09/The-Multifaceted-Impact-of-User-Experience-scaled.png.

9.4. SCALABILITY TECHNIQUES

For the category of cloud-native architectures, scalability techniques are crucial in the provision of fluctuating demand with consistent performance. Horizontal scaling, or scaling out, is one of the most widely used techniques in this category. In this approach, more instances of a service are added across multiple nodes rather than enhancing the performance of an individual machine. The practice not only enhances availability but also attains resilience by load distribution among numerous components. With the growing and evolving cloud, using a multi-provider strategy allows organizations to leverage diverse resources from multiple platforms, thereby enhancing performance and avoiding costs of inability to satisfy user demands (Buyya et al., 2017). Such flexibility is important as firms want to maintain adaptability in the context of rapidly evolving market conditions. Vertical scaling, or scaling up, means growing the capacity of single servers, perhaps by their processing power or memory. While still viable, its impact on scalability is quite different from that of horizontal scaling. For instance, vertical scaling has the potential to entail downtime, as the system will generally need to be restarted or go through maintenance intervals in order to incorporate upgrades. All that being said, there are also instances where vertical scaling is relevant, specifically legacy systems or non-distribution-oriented applications (Andrawos et al., 2019). The challenge is trying to balance between these two methods; while horizontal scaling is more cloud-native in focus, most businesses have to contend with the reality of having legacy systems that need to scale vertically to address performance gaps. Hence, a hybrid model will be needed to propel legacy systems as well as newer microservices to their optimal level. A microservices focus incorporates another layer of scalability solutions that fuel cloud-native applications. Microservices architecture makes it possible to independently develop, deploy, and scale components and thus allows the teams to enhance specific functionalities without affecting the system in general. This structure supports the idea of microservitization, where thin, autonomous services are constantly being incrementally improved and changed separately (Andrawos et al., 2019). However, identifying the optimal granularity of these services is a critical challenge; services that are overly minute can lead to inefficiencies, while services that are too large might neutralize the benefit of scalability (Andrawos et al., 2019). With the adoption of microservices by companies, understanding the principles of design and migration helps in accordance with scalability goals. Doing so helps businesses not only better manage various workloads but also increase overall resilience with varying demands.

9.4.1. Load Balancing Strategies

In cloud-native software, load balancing is the basis for achieving scalability and high performance with fluctuating workloads. Ideal load balancing practices distribute incoming traffic across instances or servers in a way that no single resource becomes a potential bottleneck. It not only enhances system responsiveness but also optimizes the usage of resources, which reduces the chances of system overload and downtime. Sophisticated techniques like round-robin, least connections, and IP hash algorithms, each have particular advantages depending on the individual need of the application. Leveraging these techniques, organizations can efficiently distribute resources, offer quicker response time, and ultimately enhance the end-user experience, the secret to staying competitive in today's digital age. Besides, the inclusion of intelligent load balancing functionality can also increase the resiliency of cloud-native applications.

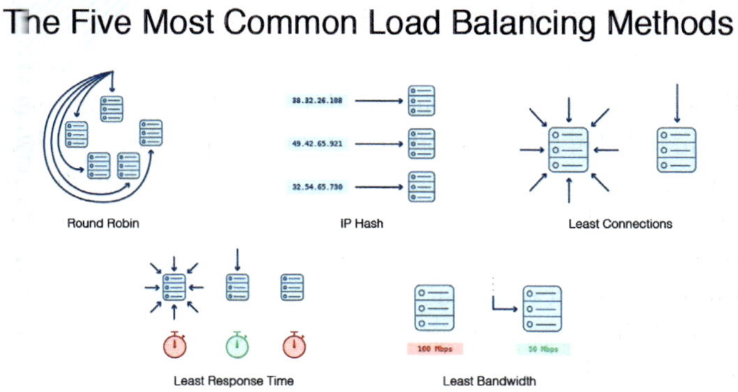

Figure 9.8. *Load balancing strategies.*

Source: https://www.dnsstuff.com/wp-content/uploads/2020/01/the-five-most-common-balancing-methods.jpg.

These advanced systems apply real-time monitoring and examination to react dynamically to changing traffic load and server condition. For instance, using machine learning algorithms, load balancers can predict potential peaks in demand and preassign resources to prevent disruptions. Such flexibility is critical in situations with constantly evolving workloads and unpredictable user behavior. Also, adoption of hybrid architectures combining cloud and edge computing resources can further distribute workloads optimally. This way not only the responsiveness is enhanced, but also fault tolerance is increased because services remain operational even in the event of server failures, thus ensuring uninterrupted access. Ongoing evolution in cloud infrastructure calls for a reconsideration of load balancing methodologies to keep pace with emerging technologies and applications. As observed by current research, the shift towards decentralized computing among multiple providers has extensive implications for load balancing strategies. The transformation from traditional data centers to hybrid and multi-cloud structures demands sophisticated load balancing processes that will function impeccably across varied platforms

(Buyya et al., 2017). Efficient application of such strategies will be essential to mitigate issues around latency, data locality, and resource utilization. Thus, organizations must invest in new load-balancing technologies that not just add to capacity but also enable agility so their cloud-native applications will be scalable and resilient in an ever-changing digital environment (Boraca et al., 2024) (Figure 9.8).

9.4.2. Auto-Scaling Mechanisms

Auto-scaling mechanisms are the core for achieving scalability for cloud-native applications such that systems can dynamically scale resources based on fluctuating demand. This is essential in maintaining performance levels without over-provisioning resources that lead to wasteful costs. Although auto-scaling is performed automatically without the intervention of humans, scaling techniques traditionally require humans to intervene so that the resource management process could be performed accordingly based on application metrics monitored in real-time like CPU usage, memory usage, and request rates. This responsiveness not only enhances performance but also renders the application overall more robust, as it enables resources to become available quickly in preparation for sudden spikes in loads. As noted, the conducting of continuous management practices such as monitoring and resource reallocation lessens dependency on humans and optimizes operational efficiency (Blöchlinger et al., 2017). Cloud-native design necessitates alterations in application architecture, and most significantly, their ability to scale automatically. Using microservice architectures, applications are broken into separate, modular components and deployed and scaled separately. The decoupling allows for the allocation of variable microservices resources based on their individual load requirements, enabling fine-grained resource allocation control. For instance, the Mobility Management Entity for Cloud Native Solution (CNS-MME) shows how microservice architectures enable auto-scaling and thereby yield improved performance levels and resource utilization compared to monolithic ones. The architecture not only enhances scalability but also service resiliency, whereby even under heavy load, the application is responsive and maintains its user experience and service integrity (Antony et al., 2018). Along with that, effective auto-scaling implementation requires effective health monitoring and recovery from failure. In cloud environments where resources are under the threat of transient failures, being able to rapidly replicate and restart components is critical to maintaining application availability. Real-time monitoring allows for immediate detection of performance degradation and supports auto-scaling in case of pre-defined thresholds. Such mechanisms not only eliminate the burden of manual management but also provide development teams with the capability to focus on innovation rather than infrastructure management. By incorporating auto-scaling into the fabric of cloud-native applications, organizations are able to ensure that their applications remain responsive and capable of handling user activity, thus establishing a competitive edge in an increasingly digital world (Blöchlinger et al., 2017).

9.4.3. Microservices Architecture and Its Effect on Scalability

Microservices architecture is a massive shift in application development and maintenance, and particularly as it pertains to scalability. Breaking down applications into separate, independent services allows organizations to manage and scale individual parts more intuitively, based on varied loads and performance needs. This granularization not only simplifies updates and support but makes it simpler to share resources, which is paramount for cloud-native ecosystems. As is evident from the systematic mapping study results, microservitization involves careful exploration of service granularity and adjustment that directly affects scalability outcomes (Andrawos et al., 2019). As each microservice can be tuned and deployed individually, systems achieve unprecedented scalability, dynamically responding to traffic requirements and resource allocation problems. Also, the modularity that is inherent in the architecture of microservices allows for easier scalability through functional modularization. Modular development enables teams to select and utilize different technologies and frameworks selectively for the requirements of each service and prefer efficiency along with innovation. Decoupling allows for deployment, scaling, and maintenance per component without weakening the system as a whole. The application of containers in this design pattern cannot be overexpressed; they provide an efficient and light-weighted way of encapsulating microservices, which enhances their performance and scalability (Amaral et al., 2015). Besides, the integration of containerization simplifies deployment operations, allowing companies to achieve quick iteration and response to changes in market conditions with high levels of service reliability. The impact of microservices architecture on scalability also encompasses the overall resilience of cloud-native applications. With services dispersed over various nodes and environments, failure in one microservice does not equate to system failure. This brings resilience for organizations to provide continuous service delivery even under adverse conditions as microservices can be redeployed or scaled up with less downtime. As research indicates, the ability to easily attach or detach elements of a system translates into more resilient architecture, which is crucial in today's rapidly evolving digital landscape (Amaral et al., 2015). In short, the collaboration of scalability and microservices architecture is not only more responsive to develop but also places organizations in a position to cope effectively with demand changes, thereby enhancing performance and long-term viability in cloud-native environments (Figure 9.9).

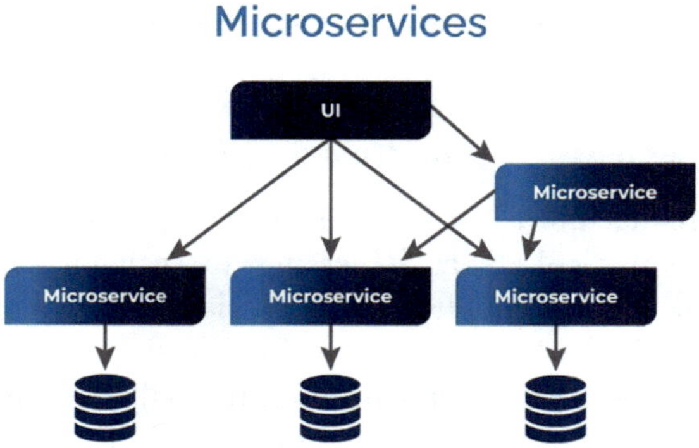

Figure 9.9. *Microservices architecture and its effect on scalability.*

Source: https://www.mytaskpanel.com/wp-content/uploads/2021/06/consulting-blog-31b.webp.

9.5. RESILIENCE STRATEGIES

In cloud-native applications, resilience mechanisms are key to the resilience of systems to recover promptly from failure. Embracing microservices has also come with a flexible style of architecture that naturally fosters resilience in the manner in which the system is spread out. Microservices are independent; therefore, if one of them fails, others can continue running, reducing the impact of such failures on the performance of the system. This approach encourages continuous deployment and scalability in accordance with the dynamic nature of cloud-based environments. Furthermore, it is observed in literature that an understanding of the principles of microservice architectures from the perspective of resiliency is essential. A systematic mapping study discovers that making technical activities involved in the transition process to microservices, also known as microservitization, transparent is essential in developing effective resilience strategies, namely managing service granularity and responding to changing operational environments (Andrawos et al., 2019). Further, incorporating resilient storage solutions is essential with companies increasingly moving their data to cloud environments. Cloud distributed storage offers scalability but resilience is still a top issue due to loss or inability to access data that results in significant disruptions. Container-based systems, such as the Rook storage operator, incorporate features to enhance resilience through self-healing mechanisms. This resilience monitoring module examines the rate at which a system can be reconstructed after failure, displaying critical information regarding performance factors like recovery time. For instance, it was observed that the mean time to recovery was 41 and 142 seconds across capacities of items to be stored, further validating the necessity of building resilient storage systems with the potential to ensure service availability upon disruption (Baumann et al., 2019). Building such methodologies not only mitigates risk but also facilitates continued operational effectiveness within cloud-native architecture. The intersection of scalability and resilience in cloud-native design points to the importance of planning and execution. As organizations transition to the model, incorporating resilience practices must be built into the architecture itself at the outset. This proactive approach includes defining failure modes and designing systems around them, testing performance under load, and implementing automated recovery processes. Moreover, the research indicates that successful resilience measures are not only technical, but also the overall organizational habits which establish a resilience and readiness culture. Ensuring that teams possess the skills and tools for addressing failures establishes a culture where innovation can emerge without compromising on reliability (Andrawos et al., 2019). As companies more and more embrace cloud-native patterns, adapting and refining resilience initiatives will be an inherent part of providing enduring performance.

9.5.1. Redundancy and Failover Mechanisms

Redundancy and failover features are essential building blocks in cloud-native systems by ensuring guaranteed availability and operation integrity. Failures in any distributed system may be caused by a variety of reasons including hardware failures, network outages, or software bugs. Redundancy is established by duplicating key components to eliminate single points of failure making the entire system more reliable. For instance, multiple copies of an application are active on different servers or geographical locations. In such a case, failover mechanisms directly divert traffic to such redundant copies whenever the master copy is unavailable, thereby cutting down on downtime. These configurations do more than just boost resilience; they also boost scalability since load distribution is feasible across numerous nodes, which eventually results in smoother operations during high usage. In the context of cloud-native applications, various redundancy strategies have to be organization needs and architectural designs-compatible. These strategies can be categorized based on the level at which they are deployed—the infrastructure, platform, or application level. On the infrastructure level, tools can replicate virtual machines or block storage asynchronously to ensure data correctness. Similarly, redundancy at the application level mostly employs load balancers and microservices-based architecture to ensure seamless handovers of user requests. With technologies such as container orchestration, companies can automate deployment and scaling of app replicas. By doing so, streamlining not only optimizes the use of resources but also prepares the environment for unscheduled failures. With increasing numbers of organizations adopting hybrid or multi-cloud setups, it is the intricacy of such failover and redundancy systems that becomes crucial to maintain performance within varied environments (Mahmoud et al., 2025). Furthermore, the intrinsic multicloud complexity demands an effective response to failover and redundancy. Geographical dispersion and regulation considerations should be integrated into resilient system design by organizations. Artificial intelligence can be incorporated to anticipate possible failures and automatically recover operations, making operations even more efficient. Such technology can make systems react to real-time changes and proactively respond against prospective disruptions. Placing a strong emphasis on strategic redundancy and innovative failover techniques, organizations can develop an ecosystem that is not only resistant to failure but also optimizes resource utilization and response times. Developing this integrated, end-to-end paradigm provides the ability to continuously optimize performance in operations and provides better user experiences, making it a critical component of effective cloud-native deployments (Dasari et al., 2023) (Figure 9.10).

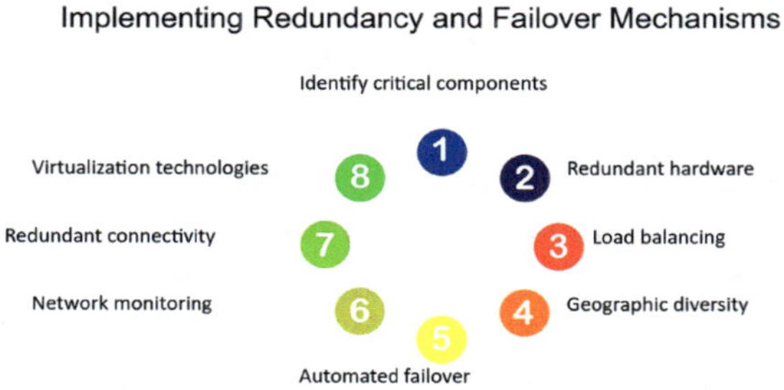

Figure 9.10. *Redundancy and failover mechanisms.*

Source: https://fastercapital.co/i/Strengthening-Network-Resilience-with-Best-Efforts-Techniques--Implementing-Redundancy-and-Failover-Mechanisms.webp.

9.5.2. Circuit Breaker Patterns

Circuit breaker patterns constitute a critical methodology for boosting the scalability, resiliency, and performance of cloud-native applications. The behind-the-scenes design is to monitor calls to services and prevent repeating the same failing request repeatedly, piling up resources. With circuit breakers, applications are able to notice failures in outside services and, instead of relentlessly sending pointless requests, halt these calls for a short time. This approach not only reduces the load on the system but also facilitates quick reset from transient faults, which allows for a more fault-tolerant system. Hence, circuit breakers are a component of cloud-native systems where service interactions are repeated and make it essential to offer seamless end-user experience. In cloud-native systems, the use of circuit breaker patterns is significant in terms of performance management by allowing a more reactive system. By defining failure thresholds, these patterns make it possible for applications to respond immediately to failures, thereby minimizing the impact on dependent services. This approach is a reflection of microservices philosophy, where applications are architected as a combination of loosely coupled services. Because microservices opt for synchronous communication protocols, as noted in Ferreira et al. (2022), application of circuit breakers helps ensure the availability of services without increasing the potential for cascading failures in multi-components. Therefore, adopting such patterns is responsible for ensuring not only operational efficiency but also the sustainability of cloud-native applications in the long term. Moreover, integrating circuit breaker patterns can even boost the auto-scaling functionality of cloud-native systems even more. Because applications automatically scale to accommodate varying loads, circuit breakers can ensure maximum resource usage by preventing over-committed instances from initiating calls to failing services. Dynamically managing the calls initiated by services, the system can cater to demand spikes without impacting performance or stability. In addition, as indicated in the results of (Blöchlinger et al., 2017), decoupling management features from application services can lead to inefficiencies. Therefore, the integration of circuit breakers also provides a self-controlling aspect that is based on scalability and fault tolerance. That self-awareness feature of applications ultimately supports continuous adjustments to the cloud ecosystem, fulfilling the essential requirements for modern enterprise offerings.

9.5.3. Chaos Engineering for Testing Resilience

The unprecedented velocity of cloud-native development has brought unprecedented challenges in system resiliency, calling for innovative solutions such as chaos engineering. Through deliberately introducing faults and observing the behavior of the system when it is stressed, chaos engineering is a critical way of ensuring the resiliency of distributed systems. This approach expands on standard testing by creating realistic conditions under which system failures can occur, thereby enabling developers to identify vulnerabilities that would otherwise not be revealed through regular test conditions. The search for these vulnerabilities is critical, particularly as systems expand and become more complex. Due to the intricate relationship between resilience and performance, chaos engineering plays a key role in making applications robust enough to handle behavior during stressful conditions, thus enhancing the scalability and performance of cloud-native systems as a whole (Jamshidi et al., 2017). Integration of chaos engineering into the software development lifecycle fosters an attitude of resilience culture that is proactive. In the past, performance engineering and DevOps have been quantified as separate disciplines, but new focus on performance-aware DevOps tries to bring them together. Seminars like the GI-Dagstuhl Seminar have realized the necessity of interaction between these disciplines to address the complexity of the existing cloud systems. It is wanted that there should be a systemic approach where resilience is not considered a secondary aspect but as the natural course of application development. Chaos engineering allows teams to develop an understanding of failure modes by actively engaging with potential interruptions and, thus, influence their design decisions and operating practices.

Figure 9.11. *Chaos engineering for testing resilience.*

Source: https://media.geeksforgeeks.org/wp-content/uploads/20240410155931/chaos-engineer.webp.

Once organizations adopt these concepts, they produce systems that do not only work effectively but can also recover quickly from surprises (Jamshidi et al., 2017). Real-life application examples of chaos engineering have been witnessed in numerous cloud-native environments such as microservices-based systems operating on environments like Kubernetes. Tests done on utilizing chaos engineering methodologies have proven that simulating failures effectively reveals systemic weaknesses, which lead to rethinking and reinforcing resilience strategies. For instance, studies have proven how network latency may lead to user account handling failure and reveal weaknesses that need to be addressed. By pointing out the requirement for resilience testing, chaos engineering also encourages companies to have constant experiments that feedback into improved architectures. Through this constant loop, teams can keep improving how they do things, building a culture of resilience that is vital in the fast-paced and highly complex IT world today (Figure 9.11).

9.6. PERFORMANCE OPTIMIZATION

The seamless operation of cloud-native applications is based on effective performance optimization strategies. When businesses migrate away from legacy infrastructures and move to the cloud, they need to reconsider their application performance strategies. This reimagining happens in varying dimensions including resource management, workload distribution, and how the system reacts to varying traffic loads. Performance optimization not only works to increase the general speed and efficiency of applications but also to counteract the difficulties of staying responsive under times of heavy usage. Cloud-native architectures, marked by their use of microservices-based frameworks, facilitate directed optimization efforts that can be applied to specific parts of an application without affecting the entire system. Thanks to containerization and orchestration technologies, companies can monitor performance measures and scale resources automatically according to real-time demands, keeping things in top working order and best of the best user experience. Thus, tactical deployment of performance optimization processes is an important aspect towards guaranteeing scalability and toughness in cloud-native ecosystems (Padma et al., 2025). One of the most important fields of cloud-native performance optimization is to leverage the latest technologies such as machine learning (ML) and artificial intelligence (AI). These technologies allow organizations to be able to predict and handle workloads more effectively, building a smart environment where resources can be allocated based on past usage and trends. Predictive scaling, driven by AI-driven insights through intelligence, enables business to provision their resources in anticipation of anticipated spikes in demand, thus cutting latency and enhancing performance. AI and ML also bring continuous performance examination and monitoring, enabling systems to gain the resiliency necessary to adjust to unanticipated traffic patterns. Convergence, besides supporting optimal application performance, also brings efficient resource utilization, hence reducing operation costs. In this regard, the confluence of emerging technologies with traditional approaches to performance optimization emerges as an essential element of cloud-native architecture, complementing the broader efficacy and resilience of applications (Mylsamy et al., 2025). In addition to that, the paramountcy of deep performance testing and monitoring within cloud-native applications cannot be overstated. Traditional testing protocols prove wanting when translated to dispersed, fluid architecture. Therefore organizations must deploy ongoing performance testing frameworks to ascertain how applications execute under varied conditions and loads continuously. Application of synthetic and real-user monitoring approaches can guarantee identification of potential bottle-necks and prevention thereof before end-users are impacted. End-to-end testing between various microservices also must be included in performance optimization, verifying their interaction and system performance as a whole. By enhancing continuous improvement culture through performance analysis and monitoring, the organizations can make sure their cloud-native applications are scalable and resilient to evolving business requirements. This end-to-end optimization of performance not only maximizes application efficiency but also the competitiveness of the organization in the dynamic digital age (Padma et al., 2025).

9.6.1. Caching Strategies for Improved Performance

Caching methods are primarily responsible for enhancing the performance of cloud-native applications when they are handling increasing volumes of data and user interactions. Caching repeats information in a buffer layer of storage, avoiding latency and backend system loads. Besides enhancing the rate of data retrieval, it also enhances resource usage, crucial when excessive demand can overflow system capabilities. Moreover, by minimizing redundant database calls and repeated calculations, caching mechanisms enable cloud-native applications to scale efficiently, rendering applications responsive and fault-tolerant even during traffic bursts. The architectures of such caching mechanisms can vary significantly, from in-memory data repositories to edge caching solutions, each being chosen depending on specific use cases and performance requirements, demonstrating the scalability of caching in the cloud. One fascinating aspect of caching methods is the choice of eviction policy for the cache, as it dictates how data is processed once the cache is full. Typical methods like Least Recently Used (LRU) and First In First Out (FIFO) help decide what to evict to make room for new data while striking a balance between the need for performance and data freshness. Applying an effective eviction policy can have a dramatic impact on application performance behavior, such as response time and throughput. Well-designed policies can enhance the user experience by making immediately available the most relevant information. Furthermore, as mature cloud-native applications emerge, integrating intelligent caching policies, leveraging real-time analytics and machine learning-driven algorithms, can learn and adapt dynamically such policies in line with the user's behavior and application needs, further balancing caching performance with scalability and resiliency objectives. As more businesses transition to cloud-native architectures, deploying cutting-edge caching techniques remains the utmost priority in addressing both scalability and performance issues. Researches have outlined the way caching is capable of significantly reducing the burden on main storage systems, generating less delay and greater application throughput rates. For instance, caching mechanisms can adapt dynamically to varying workloads, redistributing information efficiently across clusters based on real-time intelligence. This ability not only advances improved performance but also promotes system resilience against failure. Also, integrating caching with other methods, like data sharding, can quadruple such benefits, creating a robust, scalable architecture able to serve complex, data-driven applications. Thus, effective application of caching technologies within cloud-native architectures is paramount to organizations interested in optimizing their operational efficiency without sacrificing good performance under evolving demand, a conscious effort to strike a balance between scalability and performance in modern software landscapes (Alam et al., 2019; Borada et al., 2024) (Figure 9.12).

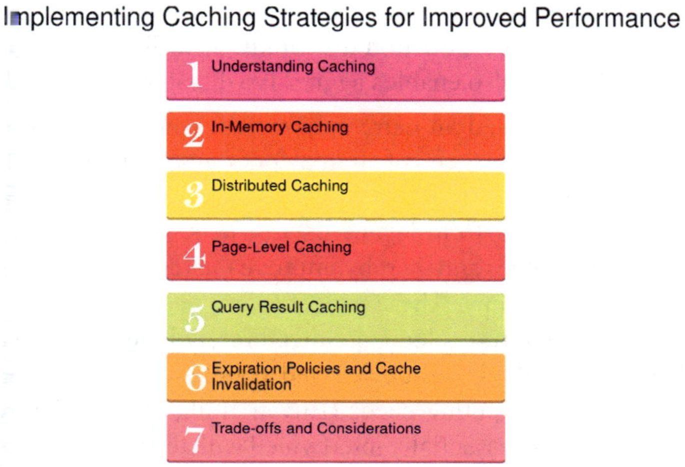

Figure 9.12. *Caching strategies for improved performance.*

Source: https://fastercapital.co/i/CTO-scalability-and-performance-Scaling-Your-Startup--A-CTO-sGuide-to-Performance-Optimization--Implementing-Caching-Strategies-for-Improved-Performance.webp.

9.6.2. Resource Allocation and Management

Resource allocation and management play important roles in enhancing cloud-native designs' performance. As more organizations shift towards cloud environments, the challenge of managing resources heightens, demanding advanced scheduling and allocation processes. The older computing patterns were generally content with conventional techniques; however, the existence of big data and transient tasks has redefined the needs. Effective job schedulers are a necessity since they function as operating systems for such cloud-native apps, specifying how resources get assigned to execute multiple processes concurrently. Schedulers' latency is of particular interest, in which even minor delay causes utilization of resources to take a hit, thereby impacting system efficiency overall. With these dynamics, businesses must concentrate on optimizing scheduler performance and leveraging adaptive dynamically resource allocation models that can adapt resource management to accommodate variability of fluctuating workloads based on resilience and scalability principles. Cloud infrastructure development further demands more decentralized resource management approaches beyond the traditional single-provider constructs. Widespread multi-provider environments offer unique advantages, including redundancy and flexibility in resource allocation. As cloud infrastructures grow in complexity, resource consolidation from multiple different suppliers not only enhances scalability but also enables aggressive disaster recovery planning.

These practices demand an extremely mature comprehension of resource orchestration, where management frameworks must intellectually balance workloads and dynamically use resources between heterogeneous environments. Decentralizing computing from legacy data centers, organizations can access different kinds of resources and thereby improve the resilience and performance of cloud-native applications. These practices are at the forefront of solving challenges related to future cloud architectures, which will strive to meet growing demands for device-to-device and people-to-people connectivity as well as data-craving computing needs (Buyya et al., 2017). The dynamics of cloud-native systems are essentially intertwined with the way in which resources are effectively allocated and managed in real-time. Enhanced job scheduling methods, as the recent thrust of research indicates, underscore the pivotal role that these systems play in optimizing resource use. Top scheduler feature analysis has demonstrated that reducing scheduler latency can significantly improve total system performance, particularly in systems with a high frequency of short computations (Arcand et al., 2017). Companies can test scheduler effectiveness categorically and enhance resource management practices by employing advanced benchmark methods and theoretical frameworks. This transition of short-burst to long-run processing necessitates the reorientation of existing paradigms such that the cloud-native systems are able to further evolve and thrive. Therefore, focusing on the intelligent management mechanisms of resources is the key to sustaining the performance and resilience of cloud-native architecture amidst the changing face of technology (Figure 9.13).

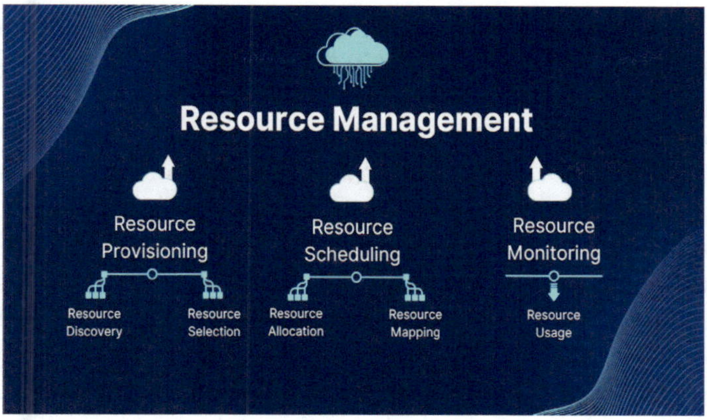

Figure 9.13. *Resource allocation and management.*

Source: https://www.bacancytechnology.com/blog/wp-content/uploads/2023/12/Resource-Management.webp.

9.6.3. Continuous Integration and Deployment Practices

Adoption of continuous integration and deployment (CI/CD) practices is now at the core of enhancing scalability, resiliency, and performance within cloud-native systems. CI practices enable developers to integrate their code changes regularly into one shared repository, leading to team collaboration and early detection of integration issues. This real-time feedback loop not only eliminates bugs but also enforces each increment as a scaled-up version. With deployment processes in combination, CI/CD facilitates automated deployment and testing processes where organizations can maintain peak performance regardless of scaling at high speeds. With microservice architecture embraced by development teams, it is essential to realize the granularity of each service as it directly affects deployment processes and system availability. Such intrinsic relationship makes CI/CD a key enabler for organizations wanting to thrive in high-velocity cloud environments. Moreover, utilization of CI/CD frameworks is ideally aligned with the principles of DevOps, which encourage a collaborative culture among development and operations teams. Utilizing CI/CD methodologies, organizations possess a well-organized means of managing issues in multi-cloud application deployments, thereby being in a better position to support heterogeneous cloud services. The utilization of these methodologies, besides speeding up the software release cycles, enhances operational efficiency. Research indicates that the management of cloud service complexities using CI/CD results in a more agile infrastructure, which is capable of responding to operational distress at short notice. The evolution of tools intended to advance this integration further endorses the effectiveness of CI/CD in optimizing cloud service deployments, creating a powerful pipeline for developers and operators (Alonso et al., 2018). Additionally, passive benefits of CI/CD practices are performance tuning for various workloads. With cloud-native applications constantly receiving updates and modifications, thorough testing combined with automated deployment ensures that the performance thresholds remain stable during and post-transitions. This proactive approach to software delivery minimizes downtime and keeps risks of service updates in a microservices world at bay. In addition, CI/CD principles can assist in more accurate understanding of microservices granularity, preventing teams from adding redundant complexity to their workflow when planning it. As emphasized in recent studies, achieving the best balance for microservice partitioning can essentially enhance scalability, where cloud environments can adjust freely to varying demands (Andrawos et al., 2019). Lastly, complementarity between CI/CD methodologies and cloud-native ideals enhances the ability of an organization to effectively adapt to market shifts, uphold high levels of performance.

SUMMARY

We find that these three building blocks are connected in nature and essential to unleashing the real potential of cloud computing. Scalability is the foundational component, allowing applications to manage increasing workloads in a cost-effective way by automatically scaling resources in line with user demand. The ability enables organizations to maintain levels of performance constant even as volumes of use explode—a highly valuable capability in today's turbocharged digital age. Utilizing scalable solutions not only minimizes the likelihood of downtime but also optimizes the cost of operation, thereby enhancing economic growth and user satisfaction in cloud-native applications. The second key feature that enhances the reliability of cloud-native systems is resilience, which has a close association with scalability. As cloud environments are susceptible to diverse kinds of transient faults and interruptions, rapid recovery from them is most critical. End-to-end management, according to the literature, allows applications to self-heal, facilitating smooth operation despite underlying infrastructural malfunctioning. By leveraging automated mechanisms of health management and replication techniques, cloud-native applications provide seamless service that is conducive to the establishment of confidence among stakeholders and users. Not only does this reduce the risk of failure, but also provides a more dynamic and responsive application environment, which is essential for modern business processes (Blöchlinger et al., 2017). Lastly, performance becomes a pivotal factor for success in cloud-native environments. Cloud-native applications, including those that make use of tools like Apache Spark, exhibit excellent performance in data handling large datasets at competitive rates (Barbary et al., 2015). This optimization capacity for data consumption and processing highlights the need to utilize cloud technology to ensure maximum computational efficiency. Through employing scalable and resilient techniques, organizations will be able to increase performance outcomes, eventually leading to higher operational efficiency and user engagement. The convergence of scalability, resilience, and performance in cloud-native architectures is a paradigm shift in the deployment and management of software, and such technologies are the enablers of future innovations in the digital landscape.

As one examines the key topics covered of how scalability is managed within cloud-native environments, it is essential to observe the shifting landscape of cloud infrastructure. With a larger role in the market by more players, the traditional model of cloud services provision, traditionally assigned to one-vendor data centers, is being decentralized. This shift highlights the requirement for cloud architectures to have the ability to mix resources transparently among several providers. Such adaptability not only enhances scalability but also aids system resilience in general, as distribution of workload to multiple infrastructures can aid in removing the threat of outages and performance bottlenecks. The ability to support diverse resources implies applications scale to diverse demand without reducing performance, a crucial concern for today's cloud services (Arcand et al., 2017). Resilience of cloud-native applications is also directly related to performance parameters, to a greater extent in job scheduling and resource usage. Efficiency of job schedulers controls the resolve of workloads, particularly in big data processing environments. Previous reliance on traditional schedulers has highlighted areas of latency and utilization ratios, particularly for transient computations. As detailed analysis demonstrates, latency can significantly hinder performance, lowering utilization of resources to below 10% for computations that require just a second or two. Such a problem necessitates the development and deployment of advanced multilevel schedulers that can better interleave short computations, increasing utilization levels well above 90% (Arcand et al., 2017). Such advancements are necessary to enable peak performance in cloud-native applications, where efficiency is the top concern. Finally, the three-way dynamic relationship between scalability, resilience, and performance highlights the pivotal importance of strategic infrastructure planning in cloud-native systems. The new computing architectures introduced through the necessity of processing data intensively necessitate a solid understanding of the compromises involved in scaling operations. Coming cloud systems will have to place emphasis on self-learning algorithms and enhanced interconnectivity among devices, further complicating this landscape.

A mitigation strategy for integrating these innovations without compromising system performance or stability is required to address these complex problems. By proactively pursuing and implementing solutions supporting scalability, resilience, and job scheduling effectiveness, organizations can finally realize the full potential of their cloud-native applications (Buyya et al., 2017). This all-encompassing approach is needed for efficiently addressing the complexity of modern cloud infrastructures.

REFERENCES

1. Alam, M., Ali, S. A., Khan, S., Liu, L., et al. (2019). Storage solutions for big data systems: A qualitative study and comparison. http://arxiv.org/abs/1904.11498 (accessed on 11th September 2025).
2. Alonso, J., Dutkowski, S., Escalante, M., Farid, A., et al. (2018). Towards supporting the extended DevOps approach through multi-cloud architectural patterns for design and pre-deployment - A tool supported approach. https://core.ac.uk/download/161652803.pdf (accessed on 11th September 2025).
3. Amaral, M., Carrera, D., Mohomed, I., Polo, J., et al. (2015). Performance evaluation of microservices architectures using containers. https://core.ac.uk/download/81578653.pdf (accessed on 11th September 2025).
4. Andrawos, M., Aßmann, U., Bass, L., Behara, D. G. K., Betts, T., Bianco, P., Bryant, D., et al. (2019). Microservice transition and its granularity problem: A systematic mapping study. https://core.ac.uk/download/426749569.pdf (accessed on 11th September 2025).
5. Andrikopoulos, V., Biro, J., García-Gómez, S., Jiménez Gañán, C., et al. (2012). Challenges for the comprehensive management of cloud services in a PaaS framework. http://oa.upm.es/15893/ (accessed on 11th September 2025).
6. Antony, F., P. C., Amogh, Rangisetti, A. K., Tamma, B., et al. (2018). A cloud native solution for dynamic auto scaling of MME in LTE. https://core.ac.uk/download/159216761.pdf (accessed on 11th September 2025).
7. Appavoo, J., Cadden, J., Dong, H., Krieger, O., et al. (2015). EbbRT: A customizable operating system for cloud applications. https://open.bu.edu/bitstream/2144/21769/1/2015-007-ebbrt.pdf (accessed on 11th September 2025).
8. Arcand, W., Bergeron, B., Bestor, D., Byun, C., et al. (2017). Scalable system scheduling for HPC and big data. http://arxiv.org/abs/1705.03102 (accessed on 11th September 2025).
9. Astorga Burgo, J., Higuero Aperribay, M. V., Jacob Taquet, E. J., Mendiola, T., et al. (2017). A survey on the contributions of software-defined networking to traffic engineering. https://core.ac.uk/download/168407472.pdf (accessed on 11th September 2025).
10. Baccarelli, E., Momenzadeh, A., & Scarpiniti, M. (2019). VirtFogSim: A parallel toolbox for dynamic energy-delay performance testing and optimization of 5G mobile-fog-cloud virtualized platforms. https://core.ac.uk/download/196295551.pdf (accessed on 11th September 2025).

11. Badia Sala, R. M., Ejarque, J., Lezzi, D., Ramón Cortés, J., et al. (2018). Transparent orchestration of task-based parallel applications in containers platforms. https://core.ac.uk/download/157811339.pdf (accessed on 11th September 2025).
12. Bairy, V. (2022). Enhancing multi-cloud network architectures for scalability and security in global enterprises. https://core.ac.uk/download/654637570.pdf (accessed on 11th September 2025).
13. Barbary, K., Franklin, M. J., Nothaft, F. A., Patterson, D., et al. (2015). Scientific computing meets big data technology: An astronomy use case. http://arxiv.org/abs/1507.03325 (accessed on 11th September 2025).
14. Baumann, L., Benz, S., Bohnert, T. M., Militano, L., et al. (2019). Monitoring resilience in a rook-managed containerized cloud storage system. https://core.ac.uk/download/222791433.pdf (accessed on 11th September 2025).
15. Blöchlinger, M., Bohnert, T. M., Brunner, S., Spillner, J., et al. (2017). Self-managing cloud-native applications: Design, implementation and experience. https://core.ac.uk/download/159415533.pdf (accessed on 11th September 2025).
16. Bohez, S., Daneels, G., De Geyter, M., Decrock, J., et al. (2013). The crowd as a cameraman: On-stage display of crowdsourced mobile video at large-scale events. https://core.ac.uk/download/147049977.pdf (accessed on 11th September 2025).
17. Bohnert, T. M., Braun, T., Carella, G. A., Cordeiro, K., et al. (2016). Toward a fully cloudified mobile network infrastructure. https://core.ac.uk/download/151536659.pdf (accessed on 11th September 2025).
18. Borada, D., & Jayaraman, S. (2024). Efficient data sharding techniques for high-scalability applications. https://core.ac.uk/download/634372818.pdf (accessed on 11th September 2025).
19. Buyya, R., & Varghese, B. (2017). Next generation cloud computing: New trends and research directions. https://core.ac.uk/download/96664300.pdf (accessed on 11th September 2025).
20. da Ferreira, J. P. R. C. (2022). Reactive microservices–An experiment. https://core.ac.uk/download/541042205.pdf (accessed on 11th September 2025).
21. Dasari, K. K. (2023). Cross-cloud continuity: A scalable framework for resilient and regulated digital infrastructure. https://core.ac.uk/download/656112784.pdf (accessed on 11th September 2025).
22. Dwivedi, Y. K., Hughes, L., Baabdullah, A. M., Ribeiro-Navarrete, S.,

Giannakis, M., Al-Debei, M. M., Dennehy, D., et al. (2022). Metaverse beyond the hype: Multidisciplinary perspectives on emerging challenges, opportunities, and agenda for research, practice and policy. International Journal of Information Management, 66, 102542–102542. https://doi.org/10.1016/j.ijinfomgt.2022.102542 (accessed on 11th September 2025).

23. Jamshidi, P., Leitner, P., van Hoorn, A., Weber, I., et al. (2017). Report from GI-Dagstuhl Seminar 16394: Software performance engineering in the DevOps world. https://core.ac.uk/download/pdf/141718346.pdf (accessed on 11th September 2025).

24. Jones, M. W., Abatzoglou, J. T., Veraverbeke, S., Andela, N., Lasslop, G., Forkel, M., Smith, A. J. P., et al. (2022). Global and regional trends and drivers of fire under climate change. Reviews of Geophysics, 60. https://doi.org/10.1029/2020rg000726 (accessed on 11th September 2025).

25. Mahgoub, A. (2025). From monolith to microservices: Building scalable applications with Kubernetes, CI/CD, and chaos engineering. https://core.ac.uk/download/657105048.pdf (accessed on 11th September 2025).

26. Mahmoud, E. (2025). Enhancing hosting infrastructure management with AI-powered automation. https://core.ac.uk/download/657100959.pdf (accessed on 11th September 2025).

27. Munnangi, S. (2022). Achieving operational resilience with cloud-native BPM solutions. https://core.ac.uk/download/654637525.pdf (accessed on 11th September 2025).

28. Mylsamy, S., & Mishra, R. K. (2025). Cloud-native development and deployment. International Journal of Research in Modern Engineering & Emerging Technology. https://www.semanticscholar.org/paper/906572deb8cdf14b98581f627527aa9be1303bb5 (accessed on 11th September 2025).

29. Vardhineedi, P. N., & Jain, A. (2025). Architecting for the cloud: Best practices for application design, scalability, and performance. International Journal of Research in Humanities and Social Sciences. https://www.semanticscholar.org/paper/9c9338d4d20ede446125366f11e4a2e0efa323cd (accessed on 11th September 2025).

30. Yang, M., Chen, L., Wang, J., Msigwa, G., Osman, A. I., Fawzy, S., Rooney, D. W., et al. (2022). Circular economy strategies for combating climate change and other environmental issues. Environmental Chemistry Letters, 21, 55–80. https://doi.org/10.1007/s10311-022-01499-6 (accessed on 11th September 2025).

CHAPTER 10

SERVERLESS AND FUTURE OF CLOUD-NATIVE

Contents

INTRODUCTION

The rapidly evolving landscape of cloud computing has led to spectacular innovations regarding the deployment and management of applications within organizations. Of the various paradigms, serverless computing has been an innovative approach that can simplify the development process and ease the operation. Rather than needing provisioning and administration of server resources, serverless models enable developers to create code with the underlying infrastructure abstracted. This paradigm shift not only minimizes latency and expenses but also optimizes scalability and resource utilization. With businesses increasingly embracing cloud-native architectures, it is essential to understand the serverless computing implications. This essay therefore discusses how serverless computing is transforming the future of cloud-native paradigms, uncovering challenges as well as opportunities ahead in this area. The significance of serverless computing is further highlighted by its potential to address severe issues in different sectors like healthcare and finance. By using edge computing and distributed machine learning techniques, according to recent studies, businesses can leverage serverless architecture to analyze and process data in real-time while maintaining stringent privacy and security provisions. For example, in the healthcare sector, edge intelligence can facilitate real-time interventions, which have a significant impact on patient outcomes. Qayyum et al. (2022) identifies challenges and technological advancements that are needed for effective deployment of machine learning at the edge, bringing to fore pioneering solutions to long-standing issues. While serverless computing is evolving, its impact resonates throughout companies, necessitating continuous research and development to fully realize its capabilities in supporting flexible and agile services. Potentially promising, the road to ubiquitous serverless computing utilization is paved with challenges that need continued examination. Vendor lock-in issues, inconsistent performance, and operation complexity are only a few of the problems companies must navigate. Despite these issues, Hassan et al. (2021) emphasizes the importance of comprehensive studies to enlighten one about the actual-world realities of serverless settings to understand their efficacy and shortcomings. Through systematic review of previous work in the field of serverless computing, key knowledge gaps can be recognized and addressed. This essay will continue to delve into these complexities, not just shining a light on the state of serverless computing today but also opening doors to ideas on where research can go next that can enable developers and researchers alike to unlock the full potential of cloud-native architectures.

Definition of Serverless Computing

The serverless paradigm represents a significant shift in application development, deployment, and management in the cloud. Unlike provisioning and hosting the server infrastructure, serverless computing abstracts the complexity so that developers can write code alone. Automatic scaling, where resources are dynamically provisioned based on application demand, resulting in optimizing performance and cost, is delivered under this model. The term serverless is a little misleading, as it does not imply that there are no servers; rather, it is a highlight of the fact that the management of infrastructure is fully handled by the cloud provider. As a result, developers get to deploy applications faster and more efficiently, thereby fueling innovation in their companies. This change is reflective of innovations in cloud program models and indicates the increasing maturity of cloud technology (Baldini et al., 2017). Beyond its operational advantages, serverless computing comes with an inventory of features adapted to the requirements of new digital needs. The model is particularly helpful to event-driven applications, which run based on pre-determined stimuli such as user inputs or data instances. This feature allows organizations to build microservices architecture that can be independently deployed and scaled, which fosters resilience and agility. Furthermore, the serverless computing economic model, often a pay-as-you-go model, enables organizations to pay only for the compute usage, which can be a significant cost-saver. This shift from legacy, expected billing has the potential to disrupt existing budgeting and spending practices in IT organizations, freeing up funds for a variety of projects (Al-Ameen et al., 2018). From now on, the consequences of serverless computing are not merely technical; they predict a future of revolution for organizations that want to remain competitive in a rapidly digitalizing world. The capability to scale fast with low operational overhead makes it easier for companies to respond fast to market demands and customer needs. However, with these benefits comes a number of issues, such as security risks and the complexity of handling monitoring and debugging serverless applications. For instance, even though defects in the servers are managed by the cloud provider, organizations are still responsible for their app security. As serverless computing evolves, it will become increasingly important for organizations to address these challenges directly in order to benefit as much as possible from its promise in shaping the future of cloud-native architecture (Baldini et al., 2017).

Overview of Cloud-Native Architecture

Cloud-native architecture represents a sea change in software system design and deployment. Essentially, this architecture gives applications the capability to access the full potential of cloud computing, with an emphasis on scalability, resilience, and agility. These kinds of architectures tend to be built on microservices principles, in which separate pieces of an application are developed, deployed, and scaled independently. This module-based structure not only enhances development time but also simplifies the management process, whereby one can alter a specific service without interrupting the system. Moreover, the cloud-native model encourages the utilization of managed services and serverless computing, which lighten the operational burden on developers. By integrating these fragments, businesses can focus on building value through innovation rather than being encumbered by infrastructure problems, a crucial shift in modern software development. Moreover, the matching of cloud-native and serverless architectures creates an entry into performance and cost-effectiveness levels unheard of previously. Serverless computing virtualizes the management of infrastructure so developers can write and run code without worrying about server provisioning or scaling. This model is also the most beneficial in cloud-native environments where the applications experience mixed workloads. With a pay-as-you-go pricing model, organizations reduce costs significantly, only paying for the run time and not for the idle server capacity. Cloud-native architecture's future also offers room for development with technology such as WebAssembly (Wasm), which enhances the performance and enables developers to compile their applications into several languages. As per the analysis of Wasm and IoT, the combination of these technologies offers a robust toolkit for developers, with possibilities for creating highly responsive and efficient applications that can run optimally on different environments (Ray, 2023). Also, with the evolution of cloud-native architectures, the multi-cloud strategy is emerging more and more crucial. The traditional dependency on a single cloud provider poses risks such as vendor lock-in and limited flexibility. Moving towards a multi-cloud environment allows organizations to take advantage of the unique strengths of each provider, enhancing resiliency and avoiding outages in the delivery of services. Heterogeneity in architecture requires a more complex design and operational strategy, under which developers must create applications that are capable of running on multiple platforms and configurations. The benefits of such approaches, such as increased redundancy, increased accessibility to services, and cost optimization, can accrue to competitive advantage in the fast-evolving digital landscape. As illustrated in current research, these new architectures will demand new tools and frameworks, overcoming issues associated with multi-cloud environments and enabling developers to maintain effective DevOps practices while accessing heterogeneous cloud resources (Alonso et al., 2023).

Importance of the Topic in Modern Software Development

The need for serverless architecture in contemporary software development cannot be exaggerated, particularly with organizations shifting towards more cloud-native methods. Serverless computing delivers effective use of resources since it allows developers to just write code without worrying about the infrastructure. The new method not only accelerates development cycles but also increases productivity, leading to an innovative culture where one can play and innovate rapidly. The annual activity report of the Zurich University of Applied Sciences Service Prototyping Lab indicates the essential role of education and collaboration with the industry in this field, emphasizing that efficient serverless implementations require complete understanding of emerging technologies and the trends of software development (Al-Ameen et al., 2018). Consequently, this approach presents an opportunity for both startups and big businesses to optimize operations and reduce costs, ultimately changing the application development landscape. Dynamic scaling of applications is one of the most powerful aspects of serverless architecture. Other architectures involve a lot of upfront resource investment that may not get utilized, which is inefficient. In contrast, serverless solutions such as AWS Lambda or Google Cloud Functions allow developers to only pay for compute resources consumed at runtime, which better aligns costs with usage. This scale-on-demand is imperative as businesses face fluctuating workloads, enabling them to deliver quality user experiences without wasted cost. In addition, the more complex applications businesses build, the more complex performance challenges pertinent to virtualization technologies are magnified.

Figure 10.1. *Importance of the topic in modern software development.*

Source: https://media.licdn.com/dms/image/v2/D4D12AQGusd7AmsrRBg/article-cover_image-shrink_720_1280/article-cover_image-shrink_720_1280/0/1696752345658?e=2147483647&v=beta&t=knpE0qk8_F8n-PZ7bBqaZG-RbsqwZozK-ktOpj233st4.

Research indicates Docker remains a high performer in terms of virtualization but that other solutions like Firecracker and gVisor also offer dramatic benefits for specific situations, illustrating that diverse solutions are needed in order to address different use cases (Kärnä et al., 2021). Moreover, security is a primary focus in current software development, particularly in serverless systems where resource isolation and execution of unknown code are extremely sensitive issues. As the rise in data breaches and cyber-attacks grows more common, developers must adopt secure development practices when leveraging cloud resources. Serverless architectures can ensure security by reducing the attack surface area and enabling rapid update of function code so that vulnerabilities can be overcome efficiently. But to ensure the security of serverless functions, there must be an enhanced insight into the implicit shared responsibility model existing in cloud environments (Kärnä et al., 2021). Hence, the transition to serverless computing requires not just insight into factors of performance but a similar strong compliance with security controls, illustrating the interrelated nature of these factors within the context of modern software design (Figure 10.1).

10.1. EVOLUTION OF CLOUD COMPUTING

Evolution of cloud computing has revolutionized the way organizations deploy as well as use their resources. Pre-cloud computing models originally defined cloud computing, with which it began to gain momentum when Software as a Service (SaaS) services and Infrastructure as a Service (IaaS) came into existence in the early 2000s. Such practices allowed businesses to transfer their hardware maintenance and software upgrades, releasing a significant amount of capital while enhancing efficiency. The increasing penetration of the Internet made this possible, with individuals beginning to utilize remote servers rather than local installations. Moreover, Platform as a Service (PaaS) introduced developers the possibility of building and deploying applications without having to worry about underlying layers of hardware or software, making way for more advanced cloud-native technologies. This transformation marks a turning point in the evolution of cloud computing, emphasizing scalability and flexibility in modern IT solutions. When the technology of cloud computing grew, serverless computing emerged as a revolution in application development. This architecture hides the infrastructure entirely, where developers can code without concern for the servers or provisioning resources. Serverless computing is particularly valuable for event-driven applications which require the highest level of scalability. In addition to optimizing the utilization of resources, the framework also optimizes deployment time, which is critical in the present high-speed digital world. Surprisingly, research has proved that serverless environments are able to achieve low inferencing latency for machine learning scenarios, although cold start latency remains an issue (Ishakian et al., 2018). These advancements show how serverless computing has its place in the general advancement of cloud technology, where efficiency and responsiveness are the main drivers in the digital economy. The future of cloud-native solutions relies heavily on the continued advancement and refining of serverless computing. As machine learning and artificial intelligence advance faster and faster, organizations are turning to incorporate these technologies into serverless architecture. The capacity to execute complex neural networks within a serverless environment will be able to help businesses significantly enhance their products, giving them a competitive edge in the marketplace. This is indicative of a broader trend where technology interfaces with business needs in a way that is supportive of innovation. Research studies and universities, such as those encompassed in the Service Prototyping Lab at Zurich University of Applied Sciences in its annual report, are critical to exploring these crossroads and advancing technological frontiers that will determine cloud computing's future (Al-Ameen et al., 2018) (Figure 10.2).

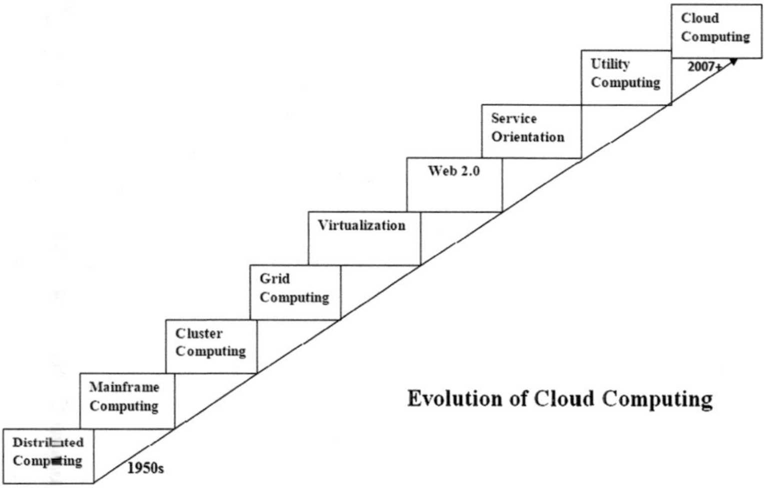

Figure 10.2 *The evolution of cloud computing.*

Source: https://media.geeksforgeeks.org/wp-content/uploads/20200512101821/Evolution_of_Cloud_computing_GFG.png.

10.1.1. Historical Context of Cloud Services

The evolution of cloud services has its origin in the early 21st century technology development, primarily driven by the widespread usage of the internet for business and personal computation. Centralized storage of information was one of the original concepts of cloud computing, which allowed users to share and access information remotely. When companies realized the possibility of increased scalability and more flexibility, it created core services, and this spawned a proliferation of Software as a Service (SaaS) and Infrastructure as a Service (IaaS). This change brought forth a new era with the outsourcing of IT infrastructure, thus enabling companies to focus on their core capabilities while having resource management and service delivery handled by cloud providers. These early developments gave rise to more sophisticated products like microservices and serverless computing, which continued to decentralize the character of computing and further encouraged software to employ agile development practices. It was during the mid-2010s that organizations began embracing serverless computing as a way to further optimize resource utilization in the dynamic market. Traditional cloud infrastructures required the user to provision and manage servers, leading to inefficiency and increased operating costs. As compared to this, serverless computing eliminates infrastructure abstraction, allowing developers to concentrate solely on code development with server resources automatically allocated regarding demand. Some of the major innovations in this period, including the introduction of Function as a Service (FaaS), were critical to the operational efficiency of cloud infrastructures. The marriage of serverless computing with microservices simplified the ability to have a scalable architecture that could efficiently scale up and down with changing workloads, a key innovation in the development and deployment of applications in the cloud. This change is part of a broader movement toward responsive, flexible IT solutions that reflect the complexities of current digital business environments. In the future, machine learning and advanced analytics convergence in serverless frameworks is viewed to enhance the effectiveness of cloud-native applications. According to recent research, for example, the proposal of the Serverless Cloud Auto Resource Framework (SCARF), predictive resource management potential that optimizes performance and reduces operational bottlenecks is monumental. The continuous evolution of microservices, fueled by cloud on-demand features, demands rigorous monitoring and inspection of the various elements of services that are embedded into an dispersed environment. Towards this end, initiatives to create global observatories to observe microservice artifacts will be significant in order to drive innovation and foster developments that increase cloud-native application flexibility and resilience (Gkikopoulos et al., 2019). Hence, understanding the historical development of cloud services and how they influence contemporary architectures will be vital to guiding future cloud directions (Trujillo et al., 2024).

10.1.2. Transition from Traditional to Cloud-Native Applications

The movement from legacy to cloud-native applications is a profound technology shift that fundamentally separates how organizations develop and run their software in terms of process composition. Legacy applications are monolithic in composition and are committed to specific environments and extremely resource-starved when performing maintenance and scaling. Cloud-native applications, however, employ microservices and containerization, which allows them to be environment-agnostic in different environments. This change facilitates more agile development patterns so that teams can release features rapidly and respond to customer needs with agility. With increasingly widespread adoption of this model, there come challenges and opportunities for them to rethink their existing IT strategy, adjusting to a world where scalability is monarch and flexibility is monarch.

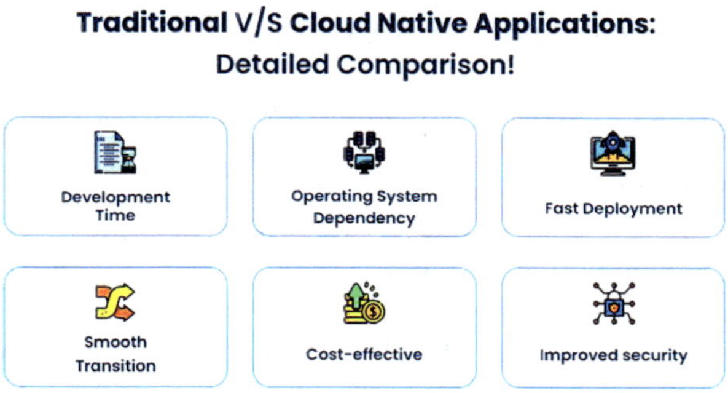

Figure 10.3. *The transition from traditional to cloud-native applications.*

Source: https://www.mtractionenterprise.com/blog/wp-content/uploads/2023/05/Traditional-v-s-Cloud-Native-Applications-detailed-comparison.png.

With organizations migrating towards paradigms that are cloud-native, the requirement for serverless computing gains even greater significance. Serverless architectures decouple compute power from application management, allowing developers to focus solely on code. This not only accelerates the development process but also optimizes resource usage since cloud providers manage resources dynamically based on demand. But with such a change comes complexity in resource management that requires innovative frameworks that do not sacrifice efficiency and performance. The Serverless Cloud Auto Resource Framework (SCARF), for instance, proposes a solution based on machine learning for predictive resource provision and thus incurs less waste as well as faster responsiveness in serverless systems (Trujillo et al., 2024). Familiarity with such developments is essential for organizations which are eager to derive utmost benefits of cloud-native applications while managing the attendant issues of scalability and operational efficiency. The cloud-native journey has also made it possible for edge computing integration, most notably as firms desire to advance performance for low-latency applications. With the applications being moved to the cloud, they must also contend with the mounting pressure of delivering smooth operations in distributed environments, just like with the convergence of cloud and edge technologies. The progress in light cloud-native runtimes and tools such as KubeEdge and K3s allows for such an integration, helping organizations deploy responsive and fault-tolerant applications at the edge (Virtanen et al., 2023). It not only facilitates varied use cases but also fuels innovation in service delivery, particularly in industries that rely on real-time data processing. Hence, the intersection of cloud-native methods with edge computing not only secures the strength of applications but also changes the very essence of application deployment and end-user experience in the digital age (Figure 10.3).

10.1.3. Emergence of Serverless as a Paradigm Shift

The serverless computing concept is a significant paradigm shift in the realm of cloud-native system designs, altering how application deployment and resource management are handled by developers. Previously, developers had substantial overhead in the form of offering and maintaining server infrastructure, which may take away from productivity levels and increase expenses. With serverless architectures, these disadvantages are circumvented as applications are broken down into microservices that scale automatically with demand. Such flexibility not only enhances operational efficiency but also allows businesses to focus on business functionality rather than infrastructure management, effectively minimizing workflow and fueling innovation. The serverless model, in this manner, propels developers to focus on creating quality apps and enjoy cost-effective and scalable cloud capabilities. Furthermore, the impacts of serverless computing are far-reaching in various sectors like healthcare and data science where rapid processing and minimal latency are critical. In the field of medical applications, for example, serverless architectures can enable the increasing complexity and volume of clinical data to support rapid insights against stringent security and privacy requirements. The union of innovative concepts, such as federated learning clustering, illustrates the potential of serverless architectures in performing intelligent data processing at the edge. With such adoption of technology, the healthcare sector can facilitate real-time diagnosis, pushing patient outcomes and operational efficiency. Such dynamic ability of serverless computing thus offers a groundbreaking prospect to industries that involve rapid and secure data processing in their operations (Qayyum et al., 2022). Despite advantages brought about by the serverless mode of operation, various challenges exist that necessitate future research and development. The most salient of these are vendor lock-in, debugging, and monitoring problems that complicate serverless application management. As the relevant literature observes, a recent survey characterized a vast number of studies addressing the state-of-the-art contributions in serverless computing, including its platforms and applications, but also remarked on the necessity for closer examination of its challenges (Hassan et al., 2021). Future efforts should be focused on building frameworks and tools to make serverless application management easy without compromising security and performance expectations. Bridging these gaps not only will enhance current implementations but also will lay the groundwork for mass adoption, solidifying serverless computing as an architecture of cloud-native development.

10.2. KEY FEATURES OF SERVERLESS COMPUTING

One of the richest features of serverless computing is its scalability by design, which automatically allows applications to grow to adapt to shifting levels of demand. This capability inherently disrupts traditional patterns of deployment, where server resource provisioning and management inherently had high overhead and complexity. With a serverless framework, cloud providers handle the underlying infrastructure, leaving developers able to focus solely on code without worrying about scaling issues. As suggested in discussions on cloud programming model development, the serverless model is a response to inefficiencies embedded within classic architectures, emphasizing the need for flexibility and resource optimization in modern application deployment (Baldini et al., 2017). Scalability, therefore, not only enhances performance but also reduces operation costs, making serverless computing an attractive option for businesses seeking flexible and cost-effective platforms in the ever-changing digital landscape. Another key feature of serverless computing is also the event-driven architecture, which provides very seamless integration of serverless with other applications and services. In this case, the model allows developers to execute functions based on events defined, such as changes in data or messages in a queue. The event-driven nature of serverless computing makes possible a more responsive and efficient application design, where functions are executed only when necessary, hence maximizing the use of the resources. This efficiency becomes particularly pertinent in the context of increasing and more intricate workload problems, as current Function as a Service (FaaS) solutions are typically optimal for frequent runs with modest working sets (Appavoo et al., 2019). With an event-driven model, serverless computing is capable of enhancing application responsiveness and user experience and constructing a more interactive system that is consistent with the expectations of present users. Lastly, cost-effectiveness is a key feature of serverless computing that fundamentally alters IT budgeting behavior for businesses. In traditional cloud computing, users have to pay for provisioned resources regardless of actual usage, and this can lead to significant wastage of financial resources.

Conversely, under serverless architecture, billing is indeed functionally associated with function execution, and firms pay for their functions only when actually in use. This pay-as-you-go model is especially valuable to startups and smaller organizations, which lack the budgetary room to maneuver of larger ones. Second, as serverless architecture matures and additional use cases come into focus, organizations benefit from more targeted application of financial capital, tying IT expenditures to project demand and business requirements, once again highlighting the flexibility and future-proofing of this architecture (Baldini et al., 2017).

10.2.1. Event-Driven Architecture

In the rapidly evolving world of cloud-native infrastructure, event-driven architecture (EDA) is a focal concept. It is an architecture that facilitates the decoupling of application pieces with greater flexibility and faster reaction to alterations in real-time information. EDA operates on the premise that events, traditionally caused by user interactions, system operations, or out-of-process events, are employed as the focal means of communication among disparate services. Through the use of event streams, developers are able to develop applications that respond dynamically to changing data inputs, a critical factor in developing cloud-native applications that are scalable and fault-tolerant. The growing use of EDA within serverless ecosystems is a strong testament to its importance; as complexity increases in applications, efficient processing of events can translate into improved performance and user experience, which is a pronounced trend towards more adaptive systems within cloud computing. Serverless computing, as a natural fit with event-driven architecture, is an appealing model for hosting event-driven applications without infrastructure management costs. In serverless environments, such as AWS Lambda, application developers are able to write code that directly responds to events, cutting the time it takes to get applications to market by orders of magnitude. This operational model not only provides usage flexibility with respect to resources but also is cost effective since it charges for actual usage compared to limited pre-provisioned resources. Notwithstanding this, issues still exist, with the main one being latency. Research indicates that serverless architectures inferencing can provide decent latencies, but problems with cold starts are likely to lead to issues, compromising service level agreements (SLAs). Making these challenges is essential to broader implementation and optimization of serverless event-driven architecture in mission-critical systems (Ishakian et al., 2018). The continuous development of cloud computing infrastructure creates a necessity for new architectural alternatives, where event-driven architectures are particularly valuable. With multi-cloud systems diversifying and increasing demands for decentralized computer systems, EDA is in accordance with trends toward multi-provider environments. These infrastructures promote the unification of different services and data sources, which ultimately contributes to more user engagement and efficiency in operation. Moreover, the future of EDA in cloud-native environments holds the potential to make self-learning systems that can learn from the event streams that reach them and thereby make the architecture proactive along with reactive. For being able to entirely take advantage of the potential of these new architectures, organizations need to overcome the issues of integration, management, and scale performance and empower the promise of next-generation cloud systems to be achieved (Buyya et al., 2017) (Figure 10.4).

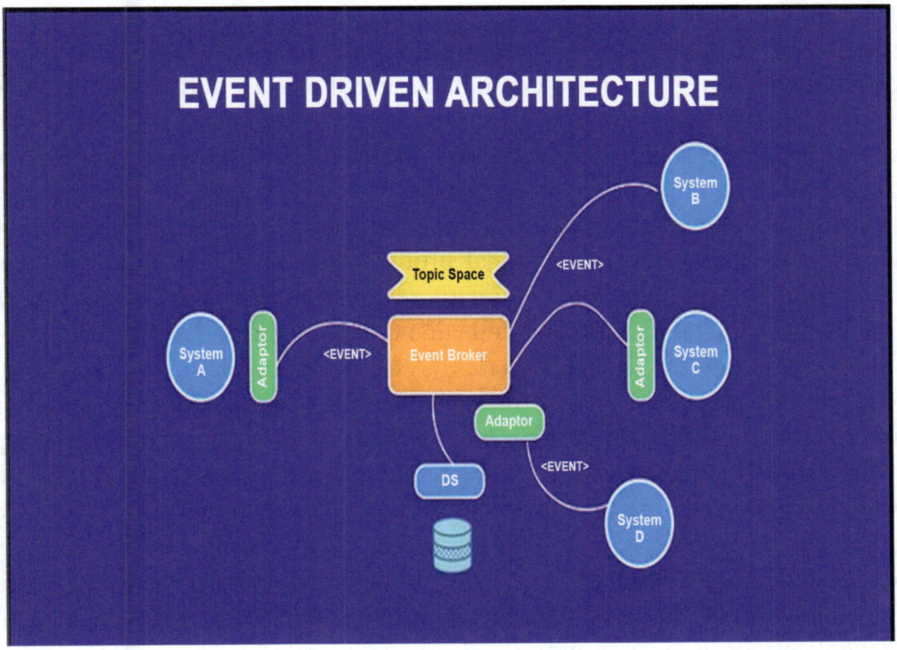

Figure 10.4. *Event-driven architecture.*

Source: https://www.tothenew.com/blog/wp-ttn-blog/uploads/2024/09/Screenshot-from-2024-09-16-16-15-50.png.

10.2.2. Automatic Scaling and Resource Management

Automatic scaling and resource management are two of the most important facets of the serverless computing paradigm, particularly as business shifts toward cloud-native applications. The ability to scale resources automatically based on demand allows applications to attain performance and responsiveness without incurring unnecessary expenses. Automatic scaling within a serverless environment cuts back on human labor, where development teams can focus more on application capabilities and innovation. This approach facilitates efficient use of resources with real-time provisioning of compute resources, thereby significantly boosting deployment flexibility. Automatic scaling methods will also become increasingly complex with cloud-native technology advancements, providing users with more tailored solutions to optimize performance across changing workloads and application profiles. The advent of such platforms as funcX is a testament to automatic scaling's ability to revolutionize computation execution in distributed environments. funcX facilitates the decomposition of monolithic applications into self-contained, concise functions that can be executed on whatever resources are on hand. Not only does function execution enhance scalability, but making certain computational resources are allocated according to individual requirements of each task further optimizes throughput even under heavy load. FuncX has been experimentally proven to scale up to over 1 million function calls per second, illustrating the impact of good resource management. By utilizing such frameworks, organizations can minimize latency and maximize computational efficiency, proving the argument, that auto-scaling is the future of cloud-native applications (Akkus et al., 2020). Besides, hybrid cloud integration and edge computing introduce new resource management opportunities in serverless systems. With the Internet of Things (IoT) extending to all corners, efficiently processing data at the edge is more important than ever. By leveraging hybrid cloud multi-access edge computing (MEC), developers can power more intelligent applications developed on localized data processing to deliver timely insights and actions. This distributed model enhances auto-scaling capabilities by distributing workloads close to data sources, reducing latency, and giving instantaneous feedback. Such architectures not only optimize throughput but also meet the gigantic scale of IoT applications, like smart city initiatives and mobile health care, by tapping into complete cloud-native environments (Bruin et al., 2019). Organizations can thus capitalize on the unpredictability of modern data needs through strategic resource management and scaling, but still maintain operational responsiveness and efficiency.

10.2.3. Cost Efficiency and Pay-as-You-Go Model

The introduction of serverless computing has transformed the way in which organizations meet cost efficiency in the cloud. By adopting the pay-as-you-go approach, companies are able to reserve their costs of hosting server infrastructure by a significant amount. This model allows firms to pay only for practical computing capacity and resources used while operational and not for the pre-allocated server capacity overheads. Therefore, organizations can dynamically scale resources based on fluctuating workloads without the cost of over-provisioning during low-demand periods. The cost advantages of serverless architectures are especially beneficial for small and startup businesses, which may be unable to afford significant server infrastructure initially. As competition in cloud services keeps increasing, providers are embracing more and more granular pricing structures that lead to overall cost-effectiveness, head-on challenging traditional pricing strategies associated with dedicated servers (Borra et al., 2025). Cost efficiencies obtained through serverless architecture is another most important impetus for embracing the pay-as-you-go model. Through infrastructure management abstraction, developers and organizations can now focus away from server maintenance and on application development and innovation.

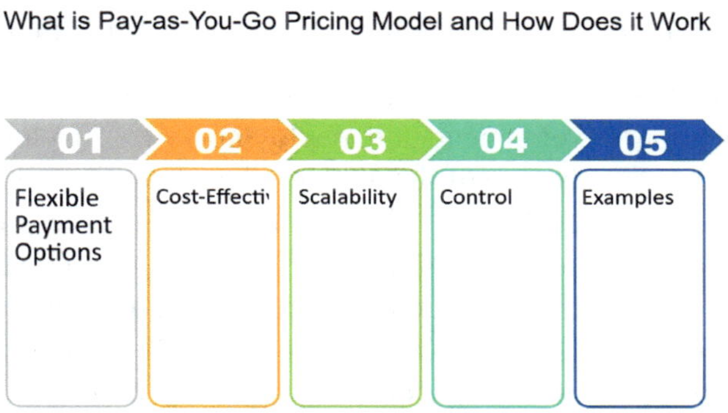

Figure 10.5. *Cost efficiency and pay-as-you-go model.*

Source: https://fastercapital.co/i/Utilization-Fee-in-Cloud-Computing--Pay-as-You-Go-Pricing-Models--What-is-Pay-as-You-Go-Pricing-Model-and-How-Does-it-Work.webp.

This not only accelerates deployment cycles, but also enables a more agile reaction to market demand. By using AWS Lambda and Azure Functions, which simplify application deployment, organizations can quickly develop and iterate on offerings without the constraints of physical hardware. Consequently, cost savings in operations are experienced beyond just financial metrics, rendering the product development environment a more nimble environment where teams can implement features more rapidly and receive user feedback in real-time. This change in operation dynamics is a desirable case in favor of many organizations adopting serverless architectures, adding to yet again the advantages of the pay-as-you-go model (Bayya, 2025). Nevertheless, while its numerous benefits make the pay-as-you-go scheme appealing to organizations, these organizations also have to deal with some challenges that serverless computing can bring. One of them is the risk of surprise bills, particularly if the workloads abruptly exceed expectations. This will result in increased fees for usage of resources whose volatility makes consumption accumulate high in a short period when usage is intense. Apart from that, the sophistication of serverless application monitoring and optimization is also exacerbated in this environment. Organizations must implement robust monitoring tools and optimize their usage patterns in a way that they can effectively assess and estimate the cost implicated with the serverless approach. Proper management of costs and ensuring cost-effectiveness is hence a must in optimizing the advantage of serverless computing while avoiding the traps of excessive expenses (Borra et al., 2025) (Figure 10.5).

10.3. BENEFITS OF SERVERLESS ARCHITECTURE

Serverless architecture is among the most compelling instances of paradigmatic shift in application development and deployment within cloud computing. Perhaps most egregiously, one of the most obvious benefits of this style is that it self-scales. Conventional approaches, with their resource provisioning for maximum load, are associated with a significant amount of advance planning and investment. Serverless architectures, by way of contrast, automatically scale compute resources as demand dictates. This adaptability not only optimizes resource utilization but also reduces the burden of operations on developers so that they can program more and worry less about infrastructure maintenance. As organizations put more pressure on being agile in reacting to shifting market scenarios, the facility for automatic scaling that serverless platforms offer is a significant advantage in guarantying competitive advantage. The cost savings that serverless architecture offers is another valuable advantage. Serverless computing adheres to a pay-as-you-go model of pricing, and hence organizations pay for the use of compute resources during the run of their functions and not otherwise. This is a contrast to the infrastructure pricing that typically requires payment for reserved instances regardless of use. Hence, business entities are able to achieve considerable cost reduction, especially for work involving varying workload patterns or volatile demand patterns. This money flexibility allows startups as well as businesses to experiment with new ideas without exposing themselves to over-spending on resources. The operational cost model that is applicable to serverless architecture thus seamlessly integrates into the lean data-driven decision-making mode in cloud-native environments. Serverless architecture also allows for increased developer productivity by masking the complexity of infrastructure management. With serverless, developers can leverage managed services that handle provisioning, scalability, and server upkeep, which previously took time and effort away from the actual work of development. Developers are now free to write code and create value, and this results in faster cycles of deployment and more iterative application development. This shift not only accelerates development but also enhances cooperation because cross-functional groups are able to quickly work on features without being bogged down by the operations. As serverless architectures advance and gain increasingly broader acceptance, they will transform software development in the future, emphasizing the importance of keeping up with the latest cloud technology and methodologies if one is to thrive in a digital economy (Buyya et al., 2017; Baldini et al., 2017).

10.3.1. Reduced Operational Overhead

The serverless architecture paradigm is revolutionizing operational activities of cloud-native applications, primarily by avoiding operational overhead. Serverless computing protects against the complex infrastructure management that previously became a standard in application deployment. This frees up developers from the difficulties of server provisioning, scaling, and upkeep to focus on coding and developing more features. With applications of such models as Function as a Service (FaaS), organizations can execute code against events and, as such, maximize usage of resources and maximize efficiency. Serverless platforms' flexibility provides developers with the option to use only compute resources when needed, significantly minimizing costs of idle infrastructure and enabling elastic response to changing workloads. As a result, organizations are able to innovate more quickly and meet market demand with less IT operation capital investment. Additionally, reduced operational overhead is experienced in terms of improved scalability and responsiveness of serverless architectures. Server-based systems have historically suffered from responsiveness and scalability problems, particularly during peak times. On the other hand, serverless architectures can scale resource provision automatically with real-time traffic, meaning application performance remains unchanged without any human intervention. For instance, advancements such as funcX reflect this capacity by enabling fast remote execution of functions with great performance upscaling to over 130,000 concurrent workers without considerable latency and high throughput (Akkus et al., 2020). This demand-based scaling functionality not only improves operating procedures but also overall user experience, thereby boosting the competitive edge of organizations employing serverless architecture. Additionally, the strategic deployment of serverless technologies provides organizations with means to manage the complexities of deployment more effectively, thereby minimizing operational overhead even further. The choice between serverful and serverless deployment has a pivotal impact on performance as well as cost savings (Grasso et al., 2025). Through a hybrid deployment strategy, companies can take advantage of serverless advantages while keeping serverful frameworks for mission-critical applications. This blending creates flexibility in application deployment, enabling smooth migrations and enhancing resource utilization as needs change. Successful deployment target management mitigates migration expense and keeps current development aligned with business goals. Implementing these strategies adds to a future-oriented operational model that minimizes both management work and costs related thereto, encouraging a greener and more innovative cloud-native ecosystem (Figure 10.6).

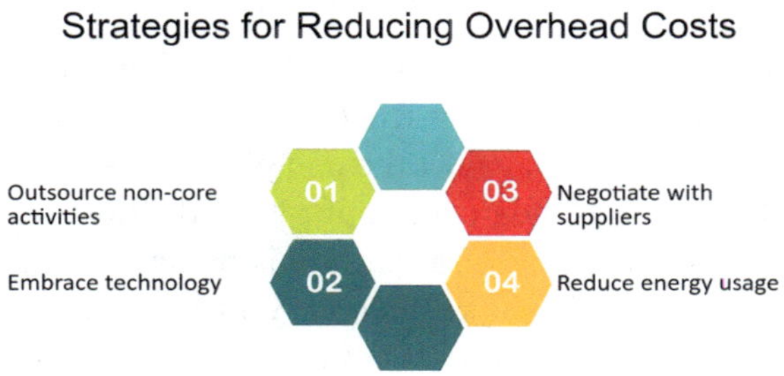

Figure 10.6. *Reduced operational overhead.*

Source: https://fastercapital.co/i/Overhead-costs--Reducing-Overhead-Costs-to-Lower-Cost-of-Revenue--Strategies-for-Reducing-Overhead-Costs.webp.

10.3.2. Enhanced Developer Productivity

With a fast-changing technological landscape, heightened developer productivity is one of the key issues to be taken into account by organizations utilizing cloud-native and serverless architectures. Through the reduction of effort in infrastructure provisioning and management, serverless platforms allow developers to concentrate on coding without being sidetracked by server management. This feature is especially crucial because developers are bombarded with an influx of new frameworks and tools, thus slowing them down. The use of artificial intelligence (AI) in coding environments aims to ease this load by proposing intelligent code suggestions, enhancing problem-solving, and thereby accelerating development processes. Studies indicate that use of AI-driven tools can result in 75% productivity improvement, significantly improving collaboration and enabling developers to focus more on creative work while AI handles repetitive tasks (Awsaf et al., 2025). Besides, serverless computing pretty much transforms the way development teams work on a project and deploy it. In the serverless paradigm, developers can deploy applications quickly, reacting to market needs with unprecedented agility. The shift in deployment strategy is geared towards iterative velocity and continuous delivery, which ultimately leads to improved quality software. When new technologies are integrated with AI in cloud-native platforms, developers can benefit from advanced learning technologies that enhance their capabilities and code quality by over 70%. This aspect not only increases productivity but also fosters an effective learning platform for technology within the team. Prioritization of collaborative coding processes allows teams to exchange information more effectively, whereby best practices can be exchanged and directly applied in development workflows (Venkata et al., 2021). However, the increasing reliance on AI and serverless environments comes with a caution call for developers. Though productivity gains are most highlighted, increased over-reliance on automated tools, threat risks of skill decay, and ethical concerns around code generated using AI must be closely monitored. Developers should balance applying AI for productivity while maintaining their coding ability so that they are innovative and flexible. The evolving trajectory of software development requires an active approach from developers, promoting a culture of lifelong learning and improvement within the teams. This approach not only prepares developers for the future challenges but also equips them to successfully counter the intricacies of cloud-native architectures while driving productivity and innovation (Awsaf et al., 2025).

10.3.3. Improved Application Performance and Reliability

The advent of serverless computing has had a dramatic impact on how applications are executed and deployed, leading to radical performance and reliability gains. Serverless technology abstracts away the underlying infrastructure, allowing developers to focus on code alone. With the provisioning of resources automated, serverless systems can dynamically adjust themselves to changing workloads, bypassing performance bottlenecks that usual configurations are prone to. Furthermore, the inborn scalability of serverless environments is such that applications will be able to withstand sudden surges in demand without collapsing, thereby enhancing user experience and satisfaction. This scalability is made possible through frameworks like the Serverless Cloud Auto Resource Framework (SCARF), which uses machine learning for resource optimization and reducing forecasting errors. By intelligent forecasting of the oscillations in demand, these frameworks offer best provisioning of resources that further improve overall application performance and reliability (Trujillo et al., 2024). In addition to scaling for power, serverless architecture induces higher reliability because it is distributed. Server-based architectures are more vulnerable to single points of failure, and this leads to future downtimes with the potential to significantly disrupt business operations. Conversely, serverless applications run on stateless computing services distributed across a number of servers or even across cloud regions, thereby spreading risk.

Figure 10.7. *Improved application performance and reliability.*

Source: https://cdn.prod.website-files.com/619e15d781b21202de206fb5/64f83a0c012c74116f8c8ab8_The-Impact-of-Improving-App-Performance-Using-the-Head-Spin-Platform.jpg.

Therefore, in case one service instance crashes, other instances may continue running, preventing application unavailability. Academic research projects, such as those cited by the Service Prototyping Lab at Zurich University of Applied Sciences, illustrate ongoing work toward further enhancing these cloud-native strategies. These are aimed at a high reliability strategy such that cloud-native apps can recover from errors in quick time and provide a seamless service, further aligning serverless computing as a reliable option for modern application deployment (Al-Ameen et al., 2018). Along with this, the future of cloud-native apps also lies in the continuous innovation of serverless technologies, which operate to marry performance enhancement with reliability upgrades. Sophisticated monitoring and logging tools now offer real-time insight into the performance of applications, thereby providing instant response to any service failure or decline in performance. Through the use of machine learning algorithms to track usage patterns and predict potential problems, developers are able to resolve reliability issues early on before they become critical ones. Such proactive handling is crucial in guaranteeing high-performance expectations in the highly competitive digital age. As companies more and more adopt serverless solutions, how improved application performance interacts with reliability will shape the destiny of cloud-native computing, subsequently driving innovation and efficiency in different industries (Trujillo et al., 2024) (Figure 10.7).

10.4. CHALLENGES AND LIMITATIONS

Serverless architecture has its built-in limitations and shortcomings, particularly where performance and resource management are concerned. With companies adopting serverless environments, they have to contend with the inherent latency due to cold starts, which can immediately affect application responsiveness. The latency occurs every time functions are invoked after being down for some time, necessitating the initial setup of infrastructure prior to being executed. Second, the ephemeral nature of serverless components could complicate state management and produce performance problems under varying loads. These are all issues that point towards embracing a more advanced model of application development, particularly as organizations shift towards optimizing the performance of their cloud-based applications while counterbalancing cost effectiveness and efficiency, ultimately placing emphasis on understanding the constraints of serverless computing (Buyya et al., 2017). Another serious drawback of serverless architectures is vendor lock-in, which can restrict an organization's strategic option and flexibility. Different providers of cloud have distinct serverless offerings with unique operational characteristics, which complicate the adoption of multi-cloud strategies. As a result, corporations may struggle to port workloads between providers due to enormous differences in APIs, cost models, and performance characteristics. This lack of standardization can render applications less portable because programmers will find it hard to rescript their codebases for deployment on other platforms if it becomes necessary. Moreover, with the growing necessity for innovation, the lack of interoperability among serverless platforms might throttle flexibility and ultimately hinder organizations from being agile in reaction to shifting market conditions (Akkus et al., 2020). Lastly, security continues to be an utmost priority in the serverless model, where conventional defensive mechanisms might not be adequate. Owing to the fact that serverless applications tend to include diverse microservices and integrations with third parties, the attack surface may greatly increase, creating vulnerabilities. The shared responsibility model typical of cloud deployments makes it incumbent on organizations to have strict security policies and continuously scan their applications for vulnerabilities. In addition to this, data privacy concerns arise in serverless architectures due to the transience of function execution and potential exposing of sensitive user information among various services. As organizations deploy serverless technology, addressing these security challenges will be core in building their trust in cloud-native applications and managing the complexities that accompany this emerging technology (Akkus et al., 2020).

10.4.1. Vendor Lock-in Concerns

As companies more and more adopt serverless designs in their cloud-native strategies, problems related to vendor lock-in have emerged as a pertinent issue. Vendor lock-in is the problem of businesses being overly dependent on a single cloud provider due to proprietary technologies, services, or APIs. This reliance would cause migrability issues when bringing applications or data to a different platform, which hampers flexibility and innovation. In the serverless setup, with services tightly coupled and abstracted, avoiding lock-in is particularly tricky. The providers typically have their own methods of deployment, scalability, and resource handling that are specific to each platform and vary from platform to platform, so it is complicated to move out of their ecosystem seamlessly. Clearly, being aware of and steering clear of vendor lock-in is critical for organizations that are trying to leverage serverless models without conceding long-term agility or control over their technology stack. The concern with vendor lock-in is further fueled by the speeding rate of innovation in cloud technologies, whose premise is to create a dynamic environment where companies must continuously adapt. As argued in recent studies, the world of cloud computing has seen a burst in the provisioning of services, with each having varying functionality and performance requirements (Buyya et al., 2017). This heterogeneity is a plus, but it also raises the stakes for businesses in making their service provider selection, as each choice has long-term scale and dependence implications. Additionally, adopting serverless architecture tends to make firms tightly committed to a provider's specific offerings, so they aren't easily able to switch vendors without great costs and operational disruption. To circumvent them, organizations must weigh their service choices carefully, utilizing multi-cloud and open-standard strategies that ensure interoperability, thus keeping themselves in minimal risk to the limitations of any one vendor. Furthermore, vendor lock-in mitigation follows not merely from strategic planning but also from having close understanding of technical issues pertaining to serverless environments. Comparison of various serverless platforms indicates that they provide unique features and uses, yet they pose identical technical issues with migration as well as integration (Baldini et al., 2017). For instance, while serverless computing improves efficiency as well as reduces the overhead of processes, it will also render code portability as well as data migration from one framework to another difficult. As organizations increasingly rely on serverless systems, promoting the collaboration of providers towards shared standards can minimize lock-in risks so that they can switch more easily and promote vendor competition. By being aware of vendor lock-in concerns and encouraging more flexible architectures, firms can achieve the full potential of serverless computing without the specter of future restriction on their development looming over them (Figure 10.8).

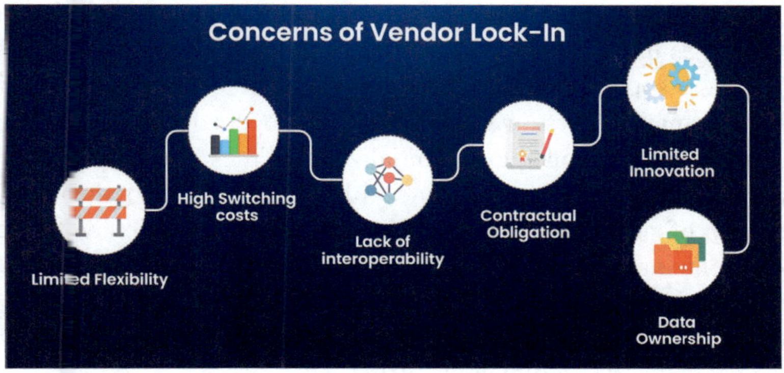

Figure 10.8. *Vendor lock-in concerns.*

Source: https://quixy.com/wp-content/uploads/2023/05/COncerns-of-vendor-lock-in-1.png.

10.4.2. Cold Start Latency Issues

The increasing adoption of serverless architecture in modern cloud-native applications has brought various advantages, such as cost savings and flexibility. However, latency issues related to cold start have also emerged as a significant concern in this model. On the first call or during idle time, there could be some perceivable latency because the cloud provider must create the necessary compute resources. This lag affects user experience, particularly in applications having stringent responsiveness requirements, such as real-time data processing or user-facing services. As cloud-native environments continue to advance, overcoming cold start issues becomes the key to delivering a seamless application experience and maintaining competitive performance benchmarks. Beyond mere basic user experience concerns, the effects of cold start delay can trickle down to contribute indirectly to system reliability and efficiency. If the initialization latency is not adequately controlled, they will also introduce bottlenecks in times of heavy usage. For instance, a program to process high volumes of data or process high-volume events will be slowed by excessive cold starts. Solutions such as function deployment optimization, pre-warming instances, or leveraging alternative architecture can be employed to mitigate against these but all have cost and complexity trade-offs. As noted by current research, designing serverless systems that minimize cold start effects is crucial in enhancing throughput and maintaining high-quality application performance (Akkus et al., 2020). In reaction to such limitations, the future of serverless computing could be in the optimization of the execution environment to address cold starts more efficiently. Optimizations might include adopting hybrid strategies that combine older infrastructure with serverless deployment or tapping more sophisticated resource management techniques that anticipate changes in demand. These would allow developers to maximize function deployment strategies and reduce initialization times effectively. Moreover, additional studies on the performance of serverless deployment highlight the necessity of additional optimization and accommodation within cloud-native environments. These advancements not only support effective system performance but also serve to enhance the overarching objective of scalable, high-fidelity remote function execution, as outlined in the context of current technological demand (Baldini et al., 2017).

10.4.3. Security and Compliance Considerations

In serverless computing and cloud-native applications, security and compliance considerations represent the issues of paramount concern that organizations must face. Transition from traditional computing architectures to serverless functions simplifies deploying applications but, in the process, opens up weaknesses to be exploited by attackers. In a typical serverless design, functions are executed without the weight of server management, but this abstraction can potentially obscure responsibility for security between consumers and providers of services. The need for utter understanding and vigilance becomes paramount, as misconfigurations or lack of joint security awareness can lead to drastic data breaches and compliance issues, particularly in deployment scenarios handling sensitive information governed by such standards as GDPR or HIPAA (Buyya et al., 2017). As cloud-native architectures advance, platform and service diversification introduces new compliance landscapes that organizations have to navigate. The availability of multiple public, private, and hybrid cloud environments can complicate the adoption of robust security frameworks, particularly where such environments contain edge computing and IoT components. For instance, the emergence of hybrid cloud MEC architectures introduces complexity around information governance and regulations compliance (Bruin et al., 2019). Organizations must take affirmative steps to establish firm policies and guidelines to ensure that data integrity and confidentiality are maintained between distinct nodes and service endpoints. This includes keeping an eye on legal considerations of data locality, retention, and processing requirements, which differ vastly with jurisdiction and the type of data being processed. To effectively manage security and compliance concerns in a serverless cloud-native environment, organizations must have a common risk management strategy. This involves embracing continuous monitoring and assessment techniques in identifying possible vulnerabilities and meeting compliance requirements. Employing automated compliance solutions can significantly speed up the process of achieving compliance across cloud systems, enabling organizations to manage security controls in a streamlined way. Besides, spending on security awareness and training initiatives for development and operations teams promotes a culture of security first, which is critical to minimize risks in the complicated serverless environment. In the end, an engaged and informed security and compliance approach will allow organizations to leverage the complete potential of serverless architecture while safeguarding their assets and meeting regulatory requirements effectively (Figure 10.9).

Figure 10.9. *Security and compliance considerations.*

Source: https://sprinto.com/wp-content/uploads/2023/04/Copy-of-Blog_199_Security-Compliance-management_Goals-and-best-practices-02-1024x744.jpg.

10.5. USE CASES OF SERVERLESS COMPUTING

Its adoption has increased in significance in software development and IT operations use cases, providing a wide variety of applications that take advantage of its natural strengths. Number one use case of serverless computing is in event-driven architectures, where serverless systems can most efficiently deal with asynchronous events brought about by user actions or system changes.

For instance, applications such as real-time data processing, API-based mobile app backends, and chatbots are greatly served by serverless models since they allow developers to develop code without concerning themselves about the infrastructure. The model not only quickens the pace of development but also enhances the usage of resources since the cloud resources automatically scale following the level of demand, an indicator of the inward flexibility that serverless environments offer. Another important example is in microservices architecture, where the applications are divided into smaller, standalone services that are tasked with single functions. Serverless computing fits into this style by making it possible to publish the microservices as standalone functions, which can be independently deployed and updated. This architectural flexibility contributes to creating rapid iteration and deployment cycles, thereby aligning the development with Agile frameworks. Organizations employing serverless in microservices realize lesser operational overhead and improved scalability since the operational management of servers can be outsourced to the cloud provider. With increasing numbers of organizations going towards microservices, serverless computing integration is going to make a fundamental contribution towards streamlining development processes and providing faster time-to-market for applications. Also, serverless computing is invaluable when it comes to data processing and analytics, where huge volumes of data can be consumed, processed, and analyzed with much less effort. Operations such as file processing, data conversion, and real-time analytics pipelines can be easily done through serverless functions, thus simplifying the data-intensive application architecture. This capability not only allows businesses to derive meaning from their data in a short while but also provides an efficient solution since computing power is accessed only during functions execute. Serverless products that allow machine learning and artificial intelligence workflows further demonstrate the congruence between advanced analytics and efficiency that serverless computing embodies. Consequently, with the future of cloud-native technology unfolding, the versatility and reactivity of serverless computing will redefine the approach to designing and scaling applications, paving the way for breakthrough solutions across industries (Buyya et al., 2017; Baldini et al., 2017).

10.5.1. Microservices and API Development

Microservices architecture has revolutionized the application development in cloud-native and serverless environments. Microservices enable complex applications to be broken into loosely coupled, independently deployed services, thereby making them more scalable and flexible. A microservice can be written, changed, or scaled without necessarily affecting the entire application, thus facilitating a more effective DevOps lifecycle. Since companies are increasingly keen on adopting multi-cloud strategies as a means to mitigate the vendor lock-in threats, the use of microservices enables them to leverage distinctive cloud strengths, as per research exploring architecture concerns surrounding multi-cloud environments (Alonso et al., 2023). This agile approach not only simplifies the development process but also enhances the ability to respond promptly to market demands and customer requirements, thereby making companies competitive in today's digital era. API development is fundamental to facilitating interoperability between microservices in serverless architecture. APIs are the communication bridge allowing standalone microservices to converse freely while still maintaining their encapsulated operations. Successful management of APIs is instrumental, particularly within the context of microservices where services grow exponentially.

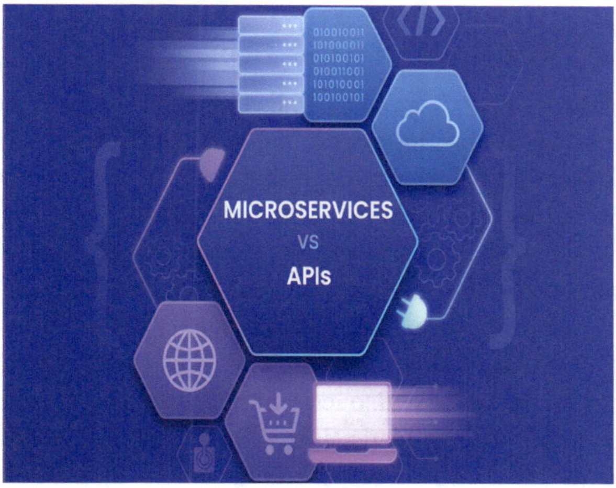

Figure 10.10. *Microservices and API development.*

Source: https://www.mindinventory.com/blog/wp-content/uploads/2022/10/microservices-vs-apis-3x.webp.

As more applications are being coded using blends of public, private, and multi-cloud services, robust API gateways become essential for effective governance, security, and performance monitoring. Thus, organizations must ensure that API development practices are in accord with the microservices ethos to realize the full potential of cloud-native applications, as previously identified within the multi-cloud application development rhetoric (Alonso et al., 2023). Synergy, besides fostering innovation, also fosters operational efficiency across various computing platforms. Although the advantages provided by microservices and API development are strong, their use within serverless environments comes with problems. Specifically, serverless solutions at present are usually marred by concerns over performance and operational overhead that can negate the advantages of a microservices pattern. Because the heavyweight components and function poor chaining can bring greater latency and less performance in microservices deployment, as recent serverless landscape criticisms, such as those involving use of platforms such as Knative, have made apparent, the solutions to such challenges necessitate continuous innovation on serverless architecture design, where attentions are placed on optimizations simplifying function execution and reducing cold-start latency. By prioritizing these improvements, developers can more closely align their microservices and APIs to the performance requirements of modern applications to make the promise of serverless computing deliver tangible value for organizations embarking on cloud-native development in the future (Figure 10.10).

10.5.2. Data Processing and Analytics

The evolution of data processing and analysis has taken a significant leap with the adoption of serverless computing, particularly when dealing with cloud-native applications. Under this paradigm, developers are able to focus primarily on writing code without worrying about managing infrastructure. As organizations become more reliant on event-driven systems, serverless platforms support seamless data ingestion and analytics in real-time. With the implementation of event triggers, such platforms are able to call functions in response to data changes, giving real-time insights and the ability to make informed decisions. Dynamic scaling of resources also contributes to the processing power of data, scaling to meet varying loads. Flexibility is particularly crucial within an environment where data sources are data-intensive, a step towards more responsive and agile analytics processes. Furthermore, serverless computing also simplifies data processing workflows by reducing the time and effort required in resource provisioning and management to a great extent. Traditional cloud infrastructures have a tendency to throttle because of the need for constant monitoring and configuration, while serverless environments offer the ability of auto-scaling based on demand. This is particularly relevant when implementing machine learning algorithms where data ingestion is unpredictable. As observed in newer studies, serverless architectures such as AWS Lambda not only provide adequate latency for inferencing calculations but also allow the seamless coexistence of complex data analytics processes. These developments hold potential for the intersection of operational efficiency and analytical precision in cloud-native architecture, with firms being able to harness vast amounts of information without the concomitant downside of having to manage resulting infrastructure (Ishakian et al., 2018). Also, the move to serverless architecture is poised to revolutionize data analytics through the introduction of new paradigms of computing that are inclined towards decentralization and collaboration across different clouds. As companies adopt a multi-cloud strategy, systems capable of processing and analyzing information coming from different sources become increasingly important. Current trends have been in the direction of auto-learned systems that can learn from evolving streams of data and stay aligned with close service level agreements (SLAs). The implications of these developments bring about the necessity for innovative solutions in processing and analyzing data, where combining multiple sets of data can yield more robust prediction models and increased operational responsiveness. Thus, organizations need to overcome the challenges of integrating these newer architectures to fully benefit from the advantage of serverless computing in an increasingly changing digital era (Buyya et al., 2017).

10.5.3. Real-Time File Processing and Event Handling

For serverless computing, event processing in real time and file processing have become essential pieces for modern-day applications. Serverless systems allow developers to create scalable applications against incoming events without any maintenance of legacy server infrastructure. It becomes possible to process large data in an efficient manner at the time an event occurs rather than batch processing, which might cause latencies. For instance, a file upload to a cloud storage server can trigger a serverless function to process the file in real time, thereby enhancing the user experience and optimizing the use of resources altogether. Therefore, making real-time capabilities available in cloud-native environments is a sea change in application writing and deployment, paving the way for more dynamic and interactive services (Baldini et al., 2017). Also, the real-time event handling is supported by cloud infrastructure through its dynamic character. Traditional data center architecture does not lend itself very well to accommodating the requirement of low-latency processing and high reliability. Serverless computing, as opposed to that, relies on a decentralized architecture where a group of cloud vendors can add resources in an on-demand manner. It does not just enhance reliability but also provides the flexibility needed for processing real-time events. For instance, in online gaming or real-time analytics, a few minutes of latency could be harmful to the user experience. Hence, the utilization of serverless architectures allows for the creation of decentralized systems that can handle events in real time effectively, showcasing the potential value proposition of this technology (Buyya et al., 2017). Greater adoption of serverless platforms and cloud-native application development is facilitating new and innovative use cases for event handling and real-time file processing. As organizations shift increasingly towards these paradigms, they realize that real-time capabilities offer competitive advantage in most sectors, including finance, health, and trade. Through enabling instant response to change in data and user actions, organizations can implement dynamic functionality, such as fraud detection software that automatically alerts against fraudulent transactions. Furthermore, real-time analytics dashboards become more important, with data continuously processed rather than intermittently. This perfect union of real-time processing power is a revolutionary shift in how applications are created, which will eventually lead to better provision of services and greater customer satisfaction (Baldini et al., 2017) (Figure 10.11).

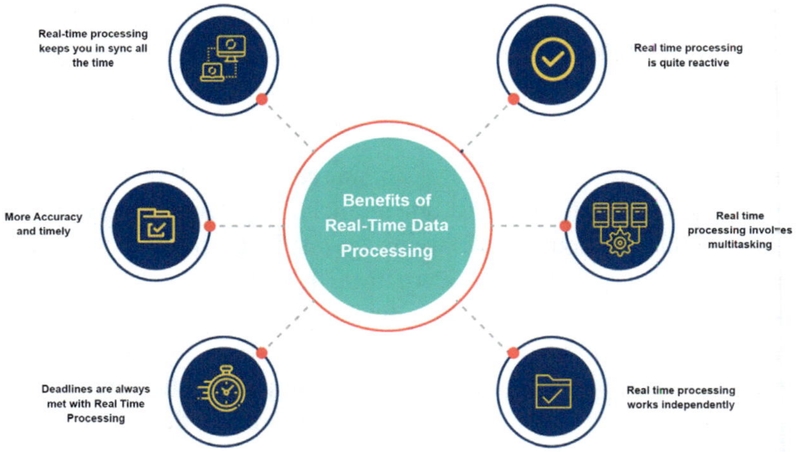

Figure 10.11. *Real-time file processing and event handling.*

Source: https://cdn.prod.website-files.com/66c240bf5ebc6be23ece104b/66e15cd4e1d035b154cc4eb5_Real-Time-Data-Processing-2-1024x683.jpeg.

10.6. FUTURE TRENDS IN CLOUD-NATIVE DEVELOPMENT

With cloud-native development maturing further, serverless computing adoption is a revolutionary trend that redefines application development and deployment. The serverless paradigm allows developers to concentrate on code writing without worrying about server infrastructure management. This is underpinned by the ever-growing need for scalable event-driven applications that naturally react to user interactions and data processing requirements. By adopting serverless architectures, organizations can save considerable amounts of money because they only pay for compute resources that are consumed on running. Moreover, fast deployment of updates allows for agility and innovation and therefore offers a compelling argument to businesses that want to innovate their service delivery in an aggressive business landscape. Serverless integration is a foundation in cloud-native development and may revolutionize best practices in app architecture and deployment models. In the years to come, the combination of serverless computing and machine learning is another game-changer in cloud-native development. As organizations increasingly embrace Artificial Intelligence in their applications, serverless architecture agility allows for fast iteration and real-time processing of large data. The benefit of this synergy is that it can achieve hard inferencing jobs on neural network models without the constraints of traditional infrastructure. Cold start latency does have an impact on performance, with ongoing optimizations and innovations within serverless frameworks (Ishakian et al., 2018). These challenges will have to be overcome for organizations to maximize the potential of machine learning in a serverless environment, potentially ushering in enhanced user experiences and intelligent applications. Moreover, the future of cloud-native development is going to be decentralized with multi-cloud strategies growing increasingly mainstream among organizations. The trend is away from dependence on single-provider data centers to a broader utilization of multiple cloud services so that organizations can leverage a broad catalog of cloud services to achieve more flexibility and resilience. The future will see cloud providers competing to serve such multi-cloud environments, with resulting customized infrastructure offerings to meet specific organizational needs (Buyya et al., 2017). Through the use of decentralized architecture, businesses are able to optimize performance and price while lowering the risks of vendor lock-in. As cloud-native apps develop to these new standards, developers will need to embrace new computing architectures that enable seamless interoperability among many different cloud services, enabling a more responsive and dynamic IT environment.

10.6.1. Integration with Artificial Intelligence and Machine Learning

The combination of machine learning (ML) and artificial intelligence (AI) into serverless architecture is building a fascinating and revolutionary future for cloud-native applications. With the help of the clouds elastic resources, organizations can enhance their AI algorithms and machine learning models without the complexities of traditional IT infrastructure. Serverless computing also facilitates deployment of such technologies more easily, allowing developers to focus on algorithm innovation rather than server management or hardware. Such transformation conserves resources and makes things more efficient as resources may be dynamically provisioned based on needs. Organizations can thus respond to real-time data in a timely manner, enhancing decision-making activities and driving business value. Here, cloud computing not only enables AI and ML in a seamless manner but also emerged as a fundamental enabler for their future advancements, changing the data-driven information collection and utilization process (Islam et al., 2023). In the field of Multi-Access Edge Computing (MEC), integration of AI, ML, and serverless architecture is full of promise for enhancing applications executed at the network edge. MECs decentralization helps bring computational capacity closer to data sources, decreasing latency and enabling real-time analysis.

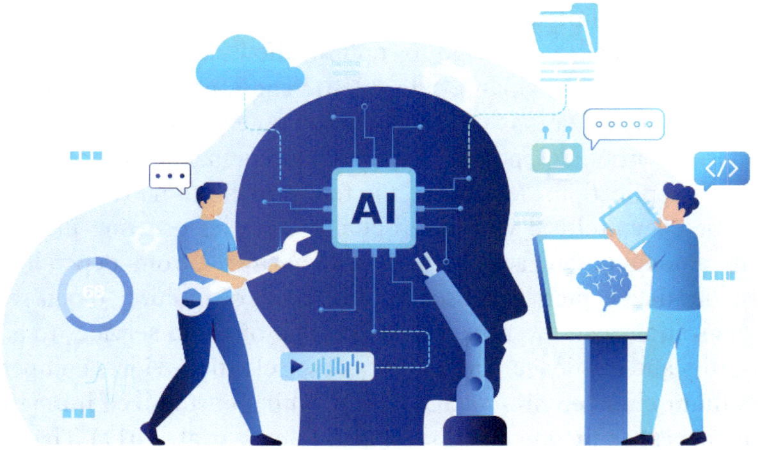

Figure 10.12. *Integration with artificial intelligence and machine learning.*

Source: https://www.ag5.com/wp-content/uploads/2023/03/1-3.jpg.

This setup is also essential for AI-driven applications that need instant response times, like autonomous vehicles or smart cities. With the integration of AI and ML in serverless MEC designs, developers can access localized data, training their models on fresh information and minimizing bandwidth consumption. As more MEC projects become a reality, a better understanding of the prevailing practical implementations will be necessary. This will allow researchers and developers to validate the efficacy of such technologies and improve their applications subsequently, subsequently leading to more effective and responsive AI solutions (Cruz et al., 2022). Furthermore, the ever-increasing cloud computing necessitates increased focus on compliance and security in AI and ML integration. Cloud service providers spend considerable amounts on security measures so that organizations can leverage AI capabilities without compromising data confidentiality and compliance. The pay-per-use aspect of serverless architectures also plays a role, with organizations able to scale their AI applications in terms of user interaction and data processing requirements. The promise of cloud-native technologies, particularly for AI and ML, relies on this delicate balance between innovation and compliance. As organizations increasingly resort to cloud-based AI solutions for competitive edge, ongoing collaboration among all parties will be essential to comprehend the complexities of both deployment and regulation. The integration of advanced technologies into serverless ecosystems represents an enormous development, enabling a more responsive and agile response to business issues (Islam et al., 2023) (Figure 10.12).

10.6.2. Growth of Hybrid and Multi-Cloud Strategies

The advent of hybrid and multi-cloud models is a result of the increasing complexity of existing computing environments, understanding that organizations require flexibility and efficiency to meet varied workload demands. Hybrid cloud combines on-premises infrastructure and outside cloud resources, allowing organizations to optimize resource use based on the needs of specific applications. This model enables organizations to distribute workloads across several environments—enhancing performance and reliability while ensuring compliance with data governance rules. Multi-cloud strategies also enable enterprises to use several vendors simultaneously, fostering vendor competition and reducing dependence on a single platform. As strategies mature over time, companies are also learning the benefit of interoperability and open data sharing, required to achieve maximum performance and cost reduction in their cloud deployments. Guiding this revolution is the concept of Distributed Computing Continuum Systems (DCCSs), which unify different computing resources, like cloud, fog, and edge computing. DCCSs effectively address the complexities of processing, as explained, and hold the capability to disrupt computing paradigms, addressing performance and user experience (Donta et al., 2023). Inclusion of DCCSs in hybrid and multi-cloud projects represents a step toward an integrated computing paradigm that responds to contemporary requirements. Businesses can distribute loads to various categories of infrastructure, enabling dynamic scalability and flexible resource allocation. The holistic paradigm provided by DCCSs is particularly important for industries that require real-time processing and feedback of information, and hybrid and multi-cloud strategies become the most important assets for today's organizations going through digital transformation. Rapid adoption of the Internet of Things (IoT) also favors the adoption of hybrid and multi-cloud strategies as these systems need guaranteed access to geographically distributed sensors and computing resources. IoT use cases demand concurrent access to multiple data sources, a requirement that conventional cloud models frequently cannot fulfill in an optimal manner. This fact has prompted the development of the Cloud-to-Things computing paradigm, emphasizing the necessity for orchestration systems that can coordinate resources across heterogeneous environments (Ullah et al., 2023). As companies shift their businesses to these architectures, they are able to harness the full potential of hybrid and multi-cloud strategies such that their applications are always running and scalable. Therefore, organizations using these strategies are able to effectively counter the threats posed by emerging technologies while remaining agile and competitive in an increasingly complex world digitally (Figure 10.13).

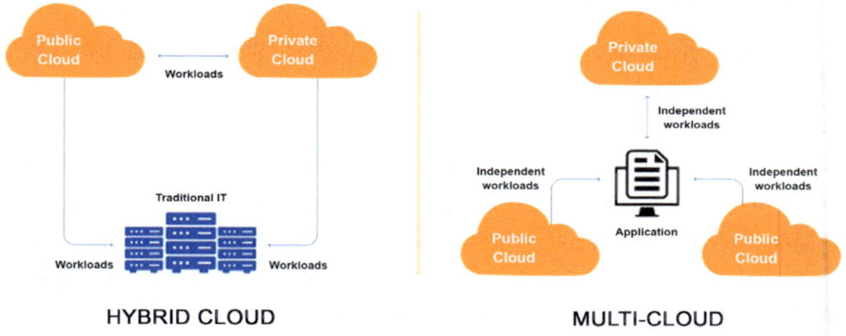

Figure 10.13. *The growth of hybrid and multi-cloud strategies.*

Source: https://www.orientsoftware.com/Themes/Content/Images/blog/2022-06-22/multi-vs-hybrid-cloud.jpg.

10.6.3. Advancements in Serverless Frameworks and Tools

Serverless tooling and frameworks are a landmark moment in the evolution of cloud-native applications. By allowing developers to code without worrying about the intricacies of infrastructure management, these tools improve productivity and stimulate innovation. One of the most significant advancements here is the addition of machine learning and artificial intelligence capabilities to serverless architectures, which enables dynamic scaling of applications and resource optimization. These enhancements are particularly beneficial for event-driven applications that require speedy response times in processing fluctuating workloads. This enhancement not only eases development workflows but also allows applications to adapt to users' demands accordingly, providing prospects for more stable and robust systems. As aspirations for interruption-free cloud experiences continue to grow, prospects offered by fresh serverless frameworks are all set to redefine the deployment landscape significantly. In addition to productivity gains, serverless tool evolution has also addressed technical challenges that have previously delayed their uptake. Of concern is the cold start latency, which, as evidenced by experimental studies, can disrupt service quality, especially in applications that are latency-sensitive (Ishakian et al., 2018). Provisioned concurrency and building warm invocation strategies are among the solutions that have emerged to solve these issues, enhancing user experience. Moreover, improvements in monitoring and debugging tools are paving the way for greater microservices performance and fault tolerance knowledge in serverless environments. In addition to providing developers with the necessary tools to keep their apps running smoothly, these improvements also facilitate enterprise-scale adoption by reducing operational overhead. As organizations increasingly adopt the promise of serverless computing, focus on bridging such technical challenges will be key. Lastly, open-source initiatives have been instrumental in supporting the development of serverless frameworks, giving the ecosystem a rich and heterogeneous pool of tools and platforms (Baldini et al., 2017). The prominent projects continue emerging, each addressing particular aspects of serverless computing, creating a rich assortment of offerings that appeal to varying use cases and developer preferences. This kind of openness of collaboration has encouraged innovation and driven rapid iteration so that the community can adopt shared challenges and experiment with new paradigms of deploying applications. In addition, cross-platform integrations are becoming increasingly prevalent, bridging the gap between serverless offerings and regular cloud offerings, increasing their flexibility and versatility even more. The sustained innovation driven by business and community involvement illustrates an interesting future for serverless computing, with these models set to be at the forefront of the development of cloud-native applications.

SUMMARY

In general, the development of serverless computing marks a revolutionary change in the cloud-native environment towards making it possible for greater efficiency and flexibility in application development. This new practice significantly reduces developers' operational burden by decoupling infrastructure control, enabling them to focus more on code and functionality. Using event-driven architectures and microservices, businesses can build a heightened agile development culture that not only enhances time-to-market but also provides higher scalability. Transition away from legacy cloud service patterns to a serverless model necessitates rethinking application design and deployment strategies, indicative of a broader shift toward multi-cloud strategies and heterogeneous computational resources. All such a paradigm shift emphasizes further is an elementary understanding that sole-provider dependence involves vendor lock-in risk, which is parallel to the need for additional heterogeneity in cloud application structure as revealed in the conceptualization of the multi-cloud phenomenon (Alonso et al., 2023). Additionally, the implications of adopting serverless architecture extend beyond operational efficiency; they resonate extremely strongly within the organizational strategy and business model paradigm. As companies continue to venture deeper into exploring the synergies of microservices and serverless, they embrace advanced multi-cloud environments that are dynamic in leveraging the benefits of multiple providers. Integration is vital to be able to navigate the sophisticated needs of modern applications, particularly in areas like Internet of Things (IoT) and cross-organizational projects. Companies utilizing serverless services are able to achieve optimal resource utilization and sensitivity to market fluctuations without losing their competitive edge in the market. However, the inherent complexities of maintaining the infrastructure of a multi-cloud native setup necessitate strict architectural designs and continuous research efforts. The insights garnered from recent literature emphasize the need for systems that are compatible with the changing needs of serverless and multi-cloud applications, making foundations for higher-level advancements in the field (Alonso et al., 2023). The future of cloud-native technologies ultimately comes down to the continuous evolution of serverless architecture and how they are well-suited to different systems. As organizations adopt these innovations, they must have an eye on performance and scalability and also steer through the associated risks of adopting new technology. The open research issues surrounding multi-cloud app development accentuate the importance of devising good methods of overcoming new complexities emerging. Alongside, as permissioned blockchains and decentralized platforms gain popularity for enterprise use cases, there is an opportunity to explore integrating the same with serverless architecture to enhance cross-organizational processes. Comprehensive performance testing of platforms like Hyperledger Fabric can serve as critical blueprints for practitioners, setting the benchmark in the configuration and deployment of cloud-native technologies that can adapt to existing demands and drive innovation across industries. And so, in the future, our focus has to be on how we can leverage these groundbreaking technologies in the building of a future that is not just cost-effective but also robust and responsive.

REFERENCES

1. Akkus, I. E., CMS, F., Forde, J., Fox, G., Hightower, K., Hindman, B., Malawski, M., et al. (2020). funcX: A federated function serving fabric for science. http://arxiv.org/abs/2005.04215 (accessed on 11th September 2025).

2. Al-Ameen, M., Dorodko, S., Harsh, P., Junker, A., et al. (2018). Service Prototyping Lab Report–2018 (Y3). https://core.ac.uk/download/160751656.pdf (accessed on 11th September 2025).

3. Alonso, J., Orue-Echevarria, L., Casola, V., Torre, A. I., Huarte, M., Osaba, E., & Lobo, J. L. (2023). Understanding the challenges and novel architectural models of multi-cloud native applications–A systematic literature review. Journal of Cloud Computing: Advances, Systems and Applications, 12. https://doi.org/10.1186/s13677-022-00367-6 (accessed on 11th September 2025).

4. Appavoo, J., Awad, Y., Cadden, J., Dong, H., et al. (2019). SEUSS: Rapid serverless deployment using environment snapshots. https://open.bu.edu/bitstream/2144/40869/1/1910.01558v1.pdf (accessed on 11th September 2025).

5. Baladari, V. (2021). The role of software developers in transitioning on-premises applications to cloud platforms. https://core.ac.uk/download/653452799.pdf (accessed on 11th September 2025).

6. Baldini, I., Castro, P., Chang, K., Cheng, P., et al. (2017). Serverless computing: Current trends and open problems. http://arxiv.org/abs/1706.03178 (accessed on 11th September 2025).

7. Bayya, A. K. (2025). The role of serverless architectures in revolutionizing FinTech solutions. Asian Journal of Mathematics and Computer Research. https://www.semanticscholar.org/paper/d1407461c84479bd9f94e6efa0fb22e21afeddb5 (accessed on 11th September 2025).

8. Borra, P., & Pamidipoola, H. P. (2025). Serverless computing: The future of scalability and efficiency with AWS, Azure, and GCP. International Journal of Advanced Research in Science, Communication and Technology. https://www.semanticscholar.org/paper/1fa0eec602eb405bd548048cc32cba107147757e (accessed on 11th September 2025).

9. Buyya, R., & Varghese, B. (2017). Next generation cloud computing: New trends and research directions. https://core.ac.uk/download/96664300.pdf (accessed on 11th September 2025).

10. Camacho Trujillo, H. D. (2024). SCARF: Serverless cloud auto resource framework. https://core.ac.uk/download/614593483.pdf (accessed on 11th September 2025).
11. Cruz, P. M., Achir, N., & Viana, A. C. (2022). On the edge of the deployment: A survey on multi-access edge computing. ACM Computing Surveys, 55, 1–34. https://doi.org/10.1145/3529758 (accessed on 11th September 2025).
12. Donta, P. K., Murturi, I., Casamayor Pujol, V., Sedlak, B., & Dustdar, S. (2023). Exploring the potential of distributed computing continuum systems. Computers, 12, 198–198. https://doi.org/10.3390/computers12100198 (accessed on 11th September 2025).
13. Gkikopoulos, P. (2019). Data distribution and exploitation in a global microserviceartefactobservatory.https://core.ac.uk/download/232207788.pdf (accessed on 11th September 2025).
14. Grasso, A. (2025). Navigating the space between serverful and serverless: Benefits, drawbacks, challenges and mitigations. https://core.ac.uk/download/667326779.pdf (accessed on 11th September 2025).
15. Guggenberger, T., Sedlmeir, J., Fridgen, G., & Luckow, A. (2022). An in-depth investigation of the performance characteristics of Hyperledger Fabric. Computers & Industrial Engineering, 173, 108716–108716. https://doi.org/10.1016/j.cie.2022.108716 (accessed on 11th September 2025).
16. Hassan, H. B., Barakat, S., & Sarhan, Q. I. (2021). Survey on serverless computing. Journal of Cloud Computing: Advances, Systems and Applications, 10. https://doi.org/10.1186/s13677-021-00253-7 (accessed on 11th September 2025).
17. Ishakian, V., Muthusamy, V., & Slominski, A. (2018). Serving deep learning models in a serverless platform. http://arxiv.org/abs/1710.08460 (accessed on 11th September 2025).
18. Islam, R., Patamsetti, V., Gadhi, A., Gondu, R. M., Bandaru, C. M., Kesani, S. C., & Abiona, O. (2023). The future of cloud computing: Benefits and challenges. International Journal of Communications Network and System Sciences, 16, 53–65. https://doi.org/10.4236/ijcns.2023.164004 (accessed on 11th September 2025).
19. Kärnä, P. (2021). Evaluating performance of serverless virtualization. https://core.ac.uk/download/428286741.pdf (accessed on 11th September 2025).
20. Masip Bruin, X., Michailidis, E. T., Nomikos, N., Trakadas, P., et al. (2019). Hybrid clouds for data-intensive, 5G-enabled IoT applications:

An overview, key issues and relevant architecture. https://core.ac.uk/download/231705343.pdf (accessed on 11th September 2025).

21. Qayyum, A., Ahmad, K., Ahsan, M. A., Al-Fuqaha, A., & Qadir, J. (2022). Collaborative federated learning for healthcare: Multi-modal COVID-19 diagnosis at the edge. IEEE Open Journal of the Computer Society, 3, 172–184. https://doi.org/10.1109/ojcs.2022.3206407 (accessed on 11th September 2025).
22. Qi, S., Monis, L., Zeng, Z., Wang, I., & Ramakrishnan, K. K. (2022). SPRIGHT. https://doi.org/10.1145/3544216.3544259 (accessed on 11th September 2025).
23. Ray, P. P. (2023). An overview of WebAssembly for IoT: Background, tools, state-of-the-art, challenges, and future directions. Future Internet, 15, 275–275. https://doi.org/10.3390/fi15080275 (accessed on 11th September 2025).
24. Ullah, A., Kiss, T., Kovács, J., Tusa, F., DesLauriers, J., Dagdeviren, H., Arjun, R., et al. (2023). Orchestration in the cloud-to-things compute continuum: Taxonomy, survey and future directions. Journal of Cloud Computing: Advances, Systems and Applications, 12. https://doi.org/10.1186/s13677-023-00516-5 (accessed on 11th September 2025).
25. Virtanen, J. (2023). Leveraging Kubernetes in edge-native cable access convergence. https://core.ac.uk/download/571679158.pdf (accessed on 11th September 2025).
26. Zaman, A. U. (2025). Empowering full-stack development: The impact of modern technologies with AIs. https://core.ac.uk/download/646459406.pdf (accessed on 11th September 2025).

INDEX

A

B

C

D

L

M

N

O

T

U

V

W